Disknowledge

Literature, Alchemy, and the End of Humanism
in Renaissance England

Katherine Eggert

PUBLISHED IN COOPERATION WITH
FOLGER SHAKESPEARE LIBRARY

PENN

UNIVERSITY OF PENNSYLVANIA PRESS

PHILADELPHIA

Copyright © 2015 University of Pennsylvania Press

Published by
University of Pennsylvania Press
Philadelphia, Pennsylvania 19104-4112
www.upenn.edu/pennpress

Printed in the United States of America on acid-free paper
10 9 8 7 6 5 4 3 2 1

A catalogue record for this book is available
from the Library of Congress.
ISBN 978-0-8122-4751-0

For Richard Eggert

CONTENTS

NOTES ON TEXTS, BIBLICAL QUOTATIONS, AND BIBLIOGRAPHY

I have retained the original spelling and typography of quotations from medieval and early modern texts, except that I have silently expanded contractions, modernized *i/j*, *u/v*, *uu/w*, long *s*, and Middle English characters, and romanized nonmeaningful italicization. The exception is in quotations from Edmund Spenser, where I have followed the scholarly convention of retaining *i/j* and *u/v* spellings and all italicization. Early modern texts are quoted by page number when pagination is present and reliable. If there is some question about the reliability of an early modern volume's pagination, I have included signature numbers as well as page numbers.

All biblical quotations, unless otherwise noted, are from *The Geneva Bible: A Facsimile of the 1560 Edition* (Madison: University of Wisconsin Press, 1969).

Full bibliographical information for every source cited is given at first mention in the notes. More frequently cited sources are also listed in the select bibliography.

Disknowledge

Introduction

"There are more things in heaven and earth, Horatio," says Hamlet to his friend, "Than are dreamt of in your philosophy."[1] On the face of it, this is a quite reasonable thing to say at this moment in the play. Occasioned by the Ghost's appearance, which has rattled both men, Hamlet's remark suggests that ghosts are not something that you can think about properly, not in the framework you have at hand. When Horatio calls the Ghost "wondrous strange," Hamlet's observation assures him that this apparition falls into the category of things not knowable (1.5.172).

The question then becomes, though, how you are to think at all. One option—one that may seem tempting at this point in *Hamlet*—is to leave off thinking altogether. Certainly thinking has gotten no one anywhere so far in act 1. The watch and Horatio alike have been utterly wrong about what the Ghost's appearance portends, and Hamlet himself has already cast the political and familial complexities of the royal household in the half-light of his own highly idiosyncratic, and hence highly questionable, speculations and emotions. Now, after the Ghost's revelation raises more questions than it answers, Hamlet recommends to the other men that they suppress any desire for knowledge they may have. "For your desire to know what is between us"—that is, between Hamlet and the Ghost—"O'ermaster it as you may" (1.5.145–46). What a relief to be permitted to remain simply ignorant! If you never have to try to know anything, you never feel the shame of coming up with a theory that is manifestly wrong.

It is quite possible, however, that what Horatio calls "wondrous strange" is not the Ghost but Hamlet himself, whose "wild and whirling words" Horatio has already noted (1.5.139). And one of the most wondrously strange things Hamlet does in this sequence is put Horatio and the soldiers of the watch in what appears to be an untenable epistemological position. First, despite the fact that Hamlet excuses them from epistemic effort, it is clear that they *do* know something, or else Hamlet would not warn them to keep their knowledge of the Ghost close: "Never make known what you have seen tonight" (1.5.149). Second, what they are not to make known includes the fact that they know what Hamlet is up to when he "put[s] an antic disposition on" so as to hide his intent: "never . . . note / That you know aught of me" (1.5.177–87). While the men don't know what Hamlet has learned from the Ghost, they know that he has deemed the Ghost "honest" and thus has established a kind of working relationship with it (1.5.144). The sum effect of these remarks is that Hamlet evidently wants them not to know about the Ghost and about Hamlet's relation to the Ghost, even while they do know about the Ghost and about Hamlet's relation to the Ghost.

It is the founding premise of this book that Hamlet's epistemological request, while perhaps "wondrous strange," is perfectly plausible. It is possible not to know what one knows. Indeed, Hamlet, Horatio, and others like them—that is to say, humanistically educated men of the turn of the seventeenth century—were especially in need of this tricky epistemological maneuver as well as especially good at it. The knowledge practices of the late sixteenth and seventeenth centuries, I will be arguing, found themselves in such a long-standing crisis that such gyrations started to make sense. In this long interval of time England saw humanism, with its faith in how classical letters could shape moral and civic virtue, becoming less and less credible. But despite calls by the likes of Francis Bacon to sweep aside antiquated learning and start fresh, there was nothing to replace humanism—not yet. A discredited knowledge system that is nonetheless the only game in town: such a thing, as I will argue toward the end of this book, is largely what Hamlet has in mind. Before I get back to *Hamlet*, though, I will establish that Hamlet's age—an age that we may call late humanism, the Counter-Renaissance, or merely England's late Renaissance—develops a number of strategies for managing knowledge that are peculiar to the needs of a society governed by a threadbare but still ubiquitously operative educational scheme.

Many of those strategies amount to means for knowing less. The equal and opposite impulse of what William West has called the "encyclopedia culture" of early modern Europe—a culture "obsessed with collecting and sorting information . . . driven by the desire to map the world's order and to construct a universal theory of everything"—is an impulse to keep knowledge small, comfortable, familiar.[2] While it is a commonplace that early modern intellectual culture experienced an explosive proliferation of knowledge at the same time that it experienced a proliferation of (mostly printed) texts, the recent work of historians like Ann Blair casts doubt on how cheerful early modern people were about this development. Blair describes a backlash of new techniques intended to organize, censor, and restrict the flow of information.[3] Another form that backlash could take was simply to ignore new knowledge, either because it seemed revolutionary or subversive or merely because it would require that people adjust their views. Lucien Febvre and Henri-Jean Martin comment, for example, on the curious fact that, despite the prominent appearance in print of accounts of Europeans' explorations of the Western Hemisphere, Africa, and the Far East, these works were unpopular and relatively uncited in comparison to familiar and inaccurate works on geography that dated from before the great age of exploration.[4] One response to the discomfort of the new is to stick with the old.

Other strategies for managing unpalatable knowledge in an age of late humanism, however, are more complicated and epistemologically interesting than simply constricting information's flow. These strategies cultivate the stance Hamlet advocates: being acquainted with something and being ignorant of it, both at the same time. I have invented my own word, *disknowledge*, for this peculiar epistemological maneuver, because neither the Renaissance nor my own age provides me with exactly the right term. True, the early modern period devised wonderful new language to express how it feels to believe one knows nothing. The sixteenth century, for example, saw the word *skeptic* enter English as a way of describing the state of epistemological anguish that Maurice Blanchot would later call "unknowing."[5] In their turn, the twentieth and twenty-first centuries have devised invaluable terminology to describe how one acts in a fashion contrary to what one knows to be true, with Sigmund Freud's "disavowal," Jean-Paul Sartre's "bad faith," and sociology's "strategic ignorance" being perhaps the most useful. Yet none of these terms adequately pinpoints the process this book describes. The term *disknowledge* describes the conscious and deliberate setting aside of one compelling mode of understanding the world—one discipline, one theory—in favor of another. The state of knowing that results from disknowledge is not pure ignorance, but rather something more like what Peter Sloterdijk calls "enlightened false consciousness."[6]

In this book I seek to catch disknowledge in action in a number of literary texts, and a few nonliterary texts, from England's late Renaissance. I ask what purpose disknowledge serves. From what kind of knowledge is the text turning, and to what other kind, and why? What I am looking for is what Harry Berger, Jr., calls "the Technique of Conspicuous Irrelevance": a text's "perverse insistence on . . . digressive elements."[7] I am interested in that "perverse insistence," however, not when it is an irruption of the text's political unconscious but when it is a demonstrably conscious choice.

One sure sign that disknowledge is operating in a text is when bad ideas—or nutty ideas, or simply irrelevant ideas—start to look good. My focus in this book is on one discipline that literary texts persistently choose as a sign or signal of epistemological digression: the discipline of alchemy, which, among its many other attributes, was dogged by the reputation of being an especially bad idea. The literature and culture of early modern England were immensely attracted to alchemy for a number of reasons, not least because alchemy offers a treasure trove of metaphors for metamorphosis, or purification, or falsehood, or capitalism. But the literary texts I discuss in this book use alchemy not merely because it is a rich source of figurative language. They use it to signal the way that one knowledge system may be used to displace another, in a manner that allows the displaced system to be both known and not known. Alchemy can serve this purpose because of its own unusual status as a discipline of study and practice. Alchemy seemed, throughout its history and especially in the period with which this book is concerned, to be both true and false, both profound and risible.

In recent decades scholars have evaluated the truth value of early modern alchemy in several different ways. The first stems from the simple fact that "practical" alchemy—using heat to transform substances, primarily through either distillation or its "dry" counterpart, calcination—was truly useful. The working practitioners that Tara Nummedal calls "entrepreneurial alchemists" provided communities with medicines and metalwork, provided the mining and smelting industries with assaying techniques and furnace management, and provided artists and artisans with everything from the composition of new pigments (Jan van Eyck's extraordinary vermilion and verdigris) to a language that could adequately describe the transformation of goldsmithing materials under the influence of heat.[8] Practical alchemists' workroom expertise has recently led a number of historians of early modern science to emphasize a second reason for alchemy's credibility: they have argued that far from being a sidetrack from the development of modern physics and chemistry, alchemy lent method, if not quite yet science, to what would become the scientific method of hypothesis and experiment. For example, William Newman and Lawrence Principe detail the similarities between the laboratory practices of

Robert Boyle, father of modern chemistry, and those of his contemporary, alchemist George Starkey, both of them translating the mystical alchemical treatises of Jean Baptiste van Helmont into recognizably modern scientific techniques such as precise material quantification and the synthetic analysis of repeated experiments.[9]

A third characterization of alchemy's truth value stems from the foundational work of Frances Yates, who argues that the "Hermetic tradition" of which alchemy was a part exerted a deep and abiding influence on early modern thought.[10] As opposed to practical alchemy, this "theoretical" or esoteric alchemy explored alchemical purification as an analogue or even a partner to the highest aims of theology, philosophy, and moral philosophy.[11] While the "Yates thesis" of a unified esoteric body of thought has been largely dismantled, her work has borne fruit in a number of fascinating studies of the seemingly endless proliferation in early modern Europe of alchemical symbology, in everything from emblem books to landscape paintings to ceramic tableware.[12] Such exploration has proved especially useful for literary criticism, since alchemical imagery and sometimes larger alchemical structures pervade Renaissance literature, including texts that do not focus explicitly on themes of the magus or the alteration of material substances. Indeed, Karen Pinkus reads alchemy as something like the work of literature itself, "as much defined by a set of images, practices, rhetorics, and fetish-objects, as it is by the goal, the finished product."[13]

So far we have covered some of the scholarship that emphasizes alchemy's truths and profundities. But it is equally the case that early modern alchemy was seen as a powerful delusion, one that possesses addled alchemical practitioners or is inflicted by alchemical con artists on greedy dupes. The connection of alchemy with falsehood and delusion applies to both its practical and its theoretical sides. Practical alchemists since the Middle Ages had garnered a reputation for counterfeiting and other forms of small-time cons and chiseling. Similarly, esoteric alchemy was labeled by any number of writers on natural philosophy as a fool's or a charlatan's game.[14] Between the unsavory reputation of practical alchemy and the charges of intellectual incoherence leveled at theoretical alchemy, by the late sixteenth and seventeenth centuries the very word *alchemy* was convenient shorthand for obfuscation, misguided learning, and outright scams. As the alchemist's apprentice in John Lyly's 1583 play *Gallathea* comments, "such a beggarly science it is, and so strong on multiplication, that the end is to have neither gold, wit, nor honesty."[15] Stanton Linden's important book on this topic directs us past the most obvious instances, stories about alchemists, into a widespread and long-standing satiric tradition that associated alchemy with falsehood; his examples include not only classic con artist tales like Geoffrey Chaucer's *Canon's Yeoman's Tale* and Ben Jonson's *The Alchemist* but also Francis Bacon, John Donne, George Herbert, John Milton, and more.[16] A separate but similarly fruitful line of inquiry—one traced by Peggy Knapp, William Sherman, and David Hawkes, among others—explores the literary associations between alchemy and counterfeit money, suggesting that the charges of falsifying or debasing coinage that were typically leveled against alchemists signal the bad faith at the heart of nascent capitalism.[17]

Alchemy as practical art; alchemy as protoscience; alchemy as esoteric knowledge and literary ally; alchemy as falsehood. It is easy to see how all of these explanations for the continued allure of alchemy can hold true in a single culture. Alchemy need not mean the same thing at all times to all people. This book, however, explores something quite different: how all of these seemingly incommensurable aspects of alchemy are, for some writers, all true at the same time. For the authors I examine in this book, alchemy can be, all at once, true (a practical art, protoscience, or syncretic philosophy), false (a delusion or a con game), and unprovable (a literary model). Crediting alchemy's reputation for creating new physical materials and new metaphysical and moral states of being but also remembering its reputation for falsehood, some writers associate alchemy with that same dual state of awareness. Alchemy, in other words, suggests for these writers a special and important epistemological status: it can be characterized as knowledge that is also nonknowledge. More precisely, as I have already suggested, these writers can deploy alchemy to signal a mode of choosing not to know what one knows.

Investigating how disknowledge works and the uses to which it may be put is part of the project that Robert Proctor and Londa Schiebinger have called "agnotology," or the study of applied ignorance.[18] While my own book is an effort in agnotology, one that also (as I will detail in Chapter 1) draws inspiration from the relatively new field of "ignorance studies," it is so because the likes of Edmund Spenser, John Donne, William Shakespeare, Ben Jonson, Margaret Cavendish, and the other authors addressed in this book are extraordinary agnotologists, thinkers who not only use but also expose and analyze their culture's reasons and methods for shunting aside certain modes of knowing. And these authors' agnotological abilities, in turn, are enabled through literature's own agnotological propensities. At even its most basic level, the level of the trope, literature depends on deliberately saying *this* in place of *that*, substituting what is understood as fictional for what is understood as real. What literature also does, however, is insinuate that *this* is preferable to *that*: as Philip Sidney puts it in the *Defense of Poetry*, we prefer literature's golden world, however not-true it is, to history's world of brass. To know something literarily is a conscious choice over knowing it factually. The authors I examine in this book not only engage in that choice but represent it, in effect undertaking their own study of the fancy footwork and clever crosstalk required to make disknowledge take hold.

Analyzing these authors' canny song and dance helps me refine my sense of this book as an undertaking in "historical epistemology," as Lorraine Daston, following Arnold Davidson, calls "the history of the categories that structure our thought, pattern our arguments and proofs, and certify our standards for explanation." Daston notes that such study "transcends the history of ideas, by asking the Kantian question about the preconditions that make thinking this or that idea possible."[19] In the case of alchemy, the structures of thought that were in place made simultaneous faith and disbelief possible. But the fact that these structures are, indeed, historical indicates that they are not prefabricated ideology. Rather, they are put in place, incrementally, each time an argument or proof explicitly depends upon them. The kinds of microchoices that reveal themselves under the lens of literary analysis constitute these incremental building blocks, and attending to the patterns they establish will help us understand how the use of alchemical imagery may signify a series of deliberate determinations of what can and cannot be known. Such an examination of epistemic choice is not at all incompatible with the Foucauldian assumption that "at any given instant, the structure proper to individual experience finds a certain number of possible choices (and of excluded possibilities) in the systems of society."[20] Of most interest to me, in fact, are the textual productions of authors who were considered, or at least considered themselves, as entrusted with making knowledge on behalf of social systems. Arguably, it is precisely their sense of privilege regarding their role as knowledge makers that makes their texts discerning and self-conscious about what disknowledge is good for. Nor is an examination of epistemic choice incompatible with a Kuhnian sense that any massive, revolutionary shift in theoretical systems effectively cancels one set of things that are known and replaces it with another, different set. After all, Thomas Kuhn himself describes the "crisis stage" between the demise of the old theoretical system and the advent of the new as one in which scientists deliberately cobble together bits of old and new in a conscious effort to think two incompatible ways at once.[21]

Disknowledge is, in the end, a deliberate means by which a culture can manage epistemological risk. Early modern England felt itself at risk in many arenas that feel quite familiar today, from credit crises to terrorism. Among those arenas, however, perhaps the most pervasive and the least subject to control was what David Glimp has called "the global flow of risky knowledge."[22] The sense among the early modern intelligentsia that knowledge was risky was both self-generated and imported. Even while they wrestled with the desirability and practicality of a humanist ideal in which, in theory at least, there was nothing that could not be safely known, early modern intellectual circles struggled to absorb challenging bodies of knowledge that came from "out there," whether they were entirely new (such as new scientific theories) or simply unorthodox (such as non-Christian theologies). Learning while not learning was a path sometimes taken to manage that epistemological risk. For example, Schiebinger has recently analyzed the curious phenomenon of botanists of the seventeenth and eighteenth centuries—the great age of not only colonial expansion but also botanical classification—who refused to transmit knowledge of particular New World plants: those that induced abortion.[23] Burgeoning European empires required a larger population, not a smaller one. Hence, their agents, despite being devoted to the advance of science, decided not to learn what they had in fact come to know. Not because they were censored, or censored themselves.[24] Not because they were like the colonizers of North America who, in Paul Mapp's account, made poor geopolitical decisions because of poor maps—that is, because they did not understand the scope of what lay before them.[25] Rather, they simply and professedly believed it dangerous for European women to have access to information about abortifacients, and thus they chose not to learn about what the New World had to offer. Like Milton's Adam, they knew to know no more.

To explain disknowledge further, then, I begin Chapter 1 by addressing the state of learning in the age of late humanism. Humanism's reading and research tools, along with its curriculum of letters, remained the standard for both education and scholarship throughout the sixteenth and seventeenth centuries. However, as I have already suggested, late humanism was beset with a crisis of confidence brought on by shifts in thinking about such issues as epistemology, matter theory, and the advisability of following classical models in shaping personal and national character. Religious and ideological divides meant that late humanism also found its ideal of syncretic knowledge impossible to maintain. One of the reasons, I believe, that authors reached so easily for alchemical metaphors when it came to considering knowledge practices was that alchemy, though it precedes humanism chronologically, adopts humanistic goals and practices and thus shares humanism's fissures. But while all of humanism's shortcomings—including, for example, the new Baconian suspicion that rhetoric was mere frippery rather than truly consequential—were also charges that could be leveled against alchemy, the discourse of theoretical alchemy undertook a magnificent rearguard action against the forces undermining humanism's legitimacy: it threw all of its resources into rhetorical extravagance and into figuration of every kind. That very process of figuration—the turn that defines the act of troping—becomes the grounds, I argue, for alchemical discourse's profitable associations with disknowledge. Proposing a theory of disknowledge that compares and contrasts it to other twentieth- and twenty-first-century models of possessing two incongruous states of knowledge at once, this chapter also begins to sketch out why, exactly, alchemy's habits of learning and expression make it such a suggestive metaphorical referent for thinking about one thing rather than another.

I focus in the succeeding chapters on three different intellectual domains that, in the literary works I discuss, are shunted aside with the specific aid of tropes from alchemy: the matter theory underlying the Roman Catholic dogma of transubstantiation; the Jewish tradition of Kabbalah; and the study of female reproductive anatomy. These were intellectual domains that sixteenth- and seventeenth-century England had particular need of disknowing, and the literary works discussed in these chapters share in the cultural project of turning from these uncomfortable topics. At the same time, however, these literary works expose the motives for disknowing these three intellectual domains and the processes by which they are disknown.

I have chosen these three topics for my focus because, in many ways, they share the peculiar epistemological status of alchemy that I described above, and thus are particularly amenable to the use of alchemical tropes. Transubstantiation, Kabbalah, and human reproduction are sixteenth- and seventeenth-century areas of inquiry in which transformation of some kind is at stake—physical, metaphysical, or biological. They are also, however, areas of inquiry in which the nature and even the possibility of genuine transformation are hotly debated. Transubstantiation, while officially discredited in post-Reformation Protestant theology, nevertheless continues to come up in discussions of Aristotelian matter theory and the newer matter theories that are beginning to challenge it. Kabbalah, which promises both physical and metaphysical transformation by means of uniquely powerful linguistic tools, is under suspicion because of its roots in Jewish learning. And the functions of female reproductive anatomy are being reevaluated in part because no one could agree on what role, if any, women's reproductive organs play in the transformation of reproductive matter from seed into child. In all three of these fields it is thus equally possible to rely on theories of transformation and to suspect that those same theories are theologically, biologically, or physically spurious.

My first focus is transubstantiation, and Chapter 2 explores how the metaphysical poetry of John Donne, George Herbert, and Henry Vaughan participates in the fits of cultural amnesia that necessarily surrounded the issue of Roman Catholicism in early modern England. Alchemical imagery in Donne, Herbert, and Vaughan facilitates the deliberate forgetting of the Roman Catholic doctrine of transubstantiation, while at the same time highlighting the fact that the Catholic physics underlying transubstantiation had shaped the Aristotelianism that still held currency in seventeenth-century matter theory. Quite ironically, it is because alchemy and transubstantiation share a status as physically dubious that these three poets find alchemy a useful replacement for transubstantiation. Their motives are quite different, however. Whereas Donne conjoins alchemical with Eucharistic imagery to provide some intellectual relief from taking the transformation of matter seriously, Herbert uses alchemy to signal how he finds such questions serious but unanswerable. Tracking Herbert closely, Vaughan—quite surprisingly, considering that he was not only the brother of a prominent alchemist but also dabbled in translating alchemical texts himself—uses alchemy to diverge from the nature of matter entirely. Vaughan's physical world is not a world of physics, and it is alchemy that signals it so.

Chapter 3 turns from alchemy's associations with Catholicism to what it and the other esoteric arts draw from Judaism. My topic here is how Christian theorists of the esoteric arts, like Christian scholars more generally, capitalize on reading techniques taught by late humanism to wrest Jewish learning from Jews. I begin with John Dee, whose hopes of purifying the physical universe through the manipulation of symbols attracted him to the alchemical use of Kabbalah. Dee's method of learning Kabbalah, however, may be fairly characterized as "skimming," a habit of learning he shares with Christian kabbalists from his age and beyond that relieves him of the responsibility for being true either to the Hebrew language or to the vast, seemingly impenetrable, and theologically suspect body of Jewish knowledge that Kabbalah represents. I then address Christopher Marlowe's *Doctor Faustus* and William Shakespeare's *The Tempest*, two plays that reference Dr. Dee but present two very different takes on Christian methods for simultaneously employing and discarding Jewish learning. Whereas *Faustus* endorses the utility of clever scholarly skimming in order to avoid unintended consequences—like, say, going to hell—*The Tempest* physicalizes the presence of the Jew in the slave Caliban, and thus reminds us of the undeniable source of the learning one has skimmed.

After attending to religion I turn to texts that use alchemy to help ponder how to handle one of the emerging adept sciences of the seventeenth century. Chapter 4 explores how anatomical and literary texts stave off the startling (and, to many, unsavory) new accounts of the female reproductive organs that became available in printed vernacular sources in England in the late sixteenth and seventeenth centuries. I begin with William Harvey, whose surprising introduction of alchemical imagery into discussions of mammalian reproduction coincides with his reading, then dismissing, his predecessor Helkiah Crooke's stout contention that women's contributions to the conception of children are as potent and as formative as men's. I then examine the way that literary texts deploy alchemical tropes in order to echo, play out, and critique the fantasies concocted by the refusal to see what could be known: women's essential part in forming children. On the one hand, in these works women are reformulated into the imagery of the alchemical experiment, in which fecund, productive vessels harbor the growth of new life. On the other, these works also tend to ironize such imagery, teasing the reader with the prospect of female bodies as either inert, dumb experimental vessels (who would want such a companion?) or powerful and perhaps incomprehensible bearers of transformation (who could control such a being?). Analyzing Spenser's *Faerie Queene* and Shakespeare's *Love's Labour's Lost*, Chapter 4 addresses how alchemy's alliances with disknowledge help frame larger issues: not only what can be known of the female body but also the ethical, social, and literary motivations for maintaining a particular epistemological relation to the feminine.

This book's final topic is different. I turn in Chapter 5 to how some authors make use of alchemical tropes to ponder the status of seventeenth-century knowledge making itself, and especially the odd form of knowledge making that is the writing of literature. It is no accident that Sidney's trope in *The Defense of Poetry* for how literature works is an alchemical one. The poet's fiction replaces the historian's fact, just as gold alchemically replaces brass. But alchemy complicates the seemingly straightforward analogy between gold and brass on the one hand, and fiction and fact on the other. "Fact," as Mary Poovey has helped us recognize (and as Sidney himself intuited), is an invented phenomenon: facts come into being in exactly the period of late humanism as a result of disciplinary pressures to account for a rapidly changing and increasingly economic existence.[26] If facts serve disciplinarity, though, so too may fiction. The alchemical metaphor serves Sidney's purpose because alchemy's straddling of the epistemological divide between known and not known, true and not true, suggests a new role for literature in the posthumanist divvying up of fields of learning.

By way of disciplinarity, alchemy comes to represent a choice for literary authorship. When Sidney's analogy is taken up by Shakespeare, Jonson, and Cavendish, it becomes the occasion for a meditation on where literature stands in an age of late humanism, when humanism's ideal of basing a perfected society on literary models was manifestly crumbling. It is true, as Anthony Grafton has argued, that the methods of emerging science continued to depend on humanist habits.[27] Nevertheless, the seventeenth century registered humanism's demotion, and the place of alchemy in these authors' works helps us understand some of the ways this demotion is felt in the literary realm: either as loss or as opportunity. Either literary endeavor may align itself with a threadbare vision of an intellectually omnivorous humanism or it may embrace a new specialism—the specialism of the writer. Those two incomparable plays bracketing the first decade of the seventeenth century, Shakespeare's *Hamlet* and Jonson's *The Alchemist*, put the case rather clearly. They distinguish between characters whose alchemical references point toward their pretensions for an all-encompassing knowledge scheme (Hamlet) and those whose alchemy indicates a willing alliance with discrete domains of disknowledge such as literature (Subtle, Face, and Dol Common). Cavendish's *Blazing World*, in the wake of Shakespeare and Jonson, reconceives literature not as a source for truth, as humanism would have it, but as so woven into the texture of the material world that it belongs to everyone, not to humanistically educated men alone.

In recent years, scholars from the humanities, social sciences, and sciences have proposed that the embrace of ignorance or nonknowledge in one fashion or another—from skepticism to the sublime to relativity to probability—marks and grounds intellectual culture's shift from the premodern to modernity.[28] In the end, alchemy can represent modernity for early modern authors in that it can demonstrate a way forward for knowledge practices otherwise mired in the no-longer-useful past. That way forward, however, may either frighten or hearten us, depending on the variety of disknowledge we see deployed. While this book's argument does not extend to the present moment, it is my hope—

even if a chagrined one—that the reader will quickly recognize how the habits of disknowledge impinge in damaging ways upon current learned discourse. The twenty-first century, at least in the United States, is an age of disknowledge redux, as elaborate systems like the theory of "intelligent design" are crafted merely so that they may replace bodies of knowledge that are subject to disapprobation. As Bruno Latour has pointed out, scholarly efforts of the last few decades to expose "facts" as socially constructed are all too easily enlisted in such causes.[29] When any scientific theory, no matter how well founded, may be viewed as a conspiracy theory, disknowledge can be a valuable way of shoving it aside. The use of alchemy by the writers I discuss might, in other words, model for modernity one of its most supple and frightening ideological strategies: not believing in what is not true, but rather knowing it is not true yet still acting as if we did believe.

Based on its affiliations with fiction, though, an alternative for early modern disknowledge is that it might model for modernity a kind of nimble epistemological and literary inventiveness. Gottfried Wilhelm Leibniz once told the story of how, hoping to consult a secret society of alchemists in Nuremberg even though he knew very little alchemy, he "read some alchemical books and put together the more obscure expressions—those he understood the least." The result was a letter of petition that not only got him admitted to the society but secured him an invitation to be its secretary and the offer of a pension.[30] On first glance, the moral of the story seems to be how to fake it. Leibniz's use of alchemical books parodies and hence undermines his own humanistic training: essentially, he mines alchemical books just as early modern schoolboys mined classical sources, extracting commonplaces they did not understand. But Leibniz is not exactly faking it. He is interested in alchemy because its physics is compelling to him, even if he has not yet mastered the lingo.[31] Thus his petition amounts to creating knowledge, even while eliding its absence. Alchemy gives Leibniz the occasion to engage in an inventiveness that is a far more cheering form of disknowledge. Turning from one kind of understanding can lead to another kind—one entirely new and, in its way, entirely true. True in a way that has never before been dreamt of, neither in your philosophy nor in any other avenue of your current habits of learning.

CHAPTER I

How to Sustain Humanism

From its beginnings in fourteenth- and fifteenth-century Italy, humanism aimed both to revolutionize learning practice and to create nations of educated men imbued with civic virtue. That optimistic program, however, had a fairly short reign. In England, a country that came late to the Renaissance, humanism was in its true ascendancy for less than a century. Arthur Kinney, in fact, dates humanism's English preeminence only from 1512, when John Colet chartered St. Paul's School in London on the principles of Christian humanist education, to 1605, when the publication of Francis Bacon's *The Advancement of Learning* brought home to England—in a way that previous European breakthrough works such as those by Nicolaus Copernicus, Andreas Vesalius, and Conrad Gessner had not—the fact that the ancient writers so revered by humanists were subpar explicators of the natural world.[1]

To be sure, Kinney's chronological exactitude has some of the disputability (and also some of the irony) of Virginia Woolf's declaration that "on or about December 1910 human character changed." As Woolf herself immediately qualifies, "The change was not sudden and definite like that."[2] The humanist curriculum thrived both in grammar schools and at Oxford and Cambridge well into the seventeenth century and even beyond, influencing writers and thinkers in every field from theater to history to natural and political philosophy, including writers and thinkers like Thomas Hobbes and John Locke who scorned humanism.[3] "But"—to quote Woolf one last time—"a change there was, nevertheless." Once English protoscientists like Bacon and William Gilbert began to echo, in their own way, Protestant suspicions that classical learning was not to be trusted, England began to share in what Brian Cummings calls the "crisis in studies" that ensued upon Protestantism's vexed relation to humanism's tenets.[4]

Demoting classical learning had the effect of undercutting three of the fundamental articles of humanistic faith. First, the idea that learning is founded on the mastery of rhetoric—most prominently, Ciceronian oratorical style. Second, the conviction that learning is furthered primarily by free access to written texts, by the skills to read and interpret those texts accurately, and by the ability to synthesize the wisdom of those texts—regardless of their origins—into a Christian knowledge base. And third, the belief that all these skills, both rhetorical and textual, should be put in the service of civic humanism: they equip the learned man with what he needs to improve himself and better his world. These principles had led an earlier generation of Tudor polemicists and schoolmasters to establish the *studia humanitatis*, including grammar, rhetoric, poetry, and moral philosophy, as the core—indeed, practically the entirety—of the grammar school curriculum. The idea was to train young men whose grounding in ancient wisdom would suit them for a civil society on a par with that of ancient Rome.[5] In the post-Baconian seventeenth century, in contrast, general learning—and hence civic and moral virtue—would ultimately be founded on expertises other than the command of humane letters. The classics and the philological skill required to parse those classics were increasingly seen as accomplishments befitting scholars, not men of the world.[6]

Humanism was undone, in the first instance, by a number of sixteenth-century sea changes in intellectual culture. Pyrrhonian skepticism, reintroduced to Europe in the 1560s with the publication in Latin of the works of Sextus Empiricus, joined other forms of skepticism already in circulation to remove, as Kinney puts it, "the possibility for precisely those absolute premises—such as the centrality and perfectibility of man, his educability and his transformation—upon which Tudor humanists erected an entire philosophy."[7] Efforts to reconcile skepticism with humanism did not allay the anxieties of educators like Philip Melanchthon, who worried that "Pyrrhonists or Academics, the destroyers of certitude" inculcate in impressionable young minds a "madness [that] annihilates the greatest gift of God, namely Truth, and overturns the arts, which preside over life."[8] Similarly, humanism's syncretic ideal, in which any newly encountered mode or body of erudition may be safely integrated into a flexible but nonetheless stable Christian worldview, also came into question. The same free access to new texts and new ideas that earlier on had fueled humanist syncretic ambitions now threatened to become too many new texts and new ideas, too much free knowledge, too many possible positions.[9] Melanchthon's early sixteenth-century vision of

a union of truth and the arts gave way in the seventeenth century to what
Frances Dolan calls a "crisis in evidence" in which any given reader might compile a version of events and their causation into a highly idiosyncratic, self-
designed story that, though purporting to be a "true relation," would bear no
resemblance to someone else's competing account.[10]

Perhaps most important of all the contributors to humanism's decline was
the fact that, generally speaking, humanism's faith in instilling personal and
national virtue by means of rhetorical and philological training proved inadequate to the religious, intellectual, and political challenges of the day. Even
before Bacon classifies practically all of humanist practice—its reliance on
classical authorities, its emphasis on rhetorical style, and its devotion to "eloquence and copia"—among the "distempers in learning" that bar humankind's
advancement in understanding the natural world, humanism's fundamental
tenets and customary procedures had been substantially undermined.[11] No
amount of philological expertise could resolve Reformation differences over
interpreting the biblical text, differences that, in the end, came down to the individual reformer's insistence that her interpretation was inspired by the Holy
Spirit.[12] Even more crucially, the most evangelical sorts of Protestantism—
like the more fundamentalist sorts of Catholicism that took hold in post-
Reformation Europe—equated the secular reading on which humanist thought
was founded with moral degradation, just as John Milton's Son of God does
when he rebukes Satan's offer of unlimited classical learning:

> Who therefore seeks in these
> True wisdom, finds her not, or by delusion
> Far worse, her false resemblance only meets.[13]

While training in rhetoric continued to be crucial for participation in politics
and government, many in the late sixteenth and seventeenth centuries, from
Queen Elizabeth I to Hobbes, began to suspect that immersion in the texts
of the Roman republic made the educated man and those who imitated him
susceptible to sedition and insurrection. That suspicion was manifested most
explicitly in the established church's backlash against the value humanism
placed on individual assertions of what the polis needed. It was not only in
post-Tridentine Catholic Europe, as Margo Todd points out, that church and
state hierarchy alike began to view humanistic training as undermining right
order.[14] If that were not enough, looking to ancient Rome as a model for the
modern state began to feel less attractive in nations like England, which was

beginning to realize its history included humiliating vassalage to Roman conquerors.[15]

Thus Hiram Haydn memorably identifies the sixteenth and early seventeenth centuries as "the Counter-Renaissance," a period in which thinkers from Martin Luther to Niccolò Machiavelli to Michel de Montaigne shared "an anti-intellectualistic, anti-moralistic, anti-synthetic, anti-authoritarian bias."[16] Prominent thinkers of all stripes, all of them humanistically trained, began to express serious doubts about the utility of humanism's text-based learning system. Gilbert complains in the preface to his book on magnetism, published in 1600, that the "Ocean of Books by which the minds of studious men are troubled and fatigued" hinders "trustworthy experiments and . . . demonstrated arguments."[17] And even the truly learned King James I, after counseling his son Henry to be well read in scripture and in history, advises that "As for the studie of other liberal artes and sciences, I would have you reasonably versed into them, but not preassing to be a passe-master in any of them," lest Henry be caught, "as Archimedes was," engrossed in his studies while his enemies storm the gates.[18]

To counter humanism is not to replace it, however. The fact that this increasing sense of humanism's intellectual, theological, and political shortcomings coexisted with the persistence of humanist education enabled a double vision for England's learned classes: they acknowledged and articulated its problems but at the same time continued to employ it as if there were nothing problematic about it. The result is a habitually ironic stance on the subject of humanistic learning. As Jeff Dolven describes the situation of letters in the later sixteenth century, writers "cannot free their books . . . from a culture of teaching that they take to be compromised, even bankrupt."[19] It is possible to be skeptical about a system while still functioning wholly within it.

Humanism was undone not only by its well-known theoretical shortcomings but also by the accretive calcification that besets all grand schemes for educational and civic reform. As I detail in the first section of this chapter, humanism as a pedagogical program and as applied textual practice inevitably acquired cookie-cutter tendencies; it also acquired techniques for shortcutting, condensing, and deracinating the more controversial portions of challenging texts. These techniques abetted charges in the late sixteenth and early seventeenth centuries that humanism's foundational attention to language—its dependence on rhetoric—amounted to a foundational commitment to fiction. A commitment, that is, not to discovering truth but rather to making things up.

Any body of knowledge developed along humanistic lines shares humanism's fate. Alchemical study and practice, having adopted humanistic principles of producing knowledge out of linguistic skill, also—in an intensified version of what happens with humanism—acquire a reputation for shortcuts and fictions. At the same time, however, alchemical discourse commits itself so thoroughly to rhetoric that it embraces linguistic invention. The second section of this chapter describes the reputation alchemical discourse developed for rhetorical innovation, especially its talent for allegory. For authors seeking tropes for all kinds of knowledge practices, both scrupulous and slipshod, alchemical discourse thus offers an irresistible set of metaphors. Most obviously, alchemy serves as an all-purpose trope for learning that is attuned to fancy rather than fact.

But the use of alchemy as metaphor goes further than that. Alchemy comes to serve as a trope for learning models that, in the manner of late humanism, persist and even flourish even when their shortcomings are manifest and well known. In the third section of this chapter I gather some historical evidence, some likely causes, and some theoretical models for how alchemy comes to be associated with this kind of dedication to insufficient or diversionary learning, and I explain why a new term, *disknowledge*, is needed to denote a specific kind of knowledge practice, one that is a deliberate turn from something else that is known. Finally, in this chapter's last section, I turn to the way that, in the protracted twilight of humanism, authors who see the advantages of retaining and developing alternative knowledge practices associated with fiction seize upon alchemy as a metaphor for the special case of learning that, insubstantial or outmoded though it may be, ought to be pursued nonetheless.

Alchemy and the Habits of Late Humanism

If humanism began its decline in England in the late sixteenth century, what replaced it? Traditionally, the answer has been science: text-based learning gave way to Baconian empiricism. This framework does not take into account, however, the long lag time between the predominance of one learning system and the ascendency of the next. This period, which some scholars of intellectual history have taught us to call "late humanism," may be demarcated in any number of ways depending on whether one emphasizes religion, socioeconomics, or politics as the causative factor of humanism's decline. But in terms of the way the acquisition of knowledge was conceived, we may trace the span of late humanism roughly from the 1580s to the 1660s, or from the popularization of skepticism in Montaigne's *Essays* to the founding of the Royal Society in London.[20]

As it happens, this same span of years marks the zenith of alchemy in England. While this coincidence is in some respects just that—coincidental—it is also the case that interest in alchemy spiked because it seemed to offer a solution to the problems besetting humanism's most cherished ideals.[21] Of course, alchemical learning since at least the late fifteenth century, like other protosciences, had mirrored, imitated, and indeed depended on the same shifts in education and scholarship that produced humanism in the first place. Marsilio Ficino's and Giovanni Pico della Mirandola's passions for reviving ancient texts did not discriminate between Plato and Hermes Trismegistus.[22] But the affiliations between humanistic and alchemical thought became all the more urgent as humanism took serious blows to its foundations. Arguably, alchemy is what kept humanism going, even if in esoteric form. For some English thinkers, as Bruce Janacek has discussed, alchemy's attractions had to do with its promise of turning schismatic and political rifts into a universal golden age; this alchemical goal may have breathed new life into humanism's fading hopes for unity under the banner of civic virtue.[23] Alchemy also rallied behind humanism's ideal of syncretic knowledge. In an age of encroaching disciplinarity, seventeenth-century alchemy resuscitated Ficino's and Pico's fifteenth-century dreams of unifying all knowledge within one system and under one purpose. It is perhaps for this reason that humanistic educational schemes devised in the seventeenth century began to encourage an attraction to alchemy despite alchemy's long-standing academic disrepute. For example, educational reformer Jan Amos Comenius, the man often credited with bringing Baconian posthumanist empiricism into late seventeenth-century educational practice, nonetheless professed a decidedly humanist "pansophism" that included alchemy within the fields of universal knowledge.[24] A better answer, then, to the question of what replaced humanism is that it was replaced by alchemy. Alchemy became humanism by other means.

Alchemy's alliances with humanism were methodological as well as ideological. As Wouter Hanegraaff notes, while alchemical experimental practice gained tremendous sophistication during this period—even becoming, for some practitioners, a prototype for the scientific empiricism that would eventually predominate—theoretical alchemy remained largely text-based, retaining both humanism's culture of books and humanism's conviction that rhetoric and the play of language could effect positive, real-world change.[25] Finally, alchemy began in this period to adopt humanism's intense focus on having ancient textual sources for its wisdom. Alchemy had long claimed its origins lay in ancient Egypt and in the occult expertise of biblical patriarchs like Moses, but seventeenth-century authors were even more eager than their predecessors to claim alchemy as "traceable not just to Hermes [Trismegistus] but to the most distant and venerable past, to a body of knowledge known as the 'original wisdom' (*prisca sapentia*) revealed by God to the ancient patriarchs— in some versions to Adam himself."[26] Alchemical philology also embraced the humanistically derived ideal of syncretism. Charles Webster argues that it was, in fact, Comenius's idea that "Perfect knowledge would be ratified by all sources" that led to Isaac Newton's determination to study the ancient texts of alchemy—which, Newton marveled, "have a concurrence with Antiquity and Theology."[27] Thus Newton's ultimate alchemical goal was not the philosopher's stone, about which he seems to have been rather skeptical, but instead a comprehensive *Index chemicus* that would compile all alchemical wisdom, ancient and modern.[28]

If alchemy absorbed and imitated humanism's aims and practices, however, it also absorbed and imitated the bad habits humanism had developed and the increasingly tenuous reputation humanism had acquired by the late sixteenth and seventeenth centuries. Specifically, alchemy marks fissures and weaknesses in Renaissance humanism that expose this greatest period of intellectual expansion as also one of intellectual contraction. Stephanie Jed has discussed how humanism's desire to recover ancient learning was always marked by equal and opposite impulses: on the one hand, to uncover and resuscitate as many new authorities and new strands of knowledge as possible and, on the other, to pare down the canon of texts so that the spurious, adulterated, and anachronistic are sheared away.[29] Both of these impulses can contribute to scholarly excellence, but both can also contribute to defensive, poor, or even simply lazy scholarly behavior.[30] Expanding the horizons of learning through infinitely expanding the library of predecessor texts can lead to a gullible or simply indolent acceptance of any kind of book—even a bad one—as legitimate. Conversely, the desire to maintain a suitably excised canon of texts can devolve, as Charles Nauert reminds us, into an educational practice that depends on a very limited set of texts deemed safe for students' consumption.[31] The early modern commonplace book, for example, often serves as the record of a practice of "snippetizing" acceptable content from which copious, but sanitized, arguments might then be built.[32] In addition, late sixteenth-century educational reforms such as those influenced by Peter Ramus encouraged the use of textbooks, rather than the humanists' beloved ancient texts themselves, in both grammar school and university instruction.[33]

We can even see the impulse to excise and excerpt books as a humanist response to the equally humanist imperative to expand the horizons of learning through infinitely expanding the library of predecessor texts. While scholars have always complained about the length of their reading lists, the sixteenth and seventeenth centuries, as I mentioned in this book's introduction, saw a notable backlash against the number of books one was now expected to have at one's command. Ann Blair calls this backlash a response to early modern "information overload."[34] Andrew Martin, in contrast, suggests that cutting back on one's reading was an ethical response to the fact that "the sheer proliferation and diversity of available texts degraded the ideal of a comprehensive intellectual synthesis to a merely eclectic juxtaposition of unreconciled manners and ideas."[35] Either way, the impulse was to read less. By 1685, French scholar Adrien Baillet was recommending simply "separating those books which we must throw [out] or leave in oblivion from those which one should save and within the latter between what is useful and what is not."[36] Immediately we spot the problem: in order to separate the keeper books from the discards and the useful from the useless, one must read them. Anyone who attempted Baillet's winnowing process would no doubt give up long before all the books were read.

Both of these seemingly contradictory responses to the proliferation of books—feeling that there are simply too many books to read, and also neglecting to read enough of them to determine which are good and which are not—crop up in alchemical theory and practice. As Tara Nummedal describes it, whereas alchemists were told they should accept the procedure detailed in one alchemical book only if it was confirmed by another, following the philological principle of *liber librum explicat*, "the book explicates the book," in practice many alchemists tended to rely on only a few books at most.[37] No doubt the high price of books limited the size of most practicing alchemists' libraries. And yet, a number of alchemical writers who were unconcerned with where the alchemist's next book was coming from still shared late humanism's notably ambivalent attitude toward the difficult work of reading, absorbing, and synthesizing a plethora of challenging texts.

As with late humanism, the problem of alchemical knowledge management is not merely one of the sheer volume of reading material. Rather, having taken on humanism's project of Christian syncretism, alchemy also tussles with the humanist dilemma of how to incorporate ideologically challenging texts—a dilemma that, as I have mentioned, looms larger as religious positions harden and splinter in the post-Reformation era. Humanism always comprises equal and opposing impulses: on the one hand, read everything, but on the other, compose and remember only what is congruent with Christian virtue. Humanistic editing and winnowing are intended to maintain not only philological standards and a reading list of a manageable size but also ideological comfort. Similarly, alchemical reading practice, while it maintains the ideal of syncretic learning with perhaps more ease than late humanism itself does, is as concerned with choosing which texts to excise as it is with which texts to assimilate.

For humanism as a whole, those opposing impulses of assimilation and excision are nicely summed up by the dual uses, bracketing the humanist era, of Horace's epigram, "I have set out to pass through all the masters of philosophy, while swearing by none." In the late fifteenth century, Pico took Horace's remark as his motto for universal erudition. By the late seventeenth century, the very same epigram had become, for the Royal Society, what Anthony Grafton calls science's "pledge to trust no book."[38] While the motto's use by the Royal Society is now taken as signifying the triumph of scientific empiricism and the rehabilitation of curiosity about the natural world from a moral vice into an intellectual virtue, its repetition from the early days of humanism invites us to query what happened in the intervening years, between Pico and the Royal Society, to early humanism's reverence for predecessor texts.[39] One answer is that in some cases intellectuals tried to justify reading less. As textual precedent was losing its preeminent status but empirical data had not yet come to replace it, it proved quite possible to "trust no book" so far as to declare that very few books were worth reading. And hence—because books were still the source from which knowledge was derived—to declare that very few things were worth learning. Thus, some writers on alchemy, like their late-humanist fellows in other disciplines, handle this state of affairs by massaging humanism's reverence for ancient sources into an explicit exhortation to read as little as possible.

Justifying reading less requires some finessing, however. It requires what Ian Hacking has labeled a "self-stabilizing technique": that which allows a particular "style" of scientific (or pseudoscientific) reasoning to persist.[40] Among the most effective self-stabilizing techniques of alchemical theory are its claims not only to antiquity but also to universality. Everything in existence, whether animal, vegetable, mineral, or spiritual, may be alchemically explained. That style of universalizing can in turn make it possible for an alchemical thinker to justify never having to expand her intellectual horizons. When faced with a problem that seems to be outside the alchemical discipline, the alchemist has the option of denying that it is outside at all. As John Locke remarks in his posthumously published treatise *Of the Conduct of the Understanding*, "A metaphysician will bring ploughing and gardening immediately to abstract notions; the history of nature shall signify nothing to him. An alchemist, on the contrary, shall reduce divinity to the maxims of his laboratory, explain morality by sal, sulphur and mercury, and allegorise the Scripture itself and the sacred mysteries thereof into the philosopher's stone."[41]

Just as alchemy's sense of its own universality potentially transmutes into its conviction that there is nothing else besides alchemy to be studied, so can its attachment to predecessor texts transmute into claims of the primacy and sole authority of an exceptionally small corpus of antique learning. As an example let us turn to Robert Fludd, who in his *Philosophia Moysaica* (1638) not only excoriates ancient Greek philosophers' inability to recognize a "sacred essence" common to all creatures but also, at some length, blames those same philosophers for failing to cite their original source, the books of Moses as preserved in the Old Testament: "they having had a view of Moses his labours, which were indited by the Spirit of God, did gather out, and confesse the truth of his doctrine, touching the principles of all things, and yet would not in open tearms acknowledge their Master, but altered the names of them." Fludd has discerned that as Aristotle cribbed from Plato, so too did Plato crib from Moses. Only Hermes Trismegistus—author of the primary texts of alchemy and supposedly Moses' Egyptian contemporary—is exempt from criticism because he acknowledges his source: "the excellent Philosopher Hermes, otherwise termed Mercurius Trismegistus, expresseth plainly, that he was not onely acquainted with Moses his books, but also was made partaker of his mysticall and secret practise."[42] Just as the divine essence is transmitted across all substances and creatures in heaven and earth (such that alchemy is merely a matter of refining a lump of stuff to get at what is already there), so too are true principles transmitted across scientific and philosophical authorities so effectively that the original text source remains primary even when the author himself claims to be inventing something new. Fludd allows his reader to leave off ancient philosophers and take up only the books of Moses and of Hermes.

The effect of this logic is to deny that there can ever be a new idea. As Fludd has it, alchemy's constant, if often mysterious, references to ancient authority and past practice mark it as the paradigmatically conservative knowledge system: it enforces a principle of continuous preservation. Thus, unlike Bacon's new inductive science—which, as Mary Poovey has argued, invents itself as something that looks new only by occluding its continuities with the past (the same charge that Fludd levels against Plato and Aristotle, who fudge their dependence on Moses)—Fludd's alchemy is proud of its staving off all that is new, defined as all writing that postdates Moses and his pupil Hermes.[43] We can thus distinguish Fludd's gesture of reverting to ancient learning from the same claim to intertextual lineage made by humanism in its most optimistic phase. Like a good humanist (or a good Protestant reformer), Fludd makes an attempt to pare away the accretions of ill-founded medievalism in order to return to the apex of an ancient past. But Fludd's insistence that all classical learning derives from "the Mosaic philosophy" means that commerce with the classics will not lend itself to an advancement of learning. Discovery does not matter; indeed, discovery is undesirable.

Similarly, Michael Sendivogius's *Novum lumen chymicum* (1604) urges the study of alchemy because it retreats from newfangled discoveries, reinforcing instead what one ought to have always known. Stick to the ancient writings on the philosopher's stone, says Sendivogius, because those writers focused on only the essential matters: "although they were contented with the plaine way alone of nature, yet they found out those things, which we now imployed about divers things could not with all our wits conceive." We misguided moderns, in contrast, "bend our wits not to things knowne, and familiar, but to such things, which not at all, or very hardly can be done. . . . And such is the disposition of mens natures, as to neglect those things they know, and to be alwaies seeking after other things."[44] Alchemy's supposed antiquity morphs into its fundamentalism: it is not subject to addition or development. Alchemy thus comports with the tension that Hanegraaff finds in discussions of the origins of wisdom after the flush of early humanism had passed. Early humanism's *prisca theologia*, "a historically/chronologically oriented narrative of ancient wisdom which held considerable revolutionary potential," comes to be matched by an idea of *philosophia perennis*, "an essentially conservative doctrine which preaches the futility of change and development by emphasizing the transhistorical continuity and universality of absolute truth."[45] As with other kinds of fundamentalism that arose in the sixteenth century, the question for alchemy then becomes one of interpreting the originary text properly and not of reading or writing new ones.

The idea that there is no new idea can be reinforced by alchemy's custom of declaring its precepts secret. Alchemical devotees urged to stick to the ancient texts may well have found themselves puzzling over how to claim a past so ancient and so occult that no one had full access to it. In keeping with the medieval and early modern tradition of *libri secretorum*, "books of secrets," many alchemical texts assert that full knowledge is available only to the man of ultimate knowledge and skill, the magus. In other words, available only to someone whose existence is always in doubt and whose knowledge is transmitted charily, if at all. Recent historians including William Eamon, Allison Kavey, and Neil Kamil have quite rightly questioned the pose of secrecy in books of secrets and in alchemical artisanal circles, analyzing instead the role of secrets in developing the kind of experimentation that will play a part in the scientific revolution (Eamon), in popularizing such experimentation among diverse groups, including women and less elite sorts (Kavey), and in maintaining the identity of a minority religious community in both Europe and the New World (Kamil).[46] Nevertheless, despite the utility of the posture of withholding secrets, such a pose of "not telling" blatantly challenges the ideal of the textual transmission of knowledge that was fundamental to humanism in its early phase.

When alchemy's humanistic devotion to ancient learning morphs into a late-humanistic desire to learn less, the kind of systematic philological analysis of the nature of one's debt to antiquity that was the hallmark of humanism in its prime also falls away. Although the scholar and master philologist Isaac Casaubon, in work published in 1614, debunked the attribution of the works of Hermes Trismegistus to ancient Egypt by making note of the *Corpus Hermeticum*'s extensive use of late-antique references, Casaubon's correction was ignored or disputed throughout the seventeenth century by several prominent alchemists and occultists including both Robert Fludd and Athanasius Kircher.[47] An air of profound continuity was so important to a certain strain of alchemical thinking that some scholars were willing to throw aside their humanist training to achieve it.

Alchemical Rhetoric: Beyond Humanism

Beyond a shared suspicion of too many books and unmanageable learning, beyond abandoning a commitment to all of antique learning and to the philology that would establish that learning as genuine, alchemy of the late sixteenth and seventeenth centuries shared one more thing with late humanism: the reputation for the excessive production of language.

From its beginnings, humanism famously saw the study and imitation of classical eloquence as intrinsic to the cultivation of personal and civic virtue. As Neil Rhodes puts Petrarch's point of view, "There is little point in knowing what virtue is . . . if you cannot move men to strive toward it."[48] Rhetoric held real-world power. By the late sixteenth and early seventeenth centuries, however, elaborately designed rhetorical display came under suspicion by some as only so much frivolous ornament, old-fashioned in style and empty of meaning.[49] This shift in opinion was not merely a shift in fashion from Ciceronian, euphuistic style to the newly popular "plain style"; it was also a reaction to a newly skeptical intellectual milieu in which, as Kinney puts it, "persuasion [could] take the place of truth."[50] By 1667, Thomas Sprat felt comfortable describing the Royal Society's preference for "the language of Artizans, Countrymen, and Merchants, before that, of Wits, or Scholars" as the only means of combating "the easie vanity of fine speaking" and the "beautiful deceipt" to which that fine speech led.[51]

It was not that late-humanist writers like Bacon disdained rhetoric entirely. Both practically speaking and as a result of their own humanist educations, they could hardly do so. As Brian Vickers has noted, it is important not to "take [late humanist] calls for the banishment of rhetoric as proof that this duly took place."[52] But Vickers himself commits the opposite error when he takes the fact that rhetoric continued to be praised and deployed in seventeenth-century education as evidence that humanism was not in decline. He forgets that something may be praised even when its faults are manifestly known.[53] A more accurate description of the late humanist period is that many began to view rhetorical skill as merely a tool needed for fine writing rather than as the basis for the public oratory that inculcates the modern state with ancient civic virtue.[54] Moreover, following Ramus, many began to reassign the foundations of good composition—proof and the arrangement of argument (*inventio* and *dispositio*)—from rhetoric, where Cicero and Quintilian had them, to logic.[55] Some recent scholarship has sought to defend Ramus against charges of discarding all that was valuable about the humanistic study of letters, and it may also be true, as Mordechai Feingold has argued, that the Ramist emphasis on logic over rhetoric did not have as much influence on English thinkers as has been claimed.[56] Nonetheless, in Ramus's insistence that discourse is best when closest to human "natural reasoning"—by which he means the reasoning of the uneducated as well as the educated—we find the germ of Sprat's Royal Society praise for the language of the artisan over the rhetoric of the humanist scholar.[57]

Just as alchemy followed early humanism in valuing a pedigree of ancient learning, so too did it follow early humanism in regarding language as productive of real-world change. Alchemy, however—like the occult sciences more generally—meant this change literally. Drawing not only from theurgic tradition but also from classical and humanist rhetoric's mythos of ancient orators as "the first leaders to bind untamed humanity together with mystical eloquence," magicians and occult philosophers, Ryan Stark argues, held the belief that "certain tropes, arranged properly and spoken forcefully by experts, had the spiritual energy to transmogrify both inanimate and animate objects alike."[58] Alchemy's version of this belief depended on the tenet that all creatures and substances, both terrestrial and celestial, partook to some degree in a shared, divinely imparted essence. While most alchemical treatises were uninterested in the topic of how the alchemist's power aligns with God's, some Christianized theories of how alchemy works posited that the divine essence manifest both in God's verbal creation of the world and in Christ's incarnation as the Word made flesh may be invoked and controlled through the alchemist's properly reverent use of language. In his introduction to a seventeenth-century English translation of the *Pimander*, a text among those attributed to Hermes Trismegistus himself, Paracelsian physician John French in fact puts Hermes in the place of the Ciceronian originary orator who civilized the world through a magical rhetoric. Crediting Hermes with the invention both of writing and of literature, French declares, rather heretically, "If God ever appeared in any man, he appeared in [Hermes]."[59]

Given alchemy's attentiveness to the power of language, not to mention the humanistic training of many sixteenth- and seventeenth-century authors of alchemical texts, it is not surprising that those texts should flourish their own rhetorical bona fides—to the extent, Lawrence Principe has argued, of attempting to lend alchemy a more legitimate air by dressing it up in Greco-Latin terminology, classical allusions, or even Latin verse form.[60] But in an era in which humanism itself started to seem past its sell-by date, such a display of rhetorical skill risked backfiring, identifying alchemy not with current scientific theory and practice but with outmoded learning. And with a rather overdone version of it, at that. Principe describes how early modern alchemists' increasing efforts to festoon their theory with antique supporting authorities led to their being ridiculed for finding alchemy in every biblical or classical story, from Jason's golden fleece to the Israelites' golden calf.[61] If alchemy's overblown claims of classical pedigree could seem absurd, so too could its overblown humanist-style claims of rhetorical power. Despite his interest in the practical application of Paracelsian "chymistry," physician and University of Wittenberg professor Daniel Sennert, in a strikingly antirhetorical comment, pooh-poohs the idea he finds in Paracelsus that words have a transformative effect. Paracelsus "said Characters would cure diseases otherwise uncurable. . . . [But] words do only declare the sense of the mind, and work no further."[62] Sennert's objections are necessary only because alchemical discourse remained fully committed in the seventeenth century to the transformative capacities of language. By the lights of its devotion to rhetoric, we see alchemy not merely as influenced by humanism but as one of humanism's last surviving outposts.

To take this point one step further, the explosion of alchemical texts in England in the late sixteenth and seventeenth centuries may be seen as a last-ditch effort at keeping humanistic rhetoric vital and imperative, alive in the discursive output of a discipline that claimed to touch upon all that is, in heaven and upon earth. Alchemical texts, as it turns out, are especially committed to certain kinds of humanist rhetorical techniques. What is interesting about these techniques is how they work very specifically to maintain the centrality of language to the alchemical enterprise in a way that mirrors and revives early humanism's dream of linguistic power. In fact, alchemical discourse seems to double down on humanist rhetoric in a way that reinvents it. Alchemical texts not only routinely deploy rhetorical strategies that are congruent in character with the alchemical goal of physical and metaphysical transmutation but also suggest that part of alchemy's mission extends to symbolic production, from the production of new words and new multisymbolic representational systems (such as diagrams) to the production of metaphor and allegory. The effect, in some instances, is not simply to reclaim invention, which had been reassigned by Ramus to the realm of logic, for rhetoric. It is also to establish a peculiarly alchemical form of rhetoric, one that freely cops to the charges that linguistic creations are merely a kind of fabrication but claims those linguistic creations' importance nonetheless.

Practical alchemy was responsible for real invention, as I have mentioned. As Bruce Moran points out, even those who derided alchemy's more far-fetched claims praised it for what Italian metallurgist Vanoccio Biringuccio called "that pleasing novelty which it shows to the experimenter in operation."[63] The novelty most obvious in theoretical alchemy, however, is the novelty of symbolic schemes: diagrams, tables, emblems, signs, and—above all—words. In some cases, the new symbology is designed to keep secret the alchemist's most treasured processes.[64] Usually, though, such new symbols, like new alchem-

ical terminology in general, were not a matter of privacy; rather, they proliferated all the more in alchemy's public productions, the printed tracts and
public demonstrations that created the public persona of the intellectual
alchemist. The second English printing of *The Last Will and Testament* of the
(probably fictional) alchemist Basilius Valentinus, for example, includes a help-
ful "Table of Chymicall & Philosophicall Characters with their significations
as they are usually found in Chymicall Authors both printed & manuscript."
This table lists no fewer than a dozen symbols for gold and nearly as many for
lead, tin, copper, mercury, and silver—far more than the typical curious reader
could have known before picking up the book.[65]

Part of the attraction of alchemy to a larger audience thus lies in its
invention of new terminology, bright shiny new words that proliferate, in a
neologistically minded age, among a literate class attracted to and apt to use the
latest lingo. Nicholas Clulee points out that "Unlike the disciplines taught in
the universities and even astrology, there was in alchemy no fixed discourse
and vocabulary and no primers providing a ready introduction to the art."[66]
Hence the field offered unlimited opportunities for concocting new vocabulary.
Writers who disdained alchemy found this habit easy to mock. As Reginald
Scot acerbically remarked, alchemists must be "learned and jollie fellowes"
because they "have in such readinesse so many mysticall termes of art."[67] Easy
to mock; but hard to resist. In Ben Jonson's 1616 masque *Mercury Vindicated
from the Alchemists at Court*, Mercury himself—despite complaining about the
perverted uses to which court alchemists put him—cannot help parading the
irresistible lexicon that accompanied the alchemical process and that was starting to transfer itself via metaphorical cross-reference to general English usage:
"I am their crude and their sublimate, their precipitate and their unctuous, their
male and their female, sometimes their hermaphrodite; what they list to stile
me."[68] In the same way, the con artists of Jonson's *The Alchemist* deploy alchemical terminology for all it's worth. They do so not merely as part of the apparatus
by which they snow their customers but also among themselves, when the cha-
rade is not needed—as if those words were too good not to pull out of one's
pocket whenever possible. Subtle uses the same terms as Jonson's Mercury
when he angrily points out that he has alchemized his colleague from servant
Jeremy to "Captain" Face, from the basest of substances to the purest:

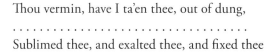

Thou vermin, have I ta'en thee, out of dung,
. . . .
Sublimed thee, and exalted thee, and fixed thee

I' the third region, called our state of grace?
Wrought thee to spirit, to quintessence, with pains
Would twice have won me the philosopher's work [that is, the
    philosopher's stone]?

Then, as if to comment on the inextricable connection between alchemy and
neologism, he also notes he has "Put [Face] in words, and fashion."[69]

    Alchemical terminology need not even be seriously posed to put people
in words as Subtle does Face. Erasmus's skeptical colloquy "Alcumistica"
details how a con man alchemist gulls a scholar—and not just any scholar, a
rhetorician. The learned Balbinus is taken in by an alchemist who comes to
him seeking his advice on a better method for transforming matter. The alchemist professes to be puzzled about how to leave off the *longatio* method of
alchemy in favor of *curtatio*: "One is shorter but a little more risky; the other
takes longer but is safer. . . . [U]p to now I've toiled in this latter path, which
does not please me, and I've been unable to find anyone willing to show me
the other path that I'm dying to find."[70] The joke is that Erasmus has made
up *longatio* and *curtatio* out of thin air, so convincingly that he eventually
dupes even Reginald Scot, who employs Erasmus's new words in the *Discoverie of Witchcraft* in their English forms, "longation" and "curtation," as if they
were authentic alchemical terms.[71] Erasmus's joke is on the educated reader who,
like Reginald Scot, takes the fabricated words for real just as Balbinus takes
the alchemist's bogus schemes for real. In the end, though, the crucial aspect
of made-up words like *longatio* and *curtatio* is not whether we are or are not
in the know about their fabricated status. What is important is that they are so
innovative and seemingly authoritative that we may want to use them, legitimate or not.

    The appeal of new alchemical words is connected to the appeal of alchem-
ical emblems, diagrams, and illustrations. Facilitated by the proliferation of
print and the increasing sophistication of illustration technique for printed
books, these verbal-visual hybrids had the practical function of helping new
symbolic associations reach a nonspecialist public. Often, however, they also
seem to be included for more than simply illustrative purposes. When George
Ripley's late fifteenth-century *Compound of Alchemy*, first printed in 1591, appears in Elias Ashmole's *Theatrum chemicum Britannicum* (1652), it features
a diagram that promises to be "the Figure conteyning all the secrets of the
Treatise both great & small."[72] But this diagram displays what Benedek Láng
calls the general tendency of diagrams in magic texts to have "lost their links

to the texts that explained their functioning": it has both less and more than Ripley's text.[73] On the one hand, whereas the text describes twelve successive "gates" or steps in the alchemical process, from calcination to projection, the diagram has only eleven concentric circles corresponding (in some fashion) to those steps. On the other hand, almost all of the circles in the diagram, though they supposedly correspond to those progressive steps, seem to refer to the alchemical end's already having been achieved. Either way, the diagram establishes itself as an alternative maker of meaning. It is alchemy's adoption of new signifying systems such as the diagram or the emblem that leads Thomas Greene to group "hermetic correspondences" with the late sixteenth century's other semiotic innovations, a newly stocked "storehouse of signifying capacities" that included everything from Protestant exegetical discourse to the nascent public theater.[74]

Alchemical discourse, in other words, is appealing not simply because it provides a new array of conventionally referential words or symbols. Rather, alchemical discourse posits a new mode of creating meaning, through aesthetic design so overabundant that it likely exceeds the text's discursive needs or the reader's capacity to comprehend. Alchemical discourse thus both confirms and tests Hacking's sense that rhetoric shapes reasoning to such an extent that any chasm between old science and new science may be explained as much by a shift in rhetorical style as by a shift in paradigm (per Thomas Kuhn) or by a shift from one concept to another, incommensurable concept (per Paul Feyerabend).[75] In alchemy's case, new rhetoric indicates new thinking, but it is not thinking that we would now call "the new science." Rather, we might think of it as "the new old rhetoric," one that confutes the late sixteenth-century chasm that, for some, had developed between words and truth. Contrary to the opinion of those who associated Ciceronian rhetoric with mere ornament, alchemy's new words and new pictorial schemes truly craft something original: *inventio*, not just *copia*.

In this way alchemical discourse establishes a third position, one that is neither the early humanist insistence that rhetoric shapes the world nor the later, Baconian plain-style implication that rhetoric is at best descriptive and at worst an extravagant flight of fancy. Alchemical discourse and alchemical diagram knowingly generate extravagant flights of fancy that nonetheless shape the world. Alchemy's revision of late-humanist rhetoric into a productively decorative, rather than merely decorative, system puts it in the company of other kinds of innovation in natural philosophy in the period of late humanism. If, as Marco Beretta argues, the alchemical mania for symbology was first developed as a way of sidestepping the habits of Aristotelian dispute that occupied the medieval university—so that "alchemists used pictograms, symbols, emblems etc. instead of disputing the philological origins of words and their precise definition"—then intellectual evasion proves the mother of alchemical invention.[76] Alchemy gives us an inventive symbology—as Beretta drily puts it, "a large number of symbols for a very small number of substances"— that comes to stand on its own, its own new heaven, new earth.[77]

In using new terms to create new horizons of symbolic possibility, alchemy also follows a trail blazed by early humanism but widened by late humanism, one that has only recently drawn the attention of scholars: not merely the quest for pure ancient languages cleansed of their medieval accretions but also the search for a new ancient language—one that, as it turns out, can be made up practically out of whole cloth. As Umberto Eco has detailed, "the search for the perfect language" often meant the invention of a language never found in nature or, for that matter, in libraries.[78] Pico, for example, crafted his syncretic humanism partly under the influence of Flavius Mithridates, the Jewish linguist whom Pico engaged to help translate Kabbalah into Latin but who proceeded to teach Pico to write what Alastair Hamilton calls "a bizarre mixture of Hebrew and Aramaic in Ethiopic characters."[79] Later experiments in producing a universal language were more systematic and also more original. In his geometrically and mathematically derived *Monas hieroglyphica* (1564), John Dee concocted his very own hieroglyphics, kabbalistically derived but consisting of new symbols rather than Hebrew, that could generate all the truths in the universe and all other human languages besides.[80] The "hieroglyphical monad" of the title of Dee's treatise, a symbol amalgamating various astrological signs (Mercury, Aries, Taurus, the sun, and the moon), is said to be capable of generating entirely new fields of knowledge, including a purified and ideally productive alchemy.[81] For Dee, in other words, language inspired in part by alchemy was not merely invented but inventive.

Thus, even while it absorbs humanism's commitment to rhetoric as foundational, alchemy also abandons early humanism's assumption that language, properly used, was firmly anchored to political, philosophical, and moral truth. Rather, in its rhetorical inventiveness, alchemy commits itself to a particular view of language as infinitely malleable. It is not simply the case that alchemical language is highly figurative—though it certainly is, as even those invested in alchemy sometimes bemoan. It is also the case that alchemical language seems to be singularly devoted to examining figuration as a process rather than just a rhetorical fillip. In this regard, alchemy is not just rhetorical; it is *metarhetorical*. As Lee Patterson puts it, "There really is a deconstructive point lurking in alchemical treatises, which is the idea that language can not unveil a pregiven truth that exists outside itself but can only provide an endlessly expanding list of synonyms, a 'chain of signifiers' that defers the signified or referent."[82] In the eighteenth century, when the new discipline of chemistry felt obliged to turn to the sets of symbols that had become familiar through alchemy as the foundation of its own symbology, chemical theorists worried, in fact, that they were partaking of a representational system that was so complex as to defer meaning endlessly. Echoing Robert Boyle's frustration in *The Sceptical Chymist* (1661) about how alchemists "do so abuse the termes they employ, that as they will now and then give divers things, one name; so they will oftentimes give one thing, many names," French chemist Pierre Joseph Macquer complained in 1749 that alchemy's "expressions were all tropes and figures, its phrases metaphorical, and its axioms so many enigmas."[83]

If, as is familiar from histories of the scientific revolution, alchemy shares premodern science's "doctrines of resemblance and similitude" explaining how all creatures and all substances are linked, then it is not surprising that tropes that assert *likeness* or *shared qualities*—that is, simile or metonymy—should be habitual in alchemical discourse.[84] But alchemy, fittingly enough, traffics adeptly in tropes not just of likeness but of substitution and shape-shifting. Which is to say that alchemy traffics in metaphor, or the trope of *substitution*. Indeed, the *Oxford English Dictionary*'s first citation of the word *metaphor* is from an alchemical poem, Thomas Norton's late fifteenth-century *Ordinal of Alchemy*, which compares its own "playne & comon speche" to the "clowdy" writing of scholarly authorities on alchemy such as Hermes Trismegistus, Roger Bacon, and Raymond Lull:

> Thei made theire bokis to many men ful derk,
> In poyses, parabols, & in methaphoris alle-so,
> which to scolers causith peyne and wo.[85]

The possibility that the word *metaphor* enters into English by way of alchemy suggests that alchemy's devotion to metaphor is more than a stylistic habit—more than just a way of burying professional secrets in obscure language, and more than just a convenient shorthand for portraying alchemical processes and ingredients (in which, for example, a reference to "the King" indicates sulfur and "the Queen" mercury).[86] Rather, as Patterson suggests in discerning a deconstructive point in alchemical treatises, alchemical discourse is metaphorical by nature.

To be "metaphorical by nature," however, suggests that alchemy partakes in an "epistemology of metaphor" that, as Paul de Man describes it, threatens to extend the substitutive power of tropes to the very texture of reality.[87] For example, the *Hieroglyphical Figures*, an early seventeenth-century alchemical text purporting to be by reputed fifteenth-century alchemist Nicolas Flamel, meditates upon alternative names one may attach to the stage of blackness that is one desired step in the heated mixture of mercury and sulfur:

> And this dissolution is by the envious Philosophers called Death, Destruction, and Perdition, because that the natures change their forme, and from hence are proceeded so many Allegories of dead men, tombes and sepulchres. . . . Others have called it Xir, or Iris, Putrefaction, Corruption, Cymmerian darknesse, a gulfe, Hell, Dragons, Generation, Ingression, Submersion, Complection, Conjunction, and Impregnation, because that the matter is black & waterish, and that the natures are perfectly mingled, and hold one of another. . . . A while after, the water beginneth to thicken and coagulate somewhat more, growing very blacke, like unto pitch, and finally comes the Body and earth, which the envious have called *Terra foetida*, that is, stinking earth: for then because of the perfect putrefaction, which is as naturall as any other can be; this earth stincks, and gives a smell like the odour of graves filled with rottennesse.[88]

This passage demonstrates how alchemy's attachment to inventive language cannot be dismissed as "mere" language. We begin here with an explication of how alchemical metaphor comes about. Because the substance obtained in this stage of the experiment is black, its color encourages "Allegories of dead men, tombes, and sepulchres" in the same way that its wateriness and its blended texture encourage the use of terms like "a gulfe" and "Conjunction." Straightforward enough. Yet by the end of the passage, the metaphor of death is no mere metaphor: it has been naturalized. The very stink of rotting bodies imbues the alchemical laboratory, permeating it with "a smell like the odour of graves." The effect is entirely contrary to Carl Jung's suggestion that alchemy was invented as a way of shaping an indifferent physical world into a projected version of the human psyche. Rather, the metaphorical substitutions that

Flamel employs bind with reality to retroject a newly formed and newly terrifying physical world back into our minds, the minds that made the words.[89]

As Flamel's casual reference to the "Allegories" to which alchemical language is liable implies, alchemical discourse's affinities with metaphor often lead to its use of allegory, the master metaphor. Treatises on alchemical theory often proceed as obscure allegorical narratives—maybe baffling or boring ones (or both), but allegories nonetheless. Alchemy's comfort with allegorical structures is another way in which alchemy unabashedly refashions its own belatedness as something uniquely innovative in an age of oncoming new science. Just as Edmund Spenser writes his allegorical epic *The Faerie Queene* in the 1590s in order to declare medieval forms not only not dead but somehow a *new* mode of English literature, just as Milton places the allegorical figures of Sin and Death both at both the beginning and in the anticipated future of Satan's career of tempting humans in *Paradise Lost*, so too does alchemy preserve and revive allegorical form in an effort both to claim a literary and biblical hermeneutic heritage and to make the decoding of allegorical mysteries seem urgent and of the moment.

The reader will be happy to hear that, in bringing up alchemical allegory, I do not intend to undertake an explication of these rather muddy allegorical alchemical texts. Rather, I wish to consider what the ubiquitous association between alchemy and allegory might offer for nonalchemist early modern authors who adopt alchemical metaphors and frameworks within their own literary works. Alchemy's allegorical habits signify, for these authors, certain habits of thought having to do with covering up, setting aside, or merely turning away from that which is allegorized. These habits of thought repurpose language from its humanist aim of effecting civic and moral change to a very different aim: sidestepping a particular construction of truth. Alchemical allegory thus comes to signify a kind of epistemic choice.

In recent years we have moved from a more deconstructive view of allegory—such as that of Maureen Quilligan, who in the late 1970s described allegory as a genre that draws attention to the reader making sense of an elaborate system of signs—to an examination of the ethical stakes of this peculiar literary structure.[90] Through the work of Gordon Teskey we have come to understand that allegory's overlay of an elaborate metaphorical scheme on a substrate of something less organized and univocal can act to repress the history of violence that characterizes relations between dominant and subordinate groups of persons.[91] The first step in creating allegory through violence, says Teskey, is to convert living beings into abstractions. The next is to characterize those beings, in their abstract form, as meriting violent sub-ordination. The last step, however, is to forget that this violent project of abstraction has ever needed to be undertaken at all. The resulting fiction suggests that the allegorical network of abstract signifiers has always, seam-lessly, been this way, occluding the trail of injustice and obliteration that led to this literary state.

Judith Anderson's dead-on description of allegory as "a process of think-ing" comes into play here, since Teskey's argument attributes epistemological maneuvers to allegory—knowing what needs to be repressed, then forgetting the act of repression—that are suggestively reminiscent of alchemical dis-course.[92] For example, theoretical alchemy's account of its textual history, as I described above, requires the effacement of how that history was crafted: the alchemical text can claim that there are no significant interim texts be-tween it and Hermes Trismegistus or between it and Moses. But more interest-ing is the way that literary authors tend to associate alchemy with a kind of "allegory lite": an allegory for which the stakes of those epistemological ma-neuvers are not as high as the ones Teskey describes and whose results are seem-ingly more benign. Rather than undertaking the violent repression of classes of persons, alchemical allegory, as these authors deploy it, thinks its way into the conscious evasion of certain venues of learning or certain modes of knowl-edge. This conscious evasion mirrors and models a kind of knowledge prac-tice that is both fundamental to and larger than the practices of alchemical allegory itself.

George Puttenham's account of allegory in *The Art of English Poesy* (1589) helps clarify how a certain mode of allegory may be associated both with an appearance of benignity and with a kind of fiction that openly acknowledges its fictiveness. Allegory is the "chief ringleader and captain of all other fig-ures," says Puttenham, one "which for his duplicity we call the Figure of False Semblant or Dissimulation."[93] While Puttenham's calling allegory a liar may be a bit disconcerting for those accustomed to thinking of it as conveying higher truths, he seems to confirm Teskey's sense that allegory can perform a massive, violent cover-up of that which was violently repressed in the service of constructing that "truth." In the course of the same description, however, Puttenham also points to allegory as constructing an alternative to the usual opposition between truth and falsehood. Allegory's fundamental "duplicity" makes it, as Angus Fletcher points out, an inherently ironic literary mode in a way that distinguishes its "False Semblant" from straightforwardly intentional lying.[94] Puttenham shrewdly notes that the allegorist dissembles—speaks other than she thinks, or speaks ironically—whether she lies or not: "And ye shall know that we may dissemble, I mean speak otherwise than we think, in earnest as well as in sport; under covert and dark terms, and in learned and apparent [that is, clear] speeches; in short sentences, and by long ambage and circumstance of words, *and finally, as well when we lie as when we tell truth*."[95] This commitment to "other-speak" regardless of whether it speaks the truth or lies makes Puttenham's allegory bear a relation to the unusual type of speech act that has recently, and memorably, been classified by philosopher Harry Frankfurt as "bullshit."[96] Because the bullshitter's primary consideration is to convince his audience, Frankfurt argues, his speech may not be classified as either honest or dishonest. For the bullshitter, the question of truth is immaterial: "His eye is not on the facts at all, as the eyes of the honest man and of the liar are, except insofar as they may be pertinent to his interest in getting away with what he says. He does not care whether the things he says describe reality correctly. He just picks them out, or makes them up, to suit his purpose."[97] The bullshitter may at times tell the truth, but that does not make his position anything other than bullshit nonetheless. An allegory that, in Puttenham's terms, dissembles whether it speaks honestly or lies—one that, in Frankfurt's terms, is bullshit—thus meliorates the violence effect that Teskey describes. While seeking to impose meaning on the chaos that is reality, as any allegory does, an allegory that conforms to the technical qualities of Frankfurtian bullshit need not hold dear the notion that its structure convey a singular truth. Multiplicity and inconsistency may be valued instead.

This multiplicity and inconsistency are the hallmarks of alchemical allegory, which tends to feature underdeveloped, contradictory, and/or mutually exclusive multiple narratives, sometimes all acting at the same time. Because alchemy enjoys a protean symbology, any inconsistency in its narrative is almost a virtue because it provides an opportunity for another aspect of the language to be invented that will bridge any gaps. Together, these characteristics tend to give alchemical allegory a crucial air of mobility. Alchemical allegory calls attention to the possible alternatives for its own troping: X might be figured as Y, but it might equally be figured as Z, and to some degree it does not matter whether we choose Y or Z. As with the flexible speech of the bullshitter, the truth or falsehood of Y or Z is immaterial. What counts is that there is a choice. In this way, alchemical allegory confirms Anderson's sense that allegory is a *narrative* construction, one always in motion.[98] Alchemical allegory demonstrates how to engage in the motion of figuration without having to settle on or commit to a final image.

Alchemy as Disknowledge

Its emphasis on allegorical mobility, I believe, is what makes alchemy so attractive to nonalchemist authors as a figurative scheme. As the chapters that follow will explore in detail, such authors frequently, indeed obsessively, bring the allegorical apparatus of alchemy to bear on situations that have little or nothing to do with trying to transmute baser substances into purer ones. As a literary critic, I am thus moved to ask: Why *this* set of metaphors, why *this* allegory? Why choose alchemy as a model rather than some other substitutive system? The answer, I suspect, is threefold. First, as I have suggested, the style of alchemical discourse suggests an activity for which the act of substitution is far more important than the coherence of the framework that is thereby created. Second, as I have described above, alchemical discourse often claims a mode of reality that exists on the level of metaphoric creation, and this reality is independent of its truth or falsehood. Third, alchemical discourse's rhetorical alliances with the style of late humanism can suggest an activity that is being carried on even though it is suspected of being no longer useful. That is to say, alchemy may be associated with the act of choosing an intellectual pursuit or direction even when—or even because—that pursuit employs faulty reading and learning practices. The sum of these associations? Alchemy suggests a fantastically creative, tremendously learned, metaphorically plausible, and rhetorically elaborate scheme for purposefully choosing the wrong way to go about knowing things. For the authors I discuss in the pages that follow, alchemy thus stands equally for a productive knowledge system and for the evasion of knowledge. Alchemy thus stands for a new sort of learning, one marked by a movement away from the empirically provable and a movement toward—always toward—the pleasures of the fictive.

Alchemy can convey this complex of associations because it had always been contradictorily associated both with deep, exciting erudition and with sheer impossibility. From the time that alchemy entered Europe in the eleventh century, it was a magnet for scholars interested in natural philosophy. At the same time, however, alchemy's fortunes were always accompanied by skepticism, a skepticism that intensified as the study of alchemy sought acceptance within the medieval university and failed to find it.[99] Beginning with Avicenna, in a text that was translated into Latin in the early thirteenth century and was taken for Aristotle's, a number of medieval thinkers rejected alchemy on the fundamental grounds that they considered it simply impossible to transform one type of matter into another by artificial means.[100] The thirteenth-century debate over alchemy's efficacy, which involved such heavy hitters as Thomas Aquinas and Roger Bacon, culminated in Pope John XXII's bull of 1317, *Spondent quas non exhibent* (They promise that which they do not produce). Although mostly concerned with foiling counterfeiters, this papal edict, as William Newman notes, also says "that the alchemists feign 'that which is not in the nature of things,' indicating that John did not believe alchemical transmutation to be physically possible."[101] Skepticism similarly punctuated the phases of enthusiasm for alchemy that marked the early modern era. In *Of the Vanity and Uncertainty of Arts and Sciences*, first published in 1530 and reprinted in multiple editions and translations throughout Europe in the sixteenth and seventeenth centuries, Heinrich Cornelius Agrippa repudiates his own devotion to alchemy, echoing the fourteenth-century papal position. Whether it is a legitimate science, an out-and-out con game, or a mode of *techne*, alchemy, says Agrippa, is false: "Alcumie then whether it ought to be termed an Arte, or a counterfaite colouringe, or a pursuite of nature, is doubtlesse a notable and a suffered deceipte, the vanitee whereof is easely perceaved in this, that it promiseth the thinges whiche nature in nowise can abide, nor attaine."[102]

Agrippa's position, however, is more complicated than a simple recantation of former alchemical beliefs, and the complexity of his situation helps explain how alchemy signifies a knowledge practice that is also knowledge's evasion. A talented scholar contemporary with Thomas More and Erasmus, Agrippa seems to have undergone a crisis in belief over humanistic practice that anticipated the later sixteenth century's widespread loss of faith in humanism. For Agrippa that crisis arose because of the difficulty of syncretizing Christianity with the Hermetic, kabbalistic, Neoplatonic, and other kinds of occult texts that so occupied and fascinated him and that were the basis of his massive and massively influential *Occult Philosophy* (*De occulta philosophia*), a work he first composed in 1509–10 and circulated in manuscript. In *The Vanity and Uncertainty of Arts and Sciences*, Agrippa in 1530 blames humanism's emphasis on rhetoric and its reclamation of ancient texts for Christianity's early sixteenth-century troubles: "nowe . . . that the skilfulness of the tongues, eloquence, and the number of authoures come to theire olde state againe, and sciences growe in use, the quietnes of the Churche is troubled, and newe

Heresies arise."[103] He therefore spectacularly renounces his scholarly dependence on books and reading in favor of the illumination of faith.

But why, then—having renounced not only his magic but the humanistic learning apparatus required to compose it—did Agrippa go on in 1531 and 1533 to publish editions of his *Occult Philosophy* rather than leaving it in manuscript or destroying it altogether? And why, contrarily, did its first published edition end with a long extract from *The Vanity and Uncertainty of Arts and Sciences*? A number of explanations have been proffered for Agrippa's vacillation between endorsing occult sciences and renouncing them: perhaps he was a charlatan, perhaps he needed the renunciation as a cover for his occult activities, perhaps he was merely composing in the specialized Renaissance genre of the paradox.[104] Michael Keefer gets closest to the mark, however, when he calls Agrippa "a man lodged between two legends, both of which he takes for truth."[105] His two books' publishing history implies Agrippa's alternating between two knowledge bases—a magic that relies on humanism and a Christianity that renounces humanism—as if it were simply a matter of moving between one and the other, depending on which is appealing at the moment. To choose occult science and its humanistic scaffolding is, in terms of Agrippa's Christian scheme, to choose wrongly, but it is a choice that is nonetheless reasonable. In this way—and quite unlike authors who merely differentiate useful, "true" alchemy (that is, the alchemy they themselves practice) from the charlatanry of "false" alchemy—Agrippa establishes alchemy, even if it is a false "deceit," as a redoubt of humanistic reading and interpretive practice to which one may resort at will.[106] The effect is the intellectual version of the ambivalence voiced by Geoffrey Chaucer's Canon's Yeoman, who in the course of his prologue and tale tells two stories debunking alchemical practice as a con game, but declares that the pursuit must continue nonetheless: "Yet is it fals, but ay we han good hope / It for to doon, and after it we grope."[107]

In the annals of "historical epistemology" as described in the introduction to this book, the kind of knowledge procedure I am describing has an unusual place and thus requires a new name: *disknowledge*. By this I mean the conscious act of choosing one system, body, or mode of knowledge over another, even if the one chosen is manifestly retrograde, ill informed, poorly supported, sloppily organized, or even simply wrong. Disknowledge is, in other words, a specialized means of defining what falls within the boundary of "the known"—and, concomitantly, of defining what counts as "not known," "not knowable," or "not worth knowing." With disknowledge, the knower may pick the fanciful over the empirical, the obfuscatory over the explanatory, and the outdated over the innovative.

Although it is a new term, *disknowledge* shares qualities with a number of twentieth- and twenty-first-century theories of the acquisition, comprehension, and management of knowledge, and it is worth explaining how the operation of disknowledge as I am describing it may be partly, if not fully, illuminated by those theories. My concept of disknowledge is indebted to recent sociological, historical, and literary-critical accounts of how and why humans, at different historical moments and in different social situations, go about not knowing things. Beginning in the mid-twentieth century, sociologists began to describe ignorance not as the absence of knowledge but as a constituent factor in knowledge production. "Ignorance studies" (or, as Robert Proctor has coined it, "agnotology"), a flourishing sociological subfield, has primarily been interested in understanding, in Foucauldian fashion, the cultural forces that draw the boundaries between what may be known and what may not be known—boundaries that distinguish practical knowledge from nonpractical, accessible knowledge from forbidden, or informed participants from the uninformed.[108] This work addresses the specific social constructions of what Eve Kosofsky Sedgwick, in regard to the way forms of sexual knowledge also require sexual ignorance, more generally refers to as "unknowing." For Sedgwick, as for sociologists of nonknowledge, ignorance is never simply the precursor and the blank of the knowledge that it precedes and to which it gives way. Rather, particular forms of knowledge require their concomitant ignorances, "ignorances . . . [that] are produced by and correspond to particular knowledges and circulate as part of particular regimes of truth."[109] Avital Ronell characterizes this particular form of ignorance as "stupidity," which for Ronell is more than just being dimwitted; it involves inventing an alternate system of counterknowledge that serves "as a replica of absolute knowledge."[110]

In addition to studying ignorance as a Foucauldian disciplinary structure, however, sociologists have also studied how it may be a tremendously useful, consciously deployed tool. The sociology of science, in particular, offers powerful explanations for deliberate ignorance that take into account how human beings—though influenced, to be sure, by preexisting networks and organizations and traditions—make deliberate choices as to what knowledge propositions are plausible and may be pursued. The sociologist most insistent upon holding individuals and groups responsible for these discriminations is Bruno Latour, whose actor-network theory postulates that the "social" is constituted by all the elements that act upon one another, both human and nonhuman, rather than by "social forces."[111] Though they are not interested in describing nonhuman actors in the way Latour directs, Barry Barnes, David Bloor, and John Henry similarly include the scientist's own will—her "goals and interests"—among the many factors that shape how moment-to-moment scientific decisions are made, and that hence bring about a "change in knowledge."[112] Such a change also requires the demarcation of nonknowledge. In scientific work, for example, conscious ignorance facilitates experimentation, either as an element of the double-blind study or as the precondition for addressing a research topic in the first place.[113] Conscious nonknowledge is just as crucial outside the lab. In corporations, "strategic ignorance" (as some sociologists have termed it) can create an aura of plausible deniability around issues of misconduct or malfeasance.[114] Michael Taussig has even argued that a sort of strategic ignorance lies at the nexus of power and knowledge that, in Michel Foucault's terms, sustains all ideology and all social structures. "Knowing what not to know"—a category that Taussig says includes "the public secret, which . . . can be defined as *that which is generally known, but cannot be articulated*"— drives individual actions that, as an aggregate, create and sustain everything from state power to the numinousness of the sacred.[115]

Disknowledge, as I define it, is a subspecies of strategic ignorance. Rather than simply marking out what is and what is not known ("I don't know that"), disknowledge articulates the choice of what is known over what is not ("I know *this* rather than *that*") or the choice of one method of knowing over another ("I know in *this* fashion rather than in *that* fashion"). In this manner, disknowledge engages in the kind of exclusionary work familiar to us from scholarship on the development of the disciplines. To cite two of the most influential such studies: Latour, following upon Steven Shapin and Simon Schaffer's *Leviathan and the Air-Pump*, describes the strategic ignorances involved in disciplinary formation when he argues that Robert Boyle and Thomas Hobbes were respectively able to invent chemistry and political science only through a reciprocal exclusion from each discourse of the other's domain of knowledge.[116] Similarly, Mary Poovey stresses that when bookkeeping replaced rhetoric as the primary technique by which to establish facts, language—its rhetorical figures doomed to opacity and imprecision in comparison to numerical figures' seeming transparency and exactitude—was both displaced and denigrated.[117]

One signal difference between disknowledge and the typical process of discipline formation, though, is the issue of precedent. In the emergence of a discipline, the new field sees itself as shunting aside the old field and in the process dropping its discourse practices. One of the exclusionary efforts of disknowledge, in contrast, can be not to carve out the new, more "accurate" science but to reinstantiate and even develop the old. Descriptions of alchemy thus force us to reexamine the way that we think of scientific displacement. Whereas chemistry shoulders aside alchemy, bookkeeping replaces rhetoric, and the new anatomy causes physicians finally to forget their Galen, in the case of alchemy, in contrast, an antique system retains surprising strength in the face of new intellectual systems. This is not an unusual circumstance, of course: the history of natural philosophy in the sixteenth and seventeenth centuries is marked by many such examples of hanging on to accustomed theories and practices despite the emergence of new explanations. Aristotle's idea of gravity and Galen's idea of human reproduction retain considerable traction even after Newton and Fallopius. But when we move to alchemy, especially as it is characterized by its skeptics and detractors, we come to a different case. Unlike other long-standing theories and practices, alchemy had always been under suspicion for being wrong. We thus now add a third quality to the operations of disknowledge: it is not only a deliberate choice of one kind of learning over another, and it is not only a deliberate choice of the old body of learning over the new. It is also often the deliberate choice of the reputedly false over the reputedly true.

This concatenation of qualities requires us to theorize disknowledge carefully, cherry-picking among the twentieth century's many and marvelous theories of intellectual displacement for analogues and explanations of disknowledge's characteristic maneuvers. The conscious (rather than unconscious or overdetermined) choice of an inapt knowledge system is not readily explained, for example, by Karl Marx's idea of a naive ideological consciousness, which Marx boils down to the phrase "Sie wissen das nicht, aber sie tun es" (They do not know it, but they are doing it"). Peter Sloterdijk's concept of an "enlightened false consciousness" holds more explanatory power.[118] In a state of enlightened false consciousness, as Slavoj Žižek explicates Sloterdijk's formulation, "They know very well what they are doing, but still, they are doing it." Žižek, who is interested in this cynically enlightened false consciousness's psychoanalytic underpinnings or what he calls "ideological fantasy," in turn extends Sloterdijk's revision of Marx into "They know very well how things really are, but still they are doing it as if they did not know."[119]

Revising Marx in the direction of cynical ideology potentially puts disknowledge in the vicinity of several other theorists who posit the conscious denial of knowledge as the condition of modern humanity. We often forget that Sigmund Freud, the twentieth century's foremost theorist of denial, characterizes those instances of denial that take place in the course of psychoanalysis as conscious, rather than unconscious, rejection. In Freud's first type of such denial, the intellective "no" of negation (*Verneinung*), the conscious mind furthers the work of repression by denying that an unpleasant and hence repressed thought was ever thought at all.[120] Freud's second and far more famous type of conscious denial, disavowal (*Verleugnung*), performs the same intellective maneuver in response to unpleasant news received from external reality. We consciously know that this news is so, and thus, splitting our ego into the part that knows and the part that refuses to know, our "disavowal is always supplemented by an acknowledgement."[121] Such a split allows us to "unknow" our knowledge even while we continue to know it.

It is important to note, however, that consciousness for Freud does not exactly imply volition or choice, and thus does not imply what we would usually think of as an action taken in a full state of knowledge. Despite the conscious nature of the negating or the disavowing thought process, the need to negate or disavow, in Freud's terms, is so overwhelming that we simply cannot help but accede to it. Friedrich Nietzsche's contention that self-deception is the true condition of humanity and especially of philosophy, and that "a renunciation of false judgments would be a renunciation of life, a negation of life," is much the same: it rests on the assumption that "the greater part of conscious thought must still be attributed to instinctive activity, and this is even the case for philosophical thought."[122] The same is true with Jacques Lacan's symbolic order, Louis Althusser's ideology, and Pierre Bourdieu's habitus: none of these admit of an "outside" from which one could examine, acknowledge, and understand one's choice of what is essentially a falsehood (or an imaginary).[123] Among Sloterdijk's and Žižek's predecessors, only Jean-Paul Sartre insists upon the wholly—if paradoxically—conscious nature of the self-deception that is "bad faith": even when lying to ourselves we are aware that we are doing so. For Sartre, the splitting of the self into the liar and the lied-to does not, unlike with Freud, minimize the consciousness's active collusion in self-deception: "That which affects itself with bad faith must be conscious (of) its bad faith."[124] Sartre's influence perhaps underlies Žižek's sense that the demystification of disavowed knowledge, its being brought to our consciousness, does not prevent us from adhering to the structures of what has been demystified.[125]

Sartre, it must be noted, defines consciousness as a prereflective state—which is not to say it is prethought, merely that consciousness does not have to take itself as an object of higher-order examination in order to exist.[126] (Hubert Dreyfus calls this state of prereflective consciousness in which one is thinking only in the moment, not self-reflectively, "absorbed coping."[127]) For my purposes, however, I must ramp up the degree to which consciousness in particular settings and situations may be self-reflective as well as prereflective, for I intend this discussion of disknowledge as conscious denial not only to distinguish my readings of various early modern authors' alchemical imagery from the realm of Jungian archetype in which studies of alchemy long languished, but also to hold those authors responsible for the way they evidence the pursuit of certain avenues of learning at the expense of other avenues.[128] The authors I discuss in this book are, naturally, as subject to the same ideological blindnesses and psychoanalytic disavowals as anyone. But in illustrating the operations of disknowledge, their work tends to reveal, to explain, and to justify—or, sometimes, critique—the founding assumptions and the choices that go into disknowledge's postulations and evidentiary claims. Here, too, alchemy proves the perfect vehicle for figuring this kind of knowledge operation. Karen Pinkus's insight that alchemy is remarkably open to revealing both its own ambivalences and the very structure of ambivalence itself suggests that alchemy is not only a field of discourse ripe for reading what has been disavowed, but also a field of discourse that expresses its willingness that those disavowals be recognized.[129] Alchemy, then, can be used to illustrate the kind of "knowledge of [its] own ambivalence" that Paul de Man attributes to Jean-Jacques Rousseau—who, says de Man, anticipates Jacques Derrida's deconstruction of his blindnesses by directing an awareness of blindness against itself.[130]

If alchemy as a field of discourse tends to reveal its ambivalences to an unusual degree, then the use of alchemical discourse to exemplify both disknowledge and its revelation takes on several salient characteristics. First of all, alchemical disknowledge may be deployed to designate situations of ethical tension and trial.[131] As Amélie Rorty puts it, the irony of conscious self-deception is that anyone who has owned up to the fact that it is the self who is doing the deceiving is at least not going to blame anyone else.[132] The second salient feature of disknowledge also involves its customarily ironic stance: it is often associated with a certain savoir faire or even pleasure. We tend to forget that Sartre's depiction of the person acting in bad faith is hardly a grim one, as ironic as that person's position may be. One of Sartre's best examples of bad faith is a woman on a first date who accepts her male companion's compliments even while understanding that they are signs not of his high-minded admiration but of his sexual desire for her. She manages to keep both of those possibilities, the true one and the false but preferred one, in play—his pure randiness, on the one hand, and his genuine esteem, on the other—by flirting with him. In this state of flirting, her deliberate turn from cold, hard truth to flattering fiction engages her erotic pleasure, even if only by delaying his. Furthermore, her act of bad faith brings her satisfaction in the sense that it gives her a continuing mode of self-aware, ongoing, active accomplishment.[133]

Self-awareness, ethical perspicuity, pleasure. Such qualities make a willfully alternative knowledge practice quite intriguing. Alchemy's associations with these qualities of disknowledge help explain those startling moments in which early modern intellectuals who believe alchemists to be generally either fools or charlatans declare the study of alchemy nonetheless useful, perhaps even crucial. Not because they believe alchemy works, but because they believe that alchemy as an intellectual system models how other disciplinary arenas might go about their business. Martin Luther, who elsewhere scorns alchemists as frauds, muses in his *Table Talk* that alchemy "liketh mee very well . . . not onely for the profits sake which it bringeth in melting of the Metalls. . . . But also, I like it for the sake of the Allegorie and secret signification, which is surpassing fair; namely, touching the Resurrection of the dead at the last daie."[134] Francis Bacon is perhaps the bluntest on this count. Although his *Advancement of Learning* joins others of his works in deriding alchemy as one of a set of emblematic errors in learning ("So have the Alchymists made a Philosophie out of a few experiments of the Furnace"), elsewhere Bacon suggests that, error-ridden as it is, we ought to study alchemy nonetheless.[135] After noting that there are three sciences—astrology, natural magic, and alchemy—"which have had better intelligence and confederacie with the imagination of man, than with his reason," Bacon offers the opinion that "neverthelesse the ends or pretences [of all three] are noble. For Astrologie pretendeth to discover that correspondence or concatenation, which is betweene the superiour Globe and the inferiour. Naturall Magicke pretendeth to call & reduce natural Philosophie from variety of speculations to the magnitude of works; And Alcumy pretendeth to make separation of all the unlike parts of bodies, which in mixtures of nature are incorporate."[136] The linguistic ambiguity of "pretend" in the early seventeenth century—alchemy *fakes* the purification of mixed substances into their pure, constituent parts, but it also *intends* that purification—suspends Bacon's opinion of alchemy between condemning it as chicanery and praising it for having a correct aim in mind.

Finally, Bacon turns in this passage toward a potent but brilliantly unreadable parable that indicates the fascination that alchemy continues to hold even for this inventor of the scientific method. Repeating first his opinion that "the derivations and prosecutions to these ends [that is, astrology, natural magic, and alchemy], both in the theories, and in the practises are full of Errour and vanitie," Bacon then adds a significant but enigmatic caveat, noting,

> and yet surely to Alcumy this right is due, that it may be compared to the Husband man whereof Aesope makes the Fable; that when he died, told his Sonnes, that he had left unto them gold, buried under ground in his Vineyard; and they digged over all the ground, and gold they found none, but by reason of their stirring and digging the mold about, the rootes of their Vines, they had a great Vintage the yeare following: so assuredly the search and stirre to make gold hath brought to light a great number of good and fruitfull inventions and experiments, as well for the disclosing of Nature; as for the use of mans life.[137]

At first the analogy seems simple. Just as the sons' seemingly fruitless digging in the vineyard nonetheless produces gold, although it is not the gold they expect, so too does the fruitless pursuit of alchemy produce "gold" in the form of "good and fruitfull inventions and experiments." The by-products of alchemy are valuable even when its end (the production of gold or of the philosopher's stone) is never achieved. Yet the "inventions and experiments" that Bacon praises are suspiciously parallel, both rhetorically and substantially, to the "derivations and prosecutions" of alchemical ends that he has just derided as being "full of Errour and vanity." What gold does the pursuit of alchemy produce? It produces gold in the form of inventions and experiments, derivations and prosecutions, error and vanity. Bacon's parallelism among all these phrases insinuates that what is golden about alchemy is the activity of alchemy. Despite the fact that it produces error, one practices alchemy for the sake of its practice, even though—or, rather, *because*—alchemy is wrongheaded. Alchemy, in other words, crystallizes for Bacon the possibility that the pursuit of learning is worthwhile even when it is not the pursuit of truth. What

Bacon calls "the search and stirre" of alchemy—by which he simply means its customary practices and motions, or what I have been calling its knowledge practices—is its virtue. Bacon wants to retain the study of alchemy because, for him, alchemy models a *kind* of knowledge, a way of thinking, that has its uses even if it is likely wrong. Even Bacon wants to watch disknowledge in action.

The Work of Disknowledge: Forgetting, Skimming, Avoiding, Fictionalizing

Its associations with the intellectual habit of disknowledge, the practice of willfully turning from one knowledge template to another, set up alchemy—a discourse already given, as I have argued, to the trope or turn—as a potentially magnificent trove of metaphors for authors who want to signify how knowledge is a motion, not a body, an activity, not an acquisition. But alchemy's affiliations with humanism, a senescent movement still lingeringly embraced by many, also make it a potentially magnificent metaphor for how every epistemic motion *toward* is also a motion *away*. Because of its reputation for being attached, like late humanism, to antiquity at all costs, alchemy can be a supple trope for demonstrating how one's chosen way of knowing fends off, evades, or waives others that are newly in place or on the horizon. In this way, alchemy may be used to figure a strange and canny conscientious objection to developing early modern teleologies of all kinds, including the teleology of scientific advancement. Whereas modern-day epistemologists speak of natural science as developing a quest for "truthlikeness"—the quality of a theory that, while necessarily falling short of the full plenitude of Truth (with a capital *T*), nonetheless displays acceptable verisimilitude to the truth given the current state of knowledge—alchemy may be depicted as happily secure in its convictions regardless of their provability.[138] Alchemy, in other words, can be a figure for how a theory forgoes "truthlikeness" for what early twenty-first century American comedian Stephen Colbert has taught us to call "truthiness," defined by the American Dialect Society as "the quality of preferring concepts or facts one wishes were true, rather than concepts or facts known to be true."[139]

In the chapters that follow I explore how authors use alchemical discourse and alchemical imagery to flesh out and nuance the microdecisions that constitute epistemic choice. For them alchemy is made to signify, as Peggy Knapp puts it, a certain kind of *work*, a conceptual structuring and maneuvering that gets the thinker to where she wants to go.[140] Seeking to uncover the roots of modernity in the least likely places, many of the best recent studies of the use of alchemy in literature have argued that it is put to the work of bringing modern social, intellectual, and economic structures into being in a metaphoric register. Lee Patterson, for example, argues that the alchemy of Chaucer's *Canon's Yeoman's Tale* presages the early modern individual's new capacity to undertake her own improvement, independent of the salvific agency of the church.[141] Other critics, including Peggy Knapp, William Sherman, and David Hawkes, have argued that alchemy as it appears in the literature of the late Middle Ages and early Renaissance ushers in the conceptual structure of capitalism, with its mystical conversion of one substance into another—lead into gold, labor into capital, material into symbol.[142] While I appreciate and agree with arguments that alchemy shares with early modernity a developing metaphorics, in their attention to the development of the modern such arguments neglect the equally interesting ramifications of alchemy's associations with outmodedness. My analysis of the work alchemy is put to in the texts I discuss has less in common with theories of progress and more in common with the important theories of Wiebe Bijker, who in studying sociotechnological change has pointed out that the delayed, dead-end, or wrongheaded technological development is as crucial an object of study as the prescient one—precisely because, in its own age and under its own terms, the laggard idea has tremendous utility.[143] In the texts that are of interest to me, alchemy is frequently put to the work of not going forward.

In what remains of this chapter, I briefly classify four ways of not going forward with which alchemy comes to be affiliated, each of which will be discussed more extensively in the chapters that follow. Each of these modes of disknowledge has a slightly different flavor, depending on the attitude demonstrated toward the field of knowledge from which disknowledge turns. Each involves volitional maneuvers and micromaneuvers that are revealed only under the lens of close literary analysis. These modes of disknowledge are the work of forgetting; the work of skimming; the work of avoiding; and the work of fiction.

Disknowledge's turn from one mode of knowing to another can take the form, first of all, of the "open secret" of conscious *forgetting*. Choosing to forget what was once known sounds impossible; it involves mastering the very "ars oblivionalis" that Umberto Eco has posited as impossible.[144] Countering Eco, however, Sybille Krämer has argued that memory and forgetting are complementary partners in the art of memory, and David Lowenthal has

emphasized forgetting as a conscious, deliberate social act.[145] As I have already discussed, both alchemy and humanistic learning are founded on the
strenuous work of forgetting: reviving ancient wisdom requires erasing the
extent to which one's scholarship and practice depend on many intervening
centuries of medieval intellectual effort. Perhaps for that reason, alchemy may
be used to signify an inattention to one's own intellectual history so willed
and so profound that it makes that history disappear.

A remarkable example of alchemy's being used to serve this purpose
appears in Thomas Browne's delightful study of wrongheaded learning, *Pseudodoxia Epidemica*, first published in 1646. Browne begins with the postulate of
Francis Bacon, one of Browne's heroes and models, that the ideal sort of scholarship involves starting fresh, sweeping away misconceptions so that one may
depend only on what is truly known. He finds Bacon's argument so powerful
that *Pseudodoxia Epidemica* shadows *The Advancement of Learning* at every
turn, so much so that Browne's book begins with the same echo of Plato that
Bacon's book does. Browne's Plato, though, comes with a difference—a difference in knowledge operations. And it is a difference that is signaled by alchemy. Whereas Bacon cites approvingly Plato's opinion that "all knowledge
is but remembrance," Browne insists in his epistle "To the Reader" that, no
matter what Plato says, we must not just discard *but also forget* that which
we think we know: "Would Truth Dispense, we could be content, with Plato,
that knowledge were but Remembrance; that Intellectuall acquisition were but
Reminiscentiall evocation, and new impressions but the colourishing of old
stamps which stood pale in the soul before. For, what is worse, knowledge is
made by oblivion; and to purchase a clear and warrantable body of Truth, we
must forget and part with much wee know."[146] This emphasis on knowledge
as forgetting eventually comes to fruition in the way that alchemy brings forth
a special kind of epistemic action for Browne, one that Bacon never imagined.
Despite otherwise tracking *The Advancement of Learning* closely on what constitutes pseudodoxy, Browne, quite unlike Bacon, astonishingly omits alchemy
from his catalog of the many false and ridiculous pseudodoxies that must be
discarded. He thus grants alchemy a privileged and indeed catalytic status.
Browne seems to have adopted, though in somewhat perverse fashion, alchemy's aim of refining matter so that nothing base remains. It is as if his reading
of Bacon acts in the manner of an alchemical refinement: distilling away and
reserving what is pure (including alchemy itself), and leaving for the matter
of Browne's own discussion only the dross of false learning.[147]

Browne thus not only portrays alchemy as part of what does not need to be forgotten but also employs it as a model for the process by which any discipline's prior associations with what he calls "credulity and supinity"—two of the primary promulgators of pseudodoxy—may be consigned to oblivion.[148] He is perfectly aware of Bacon's disdain for alchemy as acceptable learning, and yet he also forgets it. In Chapter 2 we shall see this kind of epistemic maneuver associated with alchemy in regard to the way that early modern matter theory has prior associations with the Roman Catholic doctrine of transubstantiation. For those late sixteenth- and early seventeenth-century authors who care about what the stuff of the world is made of, cutting off ties to Catholicism requires forgetting where one's matter theory came from, and that difficult undertaking of obliviscence finds alchemy a profoundly useful model.

The second and third varieties of disknowledge that I discuss in this book have to do specifically with the way scholars make use of their books. As I have described above, late humanism found itself in something of a bind in regard to its ideal of syncretizing all knowledge—an ideal that, with the early modern age's increasing proliferation of texts and increasing global circulation of ideas, became ever more difficult to uphold. Thus, the dark side of late humanistic syncretism is its tendency, even while claiming to incorporate alternative knowledge systems, to tacitly jettison facts and beliefs that for whatever reason do not comfortably fit with its own. Theoretical alchemy's reputation for selective, even sloppy reading, combined with its habit of reading all biblical and classical texts alchemically and its proclaimed aim of refining all the world into desirable gist and discardable remainder, make it an ideal metaphor for how even well-meaning scholars volitionally take shortcuts or hold fast to their ignorances. In this version of portraying disknowledge, alchemy is used to exemplify an active learning that is also an active *not* learning of other, more knotty or ideologically thorny disciplines.

Skimming texts, while a practice neutral in itself, can serve scholarly disknowledge in this fashion. As I discuss in Chapter 3, alchemists—lumped in with other masters of the occult arts—may be used to emblematize the kind of reader who, using scholarly skimming, picks and chooses what to learn so as not to be responsible for learning the whole. *Avoiding* texts, the form of disknowledge discussed in Chapter 4, requires more work. To avoid texts is to implement the kind of strategic ignorance that I noted above, where one knows a fact or body of knowledge but carries on as if that knowledge were immaterial. In order to be seen as reasonable, the scholar who refuses to admit alternative theories must know full well what those theories are. To be sure, the simultaneous knowledge of a theory and refusal to admit it is a standard operation of academic polemic—as when Cambridge Platonist Henry More, attempting in the 1660s to rebut what he saw as the atheistic materialism of Hobbes and Descartes, begged the question of divine causation by asserting that "Philosophick theorems" could be employed only if they were already "solid and rational in themselves, nor really repugnant to the word of God."[149] The type of ignorance I have in mind is even more wholesale than this, however. As an enterprise with the reputation of having an explanation for everything, alchemy and its pansophic claims easily stand in for the bad scholarly habit of sticking to one's familiar intellectual field by means of categorically rejecting all others. Alchemy can represent the intellectual and scholarly maneuvers required to stave off conceptual schemes that are more challenging, more revolutionary than the schemes one holds most dear.

The fourth mode of disknowledge discussed in this book is quite different in that, rather than proposing an old and creaky knowledge system as pansophic, it seeks to retrofit that old system into something both more up to date and more delimited. That mode of disknowledge is *fiction*. Here humanism's conviction that language shapes a world may be safely indulged because that world is restricted within narrative bounds. I earlier proposed that alchemy, in many ways, is late humanism in another form. When late sixteenth- and early seventeenth-century writers associate alchemy with fictiveness, the habits of humanism are given play in a delimited sphere. The result is a display of a new kind of disciplinarity: alchemy refines its allegiance from humanism in general to literature in specific.

As it happens, alchemy and literature were linked more in England than they were elsewhere. The English seem to have had a particular mania for alchemical poetry, producing more than any other European country.[150] Robert Schuler has found that among the many medieval English poems that were essentially scientific treatises put into verse, "more were written on alchemy than on all other scientific subjects combined." These medieval works founded what Schuler calls a "native tradition" of alchemy in English verse: they were cited, copied, and printed extensively in the sixteenth and seventeenth centuries, when many more poems in this genre were produced—to the point of tediousness.[151] As Joshua Poole complains in his poetry-writing manual *The English Parnassus* (1657), "for some centuries of years, the greatest part of English Poetry [has been] spent on those barren and indeed abstruse subjects of Chymistry, and the Philosophers stone."[152]

The existence of this tradition perhaps contributes to early modern English literature's frequent association of alchemy with literariness itself. That association between alchemy and the very nature of fiction also has to do, however, with the allegorical propensities of alchemical discourse that I have already discussed. As I have outlined above, theoretical alchemy often substitutes an ostentatiously crafted explanatory scheme (sometimes even one composed of its own invented terminology) for the physical processes it claims to depict. The heightened irony inherent in this especially far-flung relationship between the allegorical representation and its substrate means that alchemical discourse institutes a kind of second-order allegory. Rather than simply weaving a net of terms and postulates that serve as a linguistic representation of what they can only approximate, alchemy thrives on inventing yet another set of representations that in turn approximate *that* net of terms and postulates—as, for example, in George Starkey's ironically entitled treatise *Secrets Reveal'd*, which encourages the reader to understand the composition of the "Mercury Sophical" by learning "what Diana's Doves are, which do vanquish the Lion by asswaging him," a process that will first require her, however, to understand the "lion" as "the Babylonian Dragon," and so on, ad infinitum.[153] When we add this infinitely receding horizon of linguistic substitution to alchemical discourse's habitual stance of secrecy, its express intent to speak without ever exactly telling the truth about the object of discourse, we have irony that is more than structural. It is literary. Layers of tropes plus the evasion of truth (or, to put it another way, metaphor plus bullshit) equals fiction.

The inherent literariness of alchemy goes a long way toward explaining why, exactly, alchemy is such a rich source of reference for the literature that I discuss in this book. It is not simply that alchemy, in its fondness for allegorical symbology, employs a literary technique. Rather, literature recognizes its own underpinnings in the modes by which alchemical theory operates. In turn, literature's recognition of its commonalities with alchemy leads to its using alchemical tropes to designate a new place for itself in the seventeenth century, one unimagined and unimaginable by early humanism: fiction existing in a world of its own, not answerable to the requirements of the *civitas*.

Indeed, my sense of the literary works discussed in the chapters to come is that they are interested in alchemy not because they want to expose the distance between alchemical aims and alchemical ends but because they hope to exploit the ironies of alchemical disknowledge: revel in them, critique them, make them new. In these texts, alchemy is incorporated into the literary project as if it enabled and perhaps even helped constitute imaginative literature itself—as if alchemy were a productive approach to fiction. In the works I discuss in the ensuing chapters, alchemy's status as an adjuvant to fiction helps explain all its other uses in what I have been calling "the work of alchemy." Forgetting, skimming, avoiding: while these are somewhat shady epistemic motives and habits, they are also motives and habits that shadow all our more sober and upright reasons for losing ourselves in fictional narrative. Literature frequently asks that we forget, skim, and avoid reality in order to read and to write. Literature makes alchemists of us all.

CHAPTER 2

How to Forget Transubstantiation

On Christmas Day, Robert Southwell had a vision of Jesus Christ as an alchemical experiment. Or so his poem "The Burning Babe" tells us. As the poem's speaker shivers in the snow, he is surprised by "sodaine heate," and he lifts his eyes to see a "pretty Babe all burning bright" with love for humankind.[1] This vision owes much to nonalchemical sources, including the Petrarchan lover's suffering simultaneous cold and heat and Ignatius Loyola's meditations on the transcendent warmth of the Savior's birth in the cold of winter. But the fact that the fire in the incendiary babe's "faultless breast" is fueled in a "furnace" means that the vision also evokes an ideal alchemy, one that successfully purifies "The mettall in this furnace wrought, / . . . mens defiled soules" (23–24). In fact, Christ in "The Burning Babe" seems to arrive on this earth with a complete complement of alchemical apparatus. Not only with a furnace, but also with the solvent, the bath or "balneum," required to dissolve the basic ingredients with which the alchemical distillation begins. "[A]s now on fire I am / To worke them to their good," says Baby Jesus, "So will I melt into a bath, / To wash them in my blood" (25–28). A mid-seventeenth-century manual for making the philosopher's stone warns that maintaining the perfect heat for the alchemical bath is a tricky business: "Whosoever therefore keeps not this our heat, our fire, our balnium . . . continually burning in one quality and measure within our Glasse . . . shall labour in vain, and shall never attain this Science."[2] Christ's fiery alchemical bath, evidently, will present no such trouble.

It is not terribly odd that Southwell associates Christ's salvation of humankind with alchemy. Alchemists themselves felt free to imply this association—for example, readily describing the warmed bath of sulfur and mercury, the basic elements of the alchemical process, as a kind of baptism.

When Paracelsus deliberately Christianized alchemy in the early sixteenth century by revising the traditional Aristotelian four elements (earth, water, air, and fire) into a trinity (sulfur, salt, and mercury), he explicitly encouraged a sacramental interpretation of what happens when alchemists make base matter better. At the same time, though, Southwell's alchemical incarnation of Christ takes the poet-priest into both theologically and scientifically dangerous waters. With its alchemical imagery, "The Burning Babe" enters into a centuries-long debate that drives to the heart of one of the great intellectual problems of the period of late humanism: the inability to conceive what earthly matter is made of. This debate sprang from, and was inseparable from, pre- and post-Reformation Europe's wrangling over the material composition and transformation of the Eucharist—what we would now call its physics. Subject to serious question from the moment transubstantiation became Roman Catholic dogma in 1215 (and even before), the physics of the Eucharist nevertheless became the essential proving ground for the physics of the world.

Because medieval physics' theories of matter were predicated on the truth of transubstantiation, and because transubstantiation was the object of skepticism even for thinkers who accepted it as church dogma, medieval matter theory did not bear too close an examination or too firm a belief. And yet, that was the primary matter theory that was available well into the seventeenth century. For the three seventeenth-century poets I discuss in this chapter, alchemy's affinities with transubstantiation thus do not lend themselves to a settled understanding, either spiritual or scientific, of what constitutes earthly matter. Rather, they lead to an acknowledgment that the current state of this understanding is unsatisfying, and a better state of understanding impossible.

I outline in the first section of this chapter how medieval matter theory adapted Aristotle in large part to supply a prop for transubstantiation. When the Reformation discarded transubstantiation, then, it also, willy-nilly, began to dismantle a received physics: not only was transubstantiation declared bad doctrine but also the Aristotelianism on which it was based was exposed as bad matter theory. The late sixteenth and early seventeenth centuries thus saw increasing calls for an alternative to Aristotelian theories of material substance and material change. But just as Protestantism did not supply a satisfactory alternative doctrine of how, exactly, Christ could be present in the bread and wine of Holy Communion, so too did learning as it existed in the period of late humanism not immediately supply a satisfactory alternative analysis of matter and its metamorphosis. Despite flirtations with atomism, the late six-teenth and early seventeenth centuries did not agree upon a new way of imag-ining the world's essential makeup.

The absence of an adequate physics proves something of a problem for metaphysical poets. A problem, and an opportunity. For John Donne, George Herbert, and Henry Vaughan, all poets obsessed with how earthly matter (including the matter of human flesh) communes with the divine, alchemy crops up in what seem like transubstantiative contexts as a way of suggesting how contemporary physics was of little help in approaching this issue. But these poets also deploy alchemy as a poetic device for diminishing that issue or keeping it usefully at bay. Indeed, alchemy comes to signify a way in which the matter of matter may be forgotten about: not wiped from memory entirely but forgotten about in the way we say "Forget it" when a friend apologizes for a slight. It is labeled as inconsequential. And for good reason. In an age lacking a physics and tired of the religious controversy that can flare when physics comes up, forgetting about it seems like a relief. If alchemy may be used, in Claude Lévi-Strauss's terms, as a "thing to think with," it may equally be used as a "thing *not* to think with" when not thinking does some desirable textual and cultural work. For these poets, alchemy survives the demise of transubstantia-tion to become, curiously, not a way of asking what physical matter is but rather a highly sophisticated device for forgetting we ever cared about the question.

Unlikely Matter: The Shared Physics
of Transubstantiation and Alchemy

Alchemy and the doctrine of transubstantiation were first proposed in medieval Europe at about the same time, the late eleventh and the twelfth centuries. They gained traction for exactly the same reason: both attached themselves to the era's most sophisticated physics. After Aristotle's *Metaphysics*, his treatise on substance and material change, was accepted and disseminated in the thirteenth century, Europe's intellectuals came to believe that a body or object was composed of a substantial form cloaked by incidental accidents. Aristotle thus made the doctrine of transubstantiation physically possible in that the essence of the body of Jesus Christ as it appears in the Eucharist could be imagined as independent from its accidental qualities—the color, smell, taste, and mouth feel of human flesh and blood. Similarly, Aristotle made alchemy physically possible in that all substantial forms, in Aristotelian terms, originate in the prime matter that underlies them. Alchemy's aim was to return matter to prime matter so that a new substantial form could be imposed.

But Aristotle required tweaking, and both transubstantiation and alchemy help explain why. Transubstantiation and alchemy both answer to the dream of matter that does not obey ordinary rules—a dream that Aristotle, who theorizes that all matter follows the same dicta, could not be used to endorse. At the moment the Host is consecrated, it transforms into a singular body whose substantial form does not match its accidents in any way. At the moment the alchemical project succeeds, it similarly exceeds the capacities of transformational processes normally found in nature. It is because they both argued for exceptions to Aristotelian physics that theories of transubstantiation and of alchemy also share a history of being challenged from their very inception.

Furthermore, the fact that alchemy shares its physics with transubstantiation destabilizes two crucial and coinciding stories that we tell ourselves of the progression from the Middle Ages to the early modern era. First, if the shaky matter theory behind transubstantiation was linked, quite early on, to the intellectually suspect matter theory behind alchemy, then we must revise our sense that the Protestant reform of the sacraments involves the early modern disenchantment of a medieval magical belief. Rather, Protestantism merely reiterates and reinforces a skepticism about unlikely sacramental matter that had been part of Eucharistic theological debate all along. Second, if transubstantiation and alchemy share a history of dubiousness, then we must reevaluate the way they continue to be evoked in tandem in the seventeenth century. As we will see later in this chapter, seventeenth-century metaphysical poets' habit of yoking alchemy to transubstantiation does not simply evince nostalgia for old certainties now gone by. Rather, the conjunction of alchemy and transubstantiation reflects these poets' acknowledgment of the continuing utility of a physics that, however long-standing and however intriguing, had always been subject to charges of balderdash.

Transubstantiation and Matter Theory

Transubstantiation, first proposed as Eucharistic theory in the late eleventh century, became official Roman Catholic doctrine in the Fourth Lateran Council of 1215. Miri Rubin has argued that the church codified transubstantiation as part of a larger agenda of transitioning matters of faith from local to centralized control.[3] It may have been almost incidental, then, that the church's desire to consolidate spiritual and political authority required a particular theory of matter. But in the case of transubstantiation, that is exactly what happened. In turn, scrutiny of the Eucharistic sacrament brought up two crucial physics questions: What was transformed? In what sense was that transformation singular?

To be sure, the nature of the Eucharist had been under debate since the fourth century, when Ambrose's realist view of the sacraments opposed Augustine's essentially significative view.[4] It was not until the late eleventh century, though, that questions of what we would call physics arose in connection with the Eucharist, when Berengar of Tours began to query what, exactly, happens to the matter of the bread and wine when they are consecrated. Although the foremost issue for Berengar was grammatical (since Christ's meaning when he says "This is my body" and "This is my blood" depends on what the meaning of "is" is), he also questioned what nature Christ's body might possess if it appeared in the Eucharist.[5] Christ's resurrected body was at the right hand of God, not on the altar. How could it be in two places at the same time—or, really, in many places at the same time, given that many Masses may be performed simultaneously?[6]

While Berengar was forced to recant and declare that the bread and wine literally became Christ's body and blood, his questions about the physics of the Eucharist continued to bedevil the church. The Fourth Lateran Council of 1215 declared transubstantiation true, but it was the work of the following century to work out *how* it was true. That *how* was enabled, as it turned out, by historical accident. The doctrine of transubstantiation gained credence and philosophical authority only later in the thirteenth century, when the introduction and dissemination in Europe of Aristotle's *Metaphysics* meant that Aristotelian theory came to dominate scholarly discussions of material form and material change. For Aristotle, as I have mentioned, any individual physical body is made up of its substantial form—its essence, a composite of prime matter and the form that nature imposes on that prime matter—and its accidents, inherent qualities that, were they to change, would not change the essence of the physical body. (Aristotelian matter theory is thus called *hylomorphism*: "matter-form.") These accidents are nine in number: quantity, quality, relation, place (or situation), time, position, state of possession, activity, and passivity (or the quality of being acted upon).[7] Importantly, Aristotle found it nonsensical to imagine a substantial form's ever being separated from all of its accidents. He considered some accidents more loosely connected to substantial form than others, of course: a man can lose an arm, part of his "quantity" or extension in space, and still be a man; some of his "quality" may change—his hair from brown to white, for example—and he is still the same man. Still, accidents appropriate to humanity and to masculinity must inhere in his substantial form for him to be a man.

Medieval theologians found it easy to Christianize Aristotle by substituting "God" for "nature" as the agent who stamps form upon matter, and by defining the substantial form of a human being as the union of body and soul that constitutes God's creation of each individual.[8] But the Eucharist posed a conundrum for medieval Aristotelianism. What the priest consecrates at the altar must transform from the substantial forms of bread and of wine to the substantial form of the body and blood of Jesus Christ. At the same time, however, the accidents of bread and wine, their taste, smell, color, and texture, must remain; if they did not, we would be repulsed by the prospect of cannibalizing Christ and would not be able to stomach the Eucharist. Thomas Aquinas solved this problem by postulating that in this one singular case, the case of the Eucharist, a substantial form might be severed from all of its accidents. While the bread and wine's substantial forms are annihilated, replaced by the substantial form of Christ's body and blood through divine miracle, their accidents remain.[9]

Crucial for Aquinas's theory of Eucharistic matter was his reconceptualization of one particular accident: the accident of quantity. Remember the physics question that Berengar of Tours raised. If Christ's body and blood are truly in the sacrament, how could he possibly be in so many places, so many Masses, at the same time? The usual Aristotelian explanation that a body's accidents inhere in its substantial form fails to answer this question. As Aquinas points out, the accidents of the consecrated bread and wine—its taste, smell, color, and so forth—cannot inhere in the body and blood of Christ, since Christ's resurrected body is in heaven, at the right hand of God. Nor can they inhere any longer in the bread and wine, whose substantial forms have been annihilated and replaced by the substantial form of Christ. Rather, Aquinas proposes, the bread and wine's taste, smell, color, and texture inhere in the bread and wine's "dimensive quantity," their extension in space. In the special case of the Eucharist, in other words, the accident of quantity serves as a kind of substitute substantial form, one in which the rest of the bread and wine's accidents inhere. Thus, there can be endless supplies of consecrated bread and wine without there having to be infinite quantities of the body and blood of the risen Christ.[10]

It was this Thomistic revision of Aristotelian matter theory for the purposes of making transubstantiation true that became the grounds for debate over the physics of transubstantiation from the thirteenth century up through the Protestant Reformation. Although Aquinas's theory was endorsed by the Roman Catholic Church, the matter was never settled, since the physics of transubstantiation as Aquinas proposed it never did seem entirely plausible.[11] Even Scholastics who were in sympathy with the theological use of Aristotle simply could not agree with Aquinas's rather precious reclassification of the bread and wine's accident of quantity as a kind of substitute substance in which the rest of the bread and wine's accidents might inhere. William of Ockham argued that you cannot differentiate between a substantial form and its accident of quantity: a body is coextensive, axiomatically, with its extension. If Christ's substance is present in the Eucharist, his quantity must be there, as well—a logical absurdity, since that would require Christ's body and blood to multiply vastly in quantity to supply every Mass that will ever take place. On the other hand, if Christ's quantity is not there in the Eucharist, his substance is not there, either.[12] In short, William of Ockham's equation of substantial form with the accident of quantity denied the Real Presence, and he knew it. In the end he, like Duns Scotus, evaded charges of heresy only by asserting that he accepted the doctrinal version of transubstantiation simply because it was doctrinal and not because it was good physics.[13]

When later generations of dissenters and reformers critiqued the Roman Catholic Church's nonscriptural dogma of transubstantiation, they revived the Scholastic debate over the physics of the Eucharist on the grounds that transubstantiation violated Aristotelian principles. John Wyclif, for example, declared transubstantiation impossible because "accidents could never be without their substance."[14] Furthermore, he noted that if God could require Christ's substantial form to be in multiple places at once—as it must be, in transubstantiative terms, when simultaneous Masses are performed—then God could require the same of any object or body, a conclusion that would eliminate the coherence of time and space.[15] Both humanist and counter-humanist philosophical and logical innovations (Neoplatonism and Ramism) complicated the picture somewhat after Wyclif's time, but the continuing dominance of Aristotelianism in matter theory meant that theological arguments that impinged on the nature of matter continued to pick up the terms of the Scholastic debate over transubstantiation.[16] Aquinas's logical manipulation of the accident of quantity remained a major sticking point, with John Calvin arguing that to make Christ's substance ubiquitous in the Eucharist is to deny him his humanity: "The presence of Christ in the Supper . . . must, moreover, be such as neither divests him of his just dimensions, nor dissevers him by differences of place, nor assigns to him a body of boundless dimensions, diffused through heaven and earth. All these things are clearly repugnant to his true human nature."[17]

One might expect that Aquinas's designation of transubstantiation as a unique category of divine miracle, and the Eucharist as a unique category of matter, would have marginalized the Eucharist's place in post-Reformation physics. But as religious dissenters' familiarity with the Scholastic debate suggests, transubstantiation was so central to matter theory in the thirteenth through sixteenth centuries that theories of matter alternative to Aristotelianism, even if they did not mention the nature of the sacraments, were either taken up as part of the Eucharistic debate or understood as challenging the nature of the Eucharist. While Pietro Redondi overstates the case when he postulates that the Inquisition saw Galileo's real heresy as atomism, not heliocentrism, he is quite right that the Roman Catholic Church found Galileo's experiments in optics challenging because they proved transubstantiation impossible. Having observed a luminescent mineral substance (now known to be barium sulfide), Galileo proposed that light was a substance and not—as Aristotelianism declared it to be—an accident inhering in a transparent medium such as air. All the properties of light, claimed Galileo, permeate each tiny corpuscle of the substance of which light is constituted.[18] If light is a substance, and if its properties are inseparable from it, then there are two possible conclusions. Either there are no such things as accidents, which would nullify Aristotle and make Aquinas's theory of transubstantiation impossible, or accidents are inseparable from their substance, which would confirm Aristotle but also make the exceptional case of transubstantiation impossible.[19] Later experiments in optics, like seventeenth-century protobarometers that left a vacuum at the top of a glass tube, similarly were considered worthy of notice in part because they challenged transubstantiative physics. That challenge held whether light was considered a substance (as Galileo believed) or an accident (as Aristotle would have it). If the vacuum in the tube contains only light and if light is a substance, then Galileo's point of view is right and transubstantiation is impossible. Conversely, if the light in the tube is an accident rather than a substance, then this accident, because it exists in a vacuum, can exist without a substance—that is, without the air that light usually illumines: this conclusion disproves the uniqueness of the matter of the Eucharist.[20]

Given the ongoing wrangles about the physics of transubstantiation, it is perhaps not surprising that, in the religious controversies of the sixteenth and seventeenth centuries, many on the Reformed side dismissed the discussion of transubstantiative physics as a silly sidetrack to theology, something not worth bothering about. While Martin Luther remained devoted to the doctrine of the Real Presence of the body and blood of Christ in the Eucharist, and while he developed a none-too-precise theory—usually (if improperly) labeled "consubstantiation"—in which the body and blood of Christ are "in, with, and around" the bread and wine, he objected to the doctrine of transubstantiation because he found it ridiculous that it be a litmus test for orthodoxy.[21] It is possible to argue, as William West has done, that in the main, the Reformist response to Eucharistic controversy was to decline to think any longer about Holy Communion in terms of matter theory.[22] While the Thirty-Nine Articles of the Church of England, referring to the long-standing debate over Eucharistic physics, declared, "Transubstantiation (or the change of the substance of Bread and Wine) in the Supper of the Lord, cannot be proved by holy Writ," the 1562 revision of the articles removed the 1552 admonition, "A faithful man ought not either to believe or openly confess the real and bodily presence . . . of Christ's flesh and blood in the sacrament." Instead, the Book of Common Prayer ultimately makes way for the Eucharist to be viewed either of two ways: either as the transubstantiated body and blood of Jesus Christ, or as only symbolic of that body and blood.[23] Believe what you like. Or, as William Tyndale suggests, simply don't think about it too hard: "Of the presence of Christ's body in the sacrament, meddle as little as you can, that there appear no division among us."[24] Richard Hooker, evidently lumping the physical nature of the Eucharist into the category of what he elsewhere calls a "thing indifferent," makes precisely the recommendation that we simply not trouble our heads with the issue: Christ's "omnipotent power . . . maketh it his body and blood to us, whether with change or without alteration of the element such as they imagine we need not greatly to care nor inquire."[25]

Not caring or inquiring about the physics of Holy Communion has its advantages. Moreover, in the seventeenth century you did not have to be a Protestant to see what those advantages were. One of them was simply to stop fighting about it. As Michel de Montaigne remarked about centuries of dispute over the meaning of Christ's saying "This is my body" and "This is my blood," "How numerous and how important are the quarrels produced in the world by doubt about the meaning of this syllable: *hoc* [this]!"[26] Leaving matter theory aside was not, however, an option for alchemy, whose physics as it was developed in medieval Europe proved very similar to, and was even imbricated with, the physics of transubstantiation. Alchemy was like transubstantiation in that it reached Europe before the Aristotelian revolution in science and in that its credibility depended in part on an aura of mysticism and on its practitioners' belief in the efficacy of ritual. However, it was also like transubstantiation in that its survival and popularity depended on its first adopting and then revising Aristotelian theories of matter—revising them so that the alchemist, like the Thomist theologian, could claim to have proved the existence of a form of matter that was exceptional. And as with transubstantiation, alchemy's physics were called out as implausible by those who questioned whether any kind of matter could be exceptional in the fashion alchemy claimed it to be.

Alchemy and Matter Theory

Any medieval account of alchemy had to cope with Avicenna's influential axiom, mentioned in Chapter 1, that one substance cannot be changed into one another by artificial means.[27] Only God and his agent, nature, could effect such transformation. William Newman cites the Dominican chronicler Martinus Polonus, whose thirteenth-century *Margarita decreti* declares that "alchemy seems to be a false [*reprobata*] art, because he who believes one species to be able to be transferred into another, or into a similar one, except by the Creator Himself, is an infident and worse than a pagan."[28] One version of alchemy, it must be pointed out, did not lay claim to any such transformative power, asserting only that alchemy separated the components of mixed matter.[29] But just as common as this rather modest claim was the more grandiose assertion that, while alchemy merely imitated nature in being able, with God's help, to transmute one substance to another, alchemy accelerated the change. What nature spent an age forging in the earth an alchemist could spend a week (or a month or a year) forging in his furnace.

The introduction of Aristotelian physics into Europe both made this theory of alchemy as sped-up nature necessary—since it was Aristotle who originated the dictum that substantial change must come from nature—and gave it physical grounds. Some alchemists cited Aristotelian matter theory to explain the process of alchemical change, arguing that alchemy works first by breaking material down into the very source of all substantial forms, prime matter (Aristotle's *hyle*), and then by introducing a new substantial form in the place of the previous one.[30] This argument for alchemy's ability to reduce materials to prime matter drew heavy fire, however, for its encroachment upon divine prerogative.[31]Alchemy's claims to godlike power only intensified with the innovations of Paracelsus, whose revisions of Aristotelian matter theory in the first half of the sixteenth century not only granted the alchemist quasi-divine powers of transmutation but also attributed divine qualities to the very elements and processes of alchemy itself. As I have already mentioned, Paracelsus, never a cautious thinker, contravened Aristotelian orthodoxy by tossing aside the four traditional elements (earth, water, air, and fire) and putting in their place three elemental principles (sulfur, salt, and mercury). Paracelsus's sulfur, salt, and mercury signify not the common household or workshop substances given those names but rather "principles of constitution" of the particular form and features of every body and every object: sulfur is the principle of heat or organization, salt the principle of mass or solidity, and mercury the principle of activity or liquidity. The force of Paracelsus's theory is the contention that alchemy is always happening in every material that undergoes change, from metals underground to the human body to the stars above. The alchemist merely controls the emergence and interactions of these ubiquitous spiritual forces, whether in the alchemical furnace or in the human body by way of alchemical medicine.[32]

Paracelsus's tripartite elemental scheme obviously reiterates the Holy Trinity, but not after the fashion of an analogy. He means that reiteration literally. The spiritual forces of Paracelsus's three elements are, in fact, derived from and equivalent to the powers of the Triune God. Sulfur provides the heat and the organizational principles of God's fiat; salt the mass and solidity embodied in the incarnate Christ; and mercury the fluid inspiration toward activity prompted by the Holy Spirit.[33] All matter contains some degree of this Trinitarian life force; the degree of life force depends only on where the matter is on the scale from most earthy to most ethereal, from rocks to trees to animals to humans to angels. For Paracelsus, therefore, alchemically created matter is exceptional not because it demonstrates the hastening of the usual time line of natural change but because it participates more fully in the divine than ordinary matter does. One can easily see why Paracelsus was deemed theologically dangerous: the alchemist, like God Almighty, could endow dumb matter with the spirit of the angels.[34]

Paracelsus's work, intertwined as it was with his own highly eccentric desire for radical reform not just of religion but of the world and all its contents, was immediately seen as having implications for Eucharistic theology.[35] His matter theory has the effect of denying transubstantiation, because if all matter participates in the divine, then nothing special is happening in the Eucharist.[36] As he asserts in a commentary on the first chapter of the Gospel of John, Christ's Words of Institution mean not that his body and blood are (in Thomistic terms) substantially in the Eucharist but that we, like Christ, are divine: "he says, as he holds the bread in his hand, 'This is my body,' and as he holds the wine, 'This is my blood.' . . . [W]e come from that very Flesh, and are not lacking the heavenly body that has become incarnate through the Holy Spirit. . . . For this reason he is in us and we in him, so that thence we are born from God and are of his body and blood, risen from heaven; so is the Word become flesh in our hands."[37] No wonder that, when the implications of Paracelsus's work for Eucharistic theology became better known, his work—like Galileo's and René Descartes's after him—was placed on the Roman Catholic Index of Forbidden Books.[38]

Even though Paracelsus's theory of a shared divinity among all bodies nullifies transubstantiation, he liberally samples from Eucharistic terminology and imagery when describing his method's efficacy. In this he follows the example of his alchemical predecessors, who had long laid claim to transubstantiative power. Indeed, the very word *transubstantiation* seems to have entered English not in relation to the Eucharist but in relation to alchemical change. The *Ordinal of Alchemy* by fifteenth-century alchemist Thomas Norton carefully applies this useful new term to distinguish between a material that has merely changed its external properties or discardable accidents and one that has alchemically changed its substantial form. The "stone Microcosmos," or philosopher's stone, is that "wherebie of metallis is made transmutacion / Not only in colour, but transubstanciacion."[39] The popular *Aurora consurgens*, an alchemical text likely from the fifteenth century but attributed to Thomas Aquinas, also plainly puts alchemy in transubstantiative terms. As the alchemist undertakes the very final step in his great work, the production of the quintessence, he accepts a mystical Eucharistic invitation from Christ himself: "eat my bread and drink the wine which I have mingled for you, for all things are made ready for you."[40] Paracelsus cleverly integrated these Eucharistic connotations into the basic elements that governed his alchemy. His notion that the principle of salt, which grants solidity to material bodies, channels the same energies as Christ's incarnation draws from the traditional Roman Catholic association between the Real Presence of Christ's body and blood in the Eucharist and Christ's incarnation on earth as a human being.[41]

Alchemy's associations with transubstantiation only became more explicit in the seventeenth century, perhaps due to Roman Catholicism's intensified Counter-Reformation commitment both to transubstantiation as dogma and to Aquinas's transubstantiative physics as the sole scientific support of that dogma. German alchemist Johann Valentin Andreae's *Chymische Hochzeit* (Chemical wedding) of 1616 describes a mystical alchemical vision received, signally, on the eve of Easter. The alchemist, having prayed and "being now ready to prepare in my Heart, together with my dear Paschal Lamb, a small unleavened, undefiled Cake," is blessed by a vision punctuated by frequent images of altars and blood, including one episode in which the developing philosopher's stone, having been heated in the alchemical furnace, is treated as the Host, laid "upon a long Table, which was covered with white Velvet" and then itself covered "with a piece of fine white double Taffeta."[42] Even more obvious in its transubstantiative parallels is Nicholas Melchior Cibinensis's "Alchemical Mass" ("Addam [*sic*] et processum sub forma missae"), first published in 1602 in Lazarus Zetzner's encyclopedic *Theatrum chymicum* and later included in alchemist Michael Maier's popular *Symbola aureae mensae* (1617), a book that also includes an illustration of an alchemist, priest-like in Eucharistic vestments, kneeling at an altar and raising his hands as if saying the Mass.[43] Elevated behind the priest in this illustration, as if he has conjured her up in his vision, is a figure resembling the Virgin Mary suckling a child—the "philosophical child" that is the product of alchemy but also the incarnate Christ who comes down to believers in the form of the Eucharist.[44] Based on the persistence of these sorts of images, Mary Baine Campbell argues that transubstantiation "was a process that became at least potentially susceptible to 'chymical' explanation in the intellectual world of the Reformation."[45] Gabriel Naudé, librarian to Cardinal Mazarin, found exactly this kind of "chymical" explanation of transubstantiation in "our Alembick-Idolators and Alchymists," who he complained "are a sort of people so strangely besotted with the Philosophers stone, that . . . they have been so prophane as to take the sacrifice of the Masse, and the miracle of the Incarnation for Emblems and figures of . . . that Soveraign [alchemical] transmutation."[46]

In binding itself so explicitly with transubstantiation, however, alchemy ironically ran the risk of augmenting its own reputation for falsehood with the skepticism that, as we have seen, greeted transubstantiation theory from its inception. For Protestants inveighing against the suspect practices of Roman Catholicism, the equation between alchemy and transubstantiation was irresistible.[47] An especially snarky example comes from Puritan William

Prynne's *Aurum reginae* (1668), which suggests that if priests can perform transubstantiation, they might as well take up alchemy, too: "Now if every Pope and ordinary Masse-Priest can thus daily transubstantiate the Sacramental bread into the very natural body of Christ . . . then they may more confidently believe and affirm, they can transubstantiate Copper, Brasse, Tinne, Lead, and other baser metals, into real Gold and Silver, since they all agree in the genus of metals, and are not so far different from each other as bread and Christs natural body." Prynne goes on to suggest flippantly that it was for this very reason that, in the fifteenth century, England's King Henry VI had employed "Monks and Masse-Priests" whose creation of the philosopher's stone would help wipe out the national debt.[48] Similar snide comparisons between transubstantiation and alchemy come from all quarters of English Protestantism, from the most High Church to the most Puritan. The Arminian Benjamin Lany, staunch royalist and eventually Bishop of Ely, distinguishes Protestants from Catholics in noting that "we [Protestants] pretend not to that Mystical Art and Chymistry, to turn the Elements of Bread and Wine into the Natural Body and Blood of Christ."[49] The religiously moderate John Donne refers in a sermon to "Our new Romane Chymists . . . that can transubstantiate bread into God."[50] The virulently anti-Catholic George Goodwin's "Of that Loude Lye, and Fond Fiction of Transubstantiation" specifically jokes about alchemy's and Catholicism's shared claims of being able to create exceptional matter:

> But Popish Chymicks make a thousand Gods:
> Priests (then) are greater gods than God, by odds.
> . . . .
> Surely, hee hath some rare resistlesse power:
> Whereby hee makes and unmakes God, each houre.[51]

The habit of associating alchemy and transubstantiation seems so ingrained for Protestant writers that when Milton uses the verb "transubstantiate" to note that angels eat the same way humans do, "with keen dispatch / Of real hunger, and concoctive heat / To transubstantiate," he undercuts his own point with a wry comparison between angelic alimentation and the rather shady "Empiric Alchemist" who "Can turn, *or holds it possible to turn* / Metals of drossiest Ore to perfet Gold."[52]

At the base of this comparison between transubstantiation and alchemy—at least for thinkers well versed in the Thomist physics that underpins transubstantiation—is a real acquaintance with the shakiness of Aristotelian matter theory as it was used and modified in the late Middle Ages and early Renaissance. In a remarkably learned if poetically awful bit of verse, for example, seventeenth-century polymath William Vaughan (no relation to the Vaughan brothers, poet Henry and alchemist Thomas) takes us through a history of Aristotelian matter theory and its absorption by Scholasticism, arguing that the doctrine of transubstantiation was inspired by alchemy's perversion of Aristotle and alluding along the way to Berengar of Tours's skepticism about transubstantiation's plausibility. In the age of Scholasticism, he says,

> Bare Accidents by Whymsyes of the Braine
> To Substances turn'd of Promethean straine,
> . . . .
> Baals sophistry, and Chymickes Transmutation
> Begot and coyn'd Transubstantiacion.
> . . . .
> For neere about that time did Alchymy
> Begin to raigne with Schoole-Theology.
> . . . .
> Woe to the time that our West Church forsooke
> The New-Mans way, which Berengarius tooke,
> And dar'd Christ [*sic*] Body so to understand
> Which till Doomes day doth sit on Gods Right hand
> Since his Ascent, and there in Heaven stayes.[53]

As indicated by William Vaughan's affirmation that Christ's body is on God's right hand and by George Goodwin's sneer that "Popish Chymicks make a thousand Gods," the issue with transubstantiation here is truly a physics problem—namely, the problem discussed above: the accident of "quantity" or extension. To reiterate that problem, this time in the words of John Donne, "They that pretend to enlarge this [risen] body [of Christ] by multiplication, by making millions of these bodies in the Sacraments, by the way of Transubstantiation, they doe not honour this body, whose honour is to sit in the same dimensions, and circumscriptions, at the right hand of God."[54] How can Christ's body be here on earth and there in heaven at the same time? The language accompanying the discussion of quantity, however, also conflates alchemy with transubstantiation. Protestant polemicists regularly accuse priests of "multiplying" Christ during the Mass, using a term so often attached to alchemy in early modern England that it seems, for most people, that "multiplying" defines what alchemists do.[55] While alchemists like Thomas Norton take care to distinguish true alchemical savants from "such lesyngis as multipliers use," alchemists themselves also regularly referred to "multiplication" as the penultimate stage of alchemical purification.[56]

What seems like a grandiose claim on the part of alchemy, then, is actually a balloon easily deflated. Sure, alchemy is just like transubstantiation, but how good is that? Both alchemy and transubstantiation, based as they are on rather unsatisfying revisions of Aristotelian matter theory, may be derided as junk science. Nevertheless, theories of both transubstantiation and alchemy do answer, even if badly, to urgent questions related to material change: What is matter made of? How does it transform? And is all matter the same, or can some matter be exceptional? While the seventeenth century is renowned for its "new science," a *novum organum* that departed from medieval models, in this particular arena natural philosophers struggled with offering a better theory than the Scholastic Aristotelianism they suspected was wrong. Even atomism, an anti-Aristotelian theory of matter that has received much attention of late in early modern literary criticism, seemed to many in the first half of the seventeenth century to be as fanciful as Aquinas's accidents that could be separated from their substantial forms. (I discuss atomism later in this chapter, in connection with George Herbert.) Oddly enough, it is dyed-in-the-wool Aristotelian Alexander Ross, the seventeenth-century clergyman who made a place for himself in history by trying to confute Galileo, René Descartes, and William Harvey, who states the problem most cogently: "Transmutation then of species is impossible to Nature, not to Chymists, who think to transform silver into gold: not to the Roman Church, which holds a transubstantiation of bread into Christs body: not unto Poets, who sing of so many metamorphoses and transformations of men into beasts: nor of those who think Witches can transform themselves into Cats, Hares, and other creatures."[57] Here Ross offers no answers to the puzzle of matter's essential makeup and its transmutation, since his outmoded Aristotelianism gives him none that will hold water. Rather, he leaves the imagination of these things to those whose theories of the material world seem equally fanciful: the witch, the alchemist, the priest, and the poet.

Transubstantiation Doesn't Matter: John Donne

We have already seen that John Donne's sermons cite alchemy and transubstantiation as equally discreditable, equally wrong. Priests who claim to call the actual body and blood of Christ into bread and wine as they say the Words of Institution are no better than the alchemists who "multiply" gold. In contrast, Donne's secular poetry also evinces a certain nostalgia for transubstantiation, and, as we shall see, that nostalgia is sometimes expressed through alchemy.

Donne's dismissal of and interest in transubstantiation are not, however, mutually exclusive attitudes—not if both dismissal and interest are predicated on understanding transubstantiation as what Luther called it, a truly trivial doctrine. For Donne, a fascination with transubstantiation derives not from fondly remembering its former status as dogma but from fondly remembering its dependence on preposterous theories of the transmutation of matter. In other words, Donne's resuscitation of transubstantiation constitutes not a longing for an old, now unattainable certainty, but rather a longing for old nonsense.[58] In frequently emphasizing the way transubstantiation shared with alchemy a reputation for junk physics, Donne's secular alchemical poems thus present a far different picture than we might expect of both his theological commitment and his scientific engagement. These poems, in fact, present a Donnean point of view that disclaims either substantial theological commitment or significant scientific engagement. When theology is represented by transubstantiation and science by alchemy—and even more, when transubstantiation and alchemy go hand in hand—both theology and science may easily be deemed inconsequential.

The inconsequentiality of transformed matter contradicts what we might expect to be compelling about transubstantiation for Donne, both before and after his Protestant conversion—that is, its promise of the existence of singular earthly substances. Specifically, following Ramie Targoff's recent work on Donne's obsession with the perfected bodies believers will regain after the Resurrection, we might expect Donne also to be compelled by the prospect of exceptional human bodies here on earth.[59] Conjoining transubstantiation with alchemy might allow Donne to transfer the unique qualities of Christ's flesh and blood as they are present in the Eucharist to human flesh and blood that was once ordinary but is now alchemically refined.

Donne's poetry and prose, however, repeatedly debunk the dream of the alchemically refined body by demonstrating that it, like the doctrine of transubstantiation itself, is a wrong idea. Yet it is no less appealing for that. Quite the contrary, this transubstantiated, alchemical physicality is all the more important to Donne because its existence is patently impossible. Furthermore, the reason it is important does not have to do merely with Donne's propensity to devise and ponder scientific and theological puzzles. Donne means also to explore how confessing one's knowledge system false at its base neither causes that knowledge system to collapse nor puts one in a state of epistemological anguish. Through cross-referencing alchemy and transubstantiation, both of them improbable, Donne establishes an alternative way of thinking. Modeled after the history of Eucharistic theology, that alternative amounts to a third way, beyond either hoping for a theory that both compels belief and makes intellectual sense (Thomas Aquinas and his inheritors) or reluctantly swallowing a theory of physical makeup that compels belief even though it does not make intellectual sense (William of Ockham and his inheritors). This third way proposes knowing that a coherent theory of physical change does not exist, but deciding not to worry about it.

A Donne who is eager not to consider Eucharistic quandaries is not a Donne most critics would recognize. Obviously it is not the Donne of the Holy Sonnets and other sacred lyrics, which are rife with anxiety about Christ's presence and its meaning. Curiously, though, while Donne's sacred lyrics also use alchemical imagery, in these poems he cordons off alchemy from the Eucharist, never once couching explorations of the Real Presence in alchemical terms. Instead, it is his secular lyrics that take on questions about the *exact* physical mechanism of Eucharistic transformation from the realm of the sacred into the realm of the secular. This bifurcation of Eucharistic discussion—Christ's presence in the sacred lyrics, Christ's physics in the secular lyrics—sets up an equally bifurcated reaction to epistemological difficulty. Whereas Donne's sacred lyrics take on Eucharistic issues with head-splitting seriousness and genuine questions of faith, his secular lyrics often accompany Eucharistic physics with the trivializing relief of alchemy.

Why might Donne require a venue in which the Eucharist need not be taken seriously? One cause may be cultural: his audience and readers might have appreciated an alchemical digression from Eucharistic matters. Even though the Lord's Supper, once the chief sacrament, was much less emphasized in the Reformed church of the later sixteenth century than it had been in the pre-Reformation or early Reformation English church, many otherwise perfectly conformist churchgoers seem to have had trouble making it to Communion the bare minimum of once a year—indicating, perhaps, a weariness with having to confront such hot-button topics as the Eucharist's importance, and a desire to avoid the whole issue.[60] Donne's own evasive tactics, though, may have to do not only with the painfulness of this particular topic but also with the way that evasion allows him to cultivate a useful and pleasurable epistemological stance. My sense of his secular alchemical-transubstantiative poems is that collectively their intellectual process is not simply to mull over the cultural problem of the Eucharist but rather also to constitute a lyric process that ultimately excuses the speaker from having to take this serious topic seriously. By means of the tincture of alchemy, Donne rehearses all of the issues behind Eucharistic dogma. But by means of the tincture of alchemy, these issues also take on the quality of something both terribly pressing and terribly diversionary. This odd combination, however, follows perfectly from Donne's perception that the natural philosophy of his day is utterly incapable of proposing an alternative matter theory superior to the Aristotelian physics that, as we have seen, was beginning to be dismantled. In his secular poems, Donne provides the alternative of both preserving the old system of learning that one knows to be wrong and also forgetting about its errors.

In the secular poems I discuss in this section, this dynamic of exceptionally graceful sidestepping is often brought to bear on Donne's contemplation of the nature of human physicality. Frequently, as we shall see, the physics questions that unite alchemy and the Eucharist intersect in Donne's treatments of the female body—that is, exactly the kind of body that Donne finds both paramount and negligible. Another kind of alchemical flesh comes into play in this regard, as we shall also see: the compellingly disgusting, quasi-Eucharistic Paracelsian remedy of mummy.

We have no reason to think that Donne's postconversion beliefs about the Eucharist ever went outside the admittedly large tent of the Church of England's doctrine. In *Ignatius His Conclave*, Donne joins every Reformist thinker in referring to transubstantiation as an unjustified, extrascriptural innovation by the Roman Catholic Church. On his tour of hell, the narrator of this text doesn't bother to look for purgatory, pronouncing it a mere fabrication concretized into doctrine by the recent Council of Trent, which, "Beeing not satisfied with making one Transubstantiation, purposed to bring in another: which is, to change fables into Articles of faith."[61] In a sermon, Donne later puts the matter even more baldly, calling transubstantiation "repugnant to the plaine wordes of Scripture."[62]

Furthermore, Donne joins Wyclif and other similarly erudite detractors of transubstantiation in objecting to this dogma on account of its flawed physics. His anti-Catholic Christmas Day sermon of 1626 derides the way that Thomist physics twists Aristotle's theory of substantial form and accidental properties to create a singular exception for the Eucharist: "since miracles are so easie and cheape, and obvious to them, as they have induced a miraculous transubstantiation, they might have done well to have procured one miracle more, a trans-accidentation, that since the substance is changed, the accidents might have beene changed too."[63] As I have already noted, Donne joined skeptics from Duns Scotus on in recognizing that the logical problem in transubstantiative physics is the "quantity" or extensive property of Christ's body. In the sermon in which he charges Roman Catholic priests with illogically "multiplying" Christ's body, he compares the sacramental bread to a portion of air illumined by light, something whose size and substance do not change even if it is called by a different name: "You would have said at noone, this light is the Sun, and you will say now, this light is the Candle; That light was not the Sun, this light is not the Candle, but it is that portion of aire which the Sun did then, and which the Candle doth now enlighten."[64]

At moments when he is debunking transubstantiation, Donne, like many of his contemporaries, seems naturally to reach for comparisons with alchemy. Both Roman Catholics and alchemists share a habit, he suggests, of rewriting fanciful suppositions as fundamental truths. In a sermon preached to King Charles I, in the course of deriding the Gregorian calendar Donne calls Catholicism alchemical in the number of accretive, extraneous principles it requires believers to adopt as axiomatic: "If wee should admitt their Metaphysiques, their transcendent Transubstantiation, and admitt their Chimiques, their Purgatorie Fires, and their Mythologie, and Poetrie, their apparitions of Soules and Spirits, they would binde us to their Mathematiques too, and they would not let us bee saved, except wee would reforme our Almanackes to their tenne dayes."[65] Like alchemists, Roman Catholics can find textual confirmation for their fanciful theories just about anywhere, "and as our Alchymists can finde their whole art and worke of Alchymy, not onely in Virgil and Ovid, but in Moses and Solomon; so these men can finde such a transmutation into gold, such a foundation of profit, in extorting a sense for Purgatory, or other profitable Doctrines, out of any Scripture."[66] Donne has absorbed his times' habit of associating transubstantiation with alchemy on the grounds of their both being physically impossible.

And yet it is precisely because it is physically impossible that alchemy is intriguing to Donne. Alchemy's constellation of metaphors does more than supply attractive poetic devices and intellectual structures through which to imagine the purification of bodies, minds, and souls.[67] It also offers Donne a mode of imagining matter that flagrantly disobeys the laws of physics. The difference between these two uses of alchemical metaphor is like the difference between employing the trope of gold beaten to airy thinness and employing the trope of gold beaten to such airy thinness that it joins lovers' souls across any physical distance, as Donne does in "A Valediction Forbidding Mourning": whereas the first draws upon plausible metallurgy, the second grants such fantastical qualities to metal that the metaphor, lovely as it is, is as far-flung as such gold would be. When alchemy keeps company with transubstantiation, the potential for imagining unbelievable matter only becomes magnified, as does the opportunity to create extraordinary images of those implausible substances.

For Donne, however, such a conjunction of elements also provides the occasion to query why, or even if, one would pursue such a substance in the first place. And when it comes to querying why one would want an evidently desirable thing, his mind often turns to women. Even when they do not refer to transubstantiation, Donne's alchemical poems are often about the possibility of refining the female body and heterosexual union with that body into something purer. Take, for example, "The Canonization," where the "Phoenix ridle" that converts both sexes to "one neutrall thing" is derived from the alchemical progression from *coniunctio*, the marriage of masculine sulfur and feminine mercury, to *exaltatio*, the production of the nonsexed alchemical product— gold, the elixir of life, or the philosopher's stone.[68] Or take "The Ecstasy," in which, before the union of their bodies is even contemplated, the lovers' souls are so thoroughly and alchemically commingled that an onlooker "Might then a new concoction take, / And part farre purer than he came" (27–28). Something different happens, however, when Donne's alchemized female bodies also take on the qualities of the Eucharist.[69] In that case, the legitimacy of this purification comes into question, leading the way for a second-order questioning of whether the game is worth the candle. All of this transubstantiated, refined flesh, but to what end, if neither transubstantiation nor alchemical refinement works?

To begin my discussion of poems that ask this question, I turn to Donne's "Air and Angels," a poem that considers the fundamental physics that underlies both transubstantiation and alchemy even if it is not about either one. Since "Air and Angels" addresses the incarnation of the soul in the body, it engages a number of the same physical issues that transubstantiation and alchemy do, and it does so in the context of considering whether a woman may assume an exceptional kind of physical virtue. At least since the time of Aquinas, as I mentioned above, Christian thinkers had repurposed the same Aristotelian matter theory that underlay the dogma of transubstantiation for Christian theories of ensoulment: God's quickening of a human fetus with its soul occurs at the same moment—indeed, is the same action—as his imposing a substantial form upon what had previously been an indistinguishable blob of prime matter.[70] In consequence, a living human body is inseparable from its soul, just as the prime matter out of which a physical body is made is inseparable from its substantial form, which in turn is inseparable from the sum of its accidents. As "Air and Angels" puts it, "my soule . . . / Takes limmes of flesh, and else could nothing doe" (7–8). All of this is always true for every human.

Always true, that is, except in the case of the incarnate Christ, whose resurrected body must be materially different from his first and ordinary earthly body for the physics of the transubstantiated Eucharist to be valid, and for Christ's body to be present in every consecrated Host, every time, everywhere. That same issue of Christ's embodiment—how can one human body be so fundamentally different from another?—arises in "Air and Angels," and is resolved in the same way that Thomist theory resolves the physics of the Eucharist. Just as Christ's resurrected body is materially superior to his initial body, "Air and Angels" proposes one form of bodily incarnation superior to another. In this case, it is a hierarchy based on sex. Man's embodied love is superior to woman's, just as angels are purer than the bodily features—the "face, and wings" of air—they assume (23). So far, so good: Donne seems to have cleverly, if misogynistically, elaborated a scale of material analogy in which angels are more refined than air, just as men are more refined than women.

But matters (and matter) prove more complicated than this, in ways that start to take on the overtones of Eucharistic controversy. In the case of the consecrated Eucharist, as we have seen, Aquinas struggled with the exact physics of how the immaterial substantial form of Christ's body and blood acquired the material accidents of the bread and wine. Once transubstantiation occurs, these accidents must inhere in *something*, but they cannot inhere in Christ's substantial form. Thus, Aquinas theorized, the baser accidents of bread and wine (their taste, smell, color, and texture) inhere in the "prime" (and purest) accident of bread and wine, that of quantity or extension. This tripartite scheme—baser accidents inhere in another but purer accident, which in turn inheres in an entirely separate, ideal substantial form—appears in "Air and Angels" in the tripartite physics that composes the beloved woman. It cannot be as simple as her body inhering in the man's love, since her physical accidents cannot intermingle with the ideal state of his love's substantial form. Hence Donne introduces a third term: *her* love. The baser accidents of her body (her hair, her lips, etc.) inhere in her love, which as prime accident inheres in the interior purity of *his* love, the true essence and substantial form that is entirely different in kind from the accidental properties she has to offer. Just as the substantial form of Christ's body and blood deigns to "wear" the accidents of the bread and wine, and just as an angel, entirely different from and superior to the air, deigns to wear the air as its face and wings, "So thy love may be my loves sphaere" (25).

The implausible transubstantiative physics behind this transmutation, however, marks it as suspect; and indeed, upon closer examination, we see it as no transmutation at all. First of all, the change in "Air and Angels" is not a physical change but a change of mind. The female beloved is not truly refined to match the male speaker. Rather, his superior, immaterial love has simply consented to be associated with her otherwise ordinary material qualities: "and now / That [love] assume thy body, *I allow*" (12–13; emphasis added). Furthermore, even that change of mind is ultimately identified as ironic. Preceded by the same improbable physics that backs transubstantiation, the misogynistic disappointment of the poem's final tercet may be read, not as a surprise, but as an inevitability:

> Just such disparitie
> As is twixt Aire and Angells puritie,
> 'Twixt womens love, and mens will ever bee.
>
> (26–28)

Air cannot be refined into angels, women's love cannot be refined into men's.

In the end, "Air and Angels" is a poem less about any real prospect of feminine refinement and more about how far we are willing to entertain theories we know to be untrue. Clued in by the poem's reference to a jury-rigged Thomist manipulation of Aristotle that allows an accident to adhere in another accident, we never entirely trust that such refinement can occur. Nevertheless, for twenty-five lines before its three-line conclusion, "Air and Angels" strings along a promise of purer feminine matter that is underlain by patently preposterous physics. The nonsurprise of the unsuccessful refinement at the end proves that the poem has undertaken not merely a quasi-scientific study of the quasi-physical attributes of love and lovers but also an epistemological study of how long false notions can hold. The answer? Twenty-eight lines, the length of two sonnets. And they are not even perfect sonnets: the scattering of truncated rhythms (trimeter and tetrameter) across those twenty-eight lines corresponds to the strained credulity the poem induces. We can entertain the idea that women can be made purer, but not for long.

Like Lewis Carroll's White Queen, then, Donne's speakers seem to be in the business of believing six impossible things before breakfast—except that they tip their hand that this state of belief is also a state of knowing that their belief is incorrect. The speaker of "A Nocturnal upon St. Lucy's Day, Being the Shortest Day" similarly puts pressure on how, and how long, we may grant credence to incredible ideas of fantastical physical matter, this time by explicitly joining the physics of transubstantiation and the physics of alchemy—with a Paracelsian twist.[71] Here, the matter in question is that of the speaker. The poem begins with the Paracelsian assumption that there is a "generall balm" or spiritual force in which everything in the world partakes (6). In this light, the speaker's recommendation that lovers study him—in that he is "every dead thing, / In whom love wrought new Alchimie"—initially promises a Paracelsian alchemical revivification. If the general balm is currently at low ebb, then spring surely will see it coursing through the speaker as it does through all who have had the good sense to take their Paracelsian medicine. In that case the speaker, though a "dead thing," is not really dead.

But Paracelsus's version of matter theory starts to go awry as the speaker turns more specifically to how he does and does not conform to a Eucharistic physics. While the speaker continues to describe himself alchemically, in his case no alchemical renewal is achieved:

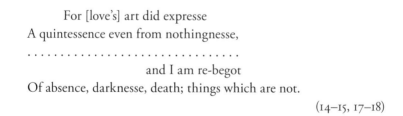

> For [love's] art did expresse
> A quintessence even from nothingnesse,
> . . . .
>   and I am re-begot
> Of absence, darknesse, death; things which are not.
>
>   (14–15, 17–18)

In the terms of Aristotelian physics, the speaker's "re-begotten" self is an impossible thing: a substantial form imposed on nothing. And not even an ordinary nothing, like a shadow—which is itself the sign, the accidental property, of a substance—but rather the "Elixer" of "the first nothing" (29). This elixir seems to be an alchemical product that is, paradoxically and impossibly, concocted not from prime matter but from the "first nothing" that existed before God created prime matter in order then to create the world *ex nihilo*.[72] If it were successful, the physics experiment of the speaker of the "Nocturnal" would be the most astounding alchemy ever achieved. More than breaking down base matter into prime matter, the speaker has broken down matter into the nothingness that preceded creation. Surely this is a position of tremendous potential.

Yet the "Nocturnal" suspends potential by suspending the operation. Circling back at its end to its beginning—the year's midnight, and the day's—the "Nocturnal" reveals that the speaker's condition is not the result of an alchemical transformation but rather the preparation for it: "Let mee prepare towards her, and let mee call / This houre her Vigill, and her Eve" (43–44). As in "Air and Angels," then, the speaker's condition is a state of mind, not a state of matter (or nonmatter). While the speaker earlier insisted that absolute nothingness has come to pass, in terms of physical change nothing has in fact yet happened. The speaker's proposal that all lovers "study" him (10) thus establishes that, like "Air and Angels," the "Nocturnal" is an exercise not in physical change but in knowledge making. What is it that lovers are supposed to learn and imitate of the speaker's claiming an impossible physical being? They cannot be that body, because even the speaker is not yet and cannot ever be that body. Rather, what they can learn and imitate is the speaker's talent for asserting a physical state that is manifestly contrary to fact, an elixir of "the first nothing" that has "grown" even though no alchemy has yet commenced (29). The speaker of the "Nocturnal," like the speaker of "Air and Angels," is interested in what kinds of knowledge-making practices he can get away with for as long as the poem can pretend that something physical has happened, even though we learn it hasn't. "Study" him, lovers, he exhorts near the poem's beginning. Yet, at the poem's end, he asks permission to commence that operation whose product they have already supposedly studied: "Let mee prepare towards her" (43). His implication is that permission, or credulity, may be denied; if so, and if the study happens nonetheless—as it must have, if we have gotten this far in the poem—then we willingly study that in which we do not believe.

The "Nocturnal" is a peculiar (and exceptionally sophisticated) Donnean variation on the matter theory that brings together alchemy and transubstantiation. Having no substantive body at all is not typically Donne's aim in either his secular or his religious poetry. In other poems, Donne's interest in Paracelsian alchemy, and particularly in Paracelsian medicine, enables him more straightforwardly to transfer the physics of exceptional matter from the transubstantiated Eucharist to the human self. I am not the first to notice that Donne is interested in appropriating the power of the sacraments: a number of critics have argued that Donne tends to invest poetry itself with a sacramental function, and others have been interested in Donne's conveyance of sacramentality to physical matter.[73] Frances Cruickshank, for example, has argued that Donne's sacramental impulses are tied to his somewhat forlorn hope that God may inhere in earthly materiality, a hope that Targoff connects to Donne's obsession with the prospect of regaining his own, individual body, in perfected form, at the time of resurrection.[74] Appropriating sacramental power thus can return Donne to the question of what the sacrament of the Eucharist, which imparts Christ's resurrected flesh and blood to living believers, is actually made of. And Donne finds Paracelsus's answers to that question, though heretical, marvelously compelling. They are, however, compelling not because they are right but rather because they are so manifestly wrong.

Donne's acquaintance with Paracelsus seems unusually thorough for even a well-educated person of his time, given that Paracelsian medicine did not really take off in England until the turn of the seventeenth century.[75] True, the Paracelsus of *Ignatius His Conclave* is a reckless physician, one who has killed any number of patients through an unfortunate habit of barely bothering to test his "uncertaine, ragged, and unperfect experiments" before administering them as medication.[76] And Donne's *Devotions upon Emergent Occasions* credits only God, not the physician, with making an effectively "powerfull Cordiall."[77] Still, Donne's poetry turns again and again to the matter theory that underlies Paracelsian medicine and that authorizes its curative capacities.

The most interesting case of that matter theory? The ostentatiously Eucharistic Paracelsian remedy of mummy. Recall that Paracelsian alchemy nullifies transubstantiation in that it envisions the Eucharist as merely another kind of body that, like all matter, contains some degree of divine energy. Recall also that this life force, often called "balm" or "balsam" by Paracelsians, was associated in Paracelsus's Trinitarian elemental scheme with the solidifying element of salt, which has preservative powers and is aligned specifically with Christ, who assumed solid form in his incarnation in human flesh. Balsam could be conveyed medicinally through the administration of one Paracelsian alchemical ingredient: *mumia*, or mummy. Paracelsus was not the first to consider mummy medicinally useful, but he seems to have been the first to theorize its operations in the context of this larger theological, physiological, and alchemical vision. Mummy, in his view, transmitted balsam's Christlike resistance to physical decay.[78]

Originally, the "mummy" valued for medicinal purposes seems to have meant the bitumen (naturally occurring asphalt) that was used to mummify Egyptian corpses and that could be retrieved when those mummies were unearthed. From this usage, however, the term was metonymically transferred to the Egyptian mummies themselves.[79] And finally, by Paracelsus's time and probably largely because of his influence, *mummy* came to mean, at least in northern Europe, either fresh or (more often) dried bits of recently deceased human corpses.[80] Following Paracelsus's lead, sixteenth- and seventeenth-century alchemical recipes for medicinal cordials began to feature mummy as a crucial ingredient. "Elixir of Mummie is made thus," advises John French in his *Art of Distillation* (1653): "Take of Mummy (*viz.* of mans flesh hardened) cut small four ounces, spirit of wine terebinthinated [that is, infused with turpentine] ten ounces, put them into a glazed vessell . . . which set in horse dung to digest for the space of a month, then take it out and express it. . . . This Elixir is a wonderful preservative against all infections, also very balsamicall."[81]

Since prescribing mummy literalizes the licensed cannibalism of the Roman Catholic doctrine of transubstantiation, associations between this alchemical medicine and the Eucharist were perhaps inevitable. Richard Sugg and Louise Noble both argue, in fact, that medicinal mummy was acceptable in parts of early modern Europe because it served as a Protestant substitute for the ingestion of Christ's divine body.[82] The association between mummy and the body and blood of Jesus Christ had two interesting consequences. On the one hand, the Reformist horror at consuming Christ in Holy Communion—a horror that never forgot Berengar of Tours's being forced to swear that Christ's body is literally "crushed by the teeth of the faithful"—acquired new waves of nausea via the alchemically endorsed consumption of mummy.[83] Reformist controversialist Daniel Featley, for example, records in his account of a debate on the nature of the Eucharist the alleged Roman Catholic opinion that eating human flesh in the form of the Eucharist was no sin because it was just the same as eating mummy in the form of medicine. In response, Featley invokes "The horror of the sinne of Anthropophagy, or eating mans flesh . . . and chamming it with the teeth."[84] On the other hand, the Paracelsian view that anthropophagy enhances health and well-being bolstered, even among Protestants, a comforting metaphorical association between Holy Communion and a sovereign cure for what ails you. As the pseudo-Paracelsian tract *De natura rerum* promises, with the administration of mummy "that which is mortified, may bee both raised again, and revived."[85] Donne, whose belief

in Paracelsus's "balsam" and whose faith in Paracelsian medicine extended—
in a letter he wrote to Henry Goodyer—to labeling mummy a product that can
restore our "naturall inborn preservative" when it "is corrupted or wasted,"
refers in his *Devotions upon Emergent Occasions* to the Eucharist as exactly a
medicinal cordial along these lines: "I have drunke of thy Cordiall Blood, for
my recoverie, from actuall, and habituall sinne."[86] Donne explains the logic by
which he extends the mummy cure to Christ's salvation of humankind later in
the *Devotions*, when he muses on the curious fact that "if my body may have
my Physicke, any Medicine from another body, one Man from the flesh of
another Man (as by Mummy, or any such composition,) it must bee from a
man that is dead."[87] His analogy is clear: it is Christ's crucified body that cures
the living man.

    One interpretation of Donne's interest in transferring Eucharistic power
from holy sacrament to alchemical medication might be that it is a benign
form of nostalgia for his Roman Catholic days. Relying on Paracelsian pharmaceuticals might allow Donne and his poetic speakers to have their balsamic
cake and eat it too. They may partake of the restorative powers of Christ's body
by imagining it as alchemical mummy while at the same time not having to
adhere to either the doctrine or the bad physics of transubstantiation. In practice, mummy does not, of course, effect such a spectacular conversion of human
flesh, and the early moderns, no fools, were well aware of mummy's failures.
Physician Ambroise Paré, expressing the frustration that many a doctor and
patient must have felt, dismissed mummy on the grounds that he had "tryed
it an hundred times" and it simply "doth nothing helpe the diseased," inducing nothing but chest pain, vomiting, and halitosis.[88] Mummy's practical inefficacy forces us to revise a reading that would have Donne safely expressing
nostalgia for transubstantiation through the medium of mummy. Why be
nostalgic for something manifestly untrue?

    To answer this question I turn now to some of Donne's most obviously
Eucharistic and/or obviously alchemical secular poems, which elucidate spectacularly how the substitution of alchemy for transubstantiation merely per-
petuates transubstantiation's failures. In the process, these poems lay out the
same epistemological framework as "Air and Angels" and "A Nocturnal upon
St. Lucy's Day": they invite—perhaps even require—us to develop an inti-
mate acquaintance with the operations of disknowledge. The issue is not
only that Donne continues to imagine the transformation of ordinary into
sublime matter and then to deflate such transformations as theoretically
impossible. The issue is also that the poems acknowledge all along that such

transformation is untenable. As a result, reading these poems is not an experience of being disappointed when Donne ultimately brings his magnificent tropes of refined physical matter down to earth. Rather, reading these poems conveys an experience of engaging viscerally, sometimes even pleasurably, in the prospect of refinement even while understanding that prospect to be wrongly theorized from the start. As I described it in this chapter's introduction, the mode of disknowledge applied here labels that understanding inconsequential. We know the physics to be all wrong, but forget we ever cared about its being right.

Since Donne, in his secular poems, demonstrates the irredeemable ordinariness of typical matter through the ordinariness of typical women, it would follow that he would choose the exceptional woman to exemplify the possibility of extraordinary matter. Indeed, several of his verse letters to aristocratic women patrons flatter his addressees by suggesting they have been alchemically refined.[89] When he is not going about cementing patronage, however, Donne considers it not so easy for even an exceptional woman to possess equally exceptional physical matter. The grounds of his skepticism about female exceptionalism, once again, have to do with whether Aristotelian physics have been violated.

"Twickenham Garden," which begins with the "Nocturnal upon St. Lucy's Day" conceit of the male speaker's command of transubstantiation—"I do bring / The spider love, which transubstantiates all, / And can convert Manna to gall" (5–7)—turns to discussing the extraordinary woman, the one who is true when ordinary women are uniformly false, in terms of whether her exterior matches her interior. The word "transubstantiate" is followed in this poem, as in "Air and Angels," by the Eucharistic physics problem of material accidents' not belonging to the substantial form they cloak. The poem draws to a close with the premise that the being of the typical woman, always a false lover, may be analyzed as a matter of misleading exterior attributes: "Nor can you more judge womans thoughts by teares, / Then by her shadow, what she weares" (24–25). The analogy between the typical woman's tears and her shadow is awkward, though. Could it be that, as a false woman's crocodile tears mask her thoughts, her shadow masks her clothing? Not really. Her shadow is, in fact, an accidental property of those clothes, and more or less truly denotes them. Following this logic, if the perfect "she" of the poem, the one true woman on earth, is unlike all ordinary women (26), then her shadow is *not* denotative; it is an accident detached from her substance. She is as extraordinary a substantial form as Christ in the Eucharist.

It is the heart of this poem's paradox, however, that this transubstantiation, like the manna transubstantiated to gall at the poem's opening, ultimately
converts the miraculous to the quotidian. Helen Gardner's commentary on
this poem's final lines, in which this extraordinary woman proves to be like
all others—"O perverse sexe, where none is true but shee, / Who's therefore
true, because her truth kills mee" (26–27)—explains why: "Although unlike all
other women she is true, she is like them in not being what she seems, for her
'truth' to another is really only cruelty" to the speaker.[90] Hence "Twickenham
Garden" joins poems like "Air and Angels" and others (for example, "Community") in developing the association between all femininity and crass matter.
No amount of transubstantiative imagery can change what women are. But
that is precisely the point: transubstantiative imagery will always confirm
femininity as crass matter because, as we see in the poem's final lines, the
physics of transubstantiation simply does not hold up. Even the speaker's declaration that his tears "are loves wine" (20) does not bear scrutiny in transubstantiative terms, since the metaphor inverts the physical structure of the
Eucharist. Unlike the transubstantiated wine of Holy Communion, in which
the accidents of ordinary wine cloak the unique substance of Christ's blood, the
uniqueness of the speaker's wine-tears resides in their unique accidents, their
unusual taste: "all [tears] are false, that tast not just like mine" (22). Nonetheless, the speaker of "Twickenham Garden" takes the typical Donnean position
of addressing an audience of "lovers" who will put his tears to the test. That
disappointed audience shares the speaker's ironic pleasure at having always
known that all women are not to be trusted. That knowledge, Donne's speaker
intimates, frames the epistemological experience of that shared knowledge
as a curious bliss of disappointment. The "True paradise" of Twickenham
Garden, he declares, is the one of failure, the one to which "I have the serpent
brought" (9).

For a palliative to this situation we might, as other critics have, turn to
"The First Anniversary: An Anatomy of the World," which proposes the dead
Elizabeth Drury as truly exceptional matter with alchemically transubstantiative properties. This poem's subject alchemically assumed female form just
to show how (unusually) pure she could be:

She in whom vertue was so much refin'd,
That for Allay unto so pure a minde
Shee took the weaker Sex, she that could drive
The poysonous tincture, and the stayne of Eve,

Out of her thoughts, and deeds; and purifie
All, by a true religious Alchimy,
Shee, shee is dead.

(177–83)

Since her death those qualities have vanished. The world is in a state of Paracelsian illness, having lost her as its balsam and preservative:

Sicke world, yea dead, yea putrefied, since shee
Thy'intrinsique Balme, and thy preservative,
Can never be renew'd, thou never live.

(56–58)

So, it seems, alchemy belongs with the other eternal verities that have been
lost with the advent of the "new Philosophy" that "cals all in doubt" (205).
The prospect of spiritual perfection was real, even if it died with Elizabeth
Drury.[91]

But not so. Elizabeth Drury's alchemy proves to have been like all alchemy,
ineffectual:

She from whose influence all Impressions came,
But, by Receivers impotencies, lame,
Who, though she could not transubstantiate
All states to gold, yet guilded every state,
. . . .
Shee, shee is dead.

(415–18, 427)

Merely "gilded" gold is, by definition, failed alchemy; the dead girl was just
as ineffective as alchemy is at inculcating virtue in the world. The comparison
of her alchemy to transubstantiation only reinforces that failure. It is not her
fault, really: her receivers' impotence lames her potency. Nevertheless, this
memory of her alchemy as a mere "gilding" puts the lie to the poem's earlier
assertion that it is only nowadays that alchemy adulterates or falsifies what it
claims to make pure (345–46). Nothing extraordinary was ever made through
Elizabeth Drury and her alchemy.

And yet, even though alchemy is ineffectual, it does valuable work
for Donne in "The First Anniversary." Specifically, it marks out a type of

epistemological maneuver that not only is useful in the moment but also serves as a device to compartmentalize memory. "The First Anniversary" extends the fundamental proposition of elegy, that "things were better then," to the materiality of the world, now distempered in every way. At the same time, the poem, as I have been arguing, discounts transubstantiative and/or alchemical material refinement as always having been a fantasy. We thus have two choices. We could simply recognize that not only are things getting worse, but they were never good. Or, while still retaining the knowledge that our always dismal world is only deteriorating, we could forget that knowledge enough to speak of improvement as on the horizon even when we know it is not. In other words, we could forget what we know even as we know it. The poem's crucial analogy in this regard is the one between transubstantiation (even if a failed transubstantiation) and gilding (which is failed alchemy). Like the speaker's wine-flavored tears in "Twickenham Garden," but now in a more explicitly theological register, the analogy posits inverted Eucharistic transubstantiation: something equivalent to a host that is gilded with the true body of Christ but stays just bread in the middle. Could the bread be the substance of the Host, and Christ its accidents? That would be preposterous. But in dangling the promise of an alchemical transubstantiation that is not occult but rather readily apparent to the senses—Christ as tangible accident—this analogy also dangles the prospect of distracting ourselves with shiny gilded objects from our certain memory of how the material refinement of transubstantiation was, as Donne well knew, always a dubious physical proposition.

This forgetting of an unforgotten memory has a poetic purpose as much as it does a theological one. As the poem comes to its end, and as it makes its argument that Elizabeth Drury's mourners are both alchemical products and alchemical agents—"her creatures, whom she workes upon / And have [their] last, and best concoction / From her example, and her vertue" (455–57)—it also defines part of their alchemized function as remembering "The First Anniversary" itself. That is, remembering it badly. As part of his final word, the speaker defends the choice of poetry, rather than chronicle, as a vehicle for Elizabeth Drury's memory by calling to mind that God's final word to Moses was in the form of "song," not law. What the poem omits, though, is that God's song to Moses was of the Israelites' inevitable future failure: "then shal they turne unto other gods, and serve them, and contemne me, & breake my covenant. And then when manie adversities and tribulacions shal come upon them, this song shal answer them to their face as a witnes . . . for I knowe their imaginacion, which they go about even now" (Deut. 31:20–21). God's warning and the Israelites' heedless "imagination"; alchemical failure and continued alchemical effort; a poem that admits as it draws to a close that it can only "emprison" its object and a poem that insists, in its final breath, that "verse the fame enroules" (470, 474). The contradictions in "The First Anniversary" are too compressed to represent authentic forgetting. Rather, they represent remembering perfectly well alongside remembering not at all.

The most compact and complex Donnean example of how alchemy stands for the simultaneous possession of two incommensurable states of knowledge is "Love's Alchemy," a poem in which alchemy is implemented as a matchless design for disknowing that which is no longer desirable to know. The poem's first stanza presents us with alchemy's stupidity:

> Some that have deeper digg'd loves Myne than I,
> Say, where his centrique happinesse doth lie:
>   I'have lov'd, and got, and told,
> But should I love, get, tell, till I were old,
> I should not finde that hidden mysterie;
>   Oh, 'tis imposture all:
> And as no chymique yet th'Elixar got,
>   But glorifies his pregnant pot,
>   If by the way to him befall
> Some odoriferous thing, or medicinall,
>   So, lovers dreame a rich and long delight,
>   But get a winter-seeming summers night.
>
>   (1–12)

The comparison here, obviously, is between alchemy and other things that are futile pursuits. Alchemy and love are fools' games, something only a "chymique" would credit, in the same way that he glorifies his "pregnant pot" of a furnace even when it yields him nothing of worth. Whatever benefits love or alchemy produces are merely "by the way," accidental by-products of a process that never achieves its intent.

Juxtaposing what begins this stanza, however—digging for something that is not found—with the accidental benefits that by chance befall the alchemist brings us into the neighborhood of Francis Bacon's Aesopian fable, discussed in Chapter 1, that alchemy is like digging for nonexistent gold in an inherited vineyard: an activity that is of no use but that ought to be undertaken anyway. If alchemy and desire amount to the same thing, and if they are both inutile but still essential diversions, from what do they divert? The answer comes in the next stanza, when, after dismissing hopes of things rarefied, Donne's speaker rather unexpectedly turns to the Paracelsian alchemical ingredient of mummy:

> Our ease, our thrift, our honor, and our day,
> Shall we, for this vaine Bubles shadow pay?
> . . . .
>
>   That loving wretch that sweares,
> 'Tis not the bodies marry, but the mindes,
>   Which he in her Angelique findes,
>   Would sweare as justly, that he heares,
> In that dayes rude hoarse minstralsey, the spheares.
>   Hope not for minde in women; at their best,
>   Sweetnesse, and wit they'are, but, Mummy, possesst.
>   (13–14, 18–24)

Donne's final image of "mummy" is less startling once we remember its alchemical associations, which are also pointedly transubstantiative associations. A woman who is "mummy, possessed" might be merely a bit of mummy that is owned, uselessly, like the bit of dried flesh kept on the alchemist's shelf until it is needed for a Paracelsian cordial. Yet she might also be "mummy, *possessed*," inhabited by a spirit, revivified in the fashion of Christ's living body in the Eucharist. Either she is dead or she raises the dead. Either way, mummy must be acquired to be eaten, in a nasty parody of what some considered the already revolting ritual of Eucharistic cannibalism.

This poem's alchemy, though, rescues us from this horror, if only by way of laying bare mummy's inefficacy. Because mummy belongs not merely to Eucharistic debates but also to alchemy, the second stanza's woman who is mummy circles back to the first stanza's "chymique" who glorifies his pregnant pot. The pot, like the woman, is possessed: possessed because his; possessed because pregnant, full of something mysterious and unexpected. But the pot is not full, as it turns out, or at least not full of anything the alchemist originally aimed for. Once we draw the thread from the alchemist's pot to the mummy possessed and back again, transubstantiation helps serve the speaker's turn of forgetting his own epistemological failure. It is not that the Eucharist emerges as the "real" topic from underneath that bitterly witty alchemical analogy. It is that the devolution of the woman's body into mummy, degraded not only as female but also as alchemical fantasy, credits the speaker with knowing *something*: he knows that pure matter—alchemical gold, true mummy, a woman with a mind—is not to be had. Admitting that there is no tenable physics of exceptional matter is preferable to admitting, as the speaker does at the beginning of the poem, that some who have "deeper digg'd loves Myne" than he know the secret of love's happiness that he does not. Forgetting about that shortfall of knowledge and experience, the speaker revels in revealing natural philosophy in dire straits.

Thus "Love's Alchemy" adds yet another tool to disknowledge's epistemological kit. Alongside the simultaneous knowing and unknowing of physical impossibility of such poems as "Air and Angels," the "Nocturnal," and "Twickenham Garden," and alongside the simultaneous remembering and not remembering of "The First Anniversary," "Love's Alchemy" adds the option of simultaneously knowing that one is in possession of junk science and not minding that fact. As I suggested earlier, this kind of epistemological movement proves quite useful for the Protestant invention of a new split between science and faith. What is the advantage of knowing but not caring? Donne's remark in his *Essays on Divinity* that "Almost all the ruptures in the Christian Church" have been caused by too much passion over physics questions—issues of "Natural Divinity" such as transubstantiation—hints at what might have come to pass had such passion never been exercised.[92] Imagining a millennium and a half of history without "ruptures in the Christian Church," Donne institutes disknowledge as the principle behind ecclesiastical harmony. In this way he takes part in what Isabel Karremann, Cornel Zwierlein, and Inga Mai Groote have described as the important, deliberate Reformation work of "forgetting faith": in an age of religious seesawing, "the forgetting of faith [is] a valid and important strategy for dealing with confessional conflict, be it in the form of religious conversion, toleration, dissimulation or de-escalating, playful disregard."[93]

But there is more in play here than a kind of theological ceasefire. Had we never cared about theological dispute, Donne proposes, we might have remained in a golden age of churchly union. It seems like a throwback strategy. But by means of percolating his theology through alchemy, Donne is in fact showing the way forward, toward a certain kind of modernity. In two important essays that I also discussed in Chapter 1, Lee Patterson has argued that alchemy ushers in modernity in two different ways: it replaces faith in the sacramental with faith in technology; and it instantiates as normal the distinction between language and the endlessly deferred truth that language claims to represent.[94] For Patterson, both of these alchemical moves toward the modern are cause for some mourning, as stability gives way to endless change. I would like to revise Patterson's sadness about modernity, though, by combining his insights and applying them to Donne. If alchemy represents, for a poet like Donne, both a defunct (because never provable) sacramental physics and a defunct (because never true) ideal of the true *logos*, then alchemy may also represent the freedom to say openly, via its link between outmoded dogma and outmoded notions of truth, that religious doctrine no longer need worry about either confirming or denying scientific theory. In that case, alchemy might usher in modernity as a cheering rather than an alienating experience. For the otherwise permanently alienated Donne, the most reassuring version of modernity might mean not developing new ways of knowing—new science or secular skepticism—but rather constructing a safe venue where knowledge is not required.[95]

Forgetting about the once crucial, always dubious foundation of matter theory in Eucharistic physics thus proves for Donne to be a good strategy for even more than smoothing over England's past religious controversy or his own past Catholicism. That forgetting also allows Donne to anticipate, even in an age when an alternative physics is not yet in place, what it would be like for religious doctrine to forget about matter theory. The secular poems I have been discussing enact, on a microlevel, what Donne's sacred lyrics enact on a macrolevel when they segregate Eucharistic from alchemical imagery. In the sacred lyrics, that segregation absolves doctrine from having to answer to this particular kind of scientific question. The secular poems, in uniting the Eucharist and alchemy, undertake a quite different process, but to the same end: they not only demonstrate that matter theory and theology are now separate intellectual enterprises but also show how the intellect, even a superb one such as Donne's, can undertake that separation and be quite content with it. These secular poems leave physics and its quandaries behind as something Donne does not wish to know.

Let me turn from this essentially theoretical, epistemological point to a more historically located one. In terms of how to assess the state of knowledge at the turn of the seventeenth century, Donne's strategic ignorance of matter theory amounts to a defense of retaining the humanist reverence for the classical text despite its manifest shortcomings. No longer caring about the makeup of matter allows him to retain Aristotelian natural philosophy, no matter how superannuated or how cockeyed it may be. In his funeral sermon for wealthy merchant Sir William Cokayne, preached on the story of the raising of Lazarus, Donne likens the outdated but still relied-upon theories of Aristotle, Galen, and Ptolemy to "a child that is embalmed to make Mummy. . . . rather conserved in the stature of the first age, then growne to be greater." And yet this mummy—at once a stunted knowledge base and an ineffective alchemical preservative of human bodies—is better than anything that has come along since: "if there be any addition to knowledge, it is rather a new knowledge, then a greater knowledge; rather a singularity in a desire of proposing something that was not knowne at all before, then an emproving, an advancing, a multiplying of former inceptions."[96] The new science is too "singular": its propositions are entirely new, rather than improving, advancing, or multiplying the old. It is possible that here Donne's diction associates the old science further with alchemy. However incorrect it may be, the old science has valuable "multiplying" capacities—a word that, especially in the context of mummy and especially given Donne's use of it elsewhere, invokes alchemy's sham physics of "multiplication." In Donne's complex analogy, then, we are urged to stick with the knowledge analogized to alchemical remedy, even though it is known to be wrong. Although bound to fail, its inventive "multiplying," as we have seen, is a welcome alternative to having to assimilate the kinds of new knowledge that will make us uncomfortable. Better mummy than novelty; better old, wrongheaded ideas than up-to-date discomfiting ones.

Donne's alchemy thus proves an all-purpose disknowledge system, one both anti-mnemonic and anti-erudite. Handy for forgetting about the disputes that were at the heart of the Reformation, however well-known their details remain, it is also handy for not allowing the new science to change cherished humanist presumptions, however erroneous they may be. When theology meets matter theory, Donne uses the occasion to construct a magnificent model of intellectual negligence. True, it is a bit strange to read Donne, one of the Renaissance's great thinkers about ideological flash points, as choosing not to think too hard. I would wager, in fact, that *not* thinking is the one intellectual strategy that has never previously been attributed to this brainy poet. Nonetheless, the undeniable pleasures of intellectual disengagement seem to be as strong a motivator for the eccentric directions of many of Donne's poems as are the ideological and theological motivators that Donne critics have stressed in the last several decades. Donne's immediate poetic successors, as it turns out, were discerning readers of his poetry in this regard. In the following two sections we shall see how George Herbert and Henry Vaughan, in chewing over the same issues of matter theory that occupied Donne, also take up the question of whether it is better not to care.

Matter Doesn't Matter: George Herbert

In George Herbert's poetry, as in John Donne's, alchemy emerges at points that gesture toward issues either of Eucharistic doctrine or of the matter theory with which the Eucharist is associated. The dynamics of the relationships among these three elements—alchemical change, Eucharistic change, and material change—have a different *telos* for Herbert than they do for Donne, however. Whereas Donne ultimately references alchemy as a way to model not caring about religious doctrine's incapacity to cope with physics, Herbert takes the alliances between alchemy and transubstantiation to discipline-specific inquiries into the physical nature of the world. Unlike Donne, who loves fripperies, Herbert thus does not emphasize alchemy's triviality. Coupled with Herbert's deep concern for the material world is a real curiosity about the nature of that world, down to the level of its physical makeup. While it is Donne who holds the reputation of delving deeply into natural philosophy, in this arena Herbert is the more thorough and more thoughtful scientist. Despite this distinction, however, Herbert does share one science-related habit with Donne: he deploys alchemy as a means of not thinking about difficult subjects. Only, however, when thinking has failed to produce an answer. And here, as with Donne, alchemy is a useful tool. Herbert designates alchemy as a way of relieving him of an intellectual responsibility that he evidently felt quite deeply: the responsibility of determining what matter is made of.

The central section of Herbert's *The Temple* (first printed in 1633), "The Church," opens by teasingly referencing the Eucharistic problem in ways that criticism has not yet remarked upon. On first glance, the famous shaped poem "The Altar," which opens this section of the volume, is a starkly uncluttered edifice, seemingly unburdened with the physical accouterments of Holy Communion. As a typographical construct, it is as plain as can be; as an altar described, it is made entirely of stone—or, metaphorically, of the speaker's stony heart for which it stands. It bears nothing, it promises nothing. As a result, "The Altar" seems to have already taken a position on the controversy over how Christ is present in the bread and wine. As in more Calvinist-leaning Reformation theology, including the official position of the Church of England

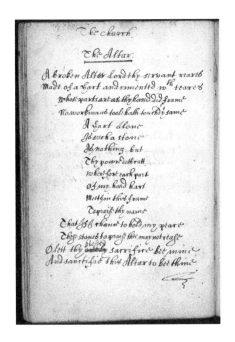

Figure 1. "The Altar" in the Williams manuscript of *The Temple* (Dr Williams's Library MS 28.169, fol. 15v). By permission of the Trustee of Dr Williams's Library.

in the Thirty-Nine Articles, the nature of the "sacrifice" referenced by the speaker of "The Altar" is Christ's sacrifice replicated in the communicant—"O let thy blessed SACRIFICE be mine"—not an event that takes place upon the altar itself.[97] The bread and wine are not even in view, much less an object of inquiry.

And yet the poem delivers a visual pun on the nature of the Eucharist that brings the question of the Eucharist's physical matter back to the table, so to speak. In both manuscript and print versions of this shaped poem, there *are* in fact two things upon the altar: the two words of the poem's title, "The" and "Altar." These words effectively mark a place for the bread and the wine, the two things that must be on the altar for Holy Communion to be celebrated. The Williams manuscript and the Bodleian manuscript of Herbert's poems both create this effect by laying a horizontal rule (or double rule) on top of line 1 of the poem, creating a surface on which "The" and "Altar" rest (see Figures 1–2). In the first printed edition of *The Temple* (1633), this portrayal of two items resting on an altar-like surface is, quite literally, embroidered (see Figure 3). The border that bounds the top and the bottom of the entire poem (including the title) is lacelike, replicating the lace edging of the "fair white linen cloth" that must be

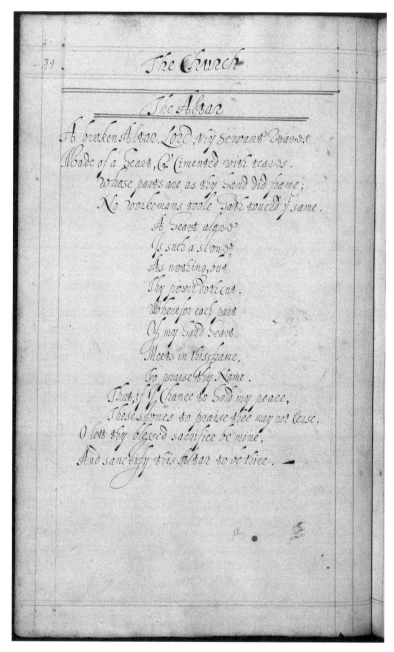

Figure 2. "The Altar" in the Bodleian manuscript of *The Temple* (Bodleian MS Tanner 307, fol. 15v). By permission of the Bodleian Libraries, University of Oxford.

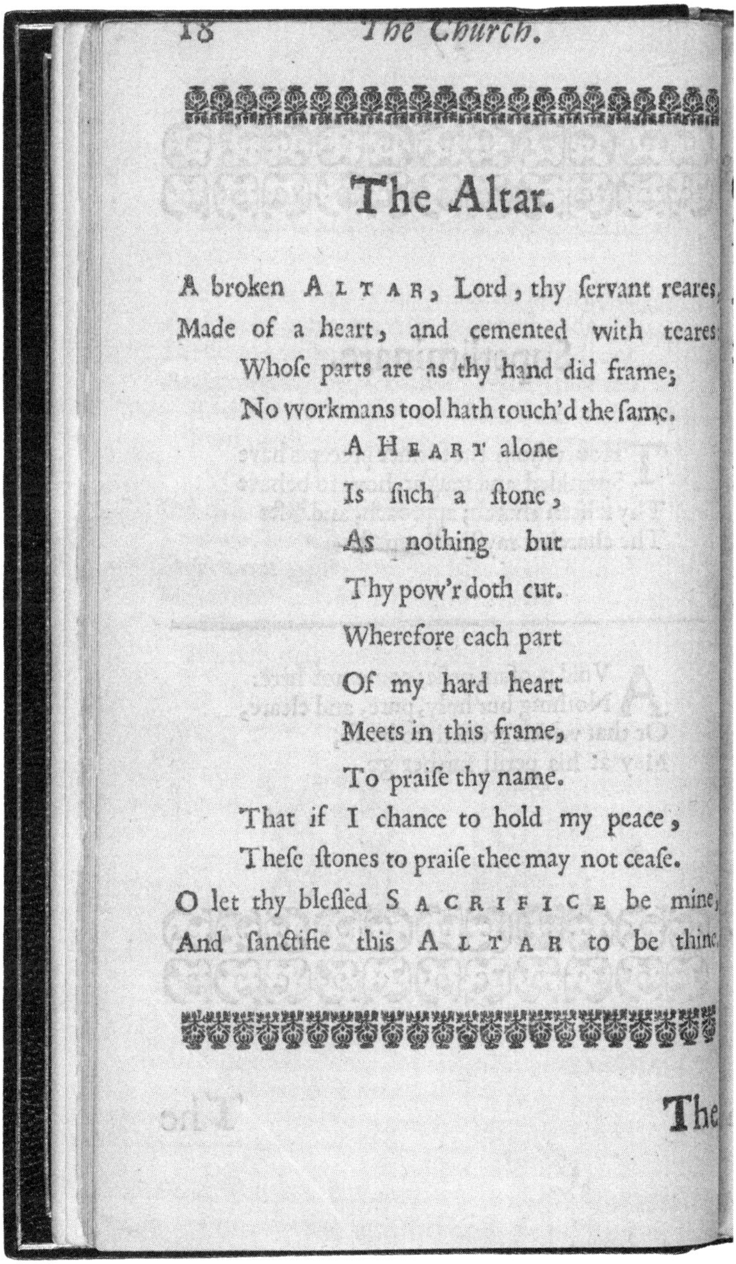

The Altar.

A broken A L T A R, Lord, thy servant reares,
Made of a heart, and cemented with teares:
   Whose parts are as thy hand did frame;
   No workmans tool hath touch'd the same.
      A H E A R T alone
      Is such a stone,
      As nothing but
      Thy pow'r doth cut.
      Wherefore each part
      Of my hard heart
      Meets in this frame,
      To praise thy name.
   That if I chance to hold my peace,
   These stones to praise thee may not cease.
O let thy blessed S A C R I F I C E be mine,
And sanctifie this A L T A R to be thine.

The

Figure 3. "The Altar" in the first print edition of *The Temple* (Cambridge, 1633). By permission of the Folger Shakespeare Library.

put on the Church of England Communion table before the holy feast is celebrated.[98] When these design elements creating the Communion table are added to the rather obvious "altar/alter" pun of the poem's title, we begin to wonder not only what two elements rest upon the altar, but also how they are altered and how that alteration might be visually apprehensible. What do we see when we see the bread and wine? Have they been transmuted? How?

Herbert, like the converted Catholic Donne and the Catholic priest Robert Southwell before him, turns out to be keenly interested in Christ's blood in a way that seems odd if he is, as some have argued, a Protestant of more Calvinist bent. Yet no matter where on the Laudian-Puritan continuum Herbert lies (a question that, I might add, I have no interest in adjudicating), his sanguinary obsession might be accounted for by the Paracelsian point of view that he seems to share with his friend Donne. When it comes to Christ's blood and sometimes even Christ himself, Herbert is, generally speaking, operating in the same vein of Paracelsian alchemical medicine that Donne is. Herbert describes Christ's blood—whether sweated in Gethsemane or shed on the cross—as "balsam" in a number of poems, and in others suggests that balsam is of alchemical derivation, a golden cordial.[99] Taken in sum, these references modulate Herbert's occasional identification of the "physick" of Christ's sacrifice with the wine of the Eucharist into Paracelsianism, as in "Conscience": "when ever at his board / I do but taste it [my Savior's blood], straight it cleanseth me" (14–15).

Along with imagining the healing effects of Christ's blood alchemically, however, Herbert also gestures toward the question of whether Christ's blood in the Eucharist is constituted according to the Thomist physics of Christic substance and comestible accidents—a question that Herbert, like Donne, knew full well was at the heart of long-standing theological controversy. In "The Agonie," in fact, Herbert portrays the wine of Holy Communion precisely as exceptional matter along Thomist transubstantiative lines, matter like which there is no other—blood for Christ, and wine for us:

> Who knows not Love, let him assay
> And taste that juice, which on the crosse a pike
> Did set again abroach;
> . . . .
> Love is that liquour sweet and most divine,
> Which my God feels as bloud; but I, as wine.
>
> (13–18)

Here the poem ends, though, leaving us hanging if we want to know *why* the crucified Christ's blood tastes like wine to the speaker. While he knows that his dual metaphor-plus-simile for what the communicant receives (love= liquor=blood, love=liquor=wine) engages the topic of material properties and material change, Herbert simply will not touch these issues.[100]

What is at stake in Herbert's going only so far and no further in investigating the nature of Eucharistic matter? We could, certainly, ally Herbert with those who, like Richard Hooker, recommended that the exact operation of the Real Presence is a question about which we ought not to worry too much. Indeed, Herbert pronounces in the Williams manuscript's poem "The H. Communion" that he simply does not care about the issue:

> I am sure, whether bread stay
> Or whether Bread doe fly away
> Concerneth bread, not mee.
>
> > (7–9)

But there's a whiff of special pleading in this assertion. When the Williams "H. Communion" poem asserts that the nature of the Host "Concerneth bread, not mee," the parallelism of the concerns of bread (which ought to care about what it is) with the concerns of the speaking self (who does not care what the bread is) not only imputes to bread the power of human concern but also reciprocally imputes to the speaking self the quality of unthinking, bready materiality. This parallelism suggests that the real issue is not narrowly the matter of the Eucharist but rather matter itself. While indeed the speaker of this poem may not be concerned with Eucharistic physics, that physics nonetheless brings up the question of the physical composition of his own self. What am I made of, and is the stuff of my body no more special than a wafer of Communion bread?

Unlike Donne, Herbert does not experiment with concocting exceptional matter out of the human body and then with analyzing why such experiments fail. Rather, Herbert's response is consistently, as in "The Agonie," to raise but then to cordon off the question of physical change and the terms in which early seventeenth-century Europe discussed this question. And it is alchemy that consistently helps him do so. In fact, alchemy marks the exact point of avoidance. For example, Herbert revises "The Elixir," his poem most explicitly on the subject of the Eucharist, to make it clear that the elixir in question is not simply a vaguely medicinal "tincture" (15) but rather the alchemical magnum opus, the philosopher's stone "That turneth all to Gold" (22).[101] This revision serves to focus attention upon the matter of the Host and its effects. Yet "The Elixir," in its revised form, turns aside the very question it raises: what the Eucharist as the miraculous philosopher's stone does, exactly. Just as "The Agonie" ends with an airy and inconclusive wave toward the physical connection between Christ's blood and the Holy Communion's wine, "The Elixir" stops at the moment it declares the Eucharist the philosopher's stone, with no elaboration of what properties in the stone effect transmutation.

We might excuse a less lettered and less well-connected poet for not delving further into what constitutes physical and creaturely bodies, but it seems rather extraordinary that Herbert, of all early seventeenth-century poets, should highlight how he retreats in the face of these questions. On the evidence of his reading and writing, Herbert's profound interest in nature ought not to stop when it comes to the makeup of natural matter. His acquaintance with and admiration for Francis Bacon, and specifically his admiration for the *Novum organum*—whose 1620 publication he lauded with Latin poems praising "the author of *The Great Instauration*"—seem to demonstrate Herbert's enthusiasm for Bacon's demolition of prior natural philosophy, including matter theory.[102] Classifying both ancient and Scholastic natural philosophy as "Idols of the Theater," or "philosophies that have been received or invented as so many stage plays creating fictitious and imaginary worlds," Bacon insists that we must discard the entirety of Aristotelian physical theory, from its assumption of four elements to its schema of a body's comprising its substantial form and its accidents: "*substance, quality, passion* [that is, being acted upon], even *existence* itself, are poor notions; much worse are *heavy, light, dense, rare, moist, dry, generation, corruption, attraction, repulsion, element, matter, form* and the like; all these are ill-defined and fantastical."[103] Bacon sets out, as the first order of business in beginning an "interpretation of nature" from scratch, a program for a new analysis of the physical makeup of material bodies, including their form, motion, transformation, and composition out of "real particles, such as are found [that is, such as truly exist]."[104]

Still, although Herbert may be taken to task for shying away from a Baconian exploration of what lies beneath material form and material change, he should also be forgiven for having no solutions to propose. Like his older contemporary Donne, Herbert would have been keenly aware that matter theory was at an impasse. As I have mentioned, while Aristotelian physics seemed patently ridiculous—at least to some—in the early seventeenth century, no satisfactory theory had as yet arisen to replace it. Recent work by

Michel Serres, Jonathan Goldberg, and Stephen Greenblatt, among others, has drawn our attention to the early modern period's flirtation with atomism, the counter-Aristotelian theory that held the universe to be made of infinitely tiny, uniform particles careening about in a vacuum and that derived from the intellectual line comprising the philosophical school of Epicureanism, especially as expressed in Lucretius's *De rerum natura*.[105] But despite the many ways in which scholars now see Renaissance atomism as anticipating modern scientific, theological, and philosophical principles, the seventeenth century was not so sure that atomism offered anything in the way of scientific truth.[106] Whatever their fascination with Lucretius, the more scientific of early modern authors feared that basing a new physics on yet another set of ancient texts would only replicate—albeit with a different classical imprimatur—the humanists' error of adhering to Aristotelianism. As Gerard Passannante has brilliantly explicated, the rediscovery of Lucretius in the early fifteenth century meant that its reception and absorption in early modern Europe were, for several centuries, the stuff of humanism rather than of natural philosophy.[107] As humanism's veneration of classical learning came to be mistrusted in the sixteenth and seventeenth centuries, then, atomism could easily share its fate. Montaigne, for example, thought of atomism as a rhetorical construct: he proposed that Epicurus's atomism, along with Plato's ideas and Pythagoras's numbers, were merely "inventions that had at least a pleasant and a subtle appearance provided that, however false, [this appearance] could be maintained against arguments to the contrary."[108]

By the time of his *Novum organum*, Bacon himself had rejected Epicurean atomism in part on the grounds that it was not experimentally provable; it was more a literary theory than a scientific one.[109] Bacon's objections were quite different from theological objections to Epicurean atomism, whose reasons included atomism's denial of divine causation and its dictum that earthly matter could not ultimately be destroyed (a principle that contradicted Christian eschatology). Nevertheless, whether taken separately or added together, the Baconian suspicion that atomism was not scientific and the doctrinal objection that atomism was not Christian should have given Herbert significant pause and may have discouraged him from seriously proposing atomism as a replacement for discredited Aristotelian physics. Indeed, it was not until well after Herbert's death in 1633 that either of these objections could even begin to be met, as Pierre Gassendi attempted to Christianize Epicurean atomism, and as Gassendi and ultimately Robert Boyle attempted (even if unsuccessfully) to give atomism some kind of empirical proof.[110]

Baconian and theological objections aside, Herbert may also have found atomism unpalatable because, in its early seventeenth-century form at least, it proposed that matter is at base nonknowable. Unlike the Aristotelian base elements of earth, water, air, and fire, Epicurean atoms do not present themselves to human perception by means of familiar properties; rather, what humans perceive is only the "effluxes" of those atoms as they collide and shed their skins.[111] This aspect of Epicurean atomism, filtered through Montaigne's "Apology for Raymond Sebond," would ultimately influence Descartes, who (despite his flat rejection of atomism) proposed that bodies have no sensible qualities at all and that whatever we believe we sense is purely a product of our own perception: "what affects our senses," noted Descartes, "is simply and solely the surface that constitutes the limit of the dimensions of the body."[112] Other than its extension in space, none of what we perceive as "qualities" of a body is a true quality of that body. Digging further into the makeup of matter might get you to exactly nothing or, worse yet, only to a reflection of your own mind.

Such a discomfiting prospect is what Herbert confronts and then evades in "The Banquet," a poem that squarely takes on—and then conspicuously veers from—the question of what happens to Eucharistic matter during Holy Communion. The poem begins with the proposition that the "delight" of the Eucharist, its "sweet and sacred cheer," "Passeth tongue to taste or tell" (1–6). What makes it delightful, then? It is not the properties retained from bread and wine, what Thomas Aquinas would call their "accidents." We cannot credit the notion that "some starre (fled from the sphere) / Melted there, / As we sugar melt in wine" (10–12) or that "sweetnesse in the bread / Made a head / To subdue the smell of sinne" (13–15). Rather, what we encounter in Holy Communion is a delightfulness imparted by God:

> Onely God, who gives perfumes,
> Flesh assumes,
> And with it perfumes my heart.
>
> (22–24)

What is consumed in the sacrament is not a flesh whose pleasant qualities we can somehow perceive truly beneath the overt qualities of bread and wine. (A thesis that would smack, in any case, of taking pleasure in cannibalism.) Rather, these lines' disjunction between "flesh" and "perfume," a disjunction that is self-evident unless Christ habitually doused himself in civet, emphasizes that we perceive "perfume" in the Eucharist not because perfume is an inherent quality of the Real Presence but because God has conditioned us to associate our ingestion of the sacramental bread with an experience of perfumed sweetness.

At this point, however, the poem swerves to avoid this proto-Cartesian implication that the qualities of Eucharistic matter are not truly known but are perceived only through preinstilled habit. The second stanza describes what we perceive of the Eucharist as a heuristic device by which God demonstrates the capacities of his divine love. The Eucharist's sweetness is neither an inherent accidental property of bread and wine nor a perception by the communicant's senses; it is a divinely added—and in that sense miraculous—property.

> But as Pomanders and wood
>   Still are good,
> Yet being bruis'd are better sented:
> God, to show how farre his love
>   Could improve,
> Here, as broken, is presented.
>
>   (25–30)

Herbert flees so swiftly from the nature of matter in this stanza that, having explicitly evoked the classic Aristotelian physics question of whether a piece of wood still bears wood's substantial form once it is broken into smaller and smaller bits or once it is burned in a fire, he then adds the caveat that the Eucharist, unlike the piece of wood, is not really split into pieces at all. The Eucharist is merely "*presented* as broken," a simulacrum of subdivided matter. We need not—indeed, we cannot—determine what it is made of if it is never anything but whole.

Refusing to consider questions of material composition puts Herbert somewhat at odds with his own poetic project, which requires the material world to aid in his longed-for conversation with the divine. I agree here with Jonathan Gil Harris, who argues against a long-standing critical tendency to "dematerialize" Herbert.[113] As Harris suggests, Herbert's attachment is not to the chimera of exceptional matter, as it was for Donne, but rather to the ordinary things of this world. The more ordinary the better, in fact. As David Glimp points out, Herbert even thinks of God's "creatures"—that is, living things of a lower order than human beings—as being capable, unlike humans, of an unproblematic, untrammeled relationship of praise toward their Lord.[114]

If God speaks through ordinary things and if ordinary things speak to and of God, then it would seem to follow that knowing the nature and makeup of those ordinary things is paramount. And yet this is a knowledge that Herbert's poetry has in sight but will not pursue.

In this regard the Eucharist's material composition is merely a special and especially knotty instance of a universal problem. Ironically enough, Herbert recommends in *A Priest to the Temple, or, the Country Parson* that the First Communion should take place "When any one can distinguish the Sacramentall from common bread, knowing the Institution, and the difference."[115] Trying to distinguish between sacramental and common bread, the unsolvable paradox of six centuries of Christian theology, inevitably leads one to inquire into the makeup of "common" and unusual matter alike. How does Herbert expect a child to conduct such an inquiry when it is one that he will not himself undertake? In the case of the nature of Eucharistic matter, Herbert expediently relieves himself of the problem by punting the question to Christ himself: "Especially at Communion times [the parson] is in a great confusion, as being not only to receive God, but to break, and administer him. Neither finds he any issue in this, but to throw himself down at the throne of grace, saying, Lord, thou knowest what thou didst, when thou appointedst it to be done thus; therefore doe thou fulfill what thou didst appoint."[116] On the question of the nature of ordinary matter, however, it is a bit more difficult to resort to the explanation that "it is whatever Christ says it is."

Hence the advantage for Herbert in not thinking terribly hard about matter theory, even when it is he himself who brought up the question. Ordinary things and ordinary creatures may speak to and of God, but neither those things nor God Almighty has anything to tell us about matter's makeup. And that is the problem. David Hawkes has described Herbert as suspicious of Baconian empiricism because it promises to disjoin the material from the spiritual.[117] And indeed Herbert seems to anticipate, as the too-close-for-comfort atomism of "The Banquet" hints, that the seventeenth century's most challenging alternatives to Aristotelian physics will begin to exclude God's participation in the properties of the stuff of this world. Descartes, who describes matter as made up of tiny corpuscles with no void or vacuum between them, defines motion as always caused by the collision of one body against another. Having surmised that the original of all material motion is God's initial "push," which was transferred into all motion that will ever take place in the universe, Descartes seems to need no God to keep things going in his mechanistic system.[118] Thomas Hobbes, following upon Bacon's somewhat Paracelsian suggestion that experiment might demonstrate a "vital spirit" common to all matter, conversely proposes in *Of Human Nature* that all spirit is corporeal and that all material objects are coextensive with material spirit.[119] Donne's evasion of matter theory leaves him happily playing in the outmoded field of learning called humanism, but Herbert's evasion has even higher rewards: it preserves a corporeal experience of God's workings in the world.

Forgotten Matter: Henry Vaughan

If George Herbert retreats from matter theory, his poetic acolyte Henry Vaughan refuses even to scout out the battlefield. To be sure, Vaughan is intensely interested in the stuff of this world. For him, Alan Rudrum argues, the nature of God is unmanifest to humans; the nature of nature, in contrast, is entirely apprehensible. Moreover, Vaughan sees nature as perfectible.[120] Sometimes, in fact, even the flesh of the speaker of Vaughan's poetry is subject to being perfected; and furthermore, sometimes that perfecting process is alchemical. Finally, Vaughan's pointed imitations of Herbert commit him to considering the effects of Holy Communion on the believer. Schooled by Vaughan's predecessor poets, as well as by the ongoing seventeenth-century doctrinal and scientific debates over the transmutation of physical matter, we would be justified in expecting Vaughan to constellate all of these themes—alchemy, materiality, and Holy Communion—into a single discussion. But in a conspicuous avoidance of the intertwined theological and physical questions engaged by Donne and especially by Herbert, Vaughan never portrays either the poetic speaker's flesh or the process by which it is perfected as Eucharistic in nature. In this way Vaughan goes Herbert one further in disknowledge. Vaughan not only avoids proposing an answer to what matter is made of and how it changes; he also avoids even the occasion for asking the question.

The absence of a topic in an author's work does not mean that she is avoiding the topic, of course. I would not accuse any run-of-the-mill metaphysical poet of neglecting matter theory on the basis of the fact that he does not mention matter theory. Of the three poets addressed in this chapter, however, Henry Vaughan has the closest relation to the debates over physics in which both alchemy and theology were engaged. Literally the closest relation: Vaughan's brother (and perhaps identical twin) Thomas Vaughan was an alchemist in the business of manufacturing Paracelsian pharmaceuticals. Under the pseudonym Eugenius Philalethes, Thomas Vaughan published prolifically in defense of alchemical principles, in treatises notable for the way they rooted Paracelsian alchemy deeply within the matter-theory controversies of the seventeenth century. Henry Vaughan's reliance on Thomas Vaughan's alchemical scholarship has long been recognized, and Thomas Vaughan even published one of his brother Henry's forays into translating alchemical treatises, his translation of Henry Nollius's *The Chymists Key*.[121] It is fairly safe to assume, therefore, that Henry Vaughan was acquainted with Thomas Vaughan's views regarding the transmutation of matter.

Thomas Vaughan's views were quite strongly stated and, in terms of mid-seventeenth-century physics, relatively advanced. First of all, Thomas Vaughan—who quarreled pugnaciously and in print with the likes of Cambridge Neoplatonist Henry More—firmly and explicitly rejects Aristotelian matter theory on the grounds that it limits new discovery: "we are still hammering of old elements, but seek not the America that lyes beyond them."[122] Specifically, Thomas Vaughan critiques Aristotle for assuming that substantial forms exist and then dwelling on their operations rather than investigating what makes up a substantial form in the first place.[123] For the most part, it must be said, Thomas Vaughan has nothing new to add to the seventeenth century's discussion of how Aristotle might be replaced; he is generally orthodox in his Paracelsianism, and indeed replicates the kind of Paracelsianism that had been available to Donne fifty years previous, at the turn of the seventeenth century. Occasionally, however, Thomas Vaughan does venture assertions that seem to anticipate Boyle in founding a new physical chemistry on experimentation rather than on prebuilt theory. While he supports a Paracelsian idea of prime matter, for example, he suggests that we not take the operations of that prime matter upon faith but instead establish them through observation and experimentation. Examining vegetables, and noting that in their previous form of seeds they did not resemble vegetables, he arrives not at the Epicurean atomist notion that the world came from seeds but rather at the supposition that even seeds must come from something prior: "This Observation I apply'd to the World, and gained by it this Inference: That the World in the beginning was no such thing as it is, but some other seed or matter out of which that Fabricke which I now behold, did arise. . . . [B]ut what that matter should be I could not guesse."[124] Here Thomas Vaughan readily classifies the nature of matter as something neither already known nor ineffably mysterious. Rather, the nature of matter is something that ought to be on his research agenda. Until you know, don't guess; but even if you don't yet know, you can confidently set a future standard by which you may judge your knowledge as better than guessing. For this reason, Thomas Vaughan headed his 1650 treatise *Anthroposophia magica* with the epigraph Bacon's *Novum organum* took from the book of Daniel: "Many shall run to and fro, and knowledge shall be increased" (Dan. 12:4).[125]

Henry Vaughan, in contrast, has evidently decided that the entire knowledge game is not worth the candle. Indeed, he pulls ahead of Herbert in the ambitiousness of his disknowledge. While Vaughan's preface to the second edition of *Silex Scintillans* (1655) declares his indebtedness to "Mr. George Herbert, whose holy life and verse gained many pious converts, (of whom I am the least)," Vaughan's tracking of *The Temple* is remarkable not only for his poems' close attention to Herbert's topics and style but also for their deliberate and blatant circumvention of the ways that Herbert comes close (though not too close) to considering matter theory.[126] "Deliberate and blatant," I say, because this circumvention occurs during the course of poems that overtly cite Herbert on the Eucharist. Indeed, we see Vaughan feinting toward and then steering clear of Herbert on matter theory from the very beginning of *Silex Scintillans*. Vaughan's opening poem, "Authoris (de se) Emblema" (The author's emblem of himself), pays homage to Herbert's opening poem "The Altar" in describing an object made of stone and the conversion of nonhuman matter into flesh. Vaughan's stony object, though, is solely the speaker's heart, not Herbert's heart-as-altar; and it is solely the heart that may undergo change. Where Herbert's concretely shaped poem demands that we query what Eucharistic transmutation, if any, might take place on the altar, Vaughan begins his volume with a deliberately non-Eucharistic transmutation. His poetry changes hearts and minds, not bread and wine.

If the truth be told, the poetic speaker of *Silex Scintillans* seems far more interested in his own blood than in Christ's; the speaker's blood is a virtual reservoir for allusions appropriated from every stage of Christ's life. Recalling Christ on the Sea of Galilee, "The Storm" recounts a tempest that needs to be calmed—in the speaker's blood, that is, and not by Christ's command. Offering to assume the place of Christ in Gethsemane, the speaker likewise vows in "Anguish," "My God, could I weep blood, / Gladly I would" (7–8). He will even happily bleed in the place of Christ on the cross. In "Misery," the speaker's plea that God "hear him, whose blood / Speaks more and better for my good" (105–6) immediately turns into a cry to God that is "not poured with tears alone, / . . . But with the blood of all my soul" (108–10). Most ambitiously Christlike of all is the speaker of the poem "Midnight," who compares the stars' "emanations, / Quick vibrations" to his own soul's "thin ejections, / Cold affections" (11–12, 15–16) and prays that God may "Shine on this blood, / And water in one beam" (22–23). While the "water" of these lines is presumably the water of baptism, since the poem's postscript is Matthew 3:11 ("he shall baptize you with the Holy Ghost, and with fire"), the syntax of the lines—"shine on this blood / And water in one beam"—joins water with the speaker's blood in such a way that it seems that the speaker, like the crucified Christ, miraculously has both blood and water in his veins. Sanguinary egotism seems to be Vaughan's watchword.

When Vaughan associates body and blood with alchemical operations, then, it is likewise the speaker's body and blood that are at issue, not Christ's. Such is the case even when Holy Communion is either the poem's explicit topic or its frame of allusive reference. Vaughan, a Paracelsian physician himself, is interested in the way that alchemical "spirits" may be curative of his body and blood, but those "spirits" are never Christ's spirit communicated in the Eucharist. Instead, cure arrives from worldly sources alone, not from heaven. In Vaughan's poetry, the stuff of this world sometimes seems to be a closed system that exists entirely for the benefit of the speaker. A signal example is "The Morning-Watch," in which the speaker is the cheerful recipient of the "dew" of a good night's sleep, which "fell on my breast; / O how it *bloods*, / And *spirits* all my earth!" (7–9; emphasis in the original). For Donne or for Herbert, the conjunction of blood and spirit would designate Christ's offering of his own spirit as sovereign Paracelsian cure. For Vaughan, in contrast, that blood that "spirits all [his] earth," though initially vaguely Eucharistic, is never identified as Christ's.

If Christ's body and blood don't matter, then certainly the nature of their matter in the Eucharist doesn't matter, either. The primacy of the speaker's own flesh and blood, and the immateriality of the material of the Eucharist, come to the fore in poems by Vaughan that follow Herbert very closely, sometimes specifically tracking Herbert's poems on the Passion and on Holy Communion. This effect is perhaps most striking in Vaughan's "The Passion," which cites Herbert's memorable final lines in "The Agonie"—"Love is that liquour sweet and most divine, / Which my God feels as bloud; but I, as wine"—in such a way as to void Herbert's query about the transmutation of one substance into another. Vaughan's revision expostulates,

> Most blessed vine!
> Whose juice so good

I feel as wine,
But thy fair branches felt as blood,
      How were thou pressed
      To be my feast!

                              (15–20)

What is felt as blood is so obscurely stated in Vaughan's imagery—"Most blessed vine! / Whose juice . . . / thy fair branches felt as blood"—that it is entirely unclear what the branches are, why branches should feel the "juice" of the "vine" as blood, or who might be feeling that juice as blood in the first place. Amid this confusion Christ's physicality recedes, as does the Real Presence, and the speaker's perceptions and sensations come to the fore instead. Moreover, the disconnection between those perceptions and sensations and the inner nature of the Eucharist causes the poem no trouble. Unlike in Herbert's "The Banquet," where the solipsism of proto-Cartesian matter theory momentarily threatens to undo the speaker's entire relationship to the sacrament, here solipsism crowds out a consideration of matter theory and thus preserves, rather than endangers, the speaker's satisfactory experience. Similarly, Vaughan's "Affliction (I)," while calling attention to the typically Herbertian word *elixir*, applies that term not to the Eucharist but to the speaker's own affliction itself, "the great *elixir* that turns gall / To wine, and sweetness" (4–5; emphasis in the original). Vaughan's alchemical terminology here signals precisely how little he cares about the precise mechanics of material transformation. In the end, even alchemy is entirely absorbed by how the speaker feels about what the poem "The Check" calls (his own) "dear flesh" (11).

Egotism abetting a lack of interest in matter theory: this Vaughanian habit might be merely a version of the poetic "detachment" from worldly affairs for which *Silex Scintillans* has been both lauded and reprehended. Several critics have viewed that detachment as Vaughan's mechanism for self-preservation during the period of the British commonwealth. As a royalist who had served in combat against Oliver Cromwell's parliamentary forces, Vaughan might have had good reason to skirt the issue of what the Eucharist is made of.[127] Under Puritan influence, the English church at the time was being encouraged to forget about the Eucharist once and for all. As Rudrum points out in his study of the value of alchemical "hiddenness" in Vaughan's poetry, the Westminster Assembly wished to abolish the Book of Common Prayer and "to end the virtually universal admission to the service of Holy Communion which had been the Anglican tradition."[128] Rudrum connects the Puritan impulse to shove aside the material aspect of this sacramental ritual with a marked Puritan tendency to degrade matter entirely and to drive a wedge between spirit and the material of this fallen world.

We should not, however, overestimate Puritanism's censorship effect on Vaughan. After all, as Rudrum notes, only one commonwealth era case of prosecution for the use of the *Book of Common Prayer* has so far been discovered, and Vaughan felt free to include material relating to Holy Communion in his *Mount of Olives, or, Solitary Devotions* (1652).[129] That freedom does not stop Vaughan, however—despite his royalist affiliations—from flirting with Puritanism's degradation of matter. For Protestant-inflected intellectual history, the ultimate consequence of that degradation was exactly what Donne's Eucharistic-alchemical poems anticipate: the separation of physics from theology.[130] (A separation that the Roman Catholic Church was not able to countenance until the twentieth century, and to which many Christians have not yet acceded.) For Vaughan, in contrast, the consequence is the separation of physics from poetry. In Vaughan's literary division of the disciplines, alchemy and poetry remain companions: no one can deny his deep and abiding attraction to alchemically imagined structures of secrecy, of transmutation, and of purification.[131] So too do the Eucharist and poetry remain companions: Vaughan writes poetic versions of his devotional prose on the restorative effects of Holy Communion.[132] And yet neither alchemical nor Eucharistic imagery ever leads Vaughan, who knew well from his alchemist brother Thomas's work what a serious inquiry into the nature of matter would look like, to venture in his poetry upon that inquiry. If Donne is eager to relieve theology of the quandaries of matter theory, and if Herbert avoids a too-close consideration of matter theory because he anticipates the answers will preclude the participation of the divine in the stuff of this world—that is to say, because physics will displace religion—Vaughan is only too happy to imply that physics is not a topic that poetry need touch at all.

What sort of cause may we posit for Vaughan's evasion of questions of matter theory? His negligence entails something other, I think, than the kind of paradoxically conspicuous forgetting that often emerges in the aftermath of historical periods of violent crisis. (For example, when individuals and groups pass over their complicity in genocide.) Vaughan's silence puzzles: we do not know why he does not care to know. We can only observe what he has declined to mention. It is as if he has simply forgotten that the topic is important. Though how could he have forgotten? And should he bear any blame for this omission? The fact that Vaughan felt perfectly comfortable, even in a

Puritan age, to write about the Real Presence in other contexts means, as I have suggested, that history will not suffice to explain his choice. An explanation deriving from the theological or philosophical context of the mid-seventeenth century seems similarly inadequate. Vaughan might protest that he, like any Protestant of the second half of the seventeenth century, need no longer care about how medieval physics was built on the admittedly shaky ground of the truth of transubstantiation. But as a close reader and imitator of Herbert, not to mention as a medical practitioner and a dabbler in alchemical theory, Vaughan ought to care what the world is made of. Or at least, like Donne, he ought to be more open to the advantages of not caring. But whereas Donne and Herbert keep track of the intellectual lineage of matter theory, Donne exploiting medieval physics' collapse and Herbert wondering what would take its place, Vaughan leaves it alone. My best guess for his reasons derives not from his historical or intellectual milieu but rather from his place in literary history. Vaughan is, in effect, a poet of the avant-garde, anticipating modernity in the form of anticipating a new kind of literary voice. With a poetry that appropriates nature to the poetic ego while abnegating the responsibility to examine nature's minutest structures, Vaughan forecasts Romanticism in its most unfortunately stereotypical form. Vaughan's version of poetry's future has the poet failing to learn natural philosophy—and proud of it, too.

CHAPTER 3

How to Skim Kabbalah

One of the most beautiful books ever produced in the cause of alchemy is alchemist and physician Heinrich Khunrath's *Amphitheatrum sapientiae aeternae* (1595).[1] A pioneering argument for the use of alchemy for the purposes of spiritual transformation and regeneration, Khunrath's volume in its next edition (1609) bore an expanded title that indicates his treatise's grand ambitions: *Amphitheatrum sapientiae aeternae, solius verae: Christiano-kabalisticum, divino-magicum, nec non physico-chymicum, tertriunum, catholicon*, which Peter Forshaw translates as "The Universal Ter-tri-une Christian-Cabalist, Divinely Magical, and Physico-Chemical Amphitheatre of the Only True Eternal Wisdom." It immediately became famous, however, less for its text than for its illustrations, which sparked a rage for sophisticated illustration techniques in alchemical emblem books.[2] In four elaborate hand-colored circular engravings, the *Amphitheatrum* illustrates alchemy in action as a process that washes clean the impurities of body and soul.[3]

But alchemy also amounts in these illustrations to another kind of cleansing, this one ethnic. From first to last, these four engravings show how alchemy washes away the taint of the alchemist's debt to Jewish learning.[4] We begin with a display of how large that debt truly is. Khunrath's first circular engraving features Christ in the center of a somewhat bewildering set of concentric circles of words, many of them in Hebrew (see Figure 4). In the volume's text, this emblem is even given a bilingual title in Hebrew and Latin: "EMES, VERITAS, DEI sigillum" (TRUTH, TRUTH, the seal of GOD). This is a caption that runs the risk of giving Hebrew truth (*emeth*) a billing equal to or perhaps even higher than Latin truth (*veritas*).[5] And indeed, the emblem's lettering reproduces copious amounts of Hebrew, both scriptural and kabbalistic, including the Ten Commandments, the Hebrew angelic names, two central tenets

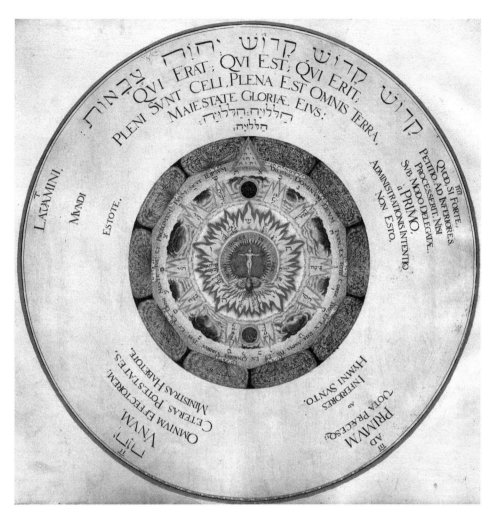

Figure 4. "EMES VERITAS." Heinrich Khunrath, *Amphitheatrum sapientiae aeternae* (Hamburg, 1595), plate 1. By courtesy of the Department of Special Collections, Memorial Library, University of Wisconsin–Madison.

about the duties of the righteous (Deuteronomy 6:5 and Leviticus 19:18), and, toward the center of the diagram, the central aspects of Kabbalah: the twenty-two letters of the Hebrew alphabet, the ten mystical aspects of God (the *sefirot*), and various divine names (Ehyeh, YHWH, El, Elohim, and so on).[6] As Raphael Patai puts it, unless one looks very closely at the emblem's text, "one has the impression of seeing a complex Jewish emblem written in Hebrew."[7]

By the time we arrive at the fourth and last circular engraving in the *Amphitheatrum*, however, Kabbalah has been thoroughly rewritten as a Christian domain and a Christian creation. This engraving, one of the most famous images of Renaissance alchemy, features the alchemist in his oratory-laboratory (see Figure 5). This time the lettering in the external circle surrounding the emblem includes, by way of Hebrew, only one word, the Tetragrammaton—the unpronounceable four-letter name of God (YHWH), and the single Hebrew word that many educated Christians of the late sixteenth century would have found familiar.[8] In one instance in the external circle, the Tetragrammaton is specifically equated with the Pentagrammaton, a Christianized conversion of the Tetragrammaton that, as I discuss later in this chapter, signifies the five-letter name of Jesus (YHSWH): "φενταγραμμος יהוה τετραγραμμος" (*pentagrammos YHWH tetragrammos*) asserts the text in a combination of Greek and Hebrew. Hebrew now serves Christian ends.

This effect of a Hebrew subservient to Christianity is intensified in the image in the fourth engraving's internal circle (see Figure 6). In this depiction of the alchemist preparing himself spiritually on the left side of the picture before he embarks on the physical work of alchemical trial using the equipment on the right side, the use of Hebrew is limited to lettering on the canopy or pavilion that covers the altar at which the alchemist prays. The top portion of the canopy again displays the Tetragrammaton; and the scalloped valance that tops the curtains, just above the Roman letters for the author's name (KHUNRA), features some Hebrew that not only conveys one of God's divine attributes—it is a (misspelled) version of "divine wisdom"—but also serves as a ham-fisted transliteration of KHUNRA into Hebrew (see Figure 7).[9] Coupled with the Tetragrammaton, this eponymous deployment of Hebrew indicates both that Hebrew exists only for Christian purposes and that its sole use beyond identifying godhead is to confirm the identity of the alchemist himself. Notably, and quite in contrast to the earlier "EMES VERITAS" depiction of Christ nearly overwhelmed by Hebrew lettering, this is the only circular engraving among the four in Khunrath's volume that features perspective, suggesting that the alchemist's scope of wisdom is, literally, deep as well as wide. Furthermore, the turn to perspective, with its "realistic" depth of field, implies that, unlike a bookish Jewish learning that exists only as text, Christianized Hebrew is the only form of Hebrew that matters in real life.[10]

What has happened to put Hebrew in its place between the first circular engraving and the fourth, the "EMES VERITAS" image and the image of

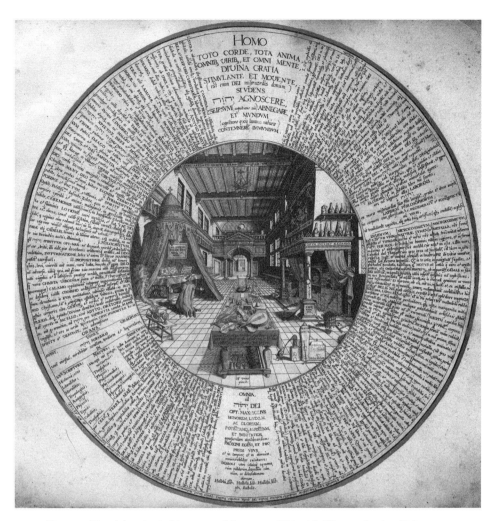

Figure 5. The alchemist in his oratory-laboratory. Heinrich Khunrath, *Amphitheatrum sapientiae aeternae* (Hamburg, 1595), plate 4. By courtesy of the Department of Special Collections, Memorial Library, University of Wisconsin–Madison.

the alchemist in his place of work and prayer? Alchemy has happened. The intervening two circular engravings, which engage the alchemical work from its origins and preparation to its completion, establish how alchemy accomplishes the Christianization of Kabbalah. In the volume's second circular engraving, a "Cabalistic Adam-Androgyne"—a single body with two heads, one male and one female—lifts its hands in prayer or rapture.[11] The Tetragrammaton

Figure 6. Hebrew subservient to Christianity in the alchemist's oratory-laboratory. Heinrich Khunrath, *Amphitheatrum sapientiae aeternae* (Hamburg, 1595), detail of plate 4. By courtesy of the Department of Special Collections, Memorial Library, University of Wisconsin–Madison.

Figure 7. The author's name in Roman letters and transliterated Hebrew. Heinrich Khunrath, *Amphitheatrum sapientiae aeternae* (Hamburg, 1595), detail of plate 4. By courtesy of the Department of Special Collections, Memorial Library, University of Wisconsin–Madison.

and especially the Pentagrammaton are sprinkled throughout this image, which seems to describe "the practice of cabbalistic contemplation."[12] The third circular engraving illustrates the result of that contemplation: it unites Neoplatonic and kabbalistic terms and symbols in an image of an accomplished alchemical work. Filled in its central image with instantly recognizable alchemical emblems such as those of the phoenix and of the hermaphroditic union (signifying the union of masculine sulfur with feminine mercury), this third engraving does feature, in its external circle, two divine names written in Hebrew.[13] But the third engraving's central image includes only one nontransliterated use of Hebrew: the word אש, *esh* ("fire"). *Esh* is the fire of alchemy. Once Kabbalah is thoroughly alchemized, tried in the fire, it is refined enough to be used in the fourth circular engraving, the one that features Hebrew in only a small part of the decor of the Christian alchemist's workplace (see Figure 6).

My topic in this chapter is how Kabbalah, a body of Jewish learning "discovered" by early humanism, was deemed by later humanism to be in need of precisely this kind of de-Judaizing. In that process of making Jewish learning not Jewish, alchemy joins with other esoteric disciplines to rewrite Kabbalah as having been Christian all along. Rewriting first requires reading, accomplished in part by means of the careful scholarship for which humanism is known. But such reading is also accomplished through that careful scholarship's very opposite: through the peculiar form of scholarly laziness that is the skimming of books. As we shall see in this chapter's examples of scholarly skimming, alchemy in this case is less a signal for a turn away from learning (as it was for transubstantiation and matter theory) than it is a partner and participant in that turn. When it comes to reading Kabbalah, alchemy and the associated esoteric arts are partners in devising a reading practice that serves an ideological purpose. Demonstrably skimming Kabbalah without learning it, Christian thinkers of all kinds, including the magicians, alchemists, and other Hermeticists who wished to use Kabbalah for Christian ends, plucked only what they needed from kabbalistic technique and style. And in so doing, they raised what we might call "bad humanism"—humanism that skims, rather than reads—to the highest of arts and to the best of ideological tools. For if a scholar can adopt an attractive veneer of Kabbalah without learning much about it, she has accomplished a major, if unspoken, goal of many early modern Christian thinkers: assimilating only what is needed from Judaism without having to accommodate Jewishness or even bother with Jews.

Christian Kabbalah and the scholarly skimming that supports it are thus a specialized type of disknowledge. Disknowledge as a whole, I have proposed, is the act of knowing and not knowing something at the same time. In the case of Kabbalah, an entire body of learning is remade so that it may be known in a new and piecemeal fashion that serves only Christian purposes. I begin this chapter with an account of how Hermetic learning in general and alchemy in particular participate in laundering Kabbalah of its Jewishness in this manner, taking as my example the way that one magus, John Dee, took up skimming Kabbalah as part of his otherwise astonishingly thorough reading practice. I then examine two plays that, in the way of all the literary works I discuss in this book, demonstrate disknowledge in action. William Shakespeare's Prospero is a rejoinder to the way that Christopher Marlowe's Faustus skims, mangles, and fabricates hermeneutic practice in a way typical of Christian scholars' uses of Kabbalah. That rejoinder is embodied in Prospero's relationship to Caliban and in Prospero's curious neglect of his books.

Alchemy and the Making of Christian Kabbalah

Despite his notorious anti-Semitism, Martin Luther was also dependent on Jewish scholarship, both as aid and as antagonist. While Jewish scholarship often pointed Luther toward some crucial theological point, he was disposed to dispute Jewish readings of the Old Testament as necessarily misguided, originating as they did in the logic of the unbeliever. At times Luther's perspec-

tive put him in the comically awkward position of declaring himself to be a
better reader of the Hebrew Bible than the Jews, even though his own Hebrew was poor. For example, while Luther acknowledges that the thirteenth-
century scholar Moses Nahmanides (Moses ben Nahman Girondi) "has an
excellent knowledge of the words [of the Hebrew Bible] (just as there are many
today who far surpass me in their knowledge of the Hebrew language)," Nahmanides' commentary on the Torah gets Genesis all wrong: "because he does
not understand the [subject] matter, he distorts the passage with which we are
dealing."[14] Luther believes that his Reformed understanding of God's Word
leads him to a better interpretation than that of those who can read the Word
in its original language. The inferior scholar is the superior reader.

In fact, Luther may be the superior reader *because* he is an inferior scholar.
Luther was able to cite Nahmanides only via Christian Hebraist Sebastian
Münster's annotations of Genesis; Luther himself did not have enough knowledge of Hebrew to read Nahmanides, much less the Hebrew Bible.[15] In this
way Luther's laser focus on the "right" reading of the Old Testament is enabled
by a scholarly aid that does the work for him of skimming Jewish scholarship.
While his own interpretation of Genesis depends on Nahmanides, Luther's use
of Münster, the Christian scholarly middleman, in effect allows him to take
advantage of Nahmanides' hermeneutic talents while also distancing his interpretation from anything smacking of Judaism.

Luther was not the only early modern Christian intellectual who did his
best to purge Jewish learning of its Jewishness. Newly important to scholarship and theology for both humanists and Protestants, acquisition of Hebrew
and access to Hebrew texts gained a novel urgency in the early modern era.
Jewish learning was, all of a sudden, not only necessary but also longed for.
That longing, however, generated the kind of backlash against learning that
I identified in Chapter 1 as characteristic of the age of late humanism. Jewish
learning also seemed dangerous and illicit insofar as it proved difficult to dis-
engage acquaintance with Hebrew books from acquaintance with actual Jews
and their recalcitrant non-Christianity. Perhaps the most attractive yet also
most dangerous strand of Jewish learning was Kabbalah, a body of texts and
a loosely integrated system of interpretive practices that became newly available, at least in digested form, to Christian readership in the late fifteenth
through the seventeenth centuries. Crafting as it does a simultaneously metaphysical and hermeneutic approach to the divine, Kabbalah became of interest
to Neoplatonists and Hermetic scholars of all stripes, including alchemists.
But Kabbalah was seen as being in pressing need of Christian Hebraism's

propensity to pluck out the most useful, most alluring strands of Jewish learning and then to claim that these strands were Christian all along.

Because the story of Christian Kabbalah is in part the story of European humanism, I begin this section by sketching the history of prominent humanists whose philosophical and theological interests, although not specifically alchemical, led them to attempt to wrench Kabbalah toward the ends of Christianity and/or Neoplatonism. I then turn to how alchemists, eager to find in Kabbalah an endorsement of and analogue for their own theories of physical and spiritual transformation, both duplicated and improved upon the de-Judaizing techniques of Christian Kabbalah. That improved technique depended, in part, on precisely the opposite of a thorough immersion in Hebrew and in kabbalistic learning: it depended on getting away with knowing as little Hebrew and as little Kabbalah as possible.

A body of esoteric and mystical Jewish literature, Kabbalah, like alchemy and like Christianity, had its origins in the Hellenic-Alexandrian-Palestinian ferment of ideas that included Gnostic and Neoplatonic inquiries into the natures of divinity and the material world.[16] The earliest extant text of Kabbalah, the brief Sefer Yetzirah (Book of Creation), proposes God created the world by means of ten *sefirot*—which are something like metaphysical principles—combined with the twenty-two letters of the Hebrew alphabet.[17] Much later, in the twelfth and thirteenth centuries, intellectual movements in France and in Germany led to the development in Provence of a significant body of kabbalistic writing systemizing the interpretation of the *sefirot*.[18] From Provence, Kabbalah spread to Spain, where the seminal Zohar (Sefer ha-Zohar, the Book of Radiance) was composed or at least compiled by Moses de Leon in the late thirteenth century.[19] After the expulsion of the Jews from Spain in 1492, Kabbalah began to reach wider, non-Jewish audiences.

As God's knowable attributes, the ten *sefirot* of Kabbalah are metaphysical, but they are also physical in that they are capacities or emanations of godhead by which the divine exerts force on, and changes, the natural and supernatural worlds.[20] The linguistic qualities of the ten *sefirot* are inseparable from their physical action in that, as Harold Bloom puts it, they are "attributes of God that need to be described by the various names of God when he is at work in creation."[21] The capacity of the *sefirot* to work simultaneously on metaphysical, physical, and linguistic planes helps explain, as we will see, why alchemy found Kabbalah so attractive.

Itself influenced, if in mediated fashion, by the Gnosticism that had helped shape early Christianity, Kabbalah developed in Christian countries and thus grew up in an atmosphere of both competition and syncretism with Christian philosophy and natural philosophy.[22] These trends might lead us to expect that Jewish kabbalists also absorbed some of the concerns, concepts, and language of alchemy, especially considering Hermeticism's historical precedence and especially given the increased opportunity for contact between Jewish intellectuals and alchemically minded Christian thinkers in the post-Expulsion era. But it turns out to be not the case that alchemy influenced Kabbalah to any great extent.[23] Rather, the vector of influence seems to have operated almost entirely in the reverse direction: Christian alchemy absorbed Kabbalah as yet more evidence of the universal truth of the Great Work.[24]

Or, to be more precise, Christian alchemy absorbed Christianized Kabbalah. It is important to understand that what late medieval and early modern Christian Europe came to regard as Kabbalah was far from what Jewish scholars regarded as Kabbalah. First of all, the Christian sense of what texts constituted Jewish Kabbalah was incorrect, owing to mistranslations and to Christian interpolations (either deliberate or not) of bits of other Jewish biblical commentary like the Talmud.[25] Second, and even more consequentially, almost every late medieval and early modern Christian thinker who sought to take Kabbalah seriously energetically reinterpreted Kabbalah as Christian.[26] In order to understand how alchemy came to be interested in Kabbalah, then, we must understand how Christians—specifically, Christian humanists—came to see Kabbalah as an instrument for controlling nature within a Christian scheme.[27]

Kabbalah's first celebrated Christian champion, Giovanni Pico della Mirandola (1463–94), seems in fact to have been interested in Kabbalah primarily for its potential for accomplishing natural magic. In the nine hundred theses of his *Conclusiones philosophicae, theologicae, et cabalisticae* (1486), to which his oration "On the Dignity of Man" was intended as a prologue, Pico goes so far as to declare that "No magical operation can be of any efficacy unless it has annexed to it a work of Cabala, explicit or implicit."[28] Pico's pioneering effort in accessing Kabbalah—he commissioned an enormous body of Latin translations from Christian convert Flavius Mithridates, and ultimately became at least somewhat competent in Hebrew himself under Mithridates' tutelage—seems to have been aimed almost entirely at understanding Kabbalah as a kind of magical system that would make divinity immanent on earth.[29]

The connection between Kabbalah and alchemy, however, began to take shape only with the work of Europe's second great Christian proponent of kabbalistic learning, humanist and Hebraist Johann Reuchlin (1455–1522), who undertook to elaborate how, exactly, Kabbalah is instrumental in natural magic.[30] Endorsed by Marsilio Ficino as an eminent humanist, and acquainted with Pico, Reuchlin departed from many of his humanist acquaintances (notably, Erasmus) in advocating Hebrew, along with Latin and Greek, as the "third language" essential for theological and scholarly expertise.[31] As with Pico, however, Reuchlin's first motive for pursuing the study of Hebrew was not to perfect his study of the Hebrew Bible but to learn Kabbalah. When he wrote the first of his two major works on Kabbalah, *De verbo mirifico* (The wonder-working word, 1494), he in fact seems not to have known much Hebrew at all: *De verbo mirifico* contains little reference to actual kabbalistic texts, and it even gets the *sefirot* wrong.[32] Nevertheless, Reuchlin forged ahead in the belief that as the Edenic language, the original in which God communicated to Adam, Hebrew held the transformative power of divine creation.[33]

This power is encoded particularly in the Hebrew Tetragrammaton, יהוה or YHWH, the unpronounceable name of God. Relying on what he knows of Kabbalah's alphabetic and numerological manipulations of these four Hebrew letters, Reuchlin composes a theory of the Tetragrammaton as the word that works miracles. Or, rather, *almost* the word that works miracles. Following a proposition in Pico's *Conclusiones*, Reuchlin reworks the Tetragrammaton YHWH into what he believes is the true worker of wonders, the Pentagrammaton—YHSWH, or "Yeshua," the name of Jesus Christ. It is here that Reuchlin's alchemical sense of Kabbalah emerges. The Hebrew letter with which Reuchlin supplements the Tetragrammaton, *shin*, is the most significant element in the word *esh*, or "fire." When *shin* is placed exactly at the center of the Hebrew name of God, it forms the name of Jesus: YHWH becomes YH-SWH. In other words, Reuchlin places fire at the center of Hebrew divinity in order to refine the Hebrew name of God into something even better, the name of the Christian Messiah.[34] Just in case we do not catch this alchemical symbolism, Reuchlin explains that the Pentagrammaton is "the philosopher's stone, far surpassing that which erring alchemists argue over."[35]

By the time of his later work on Kabbalah, *De arte cabalistica* (1517), Reuchlin had learned both Hebrew and Kabbalah well and was able to explicate Kabbalah in the same way that Jewish scholars did, as a commentary on the mystical names and attributes of God. Still, he continued to value Kabbalah for the fact that it allowed humans to traffic physically in the world of the divine.[36] Upon the wide dissemination of *De arte cabalistica*, the association between alchemy and Kabbalah was thus in the air.[37] Hard upon Reuchlin's heels, Venetian priest Johannes Augustinus Pantheus (Giovanni Agostino Panteo, d. 1535), in his *Ars transmutationis metallicae* (1518) and *Voarchadumia contra alchemiam* (1530), "pioneered in establishing a relationship between alchemy and rabbinical science, and maintained that the very word 'alchemy' was derived from the Hebrew."[38] Pantheus's method was what he called a "cabala of metals," in which the letters of the Latin alphabet correspond both to numerical values and to the weights and proportions of substances used in alchemical experiment. He also believed that the four letters of the Tetragrammaton correspond to the four Aristotelian elements that were at the heart of alchemy.[39] It was the immensely influential Heinrich Cornelius Agrippa (1486–1535), however, who made the link between Kabbalah and alchemy explicit. Indebted both to Reuchlin, on whose *De verbo mirifico* Agrippa lectured at the University of Dôle, and to Johannes Trithemius (1462–1516), whose *Steganographia* (written 1499) united the study of alchemy and magic with a kabbalistically derived number symbolism, Agrippa's master work *Occult Philosophy* (*De occulta philosophia*, 1533) puts alchemy and Kabbalah under one umbrella.[40] *Occult Philosophy* assimilates Kabbalah to alchemy in accretive rather than explicit fashion. In the volume's first book, on the magician's involvement in "natural magic," Agrippa describes the alchemical quintessence as a means of intensifying the "spirit" within any substance and turning it to gold or silver.[41] By the time of the third book, which has to do with spiritual, ceremonial magic (and which gained Agrippa his nefarious reputation, since it deals with necromancy), Agrippa has associated Kabbalah with this physically transformative power.[42] For example, Agrippa follows some suggestive passages in the Zohar in aligning the seven lower *sefirot*, those whose power is exerted on the physical world, with the seven metals, the composition of which is one of the central concerns of alchemy.[43]

The influence of Agrippa led to a common early modern refinement of Pico's earlier assertion that natural magic is no good without Kabbalah: *alchemy* is no good without Kabbalah.[44] For example, the widely read and translated alchemical *Exposition of the Hieroglyphical Figures* (1612), attributed to the reputed fifteenth-century alchemist Nicolas Flamel but almost certainly written in the late sixteenth or early seventeenth century, begins with an "editor's" introduction explaining how "no man could ever have been able to understand" the crucial "first agent" of the "transmutation of Mettalls . . . without being well skilled in their Cabala, which goeth by tradition, and without having well studied [Jewish] bookes."[45] By the early seventeenth century it had come to be understood that knowledge of the Kabbalah was not optional but rather one of alchemy's essential tools, so much so that even a popular satire of alchemists like John Taylor's poem "A Figure-Flinger" counts "the Jewish Thalmud, and Cabals" as part of the alchemist's store of learning.[46]

One reason for the association between alchemy and Kabbalah—deplorable, but not to be discounted—may have been the conceptual connections between the Jews' reputation as begetters of money and the alchemical dream of begetting gold. The Paracelsian Benedictus Figulus (Benedict Töpfer), who worked in the court of Holy Roman Emperor Rudolf II, lays out a satirical procedure for how "to acquire a great treasure in less time" by immersing sweaty Jews—ones who have been left out in the sun until they are "dark as Moors"—in a warm bath and then filtering the bathwater. With this method, a mere one hundred Jews may yield "1248 lot[h]," or 624 ounces, of gold in a year's time.[47] Another reason for the association between alchemy and Kabbalah was the reputation Jews had for their skill in medicine, as Jeffrey Shoulson points out—skill that, in the Christian imagination, could be turned to either benign or malevolent ends.[48] A third, more scholarly reason for the association between alchemy and Kabbalah was that Christian Kabbalah came to associate the originator of alchemy, Hermes Trismegistus himself, with the Hebrew of the Old Testament and with Jewish mysticism. The most prevalent account of the origins of Kabbalah said that Moses received Kabbalah as a second revelation from God on Mount Sinai: God gave Moses the law in written form, but Kabbalah in oral form.[49] Following this theory, many proposed that Hermes, an Egyptian, learned Kabbalah either from the Israelites or directly from Moses.[50] An alternative theory held by some, including Giordano Bruno, was that Moses had learned Kabbalah from Hermes in Egypt and passed it along to the Israelites.[51] No matter who taught whom, though, the assumption was that alchemy and Kabbalah merged in the wisdom of Moses and that their combination thus comported fully with Christian practice.[52]

Kabbalah's connection to Moses, who bested Pharaoh's magicians at their own game, no doubt bolstered a fourth reason for associating Kabbalah with alchemy: the changes brought about by Kabbalah were thought to be not merely an ordinary sort of magic but a transformation at the level of originary matter.[53] This theory had its origins in Adam's presumed use of Hebrew, the Edenic language. As Umberto Eco points out, Adam's naming of the animals (Genesis 2:19–20) constitutes possibly the only speech act in human history for which there is no split between sign and signifier, since Adam calls them by the "names that each animal intrinsically ought to have been given."[54] It logically follows that Adam's speech is more than just an act of naming. Because God himself creates the heavens and the earth by means of the kabbalistic technique of combining words and letters, and because God then passes along to Adam the secrets of creation in the form of the same divine language, the Hebrew that Adam then uses to name the creatures in Eden not only attaches words to creatures but also acts as a kabbalistic fiat through which the creatures become themselves.[55] Like alchemy, then, Kabbalah works upon nature at its most primordial level. The attraction for alchemists is obvious: through Kabbalah they can reproduce Edenic creation. As Reuchlin puts it, the wonder-working word allows the magus to "hold dominion over [nature] and work wonders, portents and miracles which are signs of the divinity."[56]

The final reason for attaching Kabbalah to alchemy has to do with the intricacies of Kabbalah's exegetical method, which is accomplished not only on the level of the word but also—as we have already seen with Reuchlin's expansion of YHWH into YHSWH—on the level of the letter. Indeed, early Christian kabbalists such as Reuchlin, trained as they were in Scholastic hermeneutics, seem to have gone far wilder for kabbalistic exegesis than their Jewish sources did.[57] Their enthusiasm was based on the fact that kabbalistic reading methods are extraordinarily supple in their substitutive capacity. The first of Kabbalah's four primary hermeneutic modes, *gematria*, depends upon the fact that each letter in ancient Hebrew (as in other ancient languages) has a numerical value; hence, two words whose numeric sum of letters is the same may be used interchangeably.[58] The second mode, *themura*, allows for a variety of coding/decoding techniques based on the positions of letters within the Hebrew alphabet. In the third mode, *notarikon*, each letter of a word spawns an acrostic, the whole making up a phrase. The fourth mode, *tsurif*, is simple anagrammatizing, rearranging the letters of a word to create a different word. In short, kabbalistic hermeneutics seemed endlessly productive because it potentially endowed every instance and every element of language, especially written language, with endlessly proliferative significance and multiple interpretive possibilities.

Such was the case, at least, when kabbalistic hermeneutic method was loosed from Jewish mysticism onto the intellectually inexact semiotic playground of Pico's Neoplatonism or Agrippa's magicianship. For these writers and the alchemists who read them, kabbalistic reading technique lent a kind of numinousness to any kind of symbolic pattern that one cared to make.[59]

Here too, as Raphael Patai has noted, is an analogy that proved irresistible for the more esoteric forms of alchemy: a text becomes a kind of prime matter from which any desired substance may be derived. At its extreme—such as in the case of Giordano Bruno, as Karen Silvia de León-Jones argues—Kabbalah's hermeneutics thus merge with alchemical natural magic into a system for transmuting the world as text.[60]

Despite all its attractions, Kabbalah also, however, posed special dangers for early modern Christians. Part of the problem was that access to Kabbalah provoked suspicion as well as reverence. Gabriel Naudé noted in his seventeenth-century history of magic that those who knew Hebrew were routinely suspected of being Jews: "he who was more than Ordinarily vers'd in the Hebrew tongue, went for a Jew or an Apostate."[61] Even more than merely damning by association, learning Hebrew might actually tempt a Christian to become a Jew. Erasmus voiced this suspicion when he wrote to German reformer Wolfgang Capito that the renaissance of Hebrew studies in Europe might "give Judaism its cue to plan a revival, the most pernicious plague and bitterest enemy that one can find to the teaching of Christ."[62] In its particular seductiveness, the study of Kabbalah was thought to be even more dangerous than the study of Hebrew alone. Christians proved so eager to learn Kabbalah that early sixteenth-century Venetian rabbi and kabbalist Elijah Menahem Halfan wryly commented on how potential pupils vastly outnumbered possible teachers: "seven learned men grasp a Jewish man by the hem of his garment and say: 'Be our master in this science!' "[63] Erasmus grumbled that the turn toward "Talmud, Cabbala, Tetragrammaton" in the countries where Christian scholars had become most enamored of Kabbalah, Italy and Spain, had practically made recidivist Jews of everyone who lived there: "Italy is full of Jews, in Spain there are hardly any Christians."[64] And indeed, Christian Kabbalists routinely faced charges of being closet Jews. Agrippa felt it necessary to point out "that he was a Christian, not a 'Judaizing heretic,' " and Reuchlin was actually condemned for Judaism and fined by the papal court.[65]

How could Christian kabbalists in general, and specifically Christian alchemical kabbalists, circumvent Kabbalah's reputation as Judaizing? I have already touched upon one solution, the one encapsulated by Reuchlin's "YHSWH": Christians used kabbalistic technique to read evidence of Christ into the Old Testament. In effect, Christian kabbalists read the Hebrew Bible in such a way as to assert that what looked like Judaism was really Christianity all along.[66] As the German Paracelsian Martin Ruland puts it in his *Lexicon of Alchemy* (1612), "Cabalistic Art is a most secret science which is affirmed to have been made known in a divine manner to Moses at the same time as written law; it reveals to us the doctrine of the Messiah of God."[67] This tactic began with Pico himself, who, describing Kabbalah as "necessary . . . for defending our religion against the grievous misrepresentations of the Hebrews," declares in the section of his *Conclusiones* titled "Cabalistic Conclusions Confirming the Christian Religion" that "Every Hebrew Cabalist . . . is inevitably forced to concede, without addition, omission, or variation, precisely what the Catholic faith of Christians maintains concerning the Trinity and every divine Person, Father, Son, and Holy Spirit."[68] Both Reuchlin and Agrippa are also adamant that Kabbalah works only for Christians. Reuchlin has his alter ego, the Christian Capnion, say to his Jewish interlocutor in *De verbo mirifico*, "The saving power of words, which has deserted you and has chosen us, accompanies us and, as can be observed, obeys our will. . . . Therefore you mumble in vain."[69] Agrippa argues that Kabbalah's efficacy shifted from Jewish to Christian control after Christ's dispensation on earth began.[70] Taking the de-Judaization of Kabbalah even further, some early modern thinkers determine that Kabbalah's origins weren't Jewish in the least. Paracelsus, for example, claims that Kabbalah was originally a Persian doctrine that had been perverted by the Jews.[71] Similarly, Bruno's theory that Moses had learned Kabbalah from the Egyptians separates the origins of Kabbalah, which he believes has universal application, from anything resembling Judaism: "Jews are without doubt the excrements of Egypt, and no one could ever pretend with any degree of probability that the Egyptians borrowed any principle, good or bad, from the Hebrews."[72]

Bruno's remark that there was nothing Jewish about Kabbalah reflects an increasing suspicion that early humanists were misguided in their attempts to syncretize Jewish and Christian learning. The solution was to have a Kabbalah that did not reference Jewish learning at all. During the century separating Pico from Bruno, as Gershom Scholem describes it, Christian kabbalists found it less and less necessary to be acquainted with Hebrew sources, "and consequently the Jewish element in their books became progressively slighter, its place being taken by esoteric Christian speculations whose connections with Jewish motifs were remote."[73] This was particularly the case in England, where Kabbalah was available almost exclusively through the work of Christian kabbalists—Pico, Reuchlin, and Agrippa, along with other writers like Francesco Giorgi—rather than in Hebrew.[74] It remained the case into the seventeenth century, despite the advances in Hebrew scholarship in England. Not until Christian Knorr von Rosenroth's publication of the *Kabbala denudata*

(1684) did a significant number of authentic Jewish kabbalistic texts, in Latin translation, make their way into the libraries of English intellectuals. While Kabbalah was of supreme importance to mid-seventeenth-century philosophers, alchemists, and mystics like Henry More and Thomas Vaughan, they retained as dogma the notion that "true Kabbalah" was to be distinguished from Jewish Kabbalah, which was, as Thomas Vaughan put it, "the Inventions of some dispersed wandering Rabbies [*sic*], whose braines had more of Distraction, than their fortunes."[75] Well into the seventeenth century, then, Kabbalah in England seemed entirely up for Christian grabs.

I turn next to the way that Kabbalah—its Jewish specter and its Christian repurposing—encouraged changes in the reading and interpretive practices of Christian thinkers engaged in the more esoteric forms of alchemical and associated Hermetic learning. The alliances between kabbalistic natural magic and alchemical transformation, along with Kabbalah's mystical reputation and its generative hermeneutics, made such thinkers in the sixteenth and seventeenth centuries eager consumers of the new genre of Christian kabbalistic writing. But using Kabbalah means having to manage the hazards of borrowing learning from Jews, and evidence abounds that these thinkers not only were quick to adopt Christian Kabbalah's methodologies for de-Judaizing their sources but also invented some of their own.

John Dee Skims Kabbalah

As I discussed in Chapter 1, the humanist treatment of books and the alchemical treatment of books go hand in hand. Indeed, alchemy and humanism share a bookish history. After its origins in late antiquity, alchemy, like so much of the classical learning with which it identified itself, survived only because it was taken up by Muslim scholars who collected, preserved, translated, added to, and commented on Greek alchemical texts. Following the path of so many other classical works, alchemical manuscripts entered Europe by way of the intellectual centers of Moorish Spain, where Christian scholars who hoped to absorb the wisdom of the Arabic world encountered alchemy during the course of their textual discovery and rediscovery. The first alchemical text to be transmitted to Christian Europe was even marked by the kind of authorial precision and self-promotion commonly associated with Petrarch and other founders of humanism. On 11 February 1144, Robert of Chester, who worked in Segovia, signed and dated his just-finished Latin translation of *Liber de composi-*

tione alchimiae, noting that "it hath seemed good unto me to set my name in the beginning of the preface, lest any man should attribute this our labour unto himself and also challenge the praise and desert as due unto himself."[76] In keeping with this protohumanist gesture, the further history of alchemy in late medieval and early modern Europe closely tracked what came to be humanist obsessions, all of them involving the circulation of books: the rediscovery of the classics; the syncretism of Christian theology with classical learning; and the invention of a Christian Neoplatonism that imagined a perfected earth to match the perfection of heaven.

Just as it mirrored the grander accomplishments of humanism, though, alchemy also picked up humanism's bad habits. I described a number of those bad habits in Chapter 1; here I want to focus on the habit of scholarly skimming, a skill that proves crucial to the project of selectively reading and reinterpreting Jewish learning for Christian use, including alchemical use. I do not mean the variety of skimming motivated by sheer intellectual sloth. The indolent student skims, as does the up-and-coming politician, lawyer, or cleric who, wishing to get ahead in his business without really trying, picks up just enough learning to flaunt shallow but flashy credentials. Scholarly skimming, in contrast, requires sufficient knowledge of what *might* be in a text (or sometimes knowledge of what *is* in a text one has already read) to pluck out only the portions needed. This kind of skimming is a subspecies of what Anthony Grafton and Lisa Jardine, referring to an early modern scholarly propensity not simply to accumulate information but to direct one's information to a point, have called "active reading."[77] Whereas Grafton and Jardine have in mind the exceptionally careful sifting of texts for relevant portions that was practiced by the likes of Gabriel Harvey, scholarly skimming, though employing much different means, has much the same end. As the scholar skims, she either ignores or immediately discards what is not useful for export, retaining only the desired point or argument. The act of skimming thus reminds us that the scholar is as much a nonreader as she is a reader. Furthermore, skimming is not merely a readerly practice; it is a bibliographic principle. It extends not simply to one book, but to the vast swaths of books, partly read or mostly forgotten, that do not serve the scholar's purpose.[78]

There are ideological reasons for not reading, of course, just as much as there are ideological reasons for reading. By designating most of a text as unread, unacknowledged, or unmemorable, skimming treats most of a text as not worth reading, not worth acknowledging, and not worth remembering. As difficult as the project may be, then, we must examine an era's and an author's motives for scholarly inattention, in the same way and with many of the same tools that we typically examine citation and allusion. Because books carry the aura not just of particular authors but of entire cultures and peoples, the skill of scholarly skimming, with its exquisite capacity for acquaintance without absorption, may also convey useful strategies for encountering and assimilating just so much of a culture and its learning—and no more. Skimming, for early modern Christians, thus proves to be not only one way to read Kabbalah but arguably the best way to read Kabbalah. The skimmer keeps Judaism at arm's length while still cherry-picking the most desired elements of Jewish learning's most alluring body of texts.

The esoteric arts, including alchemy, suggest a method tailor-made for this kind of reading. Though they were omnivorous and freewheeling consumers of predecessor texts, writers on alchemy—as I discussed in Chapter 1—also sometimes claimed a purity of purpose that enabled them to extract only the salutary elements from those texts, disavowing the taint of anything untrue. As *The Mirror of Alchemy*, attributed to Roger Bacon, recommends, "if in any [books] wee can meete with a worke of Nature or Art, let us make choyse of that: if not, let us leave it as suspicious, and ill beseeming a wise man. It is the part of a Magitian so to handle thinges needlesse and superfluous."[79] *The Mirror of Alchemy* here establishes a kind of ideal (if difficult to implement) reading practice, one that supports Frank Klaasen's contention that the Renaissance pictured the magician as a chooser, rewriter, and even inventor of precedent texts, a "divinely guided editor."[80] In the manner of the humanist readers described by Anthony Grafton, Lisa Jardine, Richard Halpern, and Ann Blair, the magician may even edit his texts so thoroughly that their otherwise challenging content is neutralized, perhaps even so thoroughly that they say something quite other than what they actually said.[81] I would add that editing is often a matter of choosing what deserves to be edited. Like *The Mirror of Alchemy*'s "Magitian," the Hermeticist knows when to read; he also knows when not to read. He can learn without learning.

Somewhat perversely, my test case for how a Christian alchemist skims Kabbalah in order to learn without learning is perhaps the most learned, and certainly the most bookish, Englishman of the late sixteenth century: the polymath John Dee (1527–1608/9). Dee spent the better part of his long life in pursuit of a natural magic that would bring the perfection of heaven to fruition on earth. His sources for this magic were manifold, but among them, he found tremendous inspiration in Christian Kabbalah, which lent him the authority for speaking the language of God's own alchemy.[82] If, however, we cross-reference Dee's reading efforts with his pursuits in natural magic—a task set to us by William Sherman's groundbreaking study of Dee's library and by recent work on Dee's angelology and magic by Deborah Harkness, Stephen Clucas, Glyn Parry, and others—we find evidence of Dee's having concertedly constructed his deeply kabbalistic natural magic out of as little Jewish Kabbalah as possible.[83] For Dee, scholarly skimming was crucial to implementing a magic that would change the world.

Dee's relationship to Jewish Kabbalah, and more generally to the Hebrew language, evidences the ambivalent mix of attraction and disdain I traced above in my account of early modern alchemy's kabbalistic associations. On the one hand, Dee evidently counted the Hebrew language among his most prominent intellectual concerns. According to the library catalog Dee composed in 1583 before he departed for travels in Central Europe, he owned a total of sixty-two Hebrew and Aramaic books, likely more than any other library in England at the time.[84] None of those Hebrew books was a kabbalistic text, which would have been very difficult to obtain at the time, but he owned and read works of Christian Kabbalah by Pico, Reuchlin, Agrippa, Giorgi, and others.[85] On the other hand, his interest in Hebrew books corresponds to that of Luther and others in that Dee worried that actual Jews were the keepers of Jewish learning. Hoping to locate lost texts of Apocrypha, Dee queried the angel with whom he and his scryer Edward Kelley conversed on 18 April 1583 about where the missing books were, only to learn that "The prophets of the Jues have them." To which Dee replied, "But we can hardly, trust any thing in the Jues hands, concerning the pure Veritie: They are a stiffnecked people and dispersed all the world over."[86]

As was the case with many an alchemist or syncretic Neoplatonist who preceded or followed him, Dee's tremendous interest in Kabbalah did not mean that he knew Hebrew terribly well. Here is the one point on which I disagree with Deborah Harkness's groundbreaking book on Dee's conversations with angels. Harkness ventures to defend Dee's Hebrew expertise primarily on the evidence of one of Dee's earliest angel conversations, in which he quizzes the angel Michael about whether the name of God is contained in forty letters.[87] Dee avers that he has "red in Cabala" that its number of letters is forty-two. He then cites three different Hebrew versions of those forty-two letters, immediately translating the Hebrew into Latin.[88] What Harkness has missed, however, is that Dee has copied both these Hebrew passages and their Latin translations directly from a book of Christian Kabbalah, Pietro Galatino's *De arcanis catholicae veritatis* (1518).[89] In other words, the only knowledge of

Hebrew Dee displays in this instance is the ability to copy out Hebrew letters from a predecessor text that conveniently includes the Latin translation. Dee's subsequent remark to the angel that "I am not good in the hebrue tung, but, you know my meaning," is taken by Harkness as a modesty topos, but the evidence demonstrates that he is being perfectly honest about his rudimentary Hebrew.[90] G. Lloyd Jones's assessment seems correct: Dee's interest in Hebrew and his large Hebrew book collection do not guarantee his competence in the language.[91]

More than simply not knowing Hebrew very well, however, Dee may have intended to learn Hebrew better but not gotten far in the attempt. We know that he intended to learn Hebrew because he went to the trouble and expense of obtaining multiple Hebrew primers for his library. My suspicion, however, that he did not progress very far in this education comes from the fact that Dee, an inveterate scribbler in his books—someone who, as Sherman has described it, registered his interest in and opinions about his sources by annotating them— marked up those primers very sparsely. In several cases, there is no evidence that Dee cracked his primer at all.[92] Others of Dee's Hebrew-language books show similar inattention, prompting the observation by the editors of Dee's 1583 library catalog, Julian Roberts and Andrew Watson, that "compared with books in other parts of [Dee's] library, the Hebrew books are almost without annotation."[93] Despite his immense learning and his facility with languages, the evidence suggests that Dee, like Erasmus, found more than the basics of Hebrew too much for him. "I began to take up Hebrew as well [as Greek]," Erasmus confessed in a letter, "but stopped because I was put off by the strangeness of the language, and at the same time the shortness of life and the limitations of human nature will not allow a man to master too many things at once."[94]

While it would be unwise to make any kind of argument about Dee's attitude toward Jewish learning based solely on his failure to annotate his Hebrew primers, we can draw an interesting contrast between the Hebrew books that failed to attract Dee's marginal pen and one that did. Dee's copy of Sebastian Münster's *Messias Christianorum et Iudaeorum Hebraicem & Latinem* (1539) has copious annotations that suggest that Dee's first purpose in owning Hebrew books was to find Kabbalah, and his second purpose was to supplement his well-used books of Christian Kabbalah.[95] A dual Latin and Hebrew text, Münster's *Messias* is a dialogue between a Christian and a Jew concerning both religions' messianic teachings. The Hebrew version of the text has both vowel points and Masoretic markings, indicating that it is for a student of elementary Hebrew, not for an adept.[96] But Dee does not seem to have used this book as a means of brushing up on his Hebrew. Rather, his annotations in this volume trace how he has hunted around for his own intellectual obsessions. He marks, for example, several passages describing God's creation of extrahuman persons, including Adam's procreation of (as Dee notes in the margin) "Daemones spiritus spectrae." And he seems to be especially on the lookout for Kabbalah. Adjacent to a passage discussing the movement of angels from earth to heaven and debating whether God created demons that remained on earth after the creation, Dee has written "Cabalistice[m]." A similar annotation ("Cabala") appears next to the Jewish disputant's references to the Kabbalah.[97] In short, Dee seems to have skimmed this volume for two of his special interests, angelology/spiritology and Kabbalah—the two interests being related, since among Kabbalah's primary uses is the naming and summoning of angels.[98] For skimming purposes, bad Hebrew is enough.

Once we understand that Christian Kabbalah uses Kabbalah to de-Judaize Jewish learning, it is possible to see that bad Hebrew is in fact the preferable approach to Kabbalah. Remember that, in Christian Kabbalah, the meaning of Hebrew matters less than how Hebrew may be manipulated and reinterpreted. Even if one has only bad Hebrew, one can easily fabricate Hebrew to suit one's needs. After all, Pico did it. Pico's Hebrew tutor, the converted Jew Flavius Mithridates, was perfectly qualified to teach his pupils Hebrew, Aramaic, and Greek, but in Pico's case he taught "syncretism" in the form of making up his own language, what Alastair Hamilton describes as "a bizarre mixture of Hebrew and Aramaic in Ethiopic characters."[99] As Eco explains, for the purposes of someone like Pico, fake Hebrew was all the better for being merely Hebrew-*like*. For some, "Hebrew was all the more sacred and efficacious for remaining incomprehensible. . . . Such a language no longer even had to be the original Hebrew. All it needed to do was to seem like it."[100] Equally, genuine Hebrew terms might be wrested from their proper significance and used as the Christian kabbalist desired. Paracelsus used the term "Kabbalah" (which he spelled any number of different ways) simply to designate a subfield of magic having nothing to do with kabbalistic meaning or method, perhaps a kind of magical astronomy.[101] As William West and Carla Mazzio have each recently demonstrated, intellectual confusion and rhetorical misunderstanding have their advantages: they can spark invention.[102] When a brilliant thinker like Pico or Paracelsus begins with a confused and misunderstood Hebrew, the resulting invention can be very interesting indeed.

In the context of his peers' and models' inventing a Hebrew-like kabbalistic language, Dee's skimming of his own Hebrew books is not an embarrassing failure but rather an invaluable skill. Hoping to accomplish natural magic, Dee, like many a Christian kabbalist, was interested in reviving the Adamic language: the language in which God spoke his fiat, the language with which Adam brought the creatures of the world into being even as he named them. Dee was convinced, though, that God and Adam spoke not Hebrew but pre-Hebrew—a language from which the Hebrew of the Jews is descended, but in relation to which the Hebrew of the Jews is only a faded, debased remnant. Harkness argues that Dee's conversations with angels were largely taken up with his receiving that language. What resulted had much in common with Kabbalah, but it wasn't Hebrew. Rather, as Harkness points out, Dee thought it was the original Kabbalah, communicated by the angels directly from God and uncorrupted by Jewish use.[103]

Dee explains that language in his infamously cryptic *Monas hieroglyphica* (1564), in which he invents an alphabet that operates according to kabbalistic principles but that is pointedly not Hebrew. Rather, it is strictly geometric and mathematical.[104] Furthermore, like the many kabbalistic tables and charts in Dee's angel diaries and other works, his numerical and geometric language performs what John Bender and Michael Marrinan call the diagrammatic function, creating meaning rather than simply distilling meaning.[105] Dee derives his language from his Monas, a glyph that amalgamates astrological, alchemical, geometric, and even Habsburg symbols.[106] Having already defined the Monas as the insignia of alchemy in his previous work on geometric optics, *Propaideumata aphoristica* (1558), Dee details in *Monas hieroglyphica* how the Monas, unlike a Kabbalah that combines and recombines ordinary Hebrew letters and their numerical equivalents, uses kabbalistic principles to combine and recombine geometric shapes, significant mathematical ratios, and important numerical values. For example, whereas the kabbalistic operation of *gematria* derives new meaning from the numerical equivalents of the letters in the Hebrew alphabet, Dee's *gematria* derives new meaning from the conversion of numbers into geometric shapes. The meaning of Christ's crucifixion, for example, may be derived from the Roman numeral *X*, not only because the cross is X-shaped, but also because this numeral's value, 10, performs the Pythagorean ideal of converting the quaternary (1, 2, 3, 4) into the denary ($1+2+3+4=10$) in a fashion that Dee calls a "cabbalistic expansion."[107] And whereas the kabbalistic operation of *tsurif* rearranges letters to create a new word or phrase, Dee's *tsurif* rearranges geometric elements of the Monas to create astrological signs that are not immediately apparent in the glyph itself, as well as working designs for alchemical vessels in which the Monas's transformative powers will effect physical transformation.[108]

Dee is well aware that his Monas represents not just a Christianizing of Jewish Kabbalah in the mode of Reuchlin or Khunrath but a Kabbalah in which Hebrew words and letters, the vehicles of mystical meaning in both Jewish and Christian Kabbalah, are no longer necessary. By means of his new, geometrical alphabet, Dee says, he can compose a Kabbalah that is "the real cabbala, or [the cabbala] of that which is," as opposed to "that other and vulgar one, which rests on well-known letters that can be written by man," which Dee calls "the cabbala of that which is said."[109] By "that other and vulgar" Kabbalah, Dee means both Jewish Kabbalah and the Christian Kabbalah that relied on it, mere linguistic systems that do not attend to the truly kabbalistic power of geometry. Perhaps the most telling sign of Dee's finding Hebrew immaterial to his kabbalistic Monas is that he never mentions the *sefirot* in connection with his practice. As Hebrew names for the knowable emanations of the unknowable divine nature, the *sefirot* merely interject superfluous linguistic noise into what ought to be a solely mathematical system.[110]

What Dee had in mind for his Monas, his truly Adamic language, was nothing short of an alchemy of everything. The Monas would effect both a transterrestrial, transcosmic, apocalyptic cure—a medicine to heal what was wrong in nature—and an alchemical empire on earth, one ruled by Queen Elizabeth herself. Both esoteric and physical in its power, the Monas would effectively break down all that is into prime matter and remake it into a new, irenic universe.[111] Dee's transcendent alchemy is also an alchemy, however, that depends on fabricating Hebrew, garbling Hebrew, and ignoring Hebrew. In a *Monas hieroglyphica* passage that differentiates a beginning alchemist's "common vessels" from the vessels modeled after the Monas, Dee feels compelled—even though he says he has purged his Kabbalah of the Hebrew language—to include Hebrew words. But they are nonsensical Hebrew.[112] Years later, when Dee received further elaboration of the alchemical divine language from the angels with whom he conversed, the language he received again depended on imitating Hebrew rather than comprehending it.[113] In Dee's record of a spiritual action that took place on 26 March 1583, an angel shows Dee's scryer Edward Kelley a book composed of a page with grids and identifies this book as that which with heaven and earth was created. The angel demonstrates with his finger that the grid must be read from right to left.[114] At the end of the surviving account of his angel conversations, Dee himself determines that all of the pages of diagrams he has received from the angels must be ordered "from the right hand to the left . . . as in the hebr[ew]."[115] To follow Hebrew but not to read it, to imitate Hebrew but not to use it: the alchemy of the divine language engages techniques Dee has mastered for skimming Kabbalah.

Dee, perhaps Renaissance England's most learned man, was not an inveterate skimmer. Quite the opposite: he read more than nearly any of his contemporaries, and he usually did so not to edit and censor what he had read, as we saw earlier was one habit of humanistic snippetizing, but to expand the horizons of knowledge for Europe's intellectual class. As Harkness describes them, Dee's angelic encounters were not merely wacky séances but were rather part of a program to rescue late sixteenth-century humanism by discovering new kinds of learning that did not depend on the ancient wisdom that was then being increasingly exposed as unreliable.[116] In this one case, though, a new kind of learning belonged to a people and to a tradition that Dee, like other Christian intellectuals, saw as regrettably benighted. So it is Kabbalah alone that requires this bibliographic practice. Skimming proves the best strategy for solving the humanistic crisis while not bringing the Jews along.

On 6 August 1597 Dee recorded a dream in the diary annotations that he kept in the margins and blank pages of several of his library's volumes. As might be expected for a bibliophile like Dee, it was a dream of books: "this night I had the vision and shew of many bokes in my dreame, and among the rest was one great volume thik [*sic*] in large quarto, new printed, on the first page whereof as a title in great letters was printed 'Notus in Judaea Deus.' "[117] "God is known in Judaea," the dream-book's title page proclaims. This is not news. What deserves to be "new printed . . . in great letters" on the first page of this "great volume," however, becomes clear when we understand that "Deus" was one of the never-humble Dee's self-appellations.[118] With this substitution, the dream-book's title may be read as "Dee is known in Judaea." In other words, what is known in Judea, the ancestral land of the Jews, is not Jewish learning. Rather, what is known in Judea is the reputation of that learned man who was "not good in the Hebrew tongue": John Dee himself.

Faustus's Books

I have been arguing that, when faced with the challenge of incorporating desirable books that have undesirable origins—for example, books originating with the Jews—late humanism does not quail; it skims. Putting this new-model humanism into practice, however, is another matter. First of all, scholarly skimming requires effort, even if it is not the same effort as thorough learning. Second, even a heavily excerpted and assiduously Christianized Kabbalah still runs the risk of some philological (and hence philosophical) taint of Judaism. Dee's solution, a mystic Kabbalah that purges itself of Jewish learning by also giving up letters in favor of a geometrical and mathematical symbology, goes so far as to give up humanism altogether. Dee's kabbalistic patterning becomes a matter purely of schematic and numeric arrangement rather than linguistic and philological skill.

Reading, skimming, schematizing: the progress from humanism to late humanism to a proleptic posthumanism charts, depending on your point of view, either the downfall of responsible literary exegesis or the triumph of more precise semiotic systems. This three-step progress also denotes, however, the instability of the middle term—the skimming that, I have been arguing, replaces humanism's professed commitment to scholarly thoroughness. While scholarly skimming, as I have been describing it, is a profoundly useful technique for dabbling in illicit knowledge without subscribing to it and hence for evading ideological pressure, it is not foolproof: the scholarly skimmer can still be seen as tethered to that which she skims. Thus she not only exerts considerable effort, but also potentially stands in a somewhat exposed position. Those early modern intellectuals who skimmed Kabbalah are a case in point. As I have mentioned, Pico, Reuchlin, and Agrippa all came under suspicion for Judaizing, even though all had no interest in anything but a Christianized Kabbalah.

These charges, despite their anti-Semitic foundations, do highlight a valuable question: How much is one responsible to, and for, the full body of learning from which one has plucked an idea or two? What are the moral and ethical implications of what looks like simply a handy reading practice? I turn in the remainder of this chapter to two plays that take up these questions, Christopher Marlowe's *Doctor Faustus* (ca. 1588–92) and William Shakespeare's *The Tempest* (1611). These plays reveal and examine both the advantages and the bad faith of building a body of learning that hopes or claims to be syncretic but is not. Quite contrary to what we might expect, given the respective genres of these two plays, it is Marlowe's tragedy that manifests a rather optimistic outlook for the prospects of selective reading: Faustus's damnation seems to be in part the result of his not having absorbed the skimming techniques that might have kept him on the redeemed side of the line. It is Shakespeare's romance—the genre of union and harmony—that questions syncretism's likelihood. Prospero, having developed a kind of Kabbalah of his own, is confronted with the very figure that alchemical Kabbalah hopes to elide: the person of the Jew.

Doctor Faustus arrives on the scene with one major problem of kabbalistic learning already solved for him by his author. Marlowe has obviated the uncomfortable ties between Jewish learning and the Jews of post-Expulsion Europe by cordoning them off into two different plays. *The Jew of Malta* gets the Jew; *Doctor Faustus* gets the books. Thus, although *Doctor Faustus* is set in some vaguely early Renaissance or Reformation past, Faustus—unlike early Renaissance or Reformation figures like Pico, Reuchlin, and Luther—is never forced to consider the intellectual origins of his learning. For all of Faustus's fatal attraction to what European Christianity would have called intellectual error, flirting with Jewishness is not part of his folly.

Still, Faustus does slide into folly, and I offer his reading practices as one reason why. Like John Dee (on whom he was likely based, at least in part), Faustus develops a set of reading practices that enable mastery of heaven and earth. As the play progresses, however, he neglects the hermeneutics he has learned and fails to extend the manipulation of texts into the manipulation of physical and spiritual change. As opposed to alchemical Kabbalah's strategic ignorance of its Hebrew intellectual antecedents—a strategic ignorance that marks this brand of scholarship as a modern upgrade of humanism—Faustus opts for a retro magic that regards books almost as talismanic objects, leaving him unable to grasp how his own learning might advantage him. His objectification of the book is bound up, as we might imagine, with his mishandlings of textuality in general. Thus, if we attend to the changes in Faustus's reading practice, we may assess in a new way the puzzling increase in his manifest stupidity as the play goes along.

As the play begins and Faustus undertakes his magical endeavors, he seems set on a course of learning that includes applying the methods of Christianized Kabbalah to his more generalized esotericism and demonology. Marlowe pointedly adds Kabbalah to Faustus's bag of intellectual tricks as he prepares for his conjurations. Focused as critics have been on demonic magic, few have noticed the kabbalistic elements of Faustus's preparations, but Frances Yates astutely draws the connection between his resolve to be "as cunning as Agrippa was" (1.1.119) and one of Marlowe's probable sources, Jean Bodin's horrified condemnation of Agrippa and Pico in *De la démonomanie des sorciers* (1580), a widely read and influential work that helped feed the witch craze of the 1580s

and 1590s.[119] Bodin, who names Kabbalah as a chief contributor to magicians'
and witches' "demon mania," repeatedly denounces Kabbalah for attributing
quasi-divine (and hence demonic) agency to "letters and characters."[120] Echoing
Bodin, Faustus thus invokes Kabbalah in his description of the necromantic
books that capture his attention after philosophy, medicine, law, and theology
have disappointed him:

> These metaphysics of magicians,
> And necromantic books are heavenly,
> Lines, circles, signs, *letters, and characters*—
> Ay, these are those that Faustus most desires.
>
> (1.1.51–54; emphasis added)[121]

Initially, then, Faustus's magical learning is textual in the way that kabbalistic magic is textual. Unlike in the English Faust book, from which Marlowe
heavily drew, Faustus's first foray into magic emphasizes not incantation or
physical ritual but rather the "lines, circles, signs, letters, and characters" that
can be written or printed.[122]

I would not argue that Faustus's necromantic books are *exactly* books of
Kabbalah, even Christian Kabbalah. Rather, in a way resembling Agrippa's
Occult Philosophy, they likely are meant as books that incorporate kabbalistic
technique into a compendium of natural and occult magic. We will never
know exactly what Marlowe had in mind. But that inexactitude is precisely
the point. Faustus presents himself here as quite the up-to-date magician because, like Agrippa and others described earlier in this chapter who take up
Christian kabbalism, he prefers a general, approximate, and imprecise description of what to do with "signs, letters, and characters" to a detailed study of
Jewish learning's sources and meaning. Like Dee's kabbalistic visions, Faustus's will be unsullied by encounters with Jews or even with much in the way
of Hebrew. (Marlowe's departures in this regard from the English Faust book,
where Faustus's acquaintance comprises both Hebrew and Jews, are striking.[123])
Rather, Faustus's attraction to necromantic books depends, like Dee's drawing
of the malleable Monas, on a *style* of Kabbalah: the fact that Kabbalah breaks
larger designs down into their constituent elements and rearranges them.
Faustus seems even to be groping toward the kind of schematized, nonlinguistic, freewheeling Kabbalah-style constructions that Dee hoped to perfect.
Indeed, Faustus's implicit equation of the alphabet with the design content of

magical drawings—"lines, circles, signs, letters, and characters"—implies that it is the shapes of letters, not the content they convey, that attract him.

As Faustus begins his new educational program, he takes steps that resemble training in kabbalistic alchemy. His syllabus seems a textbook blend of the kind of esoteric mastery for which Agrippa aimed, one that included alchemical, astrological, and kabbalistic approaches. First off, instructs his companion magician Cornelius, "He that is grounded in astrology, / Enriched with tongues, well seen in minerals, / Hath all the principles magic doth require" (1.1.140–42). Second, Valdes, the second magician of the pair that advises Faustus, assigns him a veritable reading list in kabbalistic alchemy: "wise Bacon's and Albanus' works, / The Hebrew Psalter, and New Testament" (1.1.156–57). Roger Bacon, a name that evoked for learned early moderns not only natural magic and alchemy but also his early work on mathematics and Hebrew, is yoked with Albanus (Pietro d'Abano, 1257–1316), a physician and astrologer known in Marlowe's day for the (spurious) *Heptameron*, a text on the conjuration of spirits that was appended as early as 1567 to the (also spurious) "Fourth Book" of Agrippa's *Occult Philosophy*. The Pseudo-d'Abano *Heptameron* draws upon a range of late medieval theurgy, especially the *Clavicula Salomonis* and texts like it; but like Agrippa's book, it also includes heavy lashings of Kabbalah, including the invocation of the divine names and the citation of the Tetragrammaton.[124] The combination of Bacon and d'Abano with not only the New Testament but also with the "Hebrew Psalter"—cited frequently in both Jewish and Christian Kabbalah for its useful invocations of the names of God—indicates that Faustus's training will unite natural magic with the project of Christian Kabbalah, in which the New Testament is used to accomplish kabbalistic rereadings of the Old Testament.[125]

When Faustus at first launches his conjurations, he seems to have learned well the combination of linguistic art and physical change that attracted alchemists and magicians to Kabbalah in the first place. Manipulating the name of God by writing "Jehovah's name, / Forward and backward anagrammatised" (1.3.8–9), Faustus also invokes the four Aristotelian elements that alchemists hope to recombine in their great work: "*Ignei, aerii, aquatici, terreni, spiritus, salvete!*" [spirits of fire, air, water, earth, all hail] (1.3.17). The dream of effecting physical change through manipulating the letter of the text is short-lived, however. The remainder of Faustus's career indicates the difficulty of bringing bookish exercise into physical practice. And even when Faustus does undertake actions that overlap with kabbalistic magic, such as his crucial calling up of demonic spirits, he drops the suggestion of alchemy: he does not comprehend how linguistic manipulation may be interlaced with physical transformation. In fact, Faustus retreats, as the play goes along, from the very notion of possessing the power to alter physical substance in any way more permanent or consequential than the detachable-leg joke he pulls on the Horse Courser. Whereas in act 1 Faustus imagines himself as the king of magi, the "great emperor of the world" whose vow to "live in speculation of this art" is inseparable from his aim to "join the hills that bind the Afric shore / And make that land continent to Spain" (1.3.106–115), by act 4 he is cautioning the Holy Roman Emperor that "it is not in my ability to present before your eyes the true substantial bodies of . . . Alexander and his paramour" (4.1.47–55).

The only exception to the rule of Faustus's decreasing power over physical substance seems to be Helen of Troy, who has a body that can be touched. In act 5 Faustus embraces her, kisses her, swears "Here will I dwell, for heaven be in these lips, / And all is dross that is not Helena" (5.1.96–97). Alchemy potentially hovers over Faustus's separation of the heavenly Helen's body from the "dross" of all other physical matter. And yet, in the end Helen comes to Faustus less as body than as text. When Faustus says that "Her lips sucks forth my soul, see where it flies" (5.1.94), Marlowe subtly undercuts the tactility of this passage by making it a tour de force of self-reflexive intertextual citation. Faustus's lines to Helen not only cite Lucian, Homer, and Ovid, they also cite Marlowe himself, both his *Dido Queen of Carthage* and the second part of his *Tamburlaine*.[126] Marlowe thus implies with a wink that Faustus's rapture over Helen is simply another version of ecstatic textual contemplation, one that never lifts its eyes from the page.[127]

Strikingly, however, as the play progresses, Faustus regresses from complex hermeneutics to the kind of magic that barely requires books at all. Rather than anagrammatizing Jehovah's name, for example, Faustus is reduced, by the point at which he is evading the pope's attempts to curse him, to an incantation reversing religious ceremony by reversing its word order, the simplest of magical formulae: "Bell, book, and candle, candle, book, and bell" (3.1.84). Similarly, Faustus is engaged with Helen, but he is not engaged with parsing the texts that bring her to him. As William West puts it, Faustus sees words "as sufficient to interpret and enforce themselves" without his intervention.[128] By this point in the play, Faustus's intellectual regression has him untouched by even the philological habits of humanism. He does no work with words.

Faustus's puzzling textual incompetence begins as early as his opening soliloquy, with his often commented upon incapacity to quote texts from

Aristotle to the Bible either correctly or completely. By the time of his panicked vigil on the night of his damnation, though, Faustus's scholarly shortcomings have taken on a hint specifically of the failure to adopt the kind of skimming techniques that enable Kabbalah, alchemy, magic, and all to be united in the service of a text-based transformation of the physical world. Here, in a scene that obviously mirrors his opening speech, Faustus wants to discard magic just as he initially cast aside other avenues of learning. But more than that, he wishes not to know how to read—or, more precisely, he wishes never to have known how to read: "Though my heart pants and quivers to remember that I have been a student here these thirty years, O, would I had never seen Wittenberg, never read book!" (5.2.18–21). In a way, his wish is granted, as he shows little evidence in this last scene of recollecting the hermeneutic skills required to read any of the books he initially found "ravishing."

And yet, an opportunity to deploy these very hermeneutic skills—picking and choosing among any number of source texts, reinterpreting them to effect a reformulation of the very stuff of the universe—is dangled before Faustus as he approaches his end. This is another moment that potentially conflates the manipulation of text with a transformative materiality:

> See, see where Christ's blood streams in the firmament!
> One drop would save my soul, half a drop.
> . . . .
> Where is it now? 'Tis gone: and see where God
> Stretcheth out his arm and bends his ireful brows!
> Mountains and hills, come, come and fall on me,
> And hide me from the heavy wrath of God!
>
> (5.2.78–85)

To the sight of the material phenomenon of Christ's blood in the heavens, Faustus replies with Hosea's prophecy about what a terrified Israel will plead in the face of God's anger: "they shal say to the mountaines, Cover us, and to the hilles, Fall upon us" (Hosea 10:8). One might imagine, then, that Faustus is doomed simply because he takes the position of the reprobate Jew who witnesses Christ's physical sacrifice only to revert stubbornly to a premessianic text, not realizing that Christ is the Word made flesh.[129]

Yet it is not his quotation of the Hebrew Bible that is Faustus's problem at this point; it is his incapacity to launch a manipulation and reinterpretation of that text after the fashion of Christian Kabbalah. Faustus's hermeneutic deficiencies here are signaled by what happens to his vision of Christ's blood streaming in the firmament. It seems a shocking image, except that early modern Protestants were perfectly comfortable with seeing a nonfigural representation of God in the heavens. That nonfigural representation, however, was typically alphabetical, and typically Hebrew—that is, the Tetragrammaton. As Tessa Watt points out, the Tetragrammaton was "The most frequent image of the deity [in English print] from the 1570s to the 1630s," having taken the place of the representations of God in human form that fell afoul of Protestant iconophobia.[130] In illustrations of biblical and other religious scenes, those Hebrew letters frequently appear in the sky to signify God's watching over his people and his creation. If Faustus sees Christ's blood in the heavens, the pictorial position of the Tetragrammaton, he potentially has already envisioned an act of Christian alchemical Kabbalah: he imagines, in the divine space made familiar by God's unpronounceable Hebrew name, the purest possible substance, the salvational blood of the Savior. According to one formulation of Christian Kabbalah, elaborated upon by Reuchlin and others, Kabbalah in fact originated at the moment at which the angel Raziel informed the newly fallen Adam of Christ's forthcoming sacrifice: "from your seed will be born . . . a hero whose name will in pity contain these four letters—*YHWH*." This revelation to Adam, says Reuchlin, is the first "handing down" of learning that "encapsulates all the principles of Kabbalah."[131] Christ's pity for humankind, the pity that moves him to shed his blood, is encoded in his name, the five-letter YHSWH that is the exfoliation and consummation of the four-letter YHWH.

But Faustus's vision shifts. In a display of what Protestants would have seen as horrific theological recidivism, he turns to a muddle of pre-Christian Judaism and pre-Protestant Christianity. Christ's blood vanishes, replaced not only by the wrathful Old Testament God of the passage from Hosea, but also a God pictorially represented, in Roman Catholic fashion: "see where God / Stretcheth out his arm, and bends his ireful brows!" (5.2.82–83). From Christian Kabbalah's conversion of Jewish hermeneutics into a tool for a Christian purification of the material world, Faustus reverts to a purely textual presentation and finally to a *pre*-textual presentation, a pictorial vision of an anthropomorphic God.

Similarly, Faustus continues in his final scene to evidence the regression from applied alchemy that also marked his encounter with Helen of Troy. Rather than mastering the elements, he wishes that he were merely among them, a physical substance broken down into its constituent parts. In what Edward Snow has evocatively described as a "reverse-birth fantasy," Faustus begs the stars that constitute his horoscope to "draw Faustus like a foggy mist / Into the entrails of yon labouring cloud, / That when you vomit forth into the air, / My limbs may issue from your smoky mouths" (5.2.91–94), and pleads, "Now, body, turn to air, / . . . O soul, be changed into little waterdrops, / And fall into the ocean, ne'er be found!" (5.2.116–19).[132] In aiming to convert himself, body and soul, to the two least localizable of the four Aristotelian elements—water and air—the now anti-alchemical Faustus omits both earth, the element from which Adam was made and from which metals emerge, and fire, the essential tool of the alchemist's art. Now Faustus can imagine fire as good for only one thing: "I'll burn my books" (5.2.123). Reverting to this traditional, even hackneyed, gesture of abjuring magic, Faustus abandons the up-to-date kabbalization of alchemy that, for Dee, marked the new intellectual frontier. He reverts to understanding the book as having thaumaturgic powers as a physical, ritual object, rather than as a receptacle of text that is subject to creative interpretation.[133]

Faustus's hermeneutic regression corresponds to an apparent transformation from overreacher to underreacher that has long troubled critics. Quite possibly, though, Faustus was never terribly interested in or fully capable of questing after omniscience in the first place. Describing Faustus's arc as an urge toward a manageable, circumscribable, fully human self that is the necessary outer bound to an otherwise frighteningly illimitable Marlovian overreaching, Snow offers a sympathetic justification for Faustus's impulse to know *less* as the twenty-four years of his bargain pass.[134] Given Snow's insight, however, we must then attend to exactly the range of options from which Faustus chooses his limitations. His is not, I have been arguing, a choice simply between trying to know everything and settling for knowing nothing. Rather, through a synthetic magic that includes everything from alchemy to the Zohar, Faustus is exposed to a third scholarly option: a reading practice that, claiming transcendent omniscience, has as its open secret the fact that its omniscience depends on selective ignorance. A Christian Kabbalah, as I have described it, offers just this means of knowing less, of skimming or even of not learning one's source material as preface to making up a pleasing scheme and taking that scheme to the project of transforming the physical world.

As a notorious misquoter and selective quoter of the texts he reads, Faustus has surely, at the beginning of the play, already shown some talent for the humanistic techniques of skimming and snippetizing that Christian Kabbalah requires. Paul Budra plausibly suggests that Faustus—like Dee with his Hebrew primers—was always more interested in *having* books than *reading* them.[135] By seemingly failing, then, through the course of his career, to apply a readerly training that includes Christian Kabbalah, Faustus has not merely become more stupid, more limited. He has become less *usefully* stupid, less *usefully* limited. Faustus's shortcoming is not, as some critics have suggested, that he becomes a worse scholar as the play progresses; it is that he does not become the best kind of bad scholar, the humanist who limits the learning she absorbs as a means of making a better argument.[136] In other words, the odd retro nature of *Doctor Faustus* is established not only by such features as its old-fashioned magic, its morality play framework, and its devolution of absolute power into childish pranks. It is also established by Faustus's failure to adopt an up-to-date intellectual strategy. Choosing sheer ignorance over strategic ignorance, Faustus misses out on the way that late humanism and its skills of disknowledge could save his very soul.

Prospero's Golem

As Shakespeare's reply to Marlowe's magus figure, Prospero, the magus monarch in *The Tempest*, engineers a plot of redemptive endings that not only corrects Faustus's failures but ought to satisfy John Dee's wildest dreams. If Faustus strains to understand, at the end of his play, how he might still partake of a salvation offered to all, Prospero has no difficulty in offering that salvation to all those who ask for pardon. If Faustus drops the natural magic that brings linguistic manipulation to bear on physical transformation, Prospero accomplishes the reconciliations at the end of *The Tempest* through a natural magic that is both cosmic and terrestrial, and that serves, like Dee's Monas, both as an esoteric theory and as a set of practical applications. Whatever reading practices it takes to put Dee's mathematically perfect, cosmic alchemy into place, Prospero seems, if we believe the way he tells it, to have perfected them. All those years in Milan spent "transported / And rapt in secret studies" seem to have paid off.[137]

Among its many other sources, Prospero's magic is, I shall shortly argue, derived in part from Christian Kabbalah, and thus also depends upon the deliberate ignorance of their learning's Jewish heritage that marks the common practice of Christian kabbalists. Yet in spite of the fact that Prospero seems to have a much less fraught relationship to intellectual endeavor than Faustus does—no critics question Prospero's scholarship as they do Faustus's—Prospero's demonstrably well-honed capacities for skimming are more undermined than Faustus's are. As if in reply to *Doctor Faustus*, *The Tempest* exposes the fact that book learning is not a deracinated acquisition. Unlike in Dee's or Faustus's study, on Prospero's island applied textuality exists only alongside and by means of the cultural other from whom one has taken that text. With these juxtapositions, Shakespeare's play raises difficult questions about the Christian assimilation of kabbalistic practice. The magus can skim Kabbalah, but can he skim over the Jew from whose culture Kabbalah came? What happens when he tries to?

To understand how *The Tempest* insists upon these questions, we must begin with how the play engages one compelling and long-lived fantasy of an early modern alchemical Kabbalah. This is the fantasy that came to be known in later centuries as the making of the golem: an artificial man fashioned of clay and brought to life through alphabetical manipulations of the Tetragrammaton. Like Julia Lupton, whose reading of *The Tempest* I discuss below, I see the Renaissance idea of the golem manifesting itself in the play's interest in Caliban's creatureliness, or the question of what he is and how he came to be.[138] Prospero's desire to see and use Caliban as his own creation not only connects the Prospero-Caliban relationship to Prospero's more generically Kabbalah-style esoteric techniques, but also challenges the extent to which Christian Kabbalah can comfortably appropriate a Jewish-derived hermeneutic system.

While the word *golem* was not yet in common use in the late sixteenth and early seventeenth centuries, several central aspects of the golem legend were in circulation, including the central conceit that the rabbi calls a spirit into the ready receptacle of a human-made earthen figure. The rabbi employs the *sefirot* as outlined in the Sefer Yetzirah (the Book of Creation) first to animate the creature made from dust, and then to de-animate him. Meaning something like "unformed" or "amorphous" in Hebrew, *golem* appears in the Hebrew Bible only in Psalm 139:15–16, a psalm that, as Scholem notes, was traditionally ascribed to Adam himself: "My bones are not hid from thee, thogh I was made in a secret place, & facioned beneth in the earth. Thine eyes did se me, when I was without forme."[139] Making a golem does not necessarily mean stepping into God's role of making man. In the first formulations of the story, the rabbi intends only the ecstatic contemplation of the divine, not the hubristic usurpation of divine creation.[140] The making of the golem acquired early on a warning about human presumption, however. The most famous version of this warning seems not to have been part of the story until the seventeenth and eighteenth centuries: after the golem goes on a rampage, his maker is obliged to deanimate him by erasing or rewriting the Hebrew letters that, written on the golem's forehead, bring it to life. In reaching up to perform this task, the rabbi is crushed by the weight of fallen mud.[141] But the version of the golem legend that was indubitably known in England in the sixteenth century involves an even more frightening possibility than the golem's physically endangering its maker—that is, the golem's capacity to alter its own linguistically determined identity. Reuchlin describes how after Jeremiah goes about making a golem, the golem subsequently manipulates the letters that animate him into a rebuke of his creator:

> On the forehead of this newly created man was written *YHVH ALHYM* [Elohim] *AMTh*, i.e. "God the Tetragrammaton is true." The man felt the writing on his forehead and without hesitation moved his hand and removed and destroyed the first letter in *AMTh*, which is aleph. There remained then these words: *YHVH ALHYM Mth*, meaning "God the Tetragrammaton is dead." Jeremiah was struck with indignation, tore his clothes and asked him: "Why do you take the aleph from Emeth?" He replied: "Because everywhere men have failed in faithfulness to the Creator who created you in his own image and likeness."[142]

The golem rebukes its maker less for usurping God's creation of Adam than for doing it badly. Having not shaped even himself as a faithful copy of God, the kabbalist is hardly qualified to make yet more creatures that would be even poorer duplicates of the divine.

The crucial element of creating a golem, then, becomes one of ethical standing and moral responsibility. And here is where the relation between Kabbalah and Christianity gets a bit dicey. The medieval Jewish instructions for creating a golem are clear on the fact that a golem falls short of human completeness, lacking such crucial components as ensoulment and human speech. In contrast, Christian Kabbalah, influenced by the Neoplatonic Hermeticism that encourages human participation in divine activity, muddles the issue enough to make the status of the golem's soul a live question.[143] For this reason, it is the rare magus indeed whose conscience is pure and purpose upright enough to qualify him to undertake creating a golem. The use of Kabbalah to animate earthen matter with a human soul puts the kabbalist in a more elevated but also more precarious position than that of an ordinary magus who merely fashions some kind of simple artificial man. In the latter case, unmaking the thing you have created is no difficult operation—as in the late medieval legend where Thomas Aquinas, who aids Albertus Magnus in animating a molded statue and putting it to work as an assistant, ends up smashing the statue to pieces, "meerely because he could not endure its excesse of prating."[144] To make a golem, in contrast, is possibly to make what the late sixteenth-century Italian kabbalist Abraham Yagel insisted was a "perfect man"—that is, one "infused also with spirit and soul."[145] And once you have made such a creature, it is your responsibility: you are all at once its parent, its owner, its God.

One way of settling the uneasy ethics of this position is to reimagine the golem as a possession. In the fifteenth- and sixteenth-century elaborations of the story by German Hasidim, the golem acquired the status of a servant, a man (or woman) of all work, even a slave. Much preferable to a human servant who has a will of its own, the golem as slave may without compunction be unmade when rebellious or dismantled when no longer needed. Writing around 1625, rabbi and physician Joseph Solomon Delmedigo reported the legend that the eleventh-century poet and philosopher Solomon ibn Gabirol "created a woman who waited on him. When he was denounced to the government [evidently for magic], he proved that she was not a real, whole creature, but consisted only of pieces of wood and hinges, and reduced her to her original components."[146]

In Prospero's eyes, that handy golem ought to be his slave Caliban. Prospero's magic derives from many sources, and its nature is not terribly precise, but a number of elements in and surrounding the play—Shakespeare's debt to Agrippa's *Occult Philosophy*, the satirical hay the King's Men had already made of John Dee in Ben Jonson's *The Alchemist*, and *The Tempest*'s generous use of both alchemical and angel-summoning language—combine to imply that Prospero imagines himself as an alchemical-hermetical-kabbalistic magus in the mode of Agrippa and Dee.[147] Prospero's claims of imitating God and mastering nature, his occasional Kabbalah-style manipulation of language (as I will discuss shortly), and his practical application of his skills support this reading.[148] While Prospero is not primarily or specifically a kabbalist, his treatment of Caliban manifests how Shakespeare taps into the constellation of desires, skills, and materials that overlap with and inform the golem legend. Prospero hopes, beyond all rationality, that Caliban is a creature made, not born. Prospero's first summoning of his slave, in fact, reads like a *summoning* in the kabbalistic sense of calling a spirit into a clay figure: "What ho! slave! Caliban! / Thou *earth*, thou" (1.2.314–15; emphasis added).[149] Caliban's account of how Miranda taught him language further suggests that, as far as Prospero and his daughter are concerned, Caliban was not initially human. He had to be made so. Even Prospero's grudging admission that the island was "honoured with / A human shape" before his and Miranda's arrival includes his hopeful qualification that Caliban is perhaps only a human *shape* rather than exactly human (1.2.283–84).

Prospero's indecision about whether Caliban was born or made corresponds to various characters' indecision about whether Caliban is currently fully formed or not yet shaped, a man or a fish, alive or dead, manservant or man-monster. Lupton identifies this ambivalence with Caliban's status as a "creature," a primal man continually in the state of emerging from base matter into higher intelligence, but never quite emerged. In this creaturely state, says Lupton, Caliban resides on the threshold between the never-human golem and the fully human Adam, both primordial creatures made of earth.[150] In kabbalistic terms, he is the Adam Kadmon: the "earth-spirit" state that Adam occupied in the hours between when God formed him and when God animated him with a soul.[151] In connection to Lupton's point, though, it is important to note that, if Caliban is created rather than begotten, the responsibility to bring him further into full humanity lies with his creator, Prospero. When he discusses techniques for making a golem, thirteenth-century Spanish kabbalist Abraham Abulafia stresses that "every wise person ought to make souls much more than he ought to make bodies, since the duty of making bodies is [solely] intended to make souls, and thereby man will imitate his maker."[152] And indeed Prospero does report that he initiated the development of Caliban's soul, teaching him from the first chapter of Genesis "To name the bigger light and how the less / That burn by day and night" (1.2.336–37). But he cut the lesson short when Caliban attempted to rape Miranda, confining Caliban in a "hard rock" (1.2.344) in a way that makes him resemble the boar in book 3 of Edmund Spenser's *Faerie Queene*, the libidinal force "emprisoned . . . / In a strong rocky Caue" beneath the Mount of Venus.[153] Golems are sterile, and Prospero makes sure that Caliban remains so.[154] It is thus Prospero who attempts to arrest Caliban in the state of golemhood, a creature not only forever enslaved but also forever defined by a corporeality that is not its own to manage.

Caliban's very corporeality, however, puts pressure on how successful Prospero has been at relegating Caliban to golem status, and this circumstance in turn, as we shall ultimately see, puts pressure on how successful Prospero has been at implementing the redemptive universal scheme that Dee imagines as the goal of Christian, alchemical Kabbalah. For Caliban, of course, is not Prospero's creature. He has desires that exceed Prospero's, including the desire to procreate and the desire to reclaim the island to which his mother immigrated. These specific wishes, for procreation and for new territory, do not code Caliban as the golem Prospero hopes him to be. Rather, they identify him with the source of the golem legend and of other kabbalistic learning—that is, with the Jews. Not the Jews as a source of fascinating texts but the Jews as a race of people who, to the horror of sixteenth- and seventeenth-century Christian thinkers, seemed only to be multiplying. With the increase in religious persecution in the sixteenth century and especially the expulsion of Jews from Spain, formerly self-contained Jewish communities were forced to disband and migrate across Europe and the Near East, a circumstance that caused Christian Europeans to notice a growing Jewish physical presence. Further, Jewish birthrates in the early modern period were (incorrectly) perceived as considerably higher than those in neighboring Christian households, so that emigrant Jewish communities had the reputation of spreading not only by means of peripateticism but also through a sheer increase in numbers.[155] Having emigrated in utero from Algiers to a new world where he hoped to couple with Prospero's daughter and to have "peopled . . . / This isle with Calibans" (1.2.351–52), Caliban as Jew plans to be the most successful representative of the diaspora in both respects, travel and reproduction.

In identifying the ways Caliban is coded as Jewish, I am entering a decades-long discussion about Caliban's race. Lupton's reading, it is important to note, rejects the terms of this discussion. In reading Caliban as a "creature," a golem, a preensouled Adam who has not yet fully entered into covenant with God, Lupton also argues that Caliban "embodies the antediluvian moment before *ethnos*."[156] Lupton's argument, however, assumes that Caliban's "thingness" is something inherent, and thus she relieves Prospero of the responsibility of having assigned Caliban the role of golem-slave. But it is Prospero and the other Europeans who call Caliban a "thing." And the qualities of "thingness" that they ascribe to him are identifiable early modern stereotypes of Jewishness: for example, that Jews were dark-skinned, and that they stank.[157]

Naturally, such racial and ethnic slurs were applied to groups other than Jews, and their application to Caliban is typical of the early modern imprecision regarding racial otherness.[158] In the context of the kabbalistic magic Prospero employs, however, imputing "thingness" to the Jew performs an important ideological function that does not apply, in European eyes, to the case of other racial and ethnic groups like Native Americans: it divides Jews from their intellectual heritage and intellectual productivity. The implicit reasoning follows this path. If Jews are things, not engaged human minds, and if Jewish books have good ideas, and if good ideas belong to engaged minds, then Jewish books belong to Christians, not to Jews. When Prospero makes Caliban his golem, he tacitly agrees with Calvin's argument that Jews who remain Jews after the advent of Christ are solely "carnal"—that is to say, neither spiritual nor properly textual, but limited to corporeal rituals and corporeal pleasures.[159]

The relation between Caliban and language is, as a result, ethnically over-determined. If, as Stephen Greenblatt argues, Prospero and the European visitors to his island energetically participate in early modern efforts to denigrate or deny the linguistic capacity of the (supposedly) nonliterate cultures that Europeans found in the New World, they also carry out Martin Luther's resolution, mentioned at the beginning of this chapter, to deprive Jews of the learning they have produced but supposedly do not deserve.[160] These efforts to deny language to Indians and written wisdom to Jews are not mutually exclusive, however. While critics have been tussling for years about *The Tempest*'s geographical location and Caliban's ethnicity, it is important to note that early modern Europeans did not see New World Indians and Old World Jews as wholly separate racial groups.[161] (We might guess this blurred boundary from the linguistic slippage of the word *tribe*, which in the sixteenth and seventeenth centuries primarily denoted the tribes of Israel but which was later transferred to the "tribes" of the Native Americans.[162]) Indeed, what some Europeans saw when they saw Indians was the Ten Lost Tribes of Israel, the ur-Jews who, in an unusual instance of self-willed Jewish diaspora, wrongheadedly broke off from the House of David to set up their own kingdom. European explorers expected to find the Ten Lost Tribes just about everywhere they went in the world, and Columbus was confident enough that he would meet them that when he made up a party of his men to reconnoiter the interior of Hispaniola, he included Luís de Torres, a *converso* who said he knew Hebrew, to serve as interpreter.[163]

While this identification of the New World natives with the Ten Lost Tribes was based on wishful thinking, it also relied on nascent modes of comparative linguistics and anthropology. Some European observers thought the gutturals of Native American languages sounded like those of Hebrew, and others that Native American tribes and Jews had similar social and religious practices, such as male circumcision and cannibalism.[164] Others noticed similarities in character; for example, the Spanish Dominican (and ultimately grand inquisitor) Gregorio Garcia's point-by-point comparison from 1607 describes both Jews and Indians as fearful, cowardly, skeptical of divine miracles, ungrateful, and lacking in charity to the poor and infirm.[165] Finally, both Jews and Indians are especially well suited to servitude, argued Christian Europeans, because behind many of these presumed commonalities—cannibalism, unrefined speech, bad manners, and so on—lies the assumption that the Indian and the Judean share a mental incapacity to recognize what is truly valuable, the pearl of great price.[166] Ungrateful, cannibalistic, rude: such attributes do not designate Caliban as *solely* a Jew, but they mesh both with the unfixedness of Caliban's racial and geographical origins and with the attempts of Prospero and Miranda to assign him a servile, distinctly non-Christian, perhaps even subhuman identity as a member of an unspecified "vile race" (1.2.359).[167]

The attributes that associate Caliban with the Ten Lost Tribes, however, reinscribe Prospero's moral responsibility toward him. Christian Europeans were intrigued by the possibility of the New World Indians as New World Jews because they saw them as a welcome alternative to Old World Jews, who had proved themselves stubbornly reprobate in the face of Christ's offered salvation. Indians were Jews who deserved a second chance since they had, through geographic and temporal accident, missed out on Christian enlightenment. At the end of *The Tempest* we find a Caliban who seems to be ripe for this Christian change of heart if only Prospero will entertain the notion. But Prospero continues to insist upon the "salvage" Caliban's unsalvageable nature, calling him

> a born devil, on whose nature
> Nurture can never stick; on whom my pains,
> Humanely taken—all, all lost, quite lost!
>
> (4.1.188–90)

Despite Caliban's promise to "seek for grace" (5.1.296), Prospero does not promise forgiveness in return, but instead merely notes that Caliban ought to "*look* / To have [his] pardon" sometime in the indefinite future (5.1.293–94; emphasis added). Combined with his calling Caliban a "born devil," Prospero's deferral of pardon suggests that Prospero waffles on his responsibility for having made Caliban right. If Caliban were truly his golem, then it is Prospero's fault that Caliban has run amok. Indeed, that is the moral of the golem story. If Caliban is born, not made, however, then Prospero's obligation is to enact Christian forgiveness and perhaps even Christian conversion. Evading both these morals, Prospero washes his hands of someone he declares a "born devil," a phrase that designates Caliban as neither Prospero's creature nor a convertible soul.

His own moral abnegation, however, means that Prospero has another problem on his hands: he becomes a magus whose Christian appropriation of Jewish learning, unlike John Dee's or Doctor Faustus's, is challenged by the presence of a living Jew. Caliban, admittedly, is not the kind of Jewish scholar whose consultation services were increasingly demanded by early modern Christians seeking access to the Hebrew Bible or to Kabbalah, and whose input seemed to open the floodgates to the Judaizing feared by the likes of Luther or of Hebraist and Protestant divine Hugh Broughton, who warned that ever since Edward Barton, the first English ambassador to Constantinople, "moved a principal Rabbi at Stanpol, to write to England for Ebrew explication of our Gospel, the Jewes of Prage, Francfurt, Hanaw & others bestir themselves" to undermine Christianity. Still, any Jew—learned or not—seems to embody the same threat. Broughton warns in the same passage that "Jewes scattered over the world," of whatever type, provoke Christians to unbelief.[168] Born devils indeed in Broughton's eyes, Jews both learned and unlearned alike, the very *fact* of them, beset the Christian scholar who attempts to make use of Jewish scholarship. Such was the problem that Dee attempted to solve with his magical, symbolic Monas, which, he imagined, would effect a universal conversion of the Jews even though it was not based in Hebrew and did not require consultation with Jewish scholars. The user of Dee's Monas need not even leave home: he may bring about universal Christianity while ensconced in his well-stocked library. No need, in Dee's view, to ask Jews for their opinions, no need to "travel to the inhabitants of India or America"—presumed locales of the Ten Lost Tribes—for his work.[169]

Unlike Dee, Prospero has already had to leave home to establish his magus's realm, and in *The Tempest*'s last act and epilogue we see how difficult Prospero finds it to make that realm comport with Dee's vision of an irenic alchemical empire. With Caliban seemingly permanently present, perhaps even on the verge of returning to Italy with the others of Old World stock, Prospero seems to fumble his technique. On the one hand, as we have seen, Prospero wants to disclaim responsibility for the stubborn reprobate who is not amenable to Christian teaching. On the other hand, though, Prospero seems to try once again to reduce Caliban to merely a golem—"this thing of darkness"—who can be unmade at the kabbalist's will. Prospero's attempt to unmake the golem through the classic kabbalistic strategy of reversing letters may be heard in the sound of his reversed syllables as he says to the Italian nobles about the play's troublemakers,

> Two of these fellows you
> Must *know* and *own*; this thing of darkness I
> Ac*know*ledge mine.
>
> (5.1.274–76; emphasis added)

The strategy is no doubt a maladroit one, since to vocalize a spell forward, then backward, then forward—*know*, *own*, *know*—is surely to reinscribe it.[170] Nevertheless, we hear here Prospero's attempt to annul Caliban's body by asserting control over text, a spell that may be unsaid in the same way that the inscription on the golem's forehead may be erased. Caliban's response, however—"I shall be pinched to death"—indicates exactly the limits of Prospero's power: upon Prospero's curse Caliban will not be unmade, but merely (if seriously) annoyed (5.1.276). In remaining a stubbornly evident Jewish body on Prospero's stage, Caliban stands, as Jeffrey Shoulson puts it in regard to the work of John Milton, as a reality principle: "the Jew's body represents that element of the text, that element of lived experience, which is necessarily unassimilable."[171]

Prospero further fumbles the technique of a good Christian kabbalist in being unable to manage his book collection in a way that is quite similar to Faustus's disregard of his books. As *The Tempest* progresses, Prospero mysteriously divests himself of books. We know that Prospero came to the island furnished with a number of volumes, books he says he "prize[s] above [his] dukedom" (1.2.168). Caliban reminds Stephano several times that in order to kill Prospero, he must

> Remember
> First to possess his books; for without them
> He's but a sot, as I am, nor hath not
> One spirit to command.
>
> (3.2.91–94)

Given how crucial these books are supposed to be, it is odd that Prospero seems to lose possession of them without even noticing. Near the end of the play he pledges to drown his single "book" (5.1.57). What happened to all the rest? It is a striking moment in a play that, as Barbara Mowat has argued, is notably bookish, where the very speech in which Prospero renounces his magic is an ostentatious quotation of a passage from Ovid's *Metamorphoses* that was in turn cited by the likes of Agrippa.[172] Despite opposing its successful magus to *Doctor Faustus*'s damned conjurer, *The Tempest* seems to be recapitulating the structure of Marlowe's play in this regard. From his whole library of essential reading, including the "necromantic books" that ravished him at the play's beginning (1.1.52), Faustus first reduces himself to the one comprehensive magic book that Mephistopheles gives him and then loses even that single book, which falls without his noticing into the hands of his clownish servants. When Faustus resolves with almost his last breath to burn his books, then, we wonder whether he has anything left to burn. Prospero's inattention to his books is even more remarkable than Faustus's: they are so unimportant to him that, as James Kearney points out, they are never even seen on stage.[173]

Prospero's mysterious deaccessioning of his books relates to his inept kabbalistic utterances in that both prove him incapable, as Faustus is incapable, of implementing a reading practice that would fully achieve what he wants. If skimming is a late-humanist mode of reading, modifying humanist ideals of being steeped in books, then Prospero, like Faustus, seemingly reverts to an outdated mode of intellectual activity when he posits his choice as being that of a well-read book or no book at all. But whereas Faustus's failure to implement skimming as a new form of learning seems to be a matter of personal temperament, the disposition of a man who is happier when more limited, Prospero's similar failure is felt more as a matter of cultural and scholarly impasse. Prospero's fantasy is also the collective fantasy of his learned culture: that an absolute distinction-in-similarity may be made between Jewish Kabbalah and a Christian kabbalistic alchemy. And yet Caliban's stubborn physical proximity to Prospero in the last scene of the play—a juxtaposition that can be very striking in stage productions—makes it impossible to forget the Jew's proximity to the Christian humanist. When Caliban proves to be not a golem who can be unmade—that is to say, when he proves to be not merely Prospero's intellectual construct—he thus lays bare the flaws both of the seamless social body Prospero imagines and of the intellectual corpus underlying Prospero's magic.

That troubled intellectual corpus, in turn, associates Caliban's nonincorporability with the crisis of humanist syncretism in the late sixteenth and early seventeenth centuries. S. A. Farmer, editor of Pico's *Conclusiones*, points out that the dream of syncretism started dying almost as soon as it was born, done in by factors that made it impossible to imagine easily absorbing every form of exciting, newly discovered knowledge into an expansive humanist Christianity. Too many new texts were being printed and disseminated; too many ideological suspicions were aroused by unfamiliar modes of learning. And if one prop in the syncretic system were pulled down, the entire structure might tumble: "due to the increasingly systematic correspondences resonating in [syncretic] systems, any assault on any one part of them—whether of a political, religious, empirical, or philological nature—potentially, at least, became an attack on them as a whole."[174] As the sixteenth century wore on, these strains became all the more evident. Beyond Kabbalah, myriad other types of new learning were not amenable to humanist incorporation—for example, New World learning, as Halpern points out.[175] For incorporating such challenging new knowledge into a Christian intellectual world view, even skimming may not suffice.

An even more innovative solution to the problem of unassimilable learning than skimming has already been suggested by one early reader of Reuchlin's *De arte cabalistica*. In a letter written in response to Erasmus's sending him a copy of Reuchlin's book, John Colet remarks, "Of books and knowledge there is no end," echoing Ecclesiastes 1:18 on the futility of wisdom. He makes this weary comment in the context of having read *De arte cabalistica* and wishing he hadn't. Wouldn't it be easier, Colet suggests, to attain the purity and holiness promised by Kabbalah simply "by an ardent love and imitation of Jesus Christ"? If so, then one would be better off skipping Reuchlin entirely: "leaving detours, let us take a short road to attain it quickly."[176] By "leaving detours," Colet surely means leaving off reading Jewish books, but his phrasing suggests leaving off reading entirely.

Colet inadvertently anticipates the practice of experimental science in the second half of the seventeenth century, whose method was involved less with repeating results (since results were seldom repeatable) and more with displaying results in a public, shared space.[177] A different—and more familiar—form of posthumanist knowledge making than John Dee's manipulation of nonlinguistic symbols and schema, social gathering and social witnessing need no book at all. As *The Tempest* comes to a close, Prospero begins to feel his way forward to this newer mode of making and confirming knowledge, one that transforms his magic from a bookish discipline to a presentist, spectacular, social one. This advance is marked by the shift to the epilogue, in which Prospero asks the audience to join him in a different, experimental kind of happy ending. Having divested himself of his magic, Prospero now famously cedes magical power to the audience, who he hopes will release him from "this bare island, by [their] spell" (Epi.8). Both their and his current work is not the kind of magic he has hitherto undertaken, one that derives from the long textual heritage of Agrippa, Marlowe, and the rest. Rather, in the epilogue Prospero commits himself to the theatrically public display of results:

> Gentle breath of yours my sails
> Must fill, or else my project fails,
> Which was to please.
>
> (Epi.11–13)

As with the experimental scientist's public show, we will know if Prospero's "project" has been successful only through the audience's voiced agreement.

Here, somewhat unexpectedly, is where Prospero's new experiment reveals itself to be alchemical. The use of *project* as a noun meaning purpose or objective was relatively new to English in the early seventeenth century. (The first citation in the *Oxford English Dictionary* is from Richard Mulcaster's *Elementarie* of 1582.[178]) While the new sense of the word as "an objective" was derived from several older usages of *project*—including the act of schematic drawing (or the drawing itself), and the act of imagining or "putting forth"— it also drew from alchemy, for which the *projection* is the moment at which the work is bound to succeed, the moment at which the philosopher's stone touches base material and turns it into gold.[179] As Pamela Smith demonstrates, once alchemy had associated *projection* with the accomplishment of its aims, *project* began to mean not just a schematic drawing or table, nor just an imaginative act, but also an intellectual concept that could then shape the material world.[180]

Smith's account of alchemical "projectors" is titled *The Business of Alchemy*: she demonstrates how the alchemist is competing, in a courtly world, with engineering, economic, mercantile, and other kinds of "projects" that aim to monetize knowledge. At the same time as *project* was shifting its meaning from alchemy to the more general idea of scheme or plan, it was also acquiring commercial resonances. These are not mutually exclusive uses of the word, of course, since alchemical schemes were often designed as commercial moneymakers.[181] The word *project* thus helps indicate how Prospero's alchemy shifts in the epilogue to a different kind of enterprise, one that is all at once commercial, alchemical, experimental, and social. The last time Prospero noted the imminent completion of his "project," at the beginning of act 5, he was following the magical-alchemical-kabbalistic agenda by the book, uniting the manipulation of words and the manipulation of material substance: "Now does my project gather to a head. / My charms crack not; my spirits obey" (5.1.1–2).[182] Words still matter in Prospero's epilogue, but they matter differently than they did in his former project. Now, "spells" are formed by means of the emanated breath of a paying audience—in approval, in prayer—rather than by means of scholarly exercises in language such as rearranging Hebrew letters. Unlike Prospero's previous speeches regarding his art, his epilogue features no intertextual allusions. His abilities in the epilogue depend upon a language that is made only in this moment, this *now*—a word used three times in twenty lines.

The Tempest's epilogue thus bestows upon theater a new variety of dis-knowledge, one that substitutes a body of people and a body of shared experience for a corpus of failed texts. Prospero's insistence upon the "now" seems like his final revision of his earlier "know/own" anagram. Know-own-*now*: the shift from knowledge to ownership to the unbookish present suggests that, having failed in mastering predecessor texts, Prospero now finds his freedom in using none. The freedom is one to move from the solitary cell of the scholar to the communal arena of the commercial theater. Unlike in act 5's final scene with Caliban, pardon here is dispensed not via a mysterious hermeneutics that requires the magus's mastery and invention but via an improvised contract for a future exchange that is both the social space of the experimental laboratory, and a tit-for-tat trade between theatrical spectacle and paying customers: "As you from crimes would pardoned be, / Let your indulgence set me free" (Epi.19–20).

Undertaking alchemy without book, Prospero pushes past skimming into a new frontier. The craft of scholarly sloth, the art of skimming Kabbalah, gives way to the genteel "indulgence" of mutual benefit; the magus with the large (if partly unread) library gives way to the audience who needs no book; the intricacies of kabbalistic method give way to the undifferentiated din of applause. This bookish play resolves, in the end, into the one Shakespearean play with a wholly original plot.[183] The one play for which our author, for once, did not make a show of having even skimmed his source.

CHAPTER 4

How to Avoid Gynecology

Structured to showcase the triumph of nature over art, Ben Jonson's 1616 masque *Mercury Vindicated from the Alchemists at Court* begins with an exasperated and complaining Mercury being tortured by alchemy, represented by "a troupe of threadbare Alchemists" and a group of "imperfect creatures, with helms of limbecks on their heads." The scene then dissolves to "a glorious bower, wherein Nature [is] placed with Prometheus at her feet."[1] With Prometheus's help, Nature demonstrates that the twelve courtly masquers, accompanied by their ladies, are her offspring, not alchemy's: "Nature [is] here no stepdame, but a mother" (183).

So far, so good. But even while it demonstrates nature's superiority to an enterprise whose practitioners "abuse the curious and credulous nation of metal-men through the world" (44–45), *Mercury Vindicated* seems anxious about one remaining arena of competition between alchemy and nature: the generation of humankind. It is easy for Mercury to mock alchemists' medicinal and cosmetological promises. He has a slightly more difficult time, though, dismissing perhaps the most audacious claim that alchemy ever made: that it could create human beings.

Mercury first brings up alchemy as a maker of men as a point of derision. Alchemists, says Mercury, claim they can "produce men, beyond the deeds of Deucalion or Prometheus (of which one, they say, had the philosophers' stone and threw it over his shoulder, the other the fire, and lost it)" (120–23). But in fact the only men the alchemists have created are the kinds of men who are shaped in venues of courtly or urban artificiality: "a master of the duel"; an astrologer or "supposed secretary to the stars"; and "a broker in suits"—either lawsuits, or second-hand clothes (132–53). These kinds of men are not, Mercury assures us, "Paracelsus' man . . . that he promised you out of white bread and deal-wine" (129–31). The sardonic reference here is to *De natura rerum*, a treatise attributed to Paracelsus that was notorious in Jonson's day for its instructions on how to create an actual person. If you heat human sperm in an alchemical vessel, says *De natura rerum*, you can make a homunculus. No, counters Mercury: the men that the alchemists can make at court are not Pseudo-Paracelsus's parthenogenetic homunculus. But such an assertion is not exactly the same thing as saying that Pseudo-Paracelsus's homunculus cannot be made at all. Indeed, *Mercury Vindicated* ends with Nature worrying that the ladies at court are not inclined to do their part in generating human beings the old-fashioned way: " 'Tis yet with them but beauty's noon, / They would not grandams be too soon" (206–7). If the women will not do their reproductive duty, Pseudo-Paracelsus's artificial offspring may be the only alternative.

Interpreting the fantasized equivalence of human reproduction and alchemical production requires gauging the status of the fantasy of masculine parthenogenesis. On the one hand, as we will see in this chapter, parthenogenesis has considerable hold on the early modern mind as a workaround for the seeming feminine mastery of the reproductive process. On the other hand, alchemy's reputation for folly can be deployed to expose the parthenogenetic dream as folly, too. When writers like Jonson both air and mock the fantasy of male parthenogenesis in terms of alchemy, they are conjoining a theory of physical change that, to many, seemed preposterous with a theory of human reproduction that was equally so.

The stakes of such exposure are high. As silly as Pseudo-Paracelsus's early modern version of test-tube babies may seem, the academic study of anatomy in late sixteenth- and seventeenth-century England continued to be committed, to a surprising extent, to a hybrid Aristotelian-Galenic model of human reproduction that is, in many ways, only a somewhat less extreme vision of male parthenogenesis. That model, too, demonstrates disknowledge in action in that it substitutes a questionable theory for others more plausible. As scholars have recently shown, and as I will discuss further, alternative and far more sensible theories of human reproduction were readily available in England and were also widely accepted. To continue to adhere to, elaborate, and refine the long-standing Aristotelian-Galenic model, then, represents not an inevitability but a choice: the choice to be wrong rather than right. To borrow a crucial word from Stanley Cavell—a borrowing whose significance I will discuss fully later in this chapter—that choice is the *avoidance* of knowledge.

Like the Christian kabbalists discussed in Chapter 3 who used Jewish books, early modern anatomists were engaged in book-bound learning that required them to assess and to incorporate (or reject) predecessor texts. Nancy Siraisi, Peter Dear, and others describe the work of early modern anatomy as a complex and often fraught interchange between a humanistic reverence for classical learning and empirical demonstrations of how Galen, Aristotle, and other paradigmatic classical authors on medicine got it wrong.[2] My interest in this chapter, as in my discussion of early modern matter theory in Chapter 2, is how the imagery of alchemy is used to signal the intellectual quandary that often results in the transition from old learning to new. I focus in this chapter on how some early modern English authors identify alchemy not simply with the fantasy of parthenogenesis but with the choice to believe that fantasy even when better explanations abound.

In the first section of this chapter I discuss the unexpected conjunctions of alchemy and anatomy in the context of early modern academic medicine's reluctance to acknowledge active feminine participation in human reproduction, and sometimes even its reluctance to acknowledge the sheer existence of the external female genitalia. My discussion here examines how alchemical imagery serves anatomists such as William Harvey and Helkiah Crooke in excluding women from an active role in the generation of children and even from the realm of knowability. Such a use for alchemy, however, has already been anticipated by Edmund Spenser's *Faerie Queene*, the focus of this chapter's second section. *The Faerie Queene*'s "marriage books" (books 3, 4, and 5) couple the fate of desired and desiring women like Florimell and Britomart with versions of alchemical reproduction, some of which, for all their absurdity, seem preferable for the poem's male characters to female fecundity. From Spenser's sharply critical commentary on the avoidance of gynecology, I turn to William Shakespeare's more ambivalent examination of the intellectual process and the intellectual venues that are required for the avoidance of female reproductive capacity: the alchemically inflected all-male academy of *Love's Labour's Lost*.

Alchemical Gynecologies and Epistemic Choice in William Harvey and Helkiah Crooke

As it did with other topics, early modern alchemy tracked the humanist use of classical learning when it came to thinking about how matter originates and grows. Humanist practice meant that alchemical theory hewed to classical tradition for this purpose—but hewing to classical tradition often meant borrowing from multiple and even contradictory strands of classical theories of mineralogy and of sexual reproduction. In the first instance, medieval and early modern alchemists declared that their theories, contrary to critics' detractions, adhered in orthodox fashion to the Aristotelian description of how metals are formed in the earth. Aristotle's *Meteorologica* describes metal as one of the products that results when the sun's heat produces "exhalations" of two sorts in the earth, moist and dry. When trapped in the earth, moist exhalations encounter the dry exhalations contained within rocks and congeal into metal.[3] With some modifications of Aristotle's account—for example, interpreting the moist exhalations as mercury and the dry exhalations as sulfur—alchemists could claim that their operations, using fire to replicate the heat of the sun, simply accelerate what takes nature many years. This version of alchemical theory has the merit, in medieval and early modern eyes, of preserving Aristotle's notion of the conservation of matter, since what goes into metal is what comes out: the four elements, recombined. At other times, however, alchemists replaced Aristotle's description of how metals are formed in the earth with his theories of sexual generation. While excoriated for violating Aristotelian earth science, a theory of alchemical production as sexual reproduction makes it possible for the alchemist to envision multiplying his product far beyond his raw ingredients. With alchemy, as with the generation of life, you can get more—infinitely more—at the end of the process than was put in at the beginning.[4]

Once alchemy is conceived as sexual reproduction it activates a rich storehouse of tropes of gender identity, gender difference, and gender roles in conception and birth. One of medieval and early modern alchemy's most attractive aspects, in fact, is the playfulness with which questions of gender identification in alchemical reproduction can be approached. As we will see, reading a large swath of alchemical texts presents an *array* of options for characterizing the gendered metaphors of alchemical reproduction, an array from which one may pick and choose. While most alchemical texts exhibit either a weak or a strong bias toward eliminating feminine influence from human procreation, as Sally Allen and Joanna Hubbs have argued, other texts—or sometimes even the same texts, as Kathleen Long has demonstrated—subvert the ideal of the normative masculinized body in a way that amounts to a queer stance on gender norms and gendered physical functions.[5] Allison Kavey makes the point that this variety of viewpoints on the nature of the "chemical wedding" corresponds, in England, to the last hurrah of a sense of gender malleability, before the institution of a stable sex-gender binary in the eighteenth century.[6]

Idiosyncrasy—a word picked up by English in about 1600, precisely to characterize the individualized "self-mixed-together-ness" (*idio-syn-crasis*) of the post-Paracelsian human body—defines how Renaissance English alchemy approaches the question of reproduction.

What I wish to do in this section and the ensuing sections of this chapter, then, is not simply describe how alchemical imagery relating to sexual reproduction does or does not depart from prevailing Aristotelian-Galenic norms. Rather, I contend that, when associated with the issue of human sexual reproduction, alchemical imagery can signal and demonstrate the very prospect of optionality. That is to say, in contrast to other medieval and Renaissance sciences that insist upon some version of classical orthodoxy, alchemy, in its very sloppiness and imprecision and in its characteristically improvisational style, insists upon the theorist's having the opportunity to make a choice, to design her own system. Alchemy signals, in this instance, the choice either to examine or to avoid examining the feminine role in reproduction.

Alchemy's identification with the possibility of choice helps explain, I think, a peculiar phenomenon in late Renaissance discussions of human reproduction. It is not just the case that alchemical theory borrows from gynecology; gynecological theory also borrows from alchemy. Both pictorial and textual descriptions of female reproductive anatomy draw from alchemical conceits. They do so, I believe, in a way that graphically demonstrates the operations of disknowledge. Alchemy is used in anatomical texts as a vehicle for disclaiming the woman's part in reproduction. At the same time, however, this figuration draws attention to that choice, and to the fact that it might have been otherwise. Alchemy surprisingly pops up at precisely those moments at which anatomists turn away from knowledge of female reproductive anatomy that they could have had—and in fact *did* have, but chose to bypass. The turn to alchemy thus represents willed ignorance. In a period of rapid changes in anatomical science, alchemy can thus cut both ways: it can signal intellectual invention, or it can signal intellectual conservatism so severe that it enacts disknowledge in its worst possible form.

Gynecological Alchemy

Early modern conjunctions between alchemical theories of material production and biological theories of human reproduction should not surprise us, since alchemy borrows from theories of sexual generation from its very beginnings.

The sexualization of alchemy became even more heightened at the end of the fifteenth century, when Marsilio Ficino, on the orders (as legend has it) of Cosimo de' Medici, interrupted his translations of Plato to render a newly unearthed manuscript supposedly by Hermes Trismegistus from Greek into Latin.[7] Titled *Pimander* when first printed in 1471, after the first of its fourteen tractates, Ficino's edition sparked numerous new translations and editions that fueled the sixteenth-century alchemical revival. The titular tractate of the *Pimander*, an elaborate myth of the relation between divinity and nature involving both sexual and asexual reproduction, joined the already influential Hermetic text *Asclepius* to present a complex and exceptionally ambiguous set of opinions on the roles played by male and female entities in natural fertility.[8] The "Pimander" tractate begins, in Judeo-Christian fashion, with a god who asexually creates a man in his own image. But then this man, identified as a "craftsman" (*dēmiourgos*), goes on to make love to a feminine nature who "took spirit from the ether and brought forth bodies in the shape of the man."[9] These bodies, the "seven governors"—taken by alchemists to be the seven metals—are conceived in a fashion that conforms to the Aristotelian model of human reproduction, in which the man's semen provides the "form" that is imprinted on the inert "matter" furnished by the woman's womb. In contrast, while the *Asclepius* also posits a single sex in natural reproduction, that single sex is the feminine principle; nature "can breed alone without conceiving by another."[10] The *Asclepius* also, however, posits that "each sex is full of fecundity, and the linking of the two or, more accurately, their union is incomprehensible."[11] If one were to construct a theory of male and female reproductive roles based on solely the "Pimander" tractate and the *Asclepius*, one would already have a number of options from which to choose.

Even before Ficino's late fifteenth-century introduction of the *Pimander* into the conversation, however, alchemy had already staked out various positions on whether the alchemical "multiplication" of minerals proceeded in the same manner as the multiplication of humans. Generally speaking, those positions came to reflect the same muddle of classical precedent that characterized much scholarly thinking about human reproduction into the seventeenth century. Along with the Aristotelian "one seed" model of masculine form imprinting itself on inert feminine matter, alchemical texts also often suggest the Galenic "two seed" model, in which both sexes contribute to human reproduction even though the man's influence is far greater than the woman's. As Joan Cadden describes it, the medieval scholarly debate over the roles of the sexes in reproduction stressed both the distinctions between Aristotle and Galen—one seed for Aristotle versus two for Galen; two ontologically different sexes for Aristotle versus one sexual continuum for Galen—and their commonalities: in both authors, women's contribution to conception is evaluated as decidedly lesser.[12] Similarly, medieval and early modern alchemists drew freely on both the congruities and the disagreements between Galen and Aristotle, often to the point of changing their imagery of the respective reproductive capacities of masculine and feminine alchemical ingredients in the middle of a description of an alchemical process.

In this malleability, too, alchemical writers were bolstered by ancient alchemical texts. For example, the early Arabic alchemical *Emerald Tablet*, a text attributed to Hermes Trismegistus that reached Europe via its translated inclusion in a thirteenth-century version of the encyclopedic *Secretum secretorum*, describes what was taken as a recipe for the philosopher's stone as a matter of the union of superior masculinity and inferior femininity: "That which is beneath [*inferius*] is like that which is above [*superius*]: & that which is above, is like that which is beneath, to worke the miracles of one thing. And as all things have proceeded from one, by the meditation of one, so all things have sprung from this one thing by adaptation. His father is the sun, his mother is the moone, the wind bore it in hir belly. The earth is his nurse."[13] A commentary frequently attached to the *Emerald Tablet* after 1541, attributed to an antique-sounding but unidentified author named Hortulanus, glosses these lines in both Aristotelian and Galenic fashion. On the one hand, the moon, identified as "Philosophers silver," is labeled in Aristotelian fashion as merely the "fitte and consonaunt receptacle for [the] seede and tincture" of the sun, or "Philosophers gold." On the other hand, the moon's character contributes to the nature of the offspring in Galenic fashion: "sonnes like to the Father, if they want [lack] long decoction [that is, preparation by heat or by boiling], shalbe like to the Mother in whitenesse, and retaine the Fathers weight."[14] To make matters even more complicated, other texts of theoretical alchemy, perhaps reflecting alchemy's debt to its earliest sources in Gnosticism, also emphasize the hermaphroditic nature of both the prime alchemical ingredient, alchemical mercury, and the desired alchemical product, either gold or the philosopher's stone.[15]

The outcome of alchemy's connections to multiple, overlapping, and sometimes conflicting theories of human sexual biology is a complex, rich, and often contradictory metaphoric system of the alchemical process as marriage and childbirth. Attempting to derive quintessentially pure matter, the alchemist begins with *prima materia*, a substance whose sex/gender role may be characterized in any number of different ways. *Prima materia* may be thought of as the "pure, basic stuff of creation," Aristotelian matter stripped of all form—in other words, the *matrix* of the Aristotelian one-seed model of reproduction, and hence essentially feminine.[16] In this connection, *prima materia* is sometimes identified, in fact, with the *menstruum*, the Latin word for menstrual fluid that was used to name the solvent in which the alchemist dissolves whatever substances are employed in the action.[17] *Prima materia* may also, however, denote the alchemist's initial mixture of sulfur and mercury, two elements that connote, respectively, masculinity and femininity, hot/dry and cold/wet humors. And finally, *prima materia* may describe, quite generally speaking, the original matter that generates the four elements of earth, water, air, and fire, each of which has gender affiliations based upon its humoral associations. The fact that the four elements may, in Aristotelian matter theory, be converted into each other is the basis for alchemical theory; their convertibility lends a certain gender fluidity to the alchemical reproductive process.[18]

Alchemists agree that one culminating step in the alchemical operation is *coniunctio*, or the "chemical wedding," a mystical marriage of male and female, and they imagine this wedding as a form of copulation and pregnancy, as many images from medieval and early modern alchemical texts illustrate (see Figures 8 and 9).[19] But what are the natures of the masculine and feminine principles that are wed, and do they play equal, subordinated, or absolutely unequal roles in their production of the pure element? For the most part, as I have already suggested, the discussions of theoretical alchemists imply that what they have in mind is a typically hybrid Aristotelian-Galenic reproductive scheme: either masculine form acts solely upon feminine matter, or the feminine component is an inferior and less developed version of the male, who thus plays the more active and more significant reproductive role. For example, at one point in his fifteenth-century *Compound of Alchemy*, monk and alchemist George Ripley seems to endorse a strictly Aristotelian view, declaring that for alchemy to succeed, the experiment must include only the masculine agent, the feminine container, and the requisite heat: "One thing, one glasse, one furnace, and no moe."[20] But even if a treatise depicts two seeds as in the Galenic system, and despite the equal roles implied by the embrace of "King" sulfur and "Queen" mercury in Figure 9, their hierarchy is clear. As the none-too-consistent Ripley would have it elsewhere, alchemy is effective because

all is sperme; and things there be no moe
But kinde with kinde in number two,
Male and female, agent and patient.[21]

The products of alchemy could bear out this same hierarchy of gender—"male and female, agent and patient." As *The Mirror of Alchemy* asserts, "Golde is a perfect masculine bodie, without any superfluitie or diminution. . . . Silver is also a body almost perfect, and feminine."[22]

But other, more radical imaginative constructions of alchemical reproduction could also be had. One option was to declare the principal gendered elements of alchemy to be equal in reproductive agency. Perhaps encouraged by the contention that alchemists' basic materials were refined, improved versions of ordinary substances, and especially by their insistence that "philosopher's mercury" was an idealized version of ordinary, lesser mercury, some alchemical theory elevated the feminine part in alchemical reproduction to a status equal to that of the masculine part. Another option was even to reach beyond binary ideas of gender. In confuting the leading classical theorists on the makeup of matter (as I discussed in Chapter 2), Paracelsus also confuted both Aristotelian and Galenic theories of gendered reproduction. For Paracelsus, the masculine Sol and feminine Luna who marry alchemically are not the traditional sulfur and mercury but instead sulfur and salt. Their child is the hermaphroditical mercury, "their Adam, who carries his own invisible Eve hidden in his body. . . . that is, the artificially prepared and true hermaphrodite Adam."[23] Significantly, all three elements possess seed. In effect, Paracelsus's gendered alchemy amounts to what neither Aristotle nor Galen could have dreamed of: a "three seed" theory. "Our man, Sol, and his wife, Luna, cannot conceive, or do anything in the way of generation, without the seed and sperm of both. Hence the philosophers gathered that a third thing was necessary. . . . Such a sperm is Mercury, which, by the natural conjunction of both bodies, Sol and Luna, receives their nature into itself in union."[24] Believing that alchemy is at work at all times and in all bodies, both terrestrial and celestial, Paracelsus envisions a universe that continually generates and incubates seeds that exist in all things and all creatures. And all of those seeds, including those possessed by the feminine salt and the hermaphroditic mercury, represent active forces.[25] The result, Amy Cislo argues, is a radically unconventional view not only of alchemical production but also of human reproduction, which Paracelsus regards as nothing other than an alchemical process.[26]

Figure 8. The alchemical coitus of Sol and Luna. Johann Daniel Mylius, *Anatomia auri* (Frankfurt, 1628). Courtesy of the Chemical Heritage Foundation Collections.

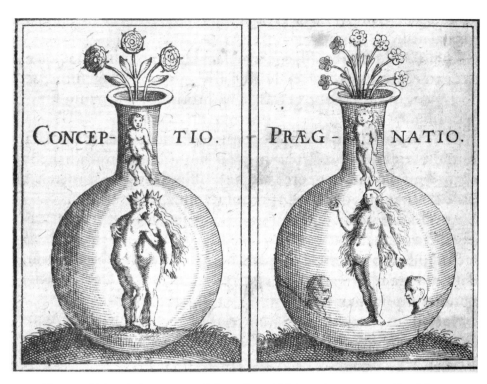

Figure 9. Alchemical conception. Johann Daniel Mylius, *Anatomia auri* (Frankfurt, 1628). Courtesy of the Chemical Heritage Foundation Collections.

As I mentioned at the beginning of this chapter, Paracelsus's name is also, however, associated with a radical theory of alchemical conception that entirely opposes the idea of equal participation by masculine and feminine elements. Under the influence of *De natura rerum* (1572), a text widely taken to be by Paracelsus even though it was published decades after his death, alchemy began to propose that the highest end to which the alchemical vessel could be put was the creation of the homunculus: a true human, perhaps one that even resembled its maker and was infused with a soul.[27] The homunculus is grown from heated male semen alone, "out [that is, outside] of the body of a Woman, and naturall matrix."[28] Elsewhere, in *De homunculis et monstris* (ca. 1529–32), the real Paracelsus shows himself wary of the creation of homunculi. He worries that misplaced male semen could create homunculi willy-nilly— for example, in the throats and intestines of men who had been the receptors in sodomitical intercourse.[29] In contrast, whoever wrote *De natura rerum* openly champions creating a homunculus as what William Newman calls "the distilled essence of masculinity . . . [free] from the gross materiality of the female."[30] While relying on the Aristotelian notion that the male seed alone provides all the form needed for conception, the creation of the homunculus triumphantly eliminates the other element of Aristotelian generation, the feminine matrix. Thus masculine alchemical reproduction is superior in every way to human reproduction, which even in Aristotle's scheme depends on the inferior content of women's wombs to produce nothing better than degraded human flesh.

With these examples I have by no means done justice to the range, variety, and sheer oddity of early modern depictions of alchemy as sexual reproduction. Indeed, this range suggests that alchemical theory is not merely a field in which sex and gender variability appears but rather a field to which questions of sex and gender variability are central. In this field, variation morphs into methodology. One not only *can* choose among a tremendous range of options for imagining the gendered roles of the participants in alchemical sexual reproduction; one *must* choose. When juxtaposed with anatomical texts, alchemical texts can therefore shed light on how the understanding of human reproductive anatomy deploys selective thinking. More than this, though, the appearance of alchemical imagery in anatomy books should alert us to moments at which that selective thinking is taking place.

Alchemical Gynecology

It is not news that early modern anatomists were as governed by patriarchalist and misogynist ideologies as any other group of intellectuals would have been at the time. It is, however, fairly new to examine how the science that academic anatomists produced reflects not an unconscious and inevitable misogyny but instead a determined and contingent misogyny. In the last decade or so, feminist historians of science and of intellectual history have demonstrated that the hybrid Aristotelian-Galenic model of human sex—with women as inferior, inadequately formed versions of men—was hardly monolithic. Thus, we can no longer assume that this hybrid scheme was an unavoidable, and hence forgivable, substrate of how early modern scholars thought of women's bodies. Instead we must examine how and why the elite anatomists of the late sixteenth and seventeenth centuries persist in not understanding the equal female part in human reproduction.

One avenue of accounting for the state of knowledge of the female reproductive organs is through an examination of medical texts' treatment of the ovaries. Such an examination might lead us, like many scholars—most prominently Thomas Laqueur in *Making Sex*—to lay the blame for the failure to modernize knowledge of female reproductive anatomy at the feet of humanist reverence for classical learning. Aristotle's one-seed version of reproduction had no use for the ovaries at all, since the nourishing "matrix" the woman furnishes in her uterus is the only thing she contributes to conception. And although Galen's two-seed version of reproduction asserted that the ovaries, analogous to the male testicles, produced female seed, this version does not necessarily lead to a valorization or even a precise examination of the ovaries' role in conception. Galen also held that the ovaries or "female testicles" were but malformed structures that had much more utility, because much more perfection, in men; as a result, early modern anatomical writers often discounted or simply did not bother to describe the ovaries' separate function in human reproduction.[31] For example, Andreas Vesalius's tremendously influential *De humani corporis fabrica* (1543) only notes, in Galenic fashion, "The function and activity of the female . . . testes are made sufficiently clear by what was said above concerning the male seminal organs."[32] A second and ancillary reason for discounting the ovaries is the influence of teachers upon their successors. Vesalius's pupil Fallopius described the female oviducts in 1561, but he still could not imagine them as anything other than conduits along the lines of the male seminal vesicles.[33] A third cause for the failure to understand female generative function was that anatomies of female corpses were rarer than those of male corpses and often hastily undertaken. One of Vesalius's anatomical subjects, for example, was the corpse of a monk's mistress, whom his students immediately skinned so that her body would be unrecognizable to her lover and her relatives. Since anatomists usually obtained their corpses from hangings, female cadavers were in shorter supply than males, and pregnant cadavers were downright difficult to come by, given that pregnant condemned criminals were allowed to give birth before an execution sentence was carried out.[34] In the second edition of *De humani corporis fabrica*, Vesalius confesses that much of his material on the human female reproductive organs had been derived from studying animals, primarily dogs.[35] For all of these reasons, it is perhaps understandable that a standard theory for the separate and equal function of the female ovaries did not take hold until the late seventeenth century.[36]

But the story of academic anatomical ignorance may also be told in much less sympathetic fashion, as one of *willed* ignorance. Recent work in the history of medicine describes early modern writers on human reproductive anatomy as having a much broader range of knowledge models to choose from than the hybrid Aristotelian-Galenic consensus. Eve Keller, for example, describes the early modern English state of knowledge regarding women's reproductive anatomy as one of eclecticism and lack of agreement, and Laura Gowing speaks of "The comparison of women's bodies to men's" in early modern popular medical texts as "part of a heterogeneous corpus of ideas and arguments."[37] If Vesalius was willing to challenge Galen on any number of anatomical points, and if Fallopius was in turn willing to challenge Vesalius, then skepticism about received wisdom might reasonably have been expected to extend to studies of the ovaries long before the late seventeenth century.[38] And indeed, skepticism seems to have been a choice available alongside acceptance of classical norms, a choice that appeared particularly in vernacular-language texts. Mary Fissell's work on vernacular anatomies from sixteenth- and seventeenth-century England reveals those writers' habits of tailoring, adapting, and confuting their sources to suit the local needs of author and audience— sometimes elevating, sometimes denigrating the extent to which female organs participate in and contribute to the generation of offspring.[39] Similarly, Janet Adelman describes English physicians writing in the vernacular in the late sixteenth and seventeenth centuries as mostly unconvinced by the hybrid Aristotelian-Galenic model of human reproductive anatomy. In their view, female reproductive organs had separate operations and perfect functions, even if these authors were not entirely sure what all those functions were.[40] This skepticism reaches its fullest expression in Helkiah Crooke's *Microcosmographia* (1615). Crooke is not exactly remarkable for his feminism, as I will discuss further below, and he generally accepts Galenist views.[41] Nevertheless, he asserts that the homology of female and male generative organs is, on the face of it, ridiculous, since those organs hardly resemble each other:

> Those things which Galen urgeth concerning the similitude, or parts of generation differing only in scite and position . . . savour little of the truth of Anatomy, as we have already prooved in the Booke going before: wherein we have shewed how little likenesse there is betwixt

the necke of the womb [vagina] and the yard [penis], the bottome of it [labia/vulva] and the cod [head of the penis]. Neither is the structure, figure, or magnitude of the testicles one and their same, nor the distribution and insertion of the spermatick vessels alike, wherefore we must not thinke that the female is an imperfect male differing onely in the position of the genitals.[42]

The lack of consensus on women's reproductive role is especially apparent in medical texts' treatment of the ovaries. Decades after Crooke, at about the same time Dutch anatomist Regnier de Graaf confirmed the perfected and separate nature of the female reproductive organs by explaining what the fallopian tubes really do, Jane Sharp's *Midwives Book* (1671) still felt obliged to note, rather tartly, that despite their continuing influence, the likes of Galen and Vesalius had no idea what the ovaries, or female "stones," look like or what function they serve: "The stones of a woman for generation of seed, are white, thick and well concocted, for I have seen one, and but one and that is more by one than many Men have seen."[43] In 1690, *Aristotle's Master-Piece, Or, the Secrets of Generation* claimed the authorship of Aristotle in order to entirely confute both Aristotle and Galen: "The Stones in Women are very useful, for where they are defective, Generation is at an end, for although those little Bladders . . . contain nothing of Seed, as the followers of Galen and Hippocrates did erroneously imagine, yet they contain several Eggs, (commonly to the number of twenty in each Testicle) one of which being impregnated by the most spirituous part of the Mans Seed in the Act of Coition, descends through the Ovi-ducts, into the Womb, and from thence, in process of time, becomes a living Child."[44]

The sturdy insistence of a range of early modern medical texts that female reproductive organs, including the ovaries, have their own, separate functions equal in importance to those of the male—perhaps even greater importance—allows us to reinterpret the ignorance of those influential early modern anatomists who clung to the hybrid Aristotelian-Galenic model. It is possible to argue that a physiologist who maintained some version of the Aristotelian-Galenic view of the ovaries was deliberately holding the female reproductive system in a kind of half-light. For the great sixteenth-century thinkers in the field, like Vesalius and Fallopius, and for those prominent seventeenth-century anatomists who followed them, female reproductive anatomy could be seen and yet not seen, described and yet not comprehended. For such thinkers the "sheer repetition" of the Aristotelian-Galenic model, as Patricia Parker asserts, requires interrogation as "symptomatic and ideological rather than as descriptive discourse."[45]

For an example of how the concerted application of ideology attempts to sidestep evidence contrary to an updated version of the hybrid Aristotelian-Galenic model, we may look to William Harvey. Potentially, the experimental findings recorded in Harvey's *Exercitationes de generatione animalium* (1651) could have prompted a crisis in the patriarchal assumptions of medical learning. Harvey's determination that there is no gain in mass in either chicken eggs after fertilization or deer uteruses after intercourse prompts him to surmise that semen does not enter the bird's egg or the mammal's womb at all. As Keller details, this is a conclusion that might have upended the entire Aristotelian-Galenic system of inherent male superiority.[46] Certainly Harvey's *De generatione* has been read as revolutionary in this fashion, both by his contemporary Alexander Ross—who grumbled that if Harvey's theory was true, the female had no need of the male—and by John Rogers, who reads *De generatione* as protofeminist and antiauthoritarian.[47]

Harvey himself, however, gets around the seeming problem of male nonparticipation in conception through a complex series of analogies, culminating in the theory that the male "genitor" imparts his influence noncorporeally, in the same way that an artist's noncorporeal idea shapes the work produced: "And from this . . . Conception it cometh to pass, that the female doth produce an offspring like the male Genitor. For as we, from the Conception of the Form, or Idea, in the Braine, do fashion a form like to it in our works, so doth the Idea or Species of the Genitor, residing in the Uterus, by the help of the formative facultie, beget a Foetus like the Genitor himself."[48] Harvey thus reinstantiates Aristotle, for whom the seminal "form" impressed on uterine "matter" also has no mass and no physicality. Furthermore, Harvey poohpoohs the very notion that mammalian ovaries produce anything like seed. At one point, he quite bluntly calls the ovaries "things utterly unconcerned in the matter of Generation" (407 [Dd4r]).[49] At another point he puts it far more polemically: "But for my part I wonder much, how they fancy, that so elaborate, concocted, and quickening semen, can arise from so imperfect and obscure parts" as the ovaries, so much so that the female semen "should exceed the Males in power, spirit, and generative ability" (175 [M8r]).

The "they" whom Harvey mocks here, specifically, is Helkiah Crooke. As evidenced by prose echoes and paraphrases, Harvey demonstrably referred to Crooke's *Microcosmographia* while composing his *De generatione*.[50] What we read as we read *De generatione*, then, is a record of Harvey's having *Micro-cosmographia* propped up in front of him, adopting its phraseology but choosing to depart from its plausible contentions of ovarian usefulness. We thus find Harvey, who is otherwise often quite pugnacious about disproving classical theory, in this case preferring the conceptual framework of the classical text over a contemporary empirical account. At this moment, Harvey's approach to his topic is overtly imparted by humanism's command: when given alternative theories, choose the one that comports with antique authority.

Studiously avoiding Crooke's assertion of ovarian function requires, however, a good deal of effort on Harvey's part, and Harvey deliberately turns to fiction to help him make the case. Specifically, he turns to the fiction of alchemy. After hundreds of pages of markedly dry analysis of chicken eggs, Harvey enters upon a much shorter and much more florid discussion of mammalian reproduction based upon his dissections of deer. This discussion engages, as Keller has analyzed, in extravagant analogies to explain how it is that the male essence determines conception even when no semen enters the uterus. Harvey's most elaborate prose, however, is reserved for *De generatione*'s last three chapters, in which he departs from his anatomies of deer species in order to mount an operatic paean to the nurturing qualities of blood, which, he argues, provides the nutrition and developmental environment that the fetus needs. The vitalist strain in Harvey that John Rogers has analyzed is on full display here.[51] Also on full display, however, is alchemy. Walter Pagel, Allen Debus, and Peter Mitchell have established that Harvey's theories of blood circulation are in large part derived from Paracelsian alchemical medical theory.[52] On the one hand, Harvey rejects Paracelsian alchemical notions such as a vital "distinct spirit, and innate heat, which is of a celestial extract . . . partaking of a fift essence" (449 [Gg1r]). On the other hand, even while he explicitly rejects Paracelsus's concept of the blood as "partaking of a fift essence," he expropriates exactly the alchemical qualities of the quintessence, the philosopher's stone, for blood. Like Paracelsian "spirit," Harvey's blood derives from primordial heat, possesses "fruitful" (that is, formative) powers, and is "answerable in proportion to the element or substance of the Stars" (452 [Gg2v]). In short, "The Blood therefore is a Spirit" (455 [Gg4r]).[53] Here Harvey recapitulates some of the alchemically derived language of his predecessor Andrea Cesalpino, who in the sixteenth century had proposed a theory of the circulation of the blood based upon alchemical processes of repeated distillation, of heating and cooling.[54] Thus, while Harvey has excluded semen from the uterus, he has, in a sense, reincorporated it by means of the old physiological association of refined blood with semen as "spirit."[55] In this case, the blood seems to have been alchemically refined.

And yet the appropriation of alchemical "spirit" to the blood is the appropriation of a fable. Who could believe that blood has such efficacy, Harvey asks rhetorically, when its name is so commonplace (460 [Gg6v])? To make his point, Harvey borrows from Jean Fernel's *On the Hidden Causes of Things* (*De abditis rerum causis*, 1548) a riddle of a "miraculous Stone" of "infinite purity" and tremendous beauty that possesses extraordinary powers: it cannot be touched; it transforms everything it touches; it has been known to fall from heaven to earth (460–61 [Gg6v–Gg7r]).[56] The philosopher's stone, surely. But no: the answer to the riddle is "flame." With this answer, the magical alchemical object is revealed as purely ordinary after all. "In like manner," analogizes Harvey, "if I should describe the Blood under the veil and covering of a Fable, calling it the Philosophers stone, and displaying all its endowments, operations, and faculties, in an aenigmatical manner; doubtless every body would set a greater price upon it, and believing it to act beyond the Activity of the elements, would ascribe another and more divine body unto it" (462 [Gg7v]). Harvey is describing his own strategy here: he *has* given blood the attributes of the philosopher's stone, proposing its qualities and operations in the "aenigmatical," fabulous, and (despite his protestations) manifestly grandiloquent language of alchemy.

Only by resorting to the fabulist terms of alchemy can Harvey cement his case about the wonders of blood. Elizabeth Spiller makes the point that Harvey's alliance between fetal and mental conception extends to Harvey's own scientific practice: "Harvey is talking not so much about women . . . as about himself and his acts of scientific creation."[57] But in resorting to alchemy, Harvey only highlights the fact that his decision to shrug off the influence of the ovaries, and even of the uterus, in conception and gestation equates to the choice of a certain kind of fiction. There is a kind of willfulness, if not exactly a kind of arbitrariness, about a biological theory that describes itself in alchemical terms. After all, as I described above, alchemy itself offers any number of models for assigning agency or passivity to one gender or another. The frontispiece of Harvey's 1651 London edition of *De generatione*, which features Jove opening an egg from which, as if from Pandora's box, creatures of all kinds are emerging, could serve equally as an alchemical emblem—drawing upon "egg" as a common term for an alchemical vessel—and as an illustration for the primacy of the female in generation. "*Ex ovo omnia*," the egg is labeled.[58] It is as plausible that "everything comes from the egg" as that everything comes from the spirit. Turning from one alchemical fiction of reproduction to another, from egg to spirit, is not so terribly difficult.[59]

To a large extent, of course, Harvey's theories of sexual reproduction do not matter. Even though Harvey saw his influential work on the circulation of the blood as a companion to his work on embryology, *De generatione* had almost no influence on the study of physiology, and it marks, as Laqueur notes, a kind of last hurrah for Aristotelianism.[60] In another sense, however, Harvey models the way in which the avoidance of female reproductive anatomy paradoxically remains a kind of academic and philosophical norm in the seventeenth century, even while the body of accurate knowledge concerning human reproductive processes increases.

Up to this point in this chapter, I have been using the word *avoid* largely to describe a kind of reading practice: for example, Harvey avoids information that is on the pages of Crooke's *Microcosmographia* in front of him. In addition, however, my use of *avoid* draws from and incorporates Stanley Cavell's usage in his classic essay on *King Lear*, "The Avoidance of Love." Cavell describes the characters' need to avoid love as a matter of their need not to acknowledge others, and thus not to own up to the responsibilities that love requires. Avoiding love brings comfort in that it brings less pain, less effort. Another aim of avoidance is certainty, which gives us "the idea that we can save our lives by knowing them."[61] When Harvey traffics in fable in *De generatione*—fable that is allied with alchemy—he does so in a way that both reaches toward certainty and reveals the leaps of comforting illogic that such knowledge requires.

In the process Harvey also, however, inches toward the same mid-seventeenth century separation of individual from world that, perfected by René Descartes, will both support epistemological certainty and enable the kinds of epistemological crisis that Cavell identifies with Shakespearean tragedy. Harvey's description of embryonic fertilization as originating in a male idea, like his description of the blood as the sole support of the self-sustained human body, tends to diminish human dependence on anyone outside the self: the man's seminal conception requires no female contribution, just as the circulation of blood requires no Galenic, humoral interpenetration of the elements of the body with the elements of its terrestrial surroundings.[62] For Cavell, this kind of separation of self from world, at its extreme, leads to the kind of misogynistic violence seen in Shakespeare's tragic heroes like Othello, whose "disowning" (to use Cavell's term) and murder of his wife reflect both the futile hope that utter knowledge of the female other is possible, and the realization that this hope will always be dashed. In adopting Cavell's analysis of Cartesian skepticism, I emphasize the extent to which the feminine epitomizes that which cannot be known. Cavell attributes the skeptical crisis whose end stage is murderous violence to both capitalist and psychic causes: to the problem of "exclusive possession, call it private property" and to "an intellectualization of . . . the child's sense of loss in separating from the mother's body."[63] If he is correct in these causes—and I think he is—then it is clear that managing this skeptical crisis without resorting to violence would require a better system of possessing and intellectualizing the feminine. Such a system, a culture-wide project of epistemological misogyny, would enact a milder, less engaged, and hence more socially functional form of Cartesian skepticism. It would enable dominance over the construction of women because otherwise women represent the incomprehensible nature of the physical world. But instead of achieving dominance through violence, it would achieve it merely by eliminating from the prevailing knowledge scheme any element of femininity that cannot be dominated.

The kind of reading and study practice I have detailed with Harvey, one that recycles classical frameworks when they preserve a male-dominated model of human reproduction, becomes an exceptionally useful component of this kind of avoidance of knowledge. Epistemological misogyny can profitably take place on the level of the cited source: which to include, which to discard. We can discern this kind of misogyny, I have argued, in Harvey's analysis of the female reproductive organs. However, this sort of studious misogyny can also take place in other bookish registers—including, paradoxically, ones that choose to discard classical authority entirely. For example, Will Fisher describes how some anatomy books of the sixteenth and seventeenth centuries depart from Galen to deemphasize the importance of the testicles, lauded by Galen as the principal part of the human body. Such a counterintuitive move, argues Fisher, is aligned with what Jean Howard and Phyllis Rackin have identified as the emergence of "performative masculinity" in the period, a more effective form of masculine dominance that came to replace the old regime of patrilineal inheritance.[64] Similarly, Jonathan Sawday identifies the "stridently aggressive language of appropriation and domination" in the Royal Society's publications with Harvey's and his culture's need to reassert royalist, masculinist psychosexual authority after the feminizing disruptions of the English Civil War.[65]

One point must be stressed in order to modify Fisher's and Sawday's insights, however. The stakes for avoiding gynecology in bookish medical culture were not only the preservation of male dominance but also the preservation of male sexual desire as the indispensable prop of that dominance. Keeping male desire alive requires knowing less about the feminine, and knowing less may be assisted by the way the knower is presented with bookish information. We see this form of useful avoidance in a number of early modern anatomy books, including the work of none other than Helkiah Crooke, who despite his championship of the ovaries' reproductive role follows upon a long tradition of anatomy books' steering clear of the facts of female sexual organs. Because Crooke's volume was written in English rather in the customary and properly obfuscatory Latin, portions of the text that circulated before publication came under attack in the Royal College of Physicians for what was deemed their overly clear descriptions of female generative parts. The Bishop of London informed Crooke's printer, William Jaggard—who was, incidentally, also the printer of Shakespeare's First Folio—that if the book was not altered it was liable to be destroyed.[66] In his preface to the chapter dealing with "the Naturall Parts belonging to generation" that ultimately appeared in print, Crooke goes to great lengths to defend himself against this charge of making too much known. Crooke worries that his book might be misconstrued as an effort to "ensnare mens mindes by sensuall demonstrations," and he admits to having been tempted by the option of skipping the topic of the reproductive organs entirely: "Being arived at this place in the tract of my Anatomicall Peregrination, I entred into deliberation with my selfe, whether I were best silently to passe it by, or to insist upon [including] it as I had done in the former [chapters]."[67]

Crooke's eventual decision not to "pass by" the place of the genitalia and to forge ahead with his descriptions contrasts, at first glance, with the many other early anatomy books that go to great lengths, even while they are ostensibly illustrating the female organs of generation, to avoid a full revelation of female bodies and thereby to maintain the typical aesthetic apparatus of male desire. This avoidance depends on several specifically print-based devices. The first of these is illustration. As Valerie Traub has shown, the female figure in the sixteenth- and early seventeenth-century anatomy book typically composes herself into the form of the classical nude, complete with the classical gesture of modesty—the hand covering the genital area—that is meant to compensate for what Traub calls the "dread of the female genital interior."[68] The illustrated woman's covering hand also indicates, however, that the dread of the female genital interior is matched by the dread of what is technically exterior—that is, the visible parts that cover and accompany the entrance to copulation and conception. For example, the extraordinary "flap book" anatomy text of Johann

Remmelin, *Catoptrum microcosmicum*, first published in Latin in 1613 and later in French, English, German, and Dutch, decently obscures the female figure's genitals not only with the customary painterly drape but also with a marvelous cloud of unknowing: one made of the smoke of a phoenix, whose caption obfuscates the facts of genital reproduction by comparing the life of man to that legendary bird's fiery death and asexual rebirth (see Figure 10).[69] (At least one copy of a later English edition accomplishes this genital occultation by replacing the drape/cloud flap with the face of Satan.[70]) Once the flaps are opened to reveal what lies beneath, the cloud cleared to expose the female form, what is found between the woman's labia is only a vacancy, nothing, a literal "avoidance" (see Figure 11).

Along with anatomical illustrations' obfuscation or omission of what lies between maids' legs, as Hamlet would put it, we must consider their frequent pictorial setting within a scene of seduction. The anatomized female figure reveals her own reproductive capacity within the somewhat reassuring context of the bedchamber, complete with soft pillows and a gestured invitation to join her in bed.[71] Together these details put the lie to Crooke's anxieties. Anatomical drawings and descriptions provoke and preserve male desire not by revealing the female sexual organs but by avoiding them.

In the end, Crooke himself makes allowance for meliorating his own book in the direction of avoiding gynecology, thus converting his reader from the man who knew too much into the man who has been relieved of too much information. That relief comes about both through Crooke's rhetoric and through his deployment of yet another print-based technique for avoiding a revelation of the feminine: a suggestion for the scholarly handling of his book. Referring to his discussion of reproductive anatomy, Crooke reassures us, "As much as was possible we have endeavoured (not frustrating our lawfull scope) by honest wordes and circumlocutions to molifie the harshenesse of the Argument." Like the woman's genitalia in Remmelin's "flap book," Crooke's rhetoric regarding female genitalia is softened, clouded, "molifie[d]" through "circumlocutions." If that is not enough, however, the offending material may be physically removed from the volume: "beside we have so plotted our busines, that he that listeth may separate this Booke [that is, the section "On . . . generation"] from the rest and reserve it privately unto himselfe."[72] If thy text offend thee, cut it out. Crooke may be secondarily suggesting that if the offensive cut-out section is "reserve[d] . . . privately," it will have a second use as an aid to masturbatory pleasure. This too, however, would be a mode of avoiding knowledge. Using the practice of scholarly reading against itself, the

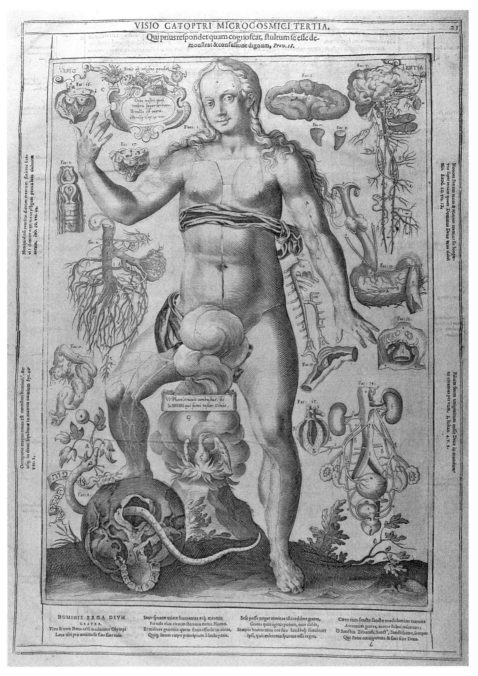

Figure 10. Anatomical figure of a woman, flaps closed. Johann Remmelin, *Catoptrum microcosmicum* (Augsburg, 1619). Photograph used by permission of the University of Iowa John Martin Rare Book Room.

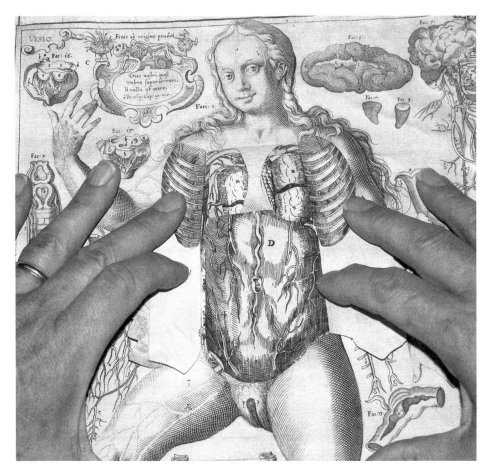

Figure 11. Anatomical figure of a woman, flaps open (detail). Johann Remmelin, *Catoptrum microcosmicum* (Augsburg, 1619). Photograph used by permission of the University of Iowa John Martin Rare Book Room.

masturbating user shunts aside academic anatomical knowledge in order to engage in sexual fantasy.

For some writers, these anatomy books' application of the technology of the printed book to the scholarly avoidance of female reproductive anatomy— via ingenious illustration or via pages typeset so as to be excisable—aligns with another fruitful set of metaphorical associations between alchemy and disknowledge. I have detailed how alchemy is a theory and practice of perfectibility that extends to perfecting the process of sexual generation. Because alchemy's ways of imagining sexual generation are so diverse, however—indeed, as I have argued, alchemy represents the very act of choosing *how* to regard human reproduction—alchemy may be used as a way to figure the process of knowledge making involved in determining how, exactly, we imagine the perfect woman and the perfect mode of reproduction. In the literary works to which I now turn, alchemical imagery surrounds exactly these issues. On the one hand, as in the anatomy books, alchemy applied to the female body may signify a choice to remain permanently in the state of seeing only her most pleasing aspects, never obliged to know more. On the other, as in the more adventurous alchemical theory I discussed above, alchemy may also signify a choice to radically reimagine the female role in reproduction along nonpatriarchal lines.

Epistemology and the Alchemical Woman in *The Faerie Queene*

When Edmund Spenser examines alchemical reproduction in *The Faerie Queene*, he introduces alchemy to explore what men desire to know, what they think they know, and what they avoid knowing about women's bodies. Not coincidentally, the most prominent instances of alchemy appear in the "marriage books" of *The Faerie Queene*: books 3, 4, and 5, which include the travels and travails of the poem's one knight whose quest is marriage, Britomart, and the poem's longest-standing object of male desire, Florimell. For Spenser, alchemy helps explain how female beauty serves, like the nonrevealing, sexy pose of the female anatomical illustration, to preserve male sexual desire while diverting men from more challenging theories of women's part in sexual reproduction. *The Faerie Queene*, however, treats this diversion as a truly stupid option, one that closes off both epistemological sophistication and—what amounts to the same thing for Spenser—literary innovation.

Throughout *The Faerie Queene* a constellation of Hermetic-Neoplatonic-Pythagorean ideas are brought to bear on questions of biological reproduction in ways that evidence Spenser's association of Hermeticism with the female body and with the feminine reproductive role. This typical Renaissance mishmash of cosmologies emerges, for example, in book 3's superfecund Garden of Adonis and in book 2's House of Alma, whose entire construction is based on an allegory of the (arguably female) body.[73] More important than their evincing this cluster of Spenserian intellectual obsessions, however, is the fact that those episodes are precisely where *The Faerie Queene* conspicuously both feints toward and veers from an examination of what human reproductive organs look like and do. The Garden of Adonis canto, while it metonymically displaces both female and male genitalia onto the landscape and its fauna (the middle of the garden features a "stately Mount" of Venus, under which is a rocky cave in which the "wilde Bore" that gored Adonis is chained), declines to explain the exact sexual function of all of these topographical features or how, exactly, the hidden Adonis manages to be "the Father of all formes" that emerge from the garden (3.6.43, 47–48).[74] And famously, Alma's house omits the genitals entirely from its allegory of the human frame.[75]

When alchemy is added to this mix, however, the question of why one would *want* to diverge from the organs of reproduction, specifically the female organs, is highlighted. This query begins in book 1, when Archimago, whose name evokes an "Arch-Magus," creates a false double for Una out of a hell-dwelling sprite,

> And fram'd of liquid ayre her tender partes
> So liuely and so like in all mens sight,
> That weaker sence it could haue rauisht quight.
>
> (1.1.45)

The "liquid air" he uses to fashion this artificial woman corresponds to the elemental qualities of alchemical mercury, that feminine component of the alchemical trial, which, as Maier's *Atalanta fugiens* puts it, is the "water of the Air . . . [that] dissolves body into spirit, and makes a living thing of a dead thing, and conducts a marriage between man and woman."[76] In particular, the stanza dwells upon how Archimago uses this liquid air to form the false Una's "tender partes." While most of the real Una's parts are no doubt "tender," Spenser plays on what A. C. Hamilton calls the "folk etymology" for "woman" (Latin *mulier*) as *molis air*, or "softened air," to imply that Archimago requires alchemical means specifically to concoct the false Una's most womanly parts, her genitalia (1.1.45n). In this way, Archimago "mollifies," softens and blurs, the false Una's sexual equipment just as Helkiah Crooke "mollifies" the language of his descriptions of the human female reproductive organs. And as with both Crooke's descriptions and the anatomy books' decorously draped female nudes, it is the "mollified" woman who proves more attractive than the authentic one. Even Archimago himself is beguiled "with so goodly sight" of his creation: sight, that is, not of the fleshy parts of an actual woman but of the liquid air of an alchemical one (1.1.45).[77] In other words, even the man who knows the difference—or, I should say, *especially* the man who knows the difference, Archimago— prefers looking imperfectly at an alchemical woman to looking plainly at a real one.

The poem also suggests, however, that when avoiding the sight of the feminine is signaled by alchemy, we can discern, as in William Harvey's account of generation, the choice of a particular kind of knowledge and a particular kind of fictionalizing. While we do not hear what ultimately happens to the false, alchemical Una, the similar replacement of a beautiful woman with her alchemical double becomes a significant story arc of books 3, 4, and 5. When the oafish son of a witch falls for Florimell ("flower honey"), the poem's sweetest woman, he is so racked with lovesickness that his mother undertakes "a wondrous worke to frame" (3.8.5), the alchemical production of a false Florimell:

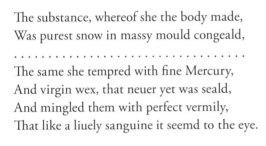

> The substance, whereof she the body made,
> Was purest snow in massy mould congeald,
> . . . .
> The same she tempred with fine Mercury,
> And virgin wex, that neuer yet was seald,
> And mingled them with perfect vermily,
> That like a liuely sanguine it seemd to the eye.
>
> (3.8.6)

What would otherwise be a standard-issue satire on the poetic construction of a woman through blazons—the witch also uses "burning lampes" for eyes and "golden wyre" for hair (3.8.7)—is transformed into an alchemical operation through three significant ingredients: "fine" or refined mercury, the kind that was usually part of the initial mixture of the alchemical work; "virgin wax," a common alchemical ingredient; and vermilion, indicative of a much-desired state called "rubification" that was a sign that the alchemical process was nearing perfection.[78] This stanza's idiosyncratic spelling of "virgin wex," the only instance of "wex" used for "wax" in Spenser's works, also indicates the moonlike "wexing" of the alchemical pregnancy that follows *coniunctio*.

Perhaps obviously, given that book 3's bipartite structure follows up its first six cantos of natural production with six cantos of unnatural, parodic production, the witch's creation, located in the eighth canto, trots out the alchemist's fantasy of a purified, nonfleshly reproduction of human bodies in order to deride it as just that—fantasy. Spenser also, however, uses the pairing of the false and true Florimells to explore an epistemological question: What is it about beautiful women, exactly, that we wish to know? The remainder of False Florimell's career challenges us to recognize how much or how little we want to understand of the female body's anatomical structures and reproductive capacity, and how satisfied we are with noticing golden hair and snowy skin instead. Just as Helkiah Crooke recommends that the squeamish or titillated reader of *Microcosmographia* remove and "reserve" the pages on human reproduction, so too does the narrative of *The Faerie Queene* remove the true Florimell from the prospect of marriage and childbirth, putting False Florimell in her place. Captured by Proteus in book 3 and imprisoned under the sea, the true Florimell languishes until book 5, when, after her rescue by her true love Marinell, she and her alchemical duplicate—who has been taken for the true Florimell in the meantime—are finally brought together at the tournament held to celebrate Florimell's and Marinell's wedding. No one, including Marinell himself, is able to distinguish the true Florimell from the false on the basis of appearance. Their exactitude sets off an epistemological crisis:

> All that behold so strange prodigious sight,
> Not knowing natures worke, nor what to weene,
> Are rapt with wonder, and with rare affright.
>
> (5.3.19)

Artegall, the knight of justice who attempts to solve the conundrum of what is "natures worke" and what is not, moves to differentiate false from true Florimell by pointing out the company False Florimell has kept: her champion is Braggadocchio, whose borrowed plumes mask the fact that he has never been in battle at all. Stripping his own sleeve to show his battle scars, Artegall asks Braggadocchio to do the same (5.3.21–22). The implication is that if the two women were stripped like Artegall's and Braggadocchio's naked arms, they would show the same difference: one woman would be wounded and one not. In the women's case, the "wounded" woman, the one who has been penetrated, would be the false one, False Florimell, whom Artegall identifies as "some fayre Franion, fit for such a fere [as Braggadocchio]" (5.3.22). Perhaps derived from the Old French *fraignant*, present participle of "to break," *franion* generally means the kind of roistering young man who breaks things: furniture, hearts, hymens.[79] Stripping a female *franion*, like stripping the upper-body armor from both a true knight and a false knight, would thus seem to be a strategy to identify her on the basis of physical breakage. Artegall proposes that a hymen, if it were found, would distinguish true from false Florimell.[80]

Such a gynecological examination is not to be had, however. As with the false Una, an alchemical apparition distracts from the uncovering of female reproductive anatomy. The minute the true and false Florimell are placed next to each other, False Florimell undergoes a new round of alchemical processing, in this case melting:

> Th'enchaunted Damzell vanisht into nought:
> Her snowy substance melted as with heat,
> . . . .
> So did this Ladies goodly forme decay,
> And into nothing goe, ere one could it bewray.
>
> (5.3.24–25)

Nor is the true Florimell "bewrayed" (revealed), either. Rather, Artegall confirms the true Florimell's chastity by presenting her with a substitute, crafted hymen, the girdle that she lost just before her capture by Proteus:

> Such power it had, that to no womans wast
> By any skill or labour it would sit,
> Vnlesse that she were continent and chast.
>
> (5.3.28)

Though crafted of gold, the purest of substances and one of alchemy's holy grails, the girdle's true usefulness seems to be as a covering that displaces the view upward toward the woman's waist, in the same fashion that the decorous hand of the anatomy book's female nude encourages us to gaze anywhere but there.

What would we see if we saw? Spenser here asks us, briefly, a different and more challenging version of that question: What would we like to see if we saw, and what would we fear to see? *The Faerie Queene* identifies one version of that desire and that fear when it becomes clear that many of the male knights would prefer to see as little as possible. When False Florimell melts instead of being stripped, Spenser indulges in a joke, much beloved of his younger contemporary Shakespeare, that he makes only twice in *The Faerie Queene*, as best as I can tell: the joke that a woman's genitals, if we saw them, might in fact be "nothing." In Shakespeare's most famous use of this bitter trope, one to which I have already alluded, Hamlet retaliates against Ophelia's assertion of will—she declines his request to "lie in [her] lap"—first by making an obscene pun ("Do you think I meant country matters?") and then by taking her shocked reply, "I think nothing, my lord," as an opportunity to convert the *cunt* in his word *country* into a vacancy, a nothing:

> Hamlet.   That's a fair thought to lie between maids' legs.
> Ophelia.   What is, my lord?
> Hamlet.   Nothing.[81]

Hamlet's need to void the feminine has been well explored and need not detain us here. What we must notice is that Spenser, in contrast to Shakespeare, associates the "nothingness" of female genitals not with a real woman but only with a woman who has been specifically constructed to have nothing real about her. Threatened with stripping, False Florimell reveals only nothing: she "vanisht into *nought*." Thus "did this Ladies goodly forme decay, / And into *nothing* goe" (5.3.24–25; emphasis added).[82] Still, when False Florimell melts into nothingness, the male knights in attendance reveal that they preferred her alchemically crafted falsehood to any other woman's true being:

> They stricken were with great astonishment,
> And their faint harts with senselesse horrour queld,
> To see the thing, that seem'd so excellent,
> So stolen from their fancies wonderment.
>
> (5.3.26)

False Florimell's "thing, that seem'd so excellent" was no thing at all, and yet this alchemical diversion is still preferable to the feminine body better left unseen.[83]

In the case of nonartificial women, in contrast, Spenser if anything makes the reverse joke: a feminine nothing is hardly a vacancy, but rather can be the most noticeable thing a man has ever met. Hence Spenser's habit of naming book 1's primary women in multiples of one—Una, Duessa—as if to emphasize from the beginning of the poem that whatever women are, they are not nothing. This feminine presence in *The Faerie Queene* in turn corresponds to an alternative alchemy, one that presents a much more challenging and less mollifying view of human reproduction than the kind of alchemy that creates the false Una or False Florimell. Among the many choices that alchemy presents regarding male and female roles in conception, Britomart's dream in book 5's Temple of Isis chooses one of the most radical options, discussed above, for male and female reproductive roles. It adopts neither Aristotle's view (masculine form imprinting upon feminine matter), nor Galen's view (active masculine seed uniting with passive feminine seed), nor Pseudo-Paracelsus's view (masculine seed acting alone, parthenogenetically). Rather, it plays out the alchemical scenario propounded by the real Paracelsus, in which all three contributors to the alchemical process—masculine sulfur, feminine salt, and their offspring, the hermaphroditic mercury—share equal potency and equal participation. This proposition proves to be a dangerous business, however, as evidenced by the fact that the episode closes out with an ostentatiously bad reading of Britomart's dream, one that attempts to render her vision palatable by avoiding any further consideration of an equal feminine reproductive role.

The Isis Church episode of book 5 is replete with alchemical meaning and iconography to an extent that has not yet been studied.[84] This episode is the only extended instance in which *The Faerie Queene* turns to ancient Egypt, the legendary origin of the wisdom of Hermes Trismegistus. Although Egypt's Nile and its fecundity are significant touchstones throughout *The Faerie Queene*, only in Isis Church does Egyptian lore acquire Hermetic and specifically alchemical connotations.[85] For example, the temple priests wear

> rich Mitres shaped like the Moone,
> To shew that *Isis* doth the Moone portend;
> Like as *Osyris* signifies the Sunne.
>
> (5.7.4; emphasis in the original)

Given these gods' associations with marriage and fecundity, it is at first glance unremarkable that the symbology of Isis and Osiris appears here.[86] Yet these two gods are mentioned by name only here in *The Faerie Queene*, and the reference seems designed to carry alchemical as well as mythographic weight. As sun god and moon goddess, Osiris and Isis denote for alchemical theory the chemical wedding of masculine and feminine elements upon which the alchemical work depends, with Osiris/Sol as sulfur and Isis/Luna as either the traditional mercury or the Paracelsian salt. Not for nothing, then, is book 5's statue of Isis framed in silver and crowned with gold (5.7.6). In this metallic context, the odd hermaphroditism of the crocodile at the statue's feet (addressed with female pronouns in the sixth stanza and male pronouns in the fifteenth) completes the alchemical scheme, since in alchemy, crocodiles and their more or less interchangeable scaly siblings—serpents, basilisks, dragons, and cockatrices—signify the hermaphroditic product of the marriage of Sol and Luna.[87] Thus, proclaims Michael Maier in his *Arcana arcanissima* (1613), the "chemist' gods" are "Osiris, Isis, Mercury, and Vulcan."[88] The full effect of the statue's fusion of emblematics and alchemy is to anticipate the kind of elaborate alchemical emblem that, having circulated throughout the Renaissance, became popular after the publication of Maier's *Atalanta fugiens* (1617).[89]

With this setup, it is perhaps inevitable that Britomart's dream is a dream of an alchemical conception, pregnancy, and birth. It is a dream that unites the four elements. Air and fire surround her, as a "hideous tempest . . . / all about did blow / The holy fire" of the temple, and as she herself, an earthy and liquid woman, brings her "earthly parts . . . deeply drowned" in sleep (5.7.12). Britomart begins by being alchemically transfigured into the statue of Isis, with the "linnen stole" she dreams herself decked in "transfigured / . . . to robe of scarlet red" and her "Moone-like Mitre" transfigured "to a Crowne of gold" like the one Isis's statue wears (5.7.13). As Peggy Muñoz Simonds has argued, the tempest marks the first stage in alchemy, the confusion of elements; and reddening or "rubification," as I have already mentioned, is a significant stage in the progress of the alchemical work.[90] Most important, however, is the fact that Britomart and the hermaphroditic crocodile become reciprocally pregnant. The crocodile devours "Both flames and tempest" and "grow[s] great, / And swolne with pride of his owne peerelesse powre"; she in turn "of his game . . . soone enwombed grew" and gives birth to "a Lion of great might" (5.7.15–16). A transvestite knight herself, Britomart mates with a hermaphroditic crocodile to produce a lion whose sex, at this point, is unspecified. The end result of this *coniunctio* is a dream of Paracelsian alchemical reproduction in which no element has the upper hand, no element is either purely masculine or purely feminine, and the child resembles its mother (since Britomart is Britain and so is the lion) as much as its father (since a crocodile is a beast and so is a lion).

Of all the radical reenvisionings of gendered reproduction in *The Faerie Queene*, Britomart's dream may be the most radical of all. Neither a conception along Aristotelian-Galenic lines, with a subordinate feminine agent, nor even a strictly feminine parthenogenesis whose agency may be safely sloughed off onto "nature" or blamed upon monstrosity (as in the case of Errour's brood in book 1), Britomart's and the crocodile's "game" is the *coniunctio* of equals. It is a dream so unnerving that Britomart, "fraught with melancholy" (5.7.17), seeks advice, and the chief priest to whom she relates her vision reacts "Like to a weake faint-hearted man . . . / Through great astonishment of that strange sight." Like the "astonied" men who appear frequently in Spenser's poetry, the priest, "with long locks vp-standing," is evidently the victim of the Medusa effect. Momentarily unable to speak, he "stifly stared / Like one adawed [daunted] with some dreadfull spright" (5.7.20).

This gender malleability does not last long, however. I use the pronoun *he* to describe the chief priest here because, in the aftermath of Britomart's dream, that is the poem's pronoun for him. When Britomart first enters Isis Church, Isis's priests, like the lion to whom Britomart gives birth in her vision, are not identified as one sex or the other. A secure pronoun assignment swiftly follows her vision, however, and it signals an effort to wrench Britomart's dream back into the typical Aristotelian-Galenic model of reproduction and of male-female gender hierarchy. Interpreting the crocodile of Britomart's dream as Artegall, Britomart's intended, the priest reads the vision as a political allegory in which Artegall defends Britomart's "iust heritage" of her father's kingdom. After marrying Artegall and joining him "in equall portion of [her] realme," Britomart "a sonne to him shalt beare, / That Lion-like shall shew his powre extreame" (5.7.23). Alchemical emblem shifts to royal coat of arms and gender complexity to gender simplicity, with Britomart's androgynous lion-child now not a lion at all, but a merely "Lion-like" son. From this point in the story, Britomart heads off to right the gender hierarchy, freeing Artegall from the Amazon Radigund's shameful captivity and handing the rule of Radigund's city-state over to him.

The outcome of the priest's reinterpretation of Britomart's vision in Isis Church is not, however, simply the loss of an alternative gender identity, as Britomart's trajectory is redirected from wandering, transvestite knight to subordinate wife and mother of British kings. It is also the loss of an alternative epistemology, which for Spenser always also means an alternative poetics. Analyzing instances in *The Faerie Queene* of feminine parthenogenesis, Elizabeth Spiller argues that the very structure and composition of the poem are imbricated in alternative early modern theories of pregnancy. Quests, which tend to be of nine-month duration in *The Faerie Queene*, are equated with gestation, and gestation with ideation and with the formulation of fiction. Spiller thus finds it important both for an Aristotelian-Galenic model of biological reproduction and for a male-centered model of authorship that, for example, Britomart's quest—which begins as her independent conception of her future lover

Artegall—is appropriated by Merlin's narrative of what she is up to. Otherwise, other, less predictable modes of biological and authorial conception could intervene.[91] The Isis Church episode, in my view, demonstrates quite openly how arbitrary—indeed, how intellectually inadequate—such an appropriation can be. As Lowell Gallagher puts it, book 5 as a whole is in the habit of showing what details must be left out of the story for ham-fisted interpretation such as the chief priest's to happen. Book 5 is also in the habit of thematizing this blindness. Thus book 5 is "about and yet not about the hegemonic economy of interpretation brought to bear in the production of pious legends" such as the pious legend of justice.[92] Or, I would add, the pious legend of male elements mastering female in the conception and gestation of children.

The interpretative choice of what story to tell is also, however, the epistemological choice of what phenomena to notice and to know. Dorothy Stephens and I have both identified moments in *The Faerie Queene*—like Britomart's dream, or the Medusan "astonishment" with which the chief priest hears of her dream—with narrative contingency: they are moments when anything might happen, and when the range of objects and events in view might expand beyond one's ken.[93] Another word for these periodic apertures of contingency might be *wonder*. According to Lorraine Daston and Katharine Park, learning in the sixteenth and seventeenth centuries included a new (and never again repeated) overlap between natural philosophy and the study of marvels. Following upon the way that thinkers such as Marsilio Ficino and Girolamo Cardano innovatively argued for the admission of contingency and chance into the physical and metaphysical structure of the universe, sixteenth- and seventeenth-century natural philosophers granted the contingent and unexplained event "a brief but key role in forging a new category of scientific experience: the fact detached from explanation, illustration, or inference."[94] The marvelous, contingent, astonishing phenomenon might lend itself to epistemological innovation.

Indeed, Descartes's efforts late in his career to construct a theory of wonder propose exactly that kind of innovation: apprehension without the attempt at ownership. When the observer is in the state of wonder, objects and persons are simply seen, not assimilated into a knowledge system that effaces them. "When our first encounter with some object surprises us and we find it novel, or very different from what we formerly know or from what we supposed it ought to be, this causes us to wonder and to be astonished at it. . . . [T]his may happen before we know whether or not the object is beneficial [*convenable*] to us."[95] What we notice about Cartesian wonder is, first of all, its potentially revolutionary application of the scientific method. It takes in new phenomena without inserting them into previously established knowledge. In contrast with the link Cavell outlines between skepticism—that other Cartesian response to the world—and a horrendous, destructive misogyny, wonder might take in, say, the visual and conceptual object of study that is female reproductive anatomy and consider it marvelous. Descartes makes it possible, in other words, for the sense of the marvelous that Daston and Park associate with premodern natural philosophy to persist in an age of scientific discovery.[96] The second thing we notice is the feminized quality of the brain in wonderment as Descartes imagines it: "objects of the senses that are novel affect the brain in certain parts where it is not normally affected; and . . . since these parts are more tender or less firm than those hardened through frequent agitation, the effects of the movements produced in them are thereby increased."[97] Descartes's tender brain in the state of wonderment brings Luce Irigaray to describe Cartesian wonder as an experience that sidesteps castration anxiety so that the feminine may be truly encountered. "A separation without a wound," Irigaray calls it.[98]

Arguing for an application of Irigarayan wonder to certain examples of blazons addressing a woman, Grant Williams suggests that Renaissance literature sometimes evidences the ability to encounter the female body as feminine alterity rather than as something to be known and mastered.[99] This literary wonder seems to have extended to some avenues of early modern anatomical science in the form of innovative curiosity about what can be seen of the external structures of female genitalia. For example, the late sixteenth and early seventeenth centuries saw in England, improbably enough, the "discovery" of the female clitoris as an anatomical feature designed for something previously unthinkable: feminine pleasure with no immediate reproductive end. On the one hand, the discovery of the clitoris and the prospect of excess female sexual pleasure drew, as Traub has shown, a tremendous amount of disapprobation.[100] On the other, as Traub, Park, and Bettina Mathes have all discussed, discovering the clitoris requires acknowledging at least some possibility of consequential female sexual difference that countervails the Aristotelian-Galenic scheme.[101]

The Spenserian equivalent of this kind of gynecological wonder occurs in book 6 of *The Faerie Queene*, when one of the knights of courtesy, Calidore, stumbles onto "An hundred naked maidens lilly white / All raunged in

a ring, and daucing in delight" (6.10.11). It is a distinctly vaginal circle, and
yet it is one that is most definitely not nothing. Rather, it is a "girland," a
"Crowne," a "goodly band, / Whose sundry parts were here too long to tell"
(6.10.13–14). In response,

> Much wondred *Calidore* at this straunge sight,
> Whose like before his eye had neuer seene,
> And standing long astonished in spright,
> And rapt with pleasaunce, wist not what to weene.
>
> (6.10.17; emphasis in the original)

Finally we see here the revolutionary approach to the study of female anatomy in action: just looking, "wisting not what to weene," observing but not
categorizing and delimiting what you cannot yet fully know. As I have previously argued, this episode, along with others in *The Faerie Queene*, proposes
an alternative kind of sexualized poetics and poetic pleasure, one associated
with female desire.[102] Moreover, Calidore's ravishing vision of the "sundry
parts" of women recognizes those parts as just that: apart, "sundered" in kind
from those of men. As opposed to the interpretive gambit practiced by the
chief priest in Isis Church, one that strategically avoids the alchemically envisioned significance of Britomart's parts, Calidore for the space of a quatrain
does not have an Aristotelian-Galenic story to tell about what women's parts
are like and what they do.

   It doesn't last, of course. Calidore decides he must classify what he sees
within a familiar knowledge scheme, "Whether it were the traine of beauties
Queene, / Or Nymphes, or Faeries, or enchaunted show, / With which his
eyes mote haue deluded beene" (6.10.17). And thus, "Therefore resoluing, what
it was, to know, / Out of the wood he rose, and toward them did go" (6.10.17).
Upon which the vision disappears. Spenser has made his point. Looking at
women in the hope of seeing only what you want to see leaves you in an epistemologically impoverished position. And a sexually impoverished one, too.
Calidore next seeks an explanation of his vision from a shepherd he runs
across—who turns out to be Spenser himself in his pastoral persona as Colin
Clout, and who proceeds to dress Calidore down for his stupidity. The nymphs'
ring, Colin explains, was meant not for Calidore's pleasure but for their own:
"For, being gone, none can them bring in place, / But whom *they of them
selues list* so to grace" (6.10.20; emphasis added). Female desire, what "they of
them selues list," is required for both male pleasure and aesthetic pleasure to

happen. And female desire requires men seeing what they see truly, and seeing what they see in wonder.

Alchemical Conceptions in *Love's Labour's Lost*

Love's Labour's Lost is William Shakespeare's most explicit portrayal of the scene of knowledge making. It is a play in love not only with the written word but also with textbooks, as Carla Mazzio has observed; it is also a play that begins with a debate over what should be studied, and to what ends.[103] The play's curriculum turns out to be an unusual one. Like one of its sources, Pierre de la Primaudaye's *L'Académie Française*, in which the discussants in an all-male academy focus largely on the nature of marriage and child rearing, *Love's Labour's Lost* seems to posit coupling and reproduction as more pressing issues than typical academic subjects. In some ways it would be a mistake to argue that *Love's Labour's Lost* engages any mode of learning deeply or consequentially: this puzzling drama of surfaces holds all knowledge at arm's length, from book learning to authentic acquaintance with one's romantic partner. But at the same time, *Love's Labour's Lost* flirts openly with alchemical modes of learning, especially with alchemical modes of converting troublesome women into a purer and more tractable form. The result is that, like the other works I have discussed in this chapter, *Love's Labour's Lost* entertains a fantasy about a mode of reproduction that might be alchemical rather than sexual. Unlike William Harvey, *Love's Labour's Lost* is not committed to eliminating women's shaping influence from the reproductive process entirely. Nor, however, is *Love's Labour's Lost* as sure as Edmund Spenser's *Faerie Queene* is that the dual-gendered generativity of true alchemy may be distinguished from the parthenogenetic fantasy of bad alchemy. Rather, the play moves ambiguously and uncertainly among alternative reproductive prospects: the mystical marriage of male and female elements; the male-only reproduction of finer bodies; and the inescapable reality of the woman's reproductive role. In turn, alchemical structures and tropes in the play become a way of figuring the impossible fantasies that pertain when men try to suture study to experience. Their approach to learning morphs into their desires regarding marriage and regarding the comedic endings that marriage signifies.

Specifically, *Love's Labour's Lost* ponders what should be studied *by a group*: we are invited to imagine learning not as the activity of an individual reader but as the activity of a collective in accord about what should be known. When

William Harvey lays aside his volume of Helkiah Crooke's anatomy—which asserts the perfection and undoubted functionality of the female ovaries—in order to argue that the ovaries are useless, he is engaging in an individual and idiosyncratic reading practice. But when that gesture is repeated in wider scholarly and scientific circles, it becomes a metonym for the efforts undertaken by scholarly communities and networks committed to downplaying the female role in reproduction.

As I mentioned in my discussion of *The Tempest* in Chapter 3, recent historical studies have emphasized how sociable an enterprise early modern science came to be. In late seventeenth-century experimentation, the public "demonstration" of such new techniques as blood transfusion or the air pump became one of the central activities of London's Royal Society. And late seventeenth-century science, as Lisa Jardine has argued, was carried out in coffeehouse discussions more than it was in solitary thought.[104] Anatomy and alchemy were both early adopters of this scientific sociability. Whether in the anatomy theater or in the practical alchemist's workshop, work took place in groups that might include the practitioner's family members, servants, friends, fellow adepts, and students. The primary conceit of Ben Jonson's *The Alchemist*—that alchemy gives an extraordinary collection of people occasion to visit an experimental space—anticipates the later age of scientists like Robert Hooke and Robert Boyle, when experimental venues were often located within private residences and were subject to unannounced social calls on the part of the curious. Boyle's attempts to get some time alone to work by posting a sign on his laboratory door, "Mr. Boyle cannot be spoken with to-day," were considered unusual.[105] That sociability, it is worth emphasizing, had its roots in the humanist culture in which seventeenth-century scientists were steeped. The group work of anatomy, alchemy, and nascent chemistry and physics alike had learned its habits from humanistic traditions of close collaboration and humanists' attempts to make their work part of the public polity.[106]

It is important, however, not to assume that "sociable" necessarily means "open-minded" or "noncoercive." Thomas Hobbes's concern that the experimental space, like the humanist classroom or closet, was still governed by the agenda of a "master" should not fall off our radar.[107] That "master" function may, of course, be implemented beyond the agenda or even the lifetime of a single individual. Hewing to an explicit or implicit agenda of "correct" knowledge, the corporate, aggregated, or networked body of scholars can, in fact, be an ideal vector for the promulgation of disknowledge. The group, whether physically present as in the anatomy theater or formed by farther-flung intellectual networks, can reinforce an agenda of not discarding outmoded ideas when those ideas prove to have their own kind of utility. The disknowledge of the female reproductive system is a case in point. Nancy Tuana argues, for example, that the medical establishment's de-emphasis on the role of the clitoris in female sexual pleasure has been perpetuated from the sixteenth century to the present, just as Marlin Ah-King, Andrew Barron, and Marie Herberstein have argued that female animal genitalia are still understudied by biologists only because of a long-standing prior assumption that female genitalia just aren't that interesting.[108] Adept at avoiding knowledge as much as creating knowledge, intellectual circles can enforce and reinforce cherished assumptions about women's part in generative reproduction.

Love's Labour's Lost is Shakespeare's examination of just what that effort of avoidance on the part of an intellectual circle looks like and what purpose that effort might serve. While feminist historians of science have begun to explore the habitual, commonplace misogyny of the rhetoric and the habits of thought of early modern science, the extent to which early modern academic relationships among men reinforced misogynistic assumptions has not yet been studied. But Shakespeare's play, in its way, conducts that very study. Just as Shakespeare, in Lynn Enterline's incisive analysis, both recapitulates and explodes the ways in which the early modern schoolroom attempted to enforce strict divisions between masculinity and femininity, so too does Shakespeare's imagination of an all-male scientific society recapitulate and critique the hothouse misogyny indulged in by male academic circles.[109]

While there is no necessary reason for an all-male intellectual circle to be any more suspicious of women than any other gathering of early modern men would be, such misogyny certainly characterized what Jesuit Robert Parsons called the "school of atheism," the loose intellectual circle around Walter Ralegh that included writers, mathematicians, and natural philosophers such as Giordano Bruno, Thomas Harriot, George Chapman, Christopher Marlowe, and the "Wizard Earl," the alchemist Henry Percy, Earl of Northumberland.[110] Shakespeare's personal, professional, and/or intellectual acquaintance with many of these men or their writings encouraged M. C. Bradbrook and Frances Yates in the 1930s each to propose a detailed topical allegory for *Love's Labour's Lost* in which the King of Navarre's retreat of gentleman scholars is modeled after this boundary-testing intellectual circle, supposedly referred to in the play's murky phrase "the school of night."[111] The particularities of this topical reading, as Mary Ellen Lamb has pointed out, are impossible either to prove or to disprove; nor does the play's "school of night" phrase require such an ingenious set of references to make it legible.[112] It is fairly clear that no such "school" existed in the way that Bradbrook or Yates imagined it. Nonetheless, I am intrigued by Bradbrook's groundbreaking assertion that Shakespeare's play specifically satirizes elite scholarly circles' misogynist habits. Stung by the consequences of unwise marriage and a queen's fury (as Ralegh was) or simply habitually disgusted by femininity (as Bruno was), the scholars associated with Ralegh seem truly to have been unusually dedicated, even in late sixteenth-century terms, to loathing the feminine.

Evidence for this loathing ranges from the portrayal of ignorance as feminine in Chapman's "Shadow of Night" (1594); to the speaker's abject whining about female authority in Ralegh's *The Ocean to Cynthia* (1590s); to the full-blown horror of female sexuality registered by Bruno's *On the Heroic Frenzies* (1585), which—despite being what Ingrid Rowland calls "a veritable anthology of love poetry"—urges its dedicatee, Philip Sidney, to leave off sonneteering about such an unworthy object as a woman's body:[113]

> Here we have written down on paper, enclosed in books, placed before the eyes and sounded in the ear a noise, an uproar, a blast of symbols, of emblems, of mottoes, of epistles, of sonnets, of epigrams, of prolific notes, of excessive sweat, of life consumed, shrieks which deafen the stars, laments which reverberate in the caves of hell, tortures which affect living souls with stupor, sighs which make the gods swoon with compassion, and all this for those eyes, for those cheeks, for that breast, for that whiteness, for that vermilion, for that speech, for those teeth, for those lips, that hair, that dress, that robe, that glove, that slipper, that shoe, that reserve, that little smile, that wryness, that window-widow, that eclipsed sun, that scourge, that disgust, that stink, that tomb, that latrine, that menstruum, that carrion, that quartan ague, that excessive injury and distortion of nature, which with surface appearance, a shadow, a phantasm, a dream, a Circean enchantment put to the service of generation, deceives us as a species of beauty.[114]

At first Bruno satirizes the contrast between high-flown poetic excess and the plain physicality of the female form to which it is applied. Surely "tortures which afflict living souls with stupor" are ill matched to something as ordinary as "those lips, that hair, that dress." But with the odd trope of "window-widow" (*vedova fenestra*), Bruno raises the specter of a female body that is not simply what it is but a window onto death for any man foolish enough to enter it. In "service of generation" (*serviggio della generazione*) and in pursuit of that "excessive injury and distortion of nature" (*estrema ingiuria e torto di natura*) that is the castrated, ill-formed female body, men are deceived into diving into their own putrid tomb.

Buried in Bruno's screed, however, is the suggestion that his description of femininity contains its own cure for the degradations it depicts. In Bruno's telling, the excremental and rotting female body—"that stink, that tomb, that latrine"—is also the stuff of an alchemical experiment. As the natural philosopher Bruno well knows, "that menstruum" and "that carrion" (*quel menstruo, quella carogna*) are among the substances on which early modern alchemists depend: menstruum as *prima materia* or wondrous solvent, carrion as the significant alchemical stage of putrefaction that signals the coming rebirth of the philosopher's stone. In other words, once converted from flesh to metaphor, femininity becomes the means for leaving the female body behind. In this regard, *The Heroic Frenzies* revises Plato's *Phaedrus* in typical humanist-Neoplatonic fashion so that the love of a beautiful woman, not a beautiful boy, might ultimately lead a man to abandon physical love in favor of contemplating the divine; *The Heroic Frenzies* also recapitulates humanism's hopes that the language arts might assist in a man's ascent from physical to metaphysical bliss.[115] Bruno's alchemical references, however, make explicit that this ascent is also a matter of disdaining and even eschewing heterosexual coupling and reproduction. He thus proves the equivalences proposed by an anonymous volume called *The Riddles of Heraclitus and Democritus* (1598). To the riddling question of who, like Paracelsus and Prometheus, "not onely maketh persons at her pleasure, but also bringeth them from hell or heaven to life againe when they be dead," the answer comes: "Paracelsus, in his booke *de natura rerum* teacheth an artificiall generation of an homunculus, or little man. Prometheus, the sonne of Iapetus, was the first maker of images, and thereupon, was fained to make men. This riddle is ment by Rhetorike, or the figure Prosopopeia, that to stirre and moove affection, attributeth speech to dead men."[116] Alchemy, art, and rhetoric—characterized here as personification—are all good for two things. First, they generate men. Second, they make dead men live, escaping the dread horrors of the killing pit that is the female body.[117]

The alchemical, rhetorical, poetic wresting of reproduction from feminine influence seems to be exactly what Navarre has in mind for his "little academe, / Still and contemplative in living art" (1.1.13–14). While "living art" means "the art of living," one cannot help but catch a whiff of Navarre's longing, in his academic retreat, to make life out of art, as Paracelsus or Prometheus did, rather than life out of sexual intercourse. The opening of *Love's Labour's Lost*, in which the gentlemen agree to Navarre's compact, draws a boundary between masculine study and feminine sexuality. The "end of study," says Navarre in response to Berowne, is limitless—"that to know which else we should not know" (1.1.55–56). Except for one thing: when Berowne suggests they study mistresses, Navarre calls women "the stops that hinder study quite / And train our intellect to vain delight" (1.1. 70–71). Berowne's proposed curriculum is in jest, but Navarre's reply suggests nonetheless that the male academic circle exclude not only women but even the *study* of women.

If the gentlemen's academy is to entertain thoughts of reproduction, it will thus require reproductive vessels alternative to women. As the play continues, male rhetoric adopts different strategies for avoiding and erasing the femininity that the men encounter—both the aristocratic women the gentlemen will woo, and Jaquenetta, a dairymaid who is pregnant by someone in the king's household, either the comic Spaniard Armado or (far more likely) the clown Costard. These rhetorical strategies are borrowed wholesale from alchemy's assays at converting the physically feminine into the metaphorically masculine: woman's base matter transmutes into purer, linguistic form, and female sexual anatomy is replaced by visions of an alchemical apparatus that is capable of a better kind of reproduction.

The alchemical imagery and terminology of *Love's Labour's Lost* have long been recognized. Both here and in his poems, Shakespeare, like John Donne (as discussed in Chapter 2), readily turns to alchemy as a reservoir of metaphors for how to purify love's less seemly aspects.[118] It is thus plausible to read the play's surprisingly frequent queries about the color of a man's beloved as an alchemically tinged investigation into how to purify the otherwise irredeemably sullied woman of her baser physicality. When the page boy Moth notes that Samson loved a woman who was of a "sea-water green" complexion, Armado protests that his own love, Jaquenetta, "is most immaculate white and red" (1.2.82, 87). Eager to translate his love into the well-worn language of love sonnets, Armado also purifies her alchemically. Green, red, white: these are progressive colors that alchemists carefully watched for in the distillation and calcination processes. Green, or the "green lion," indicates a fairly raw stage of the purification process, often called "vegetable mercury" and distinguished from the more valuable Sol and Luna.[119] Sometimes identified with copper, the "green lion"—described by a late fifteenth-century English alchemical manuscript claiming to be the "ascertations" of Raymond Lull as "quyk gold unfixed and uncomplete by nature"—replicates the liquid and unstable feminine humors in ways that must be overcome if further refinement is to be had.[120] The color green's alchemical connotations thus nicely dovetail with the early modern interpretation of women's "green sickness" as a superfluity of corrupt menstrual fluid or of female "seed."[121] If Jaquenetta is "green" alchemically as well as by virtue of her imperfect female body, it will take a great deal of rhetorical work to raise her to the "red and white" status Armado claims for her—red and white being more advanced stages of alchemy, with red as (among other things) the color of the "aurum potibile"—"an Oyl as red as Blood"—and white as the near-final version of the philosopher's stone, "the white Sulphur, not burning, and the stone of Paradice, that is, the stone which converts imperfect Mettals into fine white silver."[122]

A similar alchemical reformation of the female lover's color occurs in Berowne's discourse about Rosaline. His efforts to prove his dark love fair reflect not only his need to "whiten" his beloved into an acceptably valuable commodity, as Kim Hall has argued, but also the typical inexactitude of alchemical discourse, in which the utter whiteness that is the goal of successful experiment must be preceded by an equally utter blackness.[123] "[Y]our werk with blak must begyne," advises Thomas Norton's *Ordinall of Alchemy*, "If the end shuld be with whitnes to wyne."[124] "When thou findest it blacke," says *The Mirror of Alchemy*, "know that in that blacknesse whitenesse is hidden, and thou must extract the same from his most subtile blacknes."[125] Navarre protests in response to Berowne that black could not possibly be proximate to white: "O paradox! Black is the badge of hell, / The hue of dungeons and the school of night" (4.3.250–51). But Berowne and the ladies all insist upon the two colors' commensurability. Berowne claims that "No face is fair that is not full so black" (4.3.249), and Katherine calls Rosaline a "light condition in a beauty dark" (5.2.20).[126]

Katherine's pun on "light," however, indicates the difficulty of incorporating actual women, rather than metaphorically feminine alchemical supplies, into a refining project whose end is perfection. Women's "lightness" makes them subject to adultery, as well as adulteration, and women's commonness and commonality seed the entire action of *Love's Labour's Lost*—even past the ending of the play, as act 5's closing song features the call of the cuckoo, "word of fear, / Unpleasing to a married ear" (5.2.888–89). The fatherhood of

Jaquenetta's child, a question raised in the play's first scene, is still unsettled in the last. Is it Costard, who plays the pimpy "Pompey the huge" in the Pageant of the Nine Worthies, or is it Armado, as Costard claims (5.2.671–82)? Similarly, the aristocratic women threaten at every turn to corrupt genteel masculinity with whorishness and mean estate. Nicknaming his beloved with the commoner's name Joan, which appears in the "cuckoo" song as the name of a greasy kitchen maid (5.2.917), Berowne seems to suspect that Rosaline's darkness is accompanied by an unladylike status of two kinds, wanton behavior and low station:

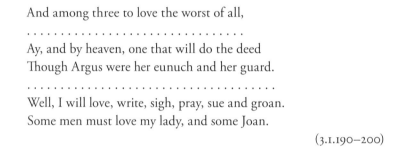

And among three to love the worst of all,
. . . .
Ay, and by heaven, one that will do the deed
Though Argus were her eunuch and her guard.
. . . .
Well, I will love, write, sigh, pray, sue and groan.
Some men must love my lady, and some Joan.

(3.1.190–200)

For reasons that are never specified, Rosaline is repeatedly accused of loose sexual conduct in the play.[127] The other three ladies are similarly at fault, though for more associative reasons. Together their names and identities either echo or anticipate a whole host of sexually problematic Shakespearean women. The generic title of the French Princess looks back to *1 Henry VI*'s whorish French Joan La Pucelle, who claims noble birth, and looks forward to the French princess of *Henry V*, who despite her sexual fastidiousness is made wanton by Henry's unwelcome kiss in that play's wooing scene. The name Katherine recalls the shrew whom Petruchio rhetorically transforms into his whorish "household Kate" and forecasts Henry V's similar domestication of his French princess into another Kate, as well as *Measure for Measure*'s Kate Keepdown. And Maria metamorphoses in *Love's Labour's Lost*'s "cuckoo" song into Marian, a name associated elsewhere in Shakespeare with lower-class women and, via the common appearance of Maid Marian characters in Morris dances and May games, with sexual availability (5.2.912n).

No wonder, then, that when Berowne calls his compatriots to the cause of love, his discourse struggles to keep the alchemical reproductive process within an Aristotelian-Galenic framework in which men are the fashioners of women rather than the other way around:

From women's eyes this doctrine I derive:
They sparkle still the right Promethean fire;
They are the books, the arts, the academes,
That *show, contain and nourish all the world*;
Else *none at all in aught* proves excellent.
. . . .
For wisdom's sake, a word that all men love,
Or, for love's sake, a word that loves all men,
Or, *for men's sake, the authors of these women,*
Or women's sake, by whom we men are men,
Let us once lose our oaths to find ourselves.

(4.3.324–35; emphasis added)

This speech in a way puts love's alchemy on safe ground in that women remain alchemical vessels, receptive to "Promethean fire." At the same time, however, the notion that women do not merely "show" and "contain" the entire world but also "nourish" it leads to some confusion over whether men are "the authors of these women" or women make men men. Buried in this endlessly reversible speculation upon who makes whom is the enigmatic suggestion that, because women are involved, perfection is unattainable. Women "show, contain and nourish all the world; / Else none at all in aught proves excellent"—they are indispensable. But there is also an aural pun here, that "none at all *in naught* proves excellent," simultaneously asserting that nothing excellent emerges from women's genitals, their "naught."

Yet even though it is uncertain about the desirability or efficacy of an alchemically purified feminine reproductive role, *Love's Labour's Lost* is equally uncertain about Pseudo-Paracelsus's all-male alternative. Not only does the gentlemen's all-male academy collapse almost as soon as it is conceived, but the play's most enthusiastic alchemist is the pedant Holofernes, whose epithet "Thrice-worthy gentleman" (5.1.135) recalls the "trimagisterial" name of Hermes Trismegistus, and whose name I am thus tempted to read as an alchemical pun on "hollow furnace."[128] Holofernes presents a ridiculous and easily debunked version of masculine parthenogenetic invention: "This is a gift that I have—simple, simple; a foolish extravagant spirit, full of forms, figures, shapes, objects, ideas, apprehensions, motions, revolutions. These are begot in the ventricle of memory, nourished in the womb of [*primater*], and delivered upon the mellowing of occasion" (4.2.65–70). This boast contains a telling textual crux. Editors of Shakespeare beginning with Nicholas Rowe have emended the Quarto and Folio editions' rendition of Holofernes' phrase, "the womb of primater," into "the womb of pia mater"—that is, the womb of the membrane protecting the brain. I find this emendation unnecessary and have restored "primater" to the passage, since "primater" as a compositor's error or eye skip is more plausibly an error for *prima mater[ia]*, alchemy's prime matter/*mater* that Holofernes appropriates for his own fertile brain.

Responding to Holofernes, the curate Nathaniel unwittingly mocks the pedant as engaging in a far less intellectual, and clearly not parthenogenetic, mode of begetting and delivering: "Sir, I praise the Lord for you, and so may my parishioners, for their sons are well tutored by you, and their daughters profit very greatly under you. You are a good member of the commonwealth" (4.2.72–75). Shakespeare's bawdy witticism here does not go as far in the direction of alchemy as Falstaff's planning to sponge off Justice Shallow enough to emasculate him entirely—"I'll make him *a philosopher's two stones* to me"— or as the apprentice Rafe's saying in John Lyly's *Gallathea* that his alchemist master, upon meeting a "pretty wench come to his shop . . . with puffing, blowing, and sweating . . . so plied her that he multiplied her . . . by the philosophers' stone."[129] Still, Holofernes' reputation for begetting recalls the joke personified by his Rabelaisian namesake and predecessor pedant, Tubal Holofernes, Gargantua's sophistical tutor. Shakespeare's sidelong glance at Rabelais's anatomical pun, "Tubal," works even better in English than it does in French: with "two balls" and a "hollow furnace" to boot, Holofernes' cognominal back story suggests no end of reproductive capacity.[130] Just not the kind of all-male, one-sex reproduction imagined by Pseudo-Paracelsus. Elsewhere the malapropisms exchanged among Armado, Costard, Moth, and Holofernes exclude women from the intellectual sphere only to substitute a sodomitical society whose product—as the genuine Paracelsus feared for misplaced semen becoming colonic homunculi—is only intestinal effluvia. Armado solemnly asserts his familiarity with Navarre to be such that "it will please his grace, by the world, sometime to lean upon my poor shoulder and with his royal finger thus dally with my excrement, with my mustachio" (5.1.94–97). Far from the textually productive homoerotic male interchanges analyzed by Jeffrey Masten, *Love's Labour's Lost*'s all-male academic enterprise produces nothing but shit, a shit that is both literal and—in the sorry spectacle of the Pageant of the Nine Worthies—literary.[131]

Thus *Love's Labour's Lost*'s male-controlled reproduction, whether it includes or does not include elements of feminine matter, falls flat, its products sometimes distasteful but always untenable. Berowne's initial dismissal of the academy scheme as an "abortive birth"—spelled "abhortive" in the 1598 Quarto of the play—nicely encapsulates both the slim likelihood of the project's success, and the abhorrence of its product (1.1.104). Male parthenogenesis must thus be added to the list of ways in which the men's activities in *Love's Labour's Lost* are failed experiments. Indeed, the ending of the play piles failure upon masculine failure. First the gentlemen swear fealty to the wrong ladies in the masque. Their mistake is interrupted by the even more egregious Pageant of the Nine Worthies—which, in another display of poor "multiplication" skills, turns out to be just three Worthies. This comically bad show is in turn interrupted by the announcement of the death of the Princess's father, which cuts off the merriment of comedy. This last development reveals the entire love plot as an experiment that has failed to come to its conclusion. When Navarre tries to make that failure right too hastily by proposing marriage, the Princess remarks that it is "A time, methinks, too short / To make a world-without-end bargain in" (5.2.782–83). And so they must meet again a year and a day hence, to see if love has failed too. It's not right, says Berowne. "Jack hath not Jill" (5.2.863). This is not how the comic experiment ought to turn out.

Still, the play's conclusion cannot give up the experiment. *Love's Labour's Lost* comes to a close with the arrival of Marcadé, the messenger who announces the Princess's father's death and shuts down the love idyll. On the one hand, Marcadé acts as the dramatic equivalent of the two-handed engine in John Milton's *Lycidas*, the inexplicable intrusion that threatens to collapse the whole frothy structure of what has come before. He is Mar-arcady, the one who mars Arcadia. On the other hand, Marcadé is Mercury: not only is he a messenger, but, as H. R. Woudhuysen argues, Shakespeare's referent here is a play by Robert Wilson called *The Cobbler's Prophecy*, where the god Mercury is alternatively called Markedy.[132] And mercury is the essential ingredient of yet another go at the alchemical process, indicating that perhaps the experimental trial is about to begin again. Perhaps it is not surprising that a play occupied, as Patricia Parker says, with "preposterous reversals"—reversals of language, of gender hierarchy, of comedic structures themselves—ultimately sustains both an irresolvable skepticism about alchemical reproduction's efficacy and an impossible desire for it to continue.[133]

Marcadé's association with death even aligns him with "putrefaction," the stage that, almost all alchemical writings agree, is crucial to the alchemical process and that is associated with the transition from blackness to whiteness. Putrefaction is, moreover, key to the alchemical process as reproduction. If the alchemist "putrifie not," says Nicolas Flamel's *Hieroglyphical Figures*, "hee doeth not corrupt nor ingender, and by consequent, the Stone cannot take vegetative life to increase and multiply."[134] Pseudo-Paracelsus's *De natura rerum* begins by citing John 12:24 on the subject: "putrefaction produceth great matters, as of this wee have a most famous example in the holy Gospel, where Christ saith: Unlesse a grain of wheat bee cast into the Earth, and be putrefied, it cannot bring forth fruit in a hundred fold."[135] Sensible enough, and in accordance with alchemy's Gnostic and Christian antecedents: death leads to conception and rebirth. Along these lines, the Mercurial death at the end of *Love's Labour's Lost* seems like a rather promising development, reversing the alchemical failures that have been seen thus far. On the other hand, though, many alchemical writings propose that the alchemical wedding either precedes alchemical putrefaction—as in Ripley's *Compound of Alchemy*, in which "conjunction" is the "Fourth Gate" and "putrefaction" the "Fifth"—or coincides with it, "for there shall be no composition / without marriage and putrefaction."[136] Conception leads to death, rather than the reverse, just as the "cuckoo" song begins with two stanzas about cuckoldry and concludes with two stanzas about winter's assaults upon physical energy, "when blood is nipped and ways be foul" (5.2.904). Given these associations, the coincidence of death with Marcadé's appearance would seem to be a natural consequence of the female fecundity and potential unchastity that have been emphasized throughout the play. An alchemically fruitful future beyond the end of the play hovers uncertainly between these two options: death producing life, female sexuality producing death.

What are we to make of the play's continued irrational faith, then, that we can start over in parthenogenetically alchemical fashion, that alchemical death will bring new life? I would suggest that in *Love's Labour's Lost* this faith is both exposed as irrational, and allowed to stand. Death is not a finality, but a postponement: the gentlemen must bear solitude and fasting for "a twelvemonth and a day" before reuniting with their ladies (5.2.865). This typically Hermetic time span, both specific and ritualistic, poignantly unites mourning and marriage. Even if it could easily turn on a dime to the kind of silly ritualized duration that is mocked in *The Alchemist*, when the con artists convince Dapper that he must await the Fairy Queen for exactly two hours with his mouth stopped with gingerbread, *Love's Labour's Lost* cannot go so far as this mockery. While the play's alchemical imagery attests to the frivolity of scholarly learning, *Love's Labour's Lost* truly wants death to be life, and hence continues to capitalize on the jumble of needlessly occult, deliberately obfuscatory confusions and crosstalk by which alchemy tries to have its parthenogenetic cake and eat it too. "The words of Mercury are harsh after the songs of Apollo" says the play in closing (5.2.918–19), but how are we supposed to take this pronouncement? Even its attribution is unclear. In the Folio version, it belongs to the braggart Armado, the same man stupid enough to think he will get ahead at court by letting the king play with his excremental mustache. In the Quarto, in contrast, it floats free and unattributed in a larger typeface that seems to conclude and comment on the play as a whole, as if Mercury's words are a harsh but necessary corrective to the play's deathly failures so far.[137] If Marcadé/Mercury has the final word, then alchemy commences again, co-opting the mercurial, feminine component of the *prima materia* as the alchemist's first step toward bringing his own offspring into the world.

CHAPTER 5

How to Make Fiction

Gabriel Naudé's early seventeenth-century history of magic rather disparagingly groups alchemists, like other fabulists and tricksters, with painters and poets. His reasons are twofold. They are all careless scholars, and they all make up stories: "For these, bestowing their time rather in gleaning what was scattered up and down, than in weighing the authority of the Authours from whom they borrowed their notes, have not onely advanced an Iliad of chimericall and ridiculous stories, but with the same labour, brought upon the stage some more improbable than the other, reporting them as most true & certain."[1]

On the face of it, Naudé's association of both alchemists and poets with bad humanistic practice—with merely "gleaning what was scattered up and down" rather than "weighing the authority of the Authours from whom they borrowed their notes"—indicates only the frustration of a scholar who frequently debunked fabricated claims of antique textual authority, including, for example, those of the Rosicrucians. But Naudé's inclusion of alchemists with poets, painters, and other bad practitioners of humanism also hints at how literature might in fact embrace alchemy's reputation for being a discipline none too attached to the truth. In the course of cautioning his readers about the need to judge carefully which historians, both ancient and modern, may be trusted to stick to the facts, Naudé indicts even the most admired poets and painters—even Homer and Apelles—as "taking the liberty to disguise [the truth], as they please, with their Chimericall imaginations."[2] Classifying these greatest of ancient artists with sources not to be trusted would startle any humanist who had been taught that to know the likes of Homer is to know truth and virtue. Naudé, in contrast, is comfortable with the increasing disciplinary divergence that, in the seventeenth century, would set literature and the other arts apart from other arenas of intellectual effort. He opens the door for literature to feel its way toward the same intellectual status that alchemy—as I discussed in Chapter 1—already occupied in some people's minds: a comprehensive, alluring scheme whose truth value was immaterial to its worth. Alchemy provides a model by which literature may divorce itself from humanism's outmoded aim to make language accurately reflect—and thus be able to influence—the world.

It is thus no accident that alchemy crops up in England's two most significant works of literary theory of the late sixteenth century. As Margaret Healy has pointed out, George Puttenham's *Art of English Poesy* (1589), through punning on metal/mettle, associates the poet's "tempered and qualified . . . mettle of his mind" with the metalwork so fundamental to alchemy.[3] In turn, poetry's metallic proclivities put us in mind of the declaration in Philip Sidney's *Defense of Poetry* (ca. 1580) that I cited in this book's introduction, that poets craft better products than nature ever could: "Her world is brazen, the poets only deliver a golden."[4] Is poetry's golden promise alchemical? Healy contends that it is, and I agree. The unusual aspect of Sidney's refining nature's brassy world into poetry's golden one, however, is his suggestion that alchemy and fiction share not simply similar operations but also a special disciplinary status. It is striking, I think, that when Sidney separates the poet as "maker" from an inclusive list of nature-bound disciplinary adepts—the astronomer, geometrician, arithmetician, musician, natural philosopher, moral philosopher, lawyer, grammarian, rhetorician, logician, physician, and metaphysician—his list does not also include the alchemist. The connection between gold and poetry suggests that, if Sidney had included alchemists in this roster, their place would have been not with the naturalists but with the poets.[5] Sidney's point about disciplinarity is the same as Naudé's, except that this time, the fact that alchemy and poetry are similar types of "making" is a compliment. Neither alchemy nor poetry is natural; neither is an art of discerning the world as it is. It is in this way that the trope of alchemy bolsters Sidney's vision of fiction making as its own realm. If disknowledge is the turn from one mode of knowing to another, then Sidney's promotion of literature into its own discipline is a paradigmatic act of disknowledge.

But simply setting poetry apart from other kinds of learning, like history or philosophy or geometry, is only Sidney's first move. His second is much more audacious: he puts poetry in the category of a mode of learning that owes no necessary allegiance to the truth. His association between alchemy and poetry is a risky one, and he knows it. When he turns to poetry's detractors,

Sidney cites Heinrich Cornelius Agrippa's *Of the Vanity and Uncertainty of Arts and Sciences* as "showing the vanity of science"—that is, the vanity of the disciplines of knowledge.[6] Given that Agrippa renounces alchemy along with poetry and all the other disciplines, Sidney's image of poetry's converting brass into gold thus conspicuously exposes poetry to the same charges of falsity that Agrippa levels against alchemy. But this liability to charges of falsehood is a risk that Sidney wants to run, because it gives him the opportunity to classify fiction, like alchemy, not only as a discipline separate from the rest but also one with ends different from all the others. As Margaret Ferguson has pointed out, Sidney's treatise has a great deal in common with Erasmus's endorsement of indecorous discourse.[7] Sidney's justification for poetry, in other words, self-consciously exploits previous defenses of the indefensible. In this light, his appropriation of alchemy for poetic creation makes more sense, since he wants them to hold the same status. Sidney's turn to alchemical imagery reflects his determination to grant poetry all the advantages of a particular variety of disknowledge—that is, turning away from fact-based modes and tenets of learning to modes and tenets that are not responsible for the truth in the same way.

Sidney's use of the alchemical trope in this fashion reminds us of how *The Defense of Poetry* comes at a turning point in the fortunes of literary knowledge. Writing around 1580, as humanism was beginning to lose its luster, Sidney looks both back and forward: back to an early humanistic era in which literature is the basis of all learning, and forward to a late humanistic era in which literature will become a thing unto itself, separate from the other disciplines.[8] While his defense of poetry shares earlier humanism's conviction that literature is uniquely positioned to inculcate virtue and "moral doctrine" in its readers—"For who will be taught, if he be not moved with desire to be taught?"—it anticipates literature's withdrawal from matters assigned to other modes of thought and inquiry: not only philosophy and history, the alternative disciplines with which Sidney is most concerned, but also all the others.[9] But all the better for that. Poetry chooses to know things its own way, not in the manner of history or philosophy or any of the other arts or sciences from which Sidney dissociates it. Poetry's golden world is advantageous not only because it is refined but also because it comprises a benign and even utopian version of deliberate strategic ignorance. True, poetry's having a delimited realm of knowledge designates the many realms it does not know. But the reverse is true as well: what poetry does not know designates its realm of knowledge as *sui generis*.

Sidney thus points the way forward for literature in a posthumanist future that he will not live to see. And through his alchemical metaphor for how that literature finds its place, he also encourages us to track alchemy's relation to literature as humanism declines. The humanistic dream of a kingdom of letters lingered in the seventeenth century, as this book has detailed. But that dream takes the form of two different ways of promoting humanistically derived rhetorical and philological accomplishment: one of them pernicious, the other delightful. The first is to insist, against all reasonable evidence, that one's theory is true because it is persuasive—persuasive to oneself, at least. The second is to invest in a kind of literary creativity that, while tremendously satisfying, is nonetheless acknowledged to be smaller in scope than other venues of intellectual endeavor are. Wedded as it is to humanistic skills and maneuvers, alchemical discourse is an ideal way to register these two different responses to humanism's decline. Tracing alchemical tropes thus allows us to see how humanism's continued existence depends on its losing its ambitions of pansophism and becoming satisfied with what fiction can do.

In this chapter I examine how three authors writing in the seventeenth century—two early, one later—take up Sidney's prognostication for the future of humanism in an era of disciplinary knowledge and how they, too, use alchemy as a trope for humanism's options and fortunes. As we follow alchemy through William Shakespeare's *Hamlet*, Ben Jonson's *The Alchemist*, and Margaret Cavendish's *Blazing World*, we find three different propositions for how to approach the enterprise of learning. As alchemy is associated less and less with the capacious aims of early humanism, and more and more with the clearly demarcated aims of fiction, both fiction and alchemy garner, quite paradoxically, more legitimacy and more unqualified endorsement, losing their shared reputation for simply being a bad idea.

My analysis of alchemical fictions in these three works will return us to themes detailed earlier in this book. In *Hamlet*, alchemy recalls transubstantiation's role in matter theory, as I discussed in Chapter 2. In *The Alchemist*, the fantasy of alchemical fulfillment picks up on the dream of the originary language that inspired the Christian kabbalists of Chapter 3. And in Cavendish's fictions, alchemically tinged reproductive ambitions take part in the early modern discussion of alternative gynecologies that I explored in Chapter 4. Following these now familiar themes will help us track the kinds of knowledge practices and knowledge values that these three authors suggest are most valuable. When the kinds of knowledge suggested by these works' alchemical plots and tropes claim universal truth, they invite mockery and disaster; but when they are devoted to the work of fiction—to fiction's allegiance to spinning out imaginative possibilities and alternative worlds—all is well.

Hamlet's Alchemical Humanism

Among the many needs that alchemy may have satisfied in the late sixteenth and seventeenth centuries was the need for a totalizing explanatory scheme—what physicists now call a theory of everything—that, in its familiarity and its safety, was not elsewhere to be found. As Alan Macfarlane suggests and as many historians and literary critics have discussed, we must revise Keith Thomas's thesis in *Religion and the Decline of Magic* that early modern England saw a smooth and unbroken transition between magical/religious thinking and mechanistic/secular thinking in order to account for what happens in between. The interregnum between old and new, Macfarlane says, is an age that had begun to aim for what John Ziman calls the "reliable knowledge" of future science but did so through old theories.[10] Even theoretical systems that looked new often betrayed their reliance on the very ideas they were meant to replace. Ramism, for example, devised a new, dialectic logic and anticipated some aspects of modern scientific thinking (for example, the emphasis on visual apprehension) but was still based on the old "certainties" of truth and knowledge.[11] The "scholastic revival" of the sixteenth and seventeenth centuries, practiced primarily by Spanish Dominicans but also evident in the work of Jesuits across Europe and even English Protestants such as Richard Hooker, was responsible for intellectual innovation in a number of ways, but nonetheless required that its adherents reject such potentially nondoctrinal theories as heliocentrism.[12]

Alchemy's affiliations with humanism, in an age when humanism was adhering to old styles of knowledge making even when they had proved themselves inadequate, thus made it an exceptionally, if oddly, suitable candidate for a placeholder theory of everything. That is the case precisely because so many thinkers of the age suspected alchemy to be—in terms I deliberately borrow from the late twentieth-century television comedy *Seinfeld*—a theory of nothing. If the sobriquet for this interim theory is mine, the idea is not new. Iain Chambers has proposed that the "in between" nature of the century between early humanism and early modern science explains the Baroque impulse to build grand schemes on slight premises: "Suspended between anterior and posterior certainties—the precedence of Renaissance humanism and the subsequent convictions of scientific logic and rationalism—the Baroque involves a self-conscious act of throwing a construction over nothing."[13] Citing Walter Benjamin's analysis of the Baroque *Trauerspiel*, Chambers ultimately argues that what makes "throwing a construction over nothing" possible are the lingering, though discredited, habits of an old-style natural philosophy that encouraged a substitutive turn of mind. Because premodern science thought of the universe as vertically integrated, a system of shared properties and mutual influences, a seventeenth century that had begun to doubt Aristotelianism but was not yet ready to accept the consequences of Galileo could still imagine a world constructed so *but no longer rationally so*: "In the interregnum between religious faith secured in the divine stability of the pre-Copernican universe and later consolation in the idolatry of science, the Baroque exposed a naked, unprotected being, in which any 'person, any object, any relationship can mean absolutely anything else.'"[14]

As Chambers and Benjamin suggest, the late sixteenth and seventeenth centuries deemed a theory of everything well suited to the age if it relied unabashedly on the endlessly proliferative substitutability attributed to rhetoric. Even though this very rhetorical proliferation, cited as a fault, contributed to humanism's decline in the seventeenth century (as I discussed in Chapter 1), nothing had yet come along to replace rhetoric's centrality to the curriculum or to civic life. The endless substitutability of terms was also, as we have seen throughout this book, the habitual operation of alchemical rhetoric. Hence alchemy's increasing attractiveness in a Baroque era: the age required a totalizing explanation that also appeared to be a totalizing fiction.

Such grand, sweeping explanatory fictions—whether alchemical or not—can, however, be tremendously damaging. When the humanistically educated Prince of Denmark takes his theory of everything for all in all, even this master of representations fails to recognize that his own fictions are likely a theory of nothing. Acting upon suppositions for which he has no independent corroboration, Hamlet acts like Francis Bacon's worst nightmare: someone who is governed by misguided precedent learning and whose rhetoric takes no care to attach *verba* to *res*. Devoted to the supremacy of the word, Hamlet's theorizing extends, as Ferguson argues, to enacting words' power to kill, in a way that hinges upon and frighteningly actualizes a humanistic understanding of rhetoric as the basis of both individual action and the state's instrumental capacities.[15] And while Hamlet promises to engage in a Baconian program to "wipe away all trivial fond records, / All saws of books, all pressures past / That youth and observation copied" in his brain, acting solely according to what he gains in the way of new and accurate knowledge, he instead implements his own, misguided version of humanistic syncretism: he enacts Marsilio Ficino and Giovanni Pico della Mirandola's dream of unifying everything he has ever known within one system and under one purpose.[16] The way he ensures that his state of knowledge is unitary, however, is to ignore any source that might disconfirm his state of knowledge—a habit that, as I have discussed in this book, is another place of overlap between the reputation of alchemy and the practice (if not the ideal) of humanism. The dark side of syncretism is the tendency, while absorbing alternative knowledge systems, to tacitly jettison facts and beliefs that do not comfortably fit with one's own.

The sense that all learning confirms one's preconceptions establishes the preconditions for the link between humanism and alchemy in *Hamlet*. Hamlet's mode of humanistic inquiry is dedicated to a pansophism that, like much alchemical theory, ignores facts that would not fit his scheme. The outcome is Hamlet's habit of large-scale theorizing that will not brook opposition, even when it is manifestly wrong. In fact, he is so certain of the truth of his theory of why things have gone rotten in Denmark that when the Ghost reveals Claudius as Old Hamlet's murderer, Hamlet claims to have predicted the revelation: "O my prophetic soul!" (1.5.41). More than colloquially speaking, he has an answer for everything.

Swayed by the attractions of Hamlet's character, we often forget, despite a century of psychoanalytic literary study, just how eccentric and solipsistic his know-it-all theorizing is. To take the most obvious example, to the extent that Hamlet undertakes a practical plan for taking his revenge on Claudius, that plan is based on rumor and similitude. Having heard that revenge is called for from a ghost who is "Most like" his father (but perhaps not his father), and having "heard / That guilty creatures sitting at a play / Have . . . proclaim'd their malefactions," Hamlet resolves to stage a play that is "something like the murder of [his] father" and to take his cue from Claudius's reaction, a reaction so apparently illegible that no one but Hamlet reads it as an admission of guilt (1.1.47, 2.2.584–91). From murky and tenuously sourced information like this, Hamlet designs an experiment that is anything but empirical. He reads whatever he likes *from* his sources and *into* his results. The result is that, while

Hamlet's soliloquizing showcases careful Tudor training in argument *in utramque partem*—arguing both sides of the question—his plots and stratagems showcase his propensity for believing only his own argument, even if that argument becomes increasingly illogical with each successive proposition.[17] If Claudius blanches at the play Hamlet stages, Claudius is a murderer; if Hamlet kills Claudius at prayer, Claudius goes to heaven; if Gertrude abstains from Claudius's bed tonight, then each successive night will be easier; if Hamlet imitates Laertes' grief, he proves he loved Ophelia more.[18]

In its totalizing solipsism, Hamlet's philosophy shares its intellectual contours with the reputed knowledge practices of alchemy. The relationship between Hamlet's thinking and alchemical thinking is more than simply analogous, however. Though it is only occasional, alchemical imagery flashes significantly in *Hamlet*, and it does so in such a way that exposes Hamlet's holistic humanism not simply as blind or erroneous but as a form of quite deliberate and easily debunked disknowledge. This illumination comes about because alchemy appears during Hamlet's encounters with—and his inexplicable inability to fathom—the fundamental nature of physical change. He approaches his queries about physical matter in the same spirit as he approaches his queries about everything else, as if his humanistic training will solve the problem. Indeed, he seems to have adopted what Gerard Passannante has described as the humanist habit of analogizing theories of materialism to theories of the transmission of texts.[19] But because Hamlet's questions about physical matter are surrounded by the penumbra of alchemy, they are also imbued with the suggestion that his humanistic approach to theorizing is irredeemably flawed.

Alchemy in *Hamlet* is deeply bound up, specifically, with Hamlet's irrational hope that flesh and spirit alike might be better than they are. His first description of physical change, his wish that "this too too [solid] flesh would melt, / Thaw and resolve itself into a dew" (1.2.129–30), evokes the alchemical goal of subjecting mineral ores to distillation and/or sublimation processes that would turn solids into a purer vapor, a "resolved" dew that releases the substance's vital spirit from its impure dross.[20] Alchemical purification seems also to be on the mind of the Ghost, whose juxtaposition in act 1, scene 5 of the "sulph'rous" fires of purgatory in which he spends his daylight hours and the "quicksilver" swiftness of the poison that killed Old Hamlet renders his very body (insofar as ghosts have bodies) a pre- and postmortem alchemical experiment (1.5.3, 66). Mercury and sulfur in alchemy, as we have seen, are presumed to be the prime metals, capable of breaking impure substances down into *prima materia* and hence preparing them to be reformed as purer and more valuable metals. Thus alchemy is also in play in *Hamlet*'s obsession with earth, which not only is the ground of nation, class, generation, inheritance, and the early modern shift from fiefdom to capitalism, as Margreta de Grazia has argued, but is also the ground of alchemy, the model and touchstone of alchemical experiment.[21] The alchemist's project replicates earth's capacity to incubate metal, but he goes earth one better in that he completes that incubation faster and perhaps even in better fashion than nature can.

Throughout the play, Hamlet proves himself interested in the metaphorics of humans as either base or refined metal/mettle. For example, he prefers to sit by Ophelia's side at the play because she is "mettle more attractive" than Gertrude (3.2.108); he worries that he is a "dull and muddy-mettled rascal" (2.2.562); and, having wept over Polonius's body despite his madness, he proves himself (says Gertrude) "like some [pure] ore / Among a mineral of metals base" (4.1.25–26).[22] But his metallic dreams go further than comparing rich to base. When he wishes that he might somehow engineer the sublimation of his own flesh into something finer, or when he hears the Ghost describe his own baser matter being purged away by fire, or when he recalls those processes of alchemical purification in his wish for a "native hue of resolution" (3.1.84) that would turn his "resolved," sublimed flesh to action, Hamlet indulges in the alchemist's fantasy of outstripping natural processes of material refinement. And so, when Hamlet greets Gertrude in the closet scene by asking her, "Now, mother, what's the matter?" (3.4.7), he not only invokes the maternal *prima materia* of which all matter is made but also paves the way for trying to bring about a reformation in Gertrude that is also the purification of her own baser matter: "O throw away the worser part" of your heart, he tells her, "And live the purer with the other half" (3.4.159–60).

Alchemy is thus part of the intellectual baggage Hamlet carries into the graveyard, where he contemplates what happens to matter in the earth. Here, however, that baggage overtly includes alchemy's reputation for impossibility. In the alchemist's mind, earth would not only yield loam and moldering skulls but also gestate gold and silver. But Hamlet is stopped short by the thought that even Alexander the Great died, was buried, and "returneth to dust," decomposing into "base uses" rather than subliming into finer material (5.1.196–203). This cemetery earth incubates nothing precious; the "bones" found there "cost no more the breeding but to play at loggets with 'em" (5.1.90–

91). The slight verbal and considerable contextual echo between "loggets" (small wooden pieces tossed in a horseshoe-like game) and the "lots" played for Christ's garments by the soldiers at his crucifixion—gaming at the scene of the king's mortality—seems to bring even Christ's resurrected flesh into question here. Earth to earth, ashes to ashes, dust to dust. The alchemical concoction's fate, to be no better in the end, is also the fate of the flesh, royal or no.

With this reference to Christ's body the graveyard scene also resuscitates the intellectual history that alchemy shares with the doctrine of transubstantiation. Stephen Greenblatt, in a brilliant reading of this scene, argues that when Hamlet muses over whether a dead king might go through the guts of a beggar, he is drawing upon the still-live debate over the possible degradation of Christ's resurrected flesh in the Eucharist—a debate that resonates deeply, psychically, with Hamlet's longing for a truly transcendent, nonfleshly corporeal being, as well as with his nagging suspicion that Gertrude is right and "all that lives must die" (1.2.72).[23] For Greenblatt, the "too too solid flesh" of Hamlet's first soliloquy leads us here: to our gorge rising at the stink of the father figure's skull. My sense, however, is that because they are associated with alchemy as well as transubstantiation, Hamlet's realizations in the graveyard undo their own profundity. As I discussed in Chapter 2, transubstantiation was questioned from the moment of its introduction into Europe in precisely the same terms that alchemy, its near identical twin, was questioned: because the matter theory invented to support it was believed to be untenable. Like alchemy, with which it came to be associated, transubstantiation's theory of matter never held water in a factual sense. It was always the object of a belief that was held because it was held, not because it was true.

When *Hamlet* brackets the fate of the flesh with alchemy and transubstantiation, then, it also exposes Hamlet's hopeless desire for a unity of body and spirit as a desire he should have always acknowledged as baseless. Understanding the relevant matter theory, in other words, allows us to view Hamlet's perspective on human physicality with something of a squinted eye: we see that it is his own version of an alternative physics. We can thus question Hamlet's fantastical presumption that there was one instance in which ideal physicality was achieved. In his son's memory, Old Hamlet holds the impossible status of a truly transcendent physical body, the product of a transubstantiation or an alchemy that indisputably worked. If he indeed possessed the body Hamlet remembers, Old Hamlet would also have been the alchemical "quintessence of dust" that, far from being debased matter, would be matter improbably refined (2.2.308).[24] Forearmed with the knowledge that neither alchemy nor transubstantiation was ever truly true, however, we may label Hamlet's memories of his father as exactly what they are: poppycock. Like Horatio, who observes what Hamlet observes but never voices agreement with the conclusions he draws, we may decline to confirm that Hamlet's deeply felt loss of a transcendent being ever meant there was such a being in the first place.[25]

Alchemy not only reveals Hamlet's penchant for a pet theory as off base, however. It also reveals it as destructive. Alchemical faith is part and parcel of the faith Hamlet has in his ability to construe all situations without corroboration, a solipsism that results only in personal and social wreckage. Hamlet rarely entertains what Paul Kottman says constitutes "the scene" of dramatic life in this play—that is, the "'joined' judgment" of mutual witnesses to an event, "wherein it matters deeply who is listening."[26] Instead, Hamlet listens to others only to ignore them, to forget almost instantly what they have said (as when he transcribes the Ghost's memorable command, "remember me," as the bromide that "one may smile, and smile, and be a villain"), or to turn their remarks instantly aside: "Seems, madam? Nay, it is. I know not 'seems'" (1.5.91, 108; 1.2.76). The results are devastating. Melancholy, callousness, cruelty, madness, death, murder: the catalog of harms directly or proximally caused by Hamlet's failure to check his convictions with anyone besides Horatio, a decided outsider (and hardly a corroborating witness, as we shall see below), is long indeed.

The harm Hamlet does himself and others is so devastating in part because it is also epistemological and epochal. Hamlet, it has been argued, is a harbinger of modernity because he displays the psychic anguish that ensues from modern skepticism in the Cartesian or at least the Montaignean mold. He has lost an assured connection to the material world and to a community of fellow souls. For example, as Stephen Greenblatt and Sarah Beckwith have each explored, he has lost faith in the sacraments either as a material manifestation of inner salvation or as the kind of shared, communal ritual that assures the believer of individual access to the divine.[27] More personally and more painfully, as Stanley Cavell discusses, Hamlet's skepticism means that he fails to understand his living mother and his dead father as individuals possessed of desires and flaws, separate from his dream of what they must be.[28] His skepticism lends itself to a narcissism so pervasive that he ultimately intends his fantasy of totalizing theory to extend to a future that will not have him in it. Despite his uncharacteristically humble acknowledgment that "no man, of aught he leaves, knows aught," the dying Hamlet imagines that Horatio will tell Hamlet's story exactly as Hamlet has instructed, "with th'occurrents more and less / Which have solicited," and he declares the power to "prophesy th'election lights / On Fortinbras" (5.2.218–19, 360–63). His mandates for the future include no consideration of Horatio's wishes in the matter—indeed, he predicts that Horatio will "draw [his] breath in pain / To tell my story"—just as they include no one's will but his own in the succession: Fortinbras "has [his] dying voice" (5.2.353–54, 361).

Though Hamlet's all-encompassing and manifestly wrong theoretical habits cause him to treat others callously and cruelly, it does not therefore follow that we must take those theories seriously. Quite the contrary; we will have been prepared to recognize the shortcomings of Hamlet's ideas of the present and schemes for the future by the alchemical tinge of his desires. That alchemical tinge, I have been arguing, exposes his pansophism for what it is, the kind of disknowledge that deliberately takes false for true. While Hamlet himself is generally uninterested in acknowledging that he acts on belief he knows to be untrue, the play structurally provides such acknowledgment in the ironizing person of Horatio, who seldom confirms Hamlet's propositions, and then only in the case of indisputable fact. Did Horatio perceive Claudio upon the talk of the poisoning? "I did very well note him" (3.2.284). Did Alexander the Great's decomposing corpse look and smell as bad as Yorick's? "E'en so, my lord" (5.1.195). On matters such as these, Horatio lets Hamlet's knowledge go unchallenged. But Horatio conspicuously declines to ratify the way Hamlet imagines his conceptions will survive into the future. While Fortinbras, the last aristocrat standing, does take the reins of power in Denmark as Hamlet prophesied, Horatio seems almost deliberately to disobey Hamlet's command to "Report me and my cause aright / To the unsatisfied" (5.2.343–44). Instead, Hamlet's posthumous story becomes, in Horatio's compressed and abstracted telling of it, quite another tale, the straightforward revenge plot that Hamlet in life evaded:

> So shall you hear
> Of carnal, bloody, and unnatural acts,
> Of accidental judgments, casual slaughters,
> Of deaths put on by cunning and forc'd cause.
>
> (5.2.385–88)[29]

While Horatio is no unalloyed empiricist, he is the play's one designated "scholar" (1.1.45).[30] And as a scholar, he points the way toward a useful disbelief in the grand, unsupported, and ethically irresponsible belief in pansophism that a lingering humanistic training seems to have instilled in Hamlet. To Hamlet's plea, "Report me and my cause aright / To the unsatisfied," Horatio replies, "Never believe it" (5.2.344–45). Horatio's ambiguous imperative—never believe *what*?—is followed by his classicizing gesture toward suicide: "I am more an antique Roman than a Dane" (5.2.346). While readers and critics usually connect these two statements, in fact they are curiously detached by means of a full stop between them. It is thus possible to read Horatio's "Never believe it" as an independent statement: not as a response to Hamlet's desire that Horatio continue to draw his breath in pain to tell Hamlet's story, but rather as a response to Hamlet's insistence that his "cause" should live on in Horatio's telling, which Hamlet believes will somehow satisfy the "unsatisfied." Hamlet, Horatio implies, would be better off if he "never believed" that his story will be given credence in future times. His cause cannot be "reported aright" because it was never a right cause in the first place.

Thomas Hobbes, who builds the foundation of a civil society in *Leviathan* on the verbal expression of true statements, worries that a humanist education interferes with this expression of truth: "in wrong or no definitions lies the first abuse [of speech]; from which proceed all false and senseless tenets, which make those men that take their instruction from the authority of books, and not from their own meditation, to be as much below the condition of ignorant men as men endued with true science are above it."[31] His implication is that humanism teaches habits of learning that exacerbate, rather than meliorate, the solitary, poor, nasty, brutish, and short existence that is the natural state of humankind. Hobbes's proposition seems to be confirmed by the utter destruction that Hamlet's bad humanism causes: not only is the stage strewn with bodies at the end of the play but Denmark itself has been conquered by a foreign power. Horatio is right. "Never believe" Hamlet's version of things, or this is what you'll get.

In this context it is odd that Horatio's consequent identification of himself as "an antique Roman," one who prefers suicide to survival, replicates the embodied revival of the classics that is humanism's foundational move. However, that classicizing is cordoned off, by that full stop after "Never believe it," from the prospect of belief itself. For Horatio, humanism is not the stuff of belief but the stuff of ending. And better so, if humanism's instruction in building a world of knowledge on a tissue of texts leads a melancholy prince to take a suspiciously alchemized ghost's word on how to live, how to kill, how to die.

The Alchemist's Alchemical Discipline

Horatio's advice, "Never believe it," would be well taken by the dupes in Ben Jonson's *The Alchemist*, a play that is practically a primer on how belief comes to no good end. Yet *The Alchemist*'s instruction in disbelief is more specific than merely teaching a person how to avoid con artists. Like Horatio, *The Alchemist* also, I shall argue, teaches a person how to discount humanism's vaunted aims of universal learning.

Despite humanism's many achievements, it is fairly clear that by the seventeenth century the dream of humanism had failed. Or, more precisely, that humanistic ideals and practice had been channeled from their initial soaring aims to more limited ambitions that could do the developing nation-state no harm, and that would likely serve its interests. Anthony Grafton and Lisa Jardine have argued, for example, that humanism gained traction in sixteenth-century educational schemes not because it extended Greek and Roman moral virtues and humanist philology's exemplary habits to the nature and conduct of civil discourse but because it raised up less inquisitive, more obedient civil servants.[32] Shifting to the modest goal of shaping tractable bureaucrats, and assailed (as I mentioned in Chapter 1) by more extreme religious reformists who advocated that believers restrict their reading programs, humanism over the course of the seventeenth century lost the ideal of an all-encompassing, syncretic learning program.[33]

Even in a world of diminished ambitions, however, humanism's skills continued to serve a valuable purpose. The humanistic practices of snippetizing and summarizing prior texts, for example, were designed not only to enable scholarly laziness or to facilitate educating uncapacious young minds. They were designed also to train the educated classes in the very useful art of not having to know all. And here is where alchemy proves its mettle. If we return to the suggestion by Francis Bacon that I brought up in this book's introduction, that we ought to study alchemy not because it is true but because it cultivates useful habits of thought, then arguably alchemy teaches the seventeenth century not how to employ apparatus and fire to induce material change but how to abandon Hamlet's misguided aim of universal learning.[34] My sense of *The Alchemist* is of a play that posits a program for exactly that: for making humanism a boutique enterprise, the enterprise of fiction. When, as Grafton and Jardine argue, the classics are no longer vehicles for training ourselves in truth and virtue, then humanistic skills are merely skills, as delimited in their scope and applicability as the surgeon's knowledge of the cardiovascular system or the lawyer's knowledge of torts and contracts.[35] Which is not to say that the humanities are not useful, just that they are useful *in their way*. And the way in which the discipline of literature, in particular, is useful is to invent fictions and purport them to be truth.

Among the many other purposes to which literature can put alchemy in the seventeenth century, then, is to register its comfort level with the anticipation or the realization of its own reduced, compartmentalized status. That is, the appearance of alchemy in a literary text sometimes signals how well that text accepts literature as a discipline rather than as a body of universal knowledge—as a branch of the humanities rather than as the grounds and mainstay of humanism. This signal is activated especially when the literary text acknowledges the affiliations between alchemy and fiction making. To the extent that literature owns up to its identity with alchemy, it gestures toward how cheerful it is at being converted from a ubiquitous, absorptive pansophic scheme to a disciplinary enterprise.

At the start of this chapter I argued that it is significant that Philip Sidney's characterization of the literary project is an alchemical one. Alchemy undertakes the work of literature by marrying a specifically literary language, the language of metaphoric substitution, to a certain laxness about truth claims. So too does Sidney's poetry substitute a golden world for a world of brass; and this literary golden world is the one in which we are presented, not with what is or what should be, but with what *might* be. I also argued that it is crucial that Sidney conceives of this alchemical literary enterprise as its own discipline, separate from others. Poetry is not history, it is not philosophy. It is certainly not natural philosophy. Sidney's vision of a separate literary domain can be fully realized, however, only once intellectual domains other than the domain of letters have been credited with facticity—that is, once veridiction has been assigned elsewhere.[36] Like others writing around the turn of the seventeenth century, Sidney anticipates a disciplinarity that will come to full fruition only in the mid-eighteenth century, when it becomes possible to imagine belles lettres both as a genre—one that Samuel Johnson defines as "polite literature"—and as a separate object of study in a university education.[37] Sidney's golden world becomes, at that point, a delimited and relatively inconsequential one, rich and gleaming though it may be.

The Alchemist's seemingly contradictory stance on alchemical language makes sense, in my view, only as a similarly prescient anticipation of literature's shift from the cornerstone of humanistic training to one small corner of learning. On the one hand, the play seems to satirize most of humanism's cherished assumptions about how rhetoric makes the world. On the other, alchemical rhetoric *does* make *The Alchemist*'s world. Before we may properly evaluate how *The Alchemist* departs from the humanistic ideal, then, we must characterize the play's simultaneous commitment to and skepticism about the modes of expression, reading, and understanding that alchemy enables.

Looked at one way, *The Alchemist* seems decidedly posthumanist in its skepticism about the efficacy of rhetoric and the primacy of books. Jonson's conservative preference of nature over artifice, as Alvin Kernan has noted, is reflected in the play's relentless debunking of cant, language that links alchemical falsehood with rhetorical balderdash.[38] The same opinion is voiced in Jonson's masque *Mercury Vindicated from the Alchemists at Court* (1616) by the god Mercury, whose complaint about alchemy is also a complaint about the corruption and misuse of language.[39] By these lights, Jonson seems to be opposed not only to alchemy but also to the wordsmithing that is the basis of the humanist enterprise. Similarly, *The Alchemist* also throws aside the humanist reliance on textual authority. Despite the play's adherence to the Aristotelian unities, it largely eschews classical models.[40] Indeed, it treats all predecessor texts, from those of Erasmus and Paracelsus to the religious belaborings of Hugh Broughton, as likely fodder for either the contrivances of the con artists or the ranting of their gulls. Relying on books in *The Alchemist* is the mark of victimhood, not of genuine learning or of civic virtue.

At the same time, however, *The Alchemist* is committed to an alchemical world in which words are everything. That commitment is, in the first instance, aesthetic. What one notices most about language in *The Alchemist* is how delightful, and how essential to the play, is the very jargon the play purports to debunk. In the same way that, as I mentioned in Chapter 1, Mercury in *Mercury Vindicated* flaunts alchemical lingo even while he claims to be weary of it, so too does *The Alchemist* deploy alchemical terminology for all it's worth.[41] The pleasure one takes in *The Alchemist*'s alchemical aesthetics derives, in part, from the fact that the play's linguistic texture, like that of all alchemical language, promises both transparency and obfuscation. As William Slights notes of Subtle's description of alchemy's "mystic symbols," Subtle's "theory of language . . . is an essentially occlusive one. . . . [but also] an invitation to interpret what he says, to find out his secret meanings."[42] The pleasure of interpretation is built into *The Alchemist*'s linguistic feats, and both the characters in the play and its audience seem to be intended, more often than not, to enjoy the guessing game.

The Alchemist's commitment to alchemical language is not only aesthetic, however; it is also metaphysical. In Chapter 3, I discussed the notion that Adam was alchemy's best practitioner. Before the fall of humankind, Adam spoke a language that, like God's fiat, transformed nature. Sir Epicure Mammon agrees: he offers to show Surly "a treatise penned by Adam. . . . / O' the philosopher's stone" (2.1.83–4). While such hopes that the perfect language would return the world to its Edenic origins are satirized in both Sir Epicure and the Anabaptist Ananias—who declares his suspicion that "All's heathen, but the Hebrew" (2.5.17)—*The Alchemist* also evidences Jonson's increasing confidence in the idea that words can have the Edenic property of expressing the true natures of things rather than arbitrarily signifying them.[43] Some of the nomenclatural correspondences in *The Alchemist* are unremarkable: names like Epicure Mammon and Kastrel (a small, fierce falcon) are merely comically apt for their bearers. With other characters, however, their names and their qualities seem to be mutually and progressively constitutive. Such is especially true with Captain Face, the former servant Jeremy whose new name, given by Subtle (1.1.81), connotes and confers a talent for falsehood as well as a capacity to "face" any challenge. Similarly, Dol Common overgoes her stereotypical whore's moniker, as Anne Barton points out, by either becoming or inventing a multitude of names and roles: Dol Proper, Dol Singular, Claridiana, Bradamante, Her Grace the Faery Queen, and so on.[44] The more personae Dol assumes, the more she seems to personify Subtle's metaphorical description of Face as the philosopher's stone, a substance that is both the product and the agent of change (1.1.68–71).

The play thus has it both ways on the efficacy of alchemical language. On the one hand, language is untrustworthy artifice; on the other, it is metaphysical transformation. It is both patently false and ravishingly true. A parallel dual status is held in the play by alchemical equipment, which is both real and imaginary, both material in its breakability and evanescent in its sometimes purely linguistic existence. While *The Alchemist*'s con artists exploit the preconception of the alchemist's occult "chamber of secrets" in gesturing toward Subtle's mysterious and possibly nonexistent offstage furnace room, at times Subtle actually seems to possess the assemblage of equipment that belongs to the working alchemist. In an exchange solely among his con artist compatriots—that is, an exchange in which he has no reason to lie—Face boasts that his aid has afforded Subtle an impressive array of both the raw matter of alchemy and the apparatus with which to manipulate it:

> I ga' you countenance, credit for your coals,
> Your stills, your glasses, your materials,
> Built you a furnace, drew you customers.
>
> (1.1.43–45)

Calling attention to the actuality of at least one of these items, Dol breaks up her confederates' initial quarrel by smashing Subtle's "glass," a generic term for an alchemical vessel (1.1.115 s.d.).[45] While Subtle's ongoing exchanges with his "assistant" Face (in his guise as Lungs) about the heat of the furnace or about the condition of the vials in process are intended to gull the likes of Sir Epicure, they also display a certain pride of ownership as well as delight at the sheer plethora and variety of alchemical gear that a successful practitioner might amass.

We thus may find ourselves rather disappointed, perhaps even disbelieving, when, at the end of the play, Lovewit describes the equipment left in his house by the grifting trio as in fact relatively minimal: "A few cracked pots, and glasses, and a furnace" (5.5.40). It is not the case, however, that Lovewit's revelation debunks the attractions of alchemical apparatus. For one thing, we are never certain whether his description is entirely true. But, more important, his description of the alchemical equipment as unimpressive merely recapitulates the entire play's unstable, shimmering, oscillatory shifts between alchemy as authentic and alchemy as sham, with that oscillation—its motion presaged in the con artists' label of their action as a "venture," a word truncated from *ad-venire*, "to come toward"—standing in the stead of the permanent transformation alchemy promises. Framed by the breaking of the alchemical glass at its beginning and the revelation of the (purportedly) ill-equipped furnace room at its end, *The Alchemist* establishes that glass and that furnace room as metonymic for alchemical discourse itself: empty, fragile, unreliable, captivating, replete, and treasured, all at once.

Examining the closing scenes of *The Alchemist* and their recalibration of the alchemical enterprise enables us to return to the question of the play's stance on humanistic learning. Language in *The Alchemist*, like alchemy itself, demands a continuous engagement of belief in the unbelievable; the grounds of humanistic endeavor are posed as simultaneously sound and illegitimate. Rather than thus simply labeling the play's attitude toward humanism "ambivalent," I would argue that Jonson at the end of *The Alchemist* is mounting a prolegomenon to an analysis of humanism's diminished function in the early seventeenth century and beyond. He does so by continuing to associate alchemy not only with language but also with literature, and by restricting the domain in which the conjoined activities of alchemy and literature make sense.

Bruno Latour's description of how processes and theories once taken for true are discredited, and vice versa, suggests an explanation for why *The Alchemist*'s disknowledge game, its continuous engagement of belief in the unbelievable, is ultimately rather narrowly delimited. An "entity"—by which Latour means a theory or process, like spontaneous generation, that a culture may endorse or not endorse—"gains in reality if it is associated with many others that are viewed as collaborating with it. It loses in reality, if, on the contrary, it has to shed associates or collaborators."[46] The schemes of Subtle, Face, and Dol work only if the con artists retain rather than shed associates and collaborators. Their success is defined—as it is in any capitalist "venture" such as theirs—by an expansion of business, but that expansion is as much a flow of persons as it is of capital. The boundaries of that flow are the boundaries of the alchemical enterprise. Through most of *The Alchemist* we are given to understand that this flow is unlimited: Face will always be able to bring in new marks, and Dol and Subtle will always be able to devise and juggle new schemes to ensnare them. The last act of the play, however, forces us to reexamine our assumptions, and to understand that the alchemical business has been strictly bounded all along.

Jonson's demarcation of alchemical collaboration in this play is, first and foremost, a spatial one. Alchemy is confined to Lovewit's house, which facilitates the con artists' schemes through their brilliant use of its exits, entrances, and unseen rooms, including the room that reputedly holds Subtle's furnace and the rather smelly "privy lodgings" in which Dapper, his mouth stuffed with gingerbread, awaits his longed-for Faery Queen (3.5.79). The house is so complete, so all in all, that we may be tempted to read it as a microcosm of all of learning itself, all there is to be known. Indeed, the play's prologue states "Our Scene" merely as "London," as if Lovewit's house bears a synecdochic relation to a city that, to Jonson, is itself synecdochic at least for Britain, if not also for the world (Pro. 5).[47] As *The Alchemist* draws toward its conclusion, however, we come to see the house less as having seemingly infinite interior space and more as having a perimeter past which the con artists' fantastical schemes are no longer tenable. This perimeter is established upon the return of Lovewit to his house in act 5, a shift in scene that is also a reduction in the con artists' command both of linguistic malleability and of the alchemical enterprise. At the same moment that the house gains, for the first time, an exterior, "Face" must revert from his Subtle-bestowed name, one emblematic of transformed and transformative capacities, to his proper (and quite prosaic) name as Lovewit's butler: Jeremy, the name of his "old shape" (4.7.120). At this same moment, we start to understand that the information we have been given so far about the con artists' business success is incomplete. The neighbors who report to Lovewit on the comings and goings at his house supply a far more comprehensive and less high-class list of alchemical customers than we ourselves have witnessed: not only aspiring "gallants" like Dapper, "Citizen's wives" like Dame Pliant, and "Tobacco-men" like Abel Drugger, but also "Oyster-women" and "Sailors' wives," a group that Lovewit classifies as "all sorts, tag-rag" (5.1.3–5, 5.2.18). It is difficult to see how such clients as oyster-women and sailors' wives could have furthered the con artists' pecuniary agenda; if anything, their possible status as prostitutes hired by Subtle and Face would have beggared, not enriched, the venture. The alchemical activity of *The Alchemist* is plausibly profitable only when its circle of confederates and victims is closely controlled. It will not survive expansion into what Lovewit calls an "open house" (5.1.17).

The limitation of alchemical efficacy to a single domicile leads us to the limitations of the kinds of knowledge in which *The Alchemist* traffics. Trained in memory systems that associated learning itself with rooms in a house, some of Jonson's audience would have been accustomed to thinking of knowledge as segmentable into subdivided domestic space.[48] What *The Alchemist* adds to that familiar trope is the proposition that one of those spaces is the space of disknowledge: a space where false notions may be freely and knowingly entertained. The corollary of that proposition, however, is that disknowledge may be explored only within those bounds and not elsewhere. Jonson's refinement of the house of memory's spatializing system is thus to assign to different spaces not just different topics of learning but different modes of epistemic activity. Anticipating and demonstrating the shift in the word *department* from its seventeenth-century sense of "taking one's leave" to its early eighteenth-century sense of "field of expertise," Jonson marries physical movement to an alteration in knowledge approaches, so that to know matters of fiction rather than matters of fact requires staying in the house of alchemy and never departing thence.[49]

In this way, Jonson also anticipates the peculiar architecture of Salomon's House, Francis Bacon's ideal site of knowledge production in his *New Atlantis* (1627).[50] Here, late in his career, Bacon depicts in clear spatial terms what he proposes much more murkily in *The Advancement of Learning*'s fable of the vineyard, discussed in Chapter 1: that alchemy should be pursued not just because it might accidentally stumble on something useful but because its manifest error is its own way of knowing. Having swept alchemy, along with other misbegotten knowledge systems, out of the program of progressive learning in *The Advancement of Learning*, Bacon nonetheless reserves in Salomon's House—in reality, more Salomon's Compound, in that it comprises a number of different houses—a space for all those fancies. "We have also houses of deceits of the senses; where we represent all manner of feats of juggling, false apparitions, impostures, and illusions; and their fallacies."[51] Notably, the separation of "impostures" from sciences implies not only a separation of false from true but also a posthumanistic separation of the language arts from more valued fields of study. As Bronwen Price has discussed, *New Atlantis* distinguishes between the less advanced humanism of the European narrator, who conceives of knowledge as a comprehensive, word-based system of learning, and the enlightened empiricism of the New Atlantis's denizens, who operate within the bounds of disciplinarity.[52] In their utopian science, "impostures" such as alchemy are strictly sequestered from legitimate, unadorned explications and manipulations of the natural world. Bacon, after years of trying to explicate how, exactly, one should differentiate true descriptions of nature from false theories such as those of alchemy, arrives at this solution: not to dispense with fallacy entirely but to designate a strictly bounded place where it may flourish.[53]

The Alchemist, I am arguing, has already made Bacon's point of disciplinary sequestration, fifteen years or more in advance of *New Atlantis*. And it has done so not only spatially but also intellectually. If Lovewit's house is where disknowledge has free rein, it is also where the interpretation of literature has free rein. Here, alchemical and literary activities are explicitly equated. After Subtle rather economically—across the space of no more than one hundred lines—sums up more or less all of alchemical theory, Surly challenges him with the declaration that the multiplicity of alchemists' "terms, / Whereon no one o' your writers 'grees with other," proves alchemy merely "a pretty kind of game, / Somewhat like tricks o' the cards, to cheat a man, / With charming" (2.3.180–83). Defending himself, Subtle then makes the typical alchemical case that this proliferation of alchemical terms is a deliberately obfuscatory tactic, an "art our writers / Used to obscure their art" (2.3.199–200) so that the vulgar should not have access to this esoteric learning. He then, however, extends the case for alchemical secrecy by reference to what amounts to a progressive and chronological construction of the work of literary criticism:

> Was not all the knowledge
> Of the Egyptians writ in mystic symbols?
> Speak not the Scriptures, oft, in parables?
> Are not the choicest fables of the poets,
> That were the fountains, and first springs of wisdom,
> Wrapped in perplexed allegories?
>
> (2.3.202–7)

Subtle begins with reading at the level of a single symbol, an Egyptian hieroglyph—which Jonson's day took to carry perfectly legible meaning, since hieroglyphs were viewed as a kind of emblem system that the adept reader could easily decode.[54] He then proceeds to the next level of interpretive difficulty, Christ's parables in the New Testament, an exegetical task made easier by the fact that Christ usually handily supplies the explanation. Finally, once trained in visual (that is, hieroglyphic) emblematics and the interpretation of parables, the reader may move on to the third and most difficult interpretive task Subtle lists, the "perplexed allegories" that mark "the choicest fables of poets."

Merely to declare alchemical writing literary, however, would be merely to allow how humanism gives us access to alchemical writing as much as it does to any other literary work. Humanistic exegetical skills may be used to parse alchemical writing just as they may be used to parse Virgil or the Song of Songs. Equally, humanistic philological skills may be used to analyze alchemical writing, as Isaac Casaubon did when he established that the *Corpus Hermeticum* was not, as alchemists claimed, as ancient as Moses. Those trained in humanistic philology will laugh knowingly, for example, at the gullible Sir Epicure for boasting that his "treatise penned by Adam . . . / O' the philosopher's stone" is written "in High Dutch" (2.1.83–84). But *The Alchemist* does more than identify alchemical writing as literary. It also makes a point of putting humanism in its place—a narrow, delimited, disciplinary place—by identifying literary writing as alchemical. After claiming he owns Adam's treatise, Sir Epicure goes on to brag to Surly that he possesses "a piece of Jason's fleece, too, / Which was no other, than a book of alchemy, / Writ in large sheepskin, a good fat ram-vellum" (2.1.89–91). While the Golden Fleece was frequently cited by alchemical writing as an allegory for the gold alchemists themselves pursued, something else is at work here. "Jason's fleece" is not gold or the philosopher's stone, it is a book on vellum whose only content is alchemical. So too, says Sir Epicure, are all the Greek myths purely alchemical guides:

> Both [the golden fleece], th' Hesperian garden, Cadmus' story,
> Jove's shower, the boon of Midas, Argus' eyes,
> Boccace his Demogorgon, thousands more,
> All abstract riddles of our stone.
>
> (2.1.101–4)

The implication is that the very foundation of a humanistic education, the stories from Ovid's *Metamorphoses* that every Renaissance schoolboy knew by heart, is not universally applicable but rather the base of a narrow alchemical specialization—and a frivolous one at that.

While it is softened by being associated with the silly Sir Epicure, Jonson's constriction of humanistic learning is nevertheless real. As I have mentioned, *The Alchemist* is a Jonsonian exercise in eschewing classical models for something new and different. One of the experiments Jonson undertakes in this play is in drawing a line between the humanism that endorsed those classical models and all other kinds of learning. The figure at the interface between the house of humanism and the public space of knowledge is also the person who determines which activity belongs where: Lovewit, whose pleasure at the alchemical stratagems of Jeremy/Face, Subtle, and Dol—"I love a teeming wit, as I love my nourishment" (5.1.16)—does not preclude his wresting control of those stratagems to keep them in their place. After extracting the truth from Jeremy/Face and using that truth to claim for himself the prize of Dame Pliant, the rich widow pursued by nearly every man in the play, Lovewit turns away the enraged victims of the con artists by redefining the scene of their gulling as the scene of both failed alchemy and truly juvenile writing. He claims to the assembled victims that the only evidence of alchemy to be found in his house are

> The empty walls, worse than I left 'em, smoked,
> A few cracked pots, and glasses, and a furnace,

The ceiling filled with poesies of the candle:
And **MADAM**, with a dildo, writ o' the walls.

(5.5.39–42; emphasis in the original)

With alchemical effort reduced to "a few cracked pots, and glasses" and literary effort reduced to the candle's involuntary creation of "poesies" on the ceiling and to the single word "MADAM" appended to a crude pornographic drawing, Lovewit has taken the identification of the literary with the alchemical to its basest and most easily ridiculed level. Just as alchemical experiments may be characterized as a couple of evidently none-too-ambitious failed attempts, so too may Ovid, with his heady sexuality, be characterized as useful for far less refined purposes than the kind of universal edification that humanists imagined for literature.

In the end, Lovewit allows Jeremy/Face's schemes to prevail—"I will be ruled by thee in anything, Jeremy" (5.5.143)—not because they are true but because they are advantageous. Disknowledge in the right context, such as outflanking one's rivals for the favors of a rich young widow, is all to the good. But it is good only in its place. Lovewit apologizes for his indecorous actions with the plea,

> if I have outstripped
> An old man's gravity, or strict canon, think
> What a young wife, and a good brain may do:
> Stretch age's truth sometimes, and crack it, too.

(5.5.153–56)

Possessed of a very "good brain" and spurred by a libido reinvigorated by his young bride, Lovewit "cracks" the truth as alchemy has cracked the pots. Still, he has done so only "sometimes," only in the service of bringing his part in this plot to a satisfactory end.

And there, in the realm of the literal crack-pot, is where Lovewit leaves alchemy, literature, and those of us who love them.[55] Jeremy/Face's brief epilogue makes it clear that alchemy ends when the play does. All the others involved in alchemy are gone; he is "clean / Got off, from Subtle, Surly, Mammon, Dol, / Hot Ananias, Draper, Drugger, all / With whom I traded" (5.5.159–61). Those who remain are the audience, identified not as participants in alchemy but as the "country" (jury) that Jeremy/Face must bribe to earn his forgiveness—that is, the applause that will see him off the stage:

> this pelf,
> Which I have got, if you do quit me, rests
> To feast you often.
>
> (5.5.163–65)

His references to paying and owning place *The Alchemist*, despite its free-wheeling, improvisational plot, securely within the orbit of what Joseph Loew-enstein has called early modern "possessive authorship." No Renaissance playwright was more committed to the literary basis of humanism than Jonson was; none was more learned in the classics. But in addition, none was more concerned to "control all aspects of dissemination and reception" of his work.[56] Something that is individually owned and managed is, by definition, no longer a public good. As Henry Turner has argued, a side effect of Jonson's "autono-mization" of his work is the disassociation of the theater from any kind of knowledge that might have application in the world. Feeling his way toward conceiving of plays—plays in print, at least—as a matter of copyright, Jonson rejects the idea that the theater might be a showcase for a kind of popular humanism: a porous, socially open venue revivifying classical forms in vernac-ular terms.

In his epistle to *Volpone* (1606), Jonson had (perhaps ironically) declared his allegiance to the foundational humanist principle of making classical knowledge the model for the way we live now. "[T]he principal end of poesy," he says, is "to inform men in the best reason of living."[57] *The Alchemist* has other ideas about the relation between literature and useful knowledge prac-tices. True, Jeremy/Face promises in his epilogue to "invite new guests" to this feast (5.5.165). But to invite new guests to a playhouse—one that *The Alche-mist* has made coterminous with the house of alchemy, as Ian Donaldson re-minds us—is not to ask them to fashion themselves or their nation upon the literary repast they have just consumed. It is to ask them to make literature an occasional pastime.[58] Like the place made for alchemy in Salomon's House in *New Atlantis*, the playhouse is designated for "deceits of the senses." It is a place to which we choose sometimes to resort, but it is not where we live.

The Blazing World's Alchemical Fiction

With a self-acquired education, an oddball and exiled social status, and a non-standard, noncommercial publishing program that puts her in quite a different category from either William Shakespeare or Ben Jonson, Margaret Cavendish would be expected to have a relation to the process of knowledge acquisition and knowledge management that is very different from the ones displayed in *Hamlet* and *The Alchemist*. Nonetheless, Cavendish's work shares with those plays a concern about the legitimacy of universal knowledge systems in an era in which the kingdom of letters was being dismantled. In a posthumanist intellectual culture, fiction's ultimate fate—a fate prophesied by Sidney and celebrated by Jonson—was to be cordoned off into its own disciplinary environs. Cavendish, however, proposes an alternative future for fiction. Unlike Jonson's boutique house of literature, Cavendish goes big.

By the mid-seventeenth century, as I have detailed throughout this book, skepticism about humanism's grand schemes was playing out in an intellectual atmosphere that routinely both questioned received wisdom and agonized over what was to replace it. Cavendish participated in that conversation in many arenas, from the debate over whether and how Aristotelian science was to be supplanted to the debate over whether the study of rhetoric was the study of mere sophistry.[59] While the later seventeenth century's questioning of previously settled truth had to do most prominently with the interrelated realms of natural philosophy and political theory, it also had to do with the fortunes of fiction in an intellectual world. Shakespeare's critique of pansophism and Jonson's prescient remaking of large-scale humanism into small-scale fiction writing overlap with Cavendish's complex sense of the importance of her own writing—especially her own "fancies," as she termed her poems, plays, and fiction. But Cavendish's innovation is to weave scientific and literary questions together as versions of the same question: What is the role of the imagination? Rather than sequester literary achievement into its own narrow discipline, as *The Alchemist* does, Cavendish proposes that the kinds of imaginative capacities that only literary language can capture are ubiquitously present in earthly matter. This variant on vitalism has Cavendish proposing an alternative pansophism that rescues literature from humanism's elitist educational delivery system, giving it to whoever has the imagination to give it shape.

Like Jonson, Cavendish finds alchemy a useful trope for thinking about the status of fiction because it allows her to consider the distinctions between the products of nature and the productions of art. Whereas Jonson associates alchemy with the artificial and thus builds literature upon the model of alchemy as grand artifice, however, Cavendish goes another direction. Returning to the associations among human reproduction, alchemical reproduction, and epistemological perspicuity brought up by Edmund Spenser's *Faerie*

Queene (and discussed in Chapter 4), Cavendish uses alchemical tropes to help theorize the female mind as fecund in both a wholly natural and a wholly artificial fashion, and the female authorial mind as one that is fully capable, in Sidney's terms, of "grow[ing] in effect another nature."[60] The result is a manifestly capacious, rather than delimited, role for literature. Cavendish's expansive vision does not, however, replicate early humanism's faith in studying literature as a precedent and a model for morality, civic virtue, and persuasive expression. Instead, Cavendish's posthumanist literary enterprise is far more fundamental: she makes the literary imagination part of the very preconditions—the growth medium, as it were—of all thought and all physical matter. If alchemical imagery gives Cavendish a toehold in the topic of art's status in relation to nature, reproductive imagery gives Cavendish a toehold in the topic of fiction. By combining alchemical and reproductive imagery, then, Cavendish develops a constellation of tropes that makes a natural fiction seem possible.

It is in the cause of a natural fiction, in fact, that Cavendish dwells upon the fantasy of parthenogenesis that, as we saw in Chapter 4, was one of the versions of reproduction that alchemy entertained. There is no historical imperative for Cavendish's keeping parthenogenesis, or any other version of the one-sex model of human reproduction, in mind. While the exact nature of women's seed was still under debate in the mid-seventeenth century, its contribution to conception was by then undisputed, and the one-sex model of reproduction had lost its hold in gynecological writing.[61] Nonetheless, Cavendish's various musings and fantasias on alchemical reproduction oddly—and perhaps deliberately—repurpose many of the same rhetorical and imagistic maneuvers by which William Harvey (as we saw in Chapter 4) deploys alchemy to declare that only one sex, not two, contributes to conception.[62] For Cavendish, however, this avoidance has a utility quite unlike Harvey's insistent masculinizing of the regimes of knowledge: her alchemical reproductive digressions create an innovative space for female (as well as male) authorship. Cavendish uses conspicuous acts of Harvey's brand of disknowledge, turning from true to impossible theories of reproduction, to further her proposition that fiction is central to the mental and physical workings of the universe. As we will see, when Cavendish deploys a kind of retro one-sex model of reproduction, it is one that she reappropriates for the female mind and the female pen, to the extent of its contributing even to her revision of Cartesian cognition. By means of alchemical detours, Cavendish revises apperception itself so that it is no longer a mode of masculine avoidance of femininity but rather a mode of acknowledging the multivalent, multigendered creativity that lies at the heart of all interactions with and within the physical world.

Cavendish's antipathy to the ordinary sort of womanly reproduction is well known.[63] For her, conception and generation are always, and from the first, activities of the mind rather than activities of the body. Thus, *The Blazing World*'s epistle "To the Reader" contrasts the "laborious" work of her philosophical writing to the fanciful "issue" of her fiction in a way that—rather than belaboring the analogy between writing and childbirth—makes writing fiction a form of reproduction appropriate to either sex: *"fictions* are an issue of a man's fancy, framed in his own mind, according as he pleases" (123–24; emphasis in the original). But calling something fanciful is not, for Cavendish, the same as calling it either intangible or unnatural. Initially in *The Blazing World*'s preface, she seems to deny that fiction finds an analogue in the real world; she contrasts fiction's fancifulness with philosophy's "rational" (what philosophy would now call "truthlike") propositions about nature that, while they may not be exactly accurate, represent the best state of current knowledge (123). But like Sidney, who solidifies the status of fiction to allow it to create a golden world better than history's brassy one, Cavendish alchemizes her fictional "fancy" into something tangible. She declares of *The Blazing World* that "I cannot call it a poor world, if poverty be only want of gold, silver, and jewels; for there is more gold in it than all the chemists ever did, and (as I verily believe) will ever be able to make" (124).

Cavendish's *Blazing World* finds alchemy important, then, precisely because of its ambiguous claims both to natural transformation and to powers that go beyond nature's capacities. As Cavendish points out in her *Observations upon Experimental Philosophy* (to which *The Blazing World* was appended in its first publication), alchemy's products "are but hermaphroditical effects, that is, between natural and artificial; just as a mule partakes both of the nature or figure of a horse, and of an ass: Nevertheless, as mules are very beneficial for use, so are many chemical effects" (232).[64] Breeding fictions as the animal husbander breeds mules, but also crafting fictions as the alchemist crafts chemical effects, Cavendish embraces rather than disdains the association of her text with alchemy's uncertain straddling of nature and artifice.

Cavendish's description of herself as "a happy *creatoress*" of her Blazing World—not parent, not artificer, but something in between: creator—similarly suggests alchemy's contradictory insistence that it accomplishes natural reproduction by artificial processes (124; emphasis in the original). In *The Blazing*

World's narrative itself, the immaterial spirits whom the Empress consults assure her that "every human creature can . . . create a world of what fashion and government he will . . . also he may alter that world as often as he pleases, or change it from a natural world, to an artificial; he may make a world of ideas, a world of atoms, a world of lights, or whatsoever his fancy leads him to" (185–86). Fictional fancy does more than spin baseless imaginative visions; it converts the stuff of nature into the stuff of art. Thus, in her play *The Comical Hash* (1662), Cavendish has two gentlemen engage in the classic debate about whether alchemy is improper because it is unnatural. Significantly, she joins that debate to the question of whether poets may also create a nature of their own. "[S]ome Poets are like Chymists," says one gentleman who wants to make the point that "Art cannot out-do Nature." They "strive and labour to make as Nature makes, but most fail in their work, and lose their labours, wanting that Natural heat, or well-tempered matter, which should produce such Creatures as Nature makes." Having made an analogy between poor poets and poor alchemists, however, this gentleman and his companion go on to make the corresponding analogy, one between good poets and good alchemists:

> 2. Gent.   . . . yet some [alchemists] 'tis said have made gold, as
>   Raimond Lully.
> 1 Gent.   Then Homer is a Raimond Lully in Poetry.
> 2 Gent.   Nay rather Raimond Lully is a Homer in Chymistry: for
>   no man ought to compare Homer to any Creature, by
>   reason he hath out-wrought Nature, having done that
>   which she never did; for Nature never made Gods,
>   Devils, Hells, and Heavens, as Homer hath done.[65]

Producing "such creatures as Nature makes" and more, the poet and the alchemist are more or less indistinguishable in their talents: Homer is the Raymond Lull of poetry, Raymond Lull the Homer of alchemy. They are indistinguishable, that is, until one of the two gentlemen declares that whereas a good alchemist produces only that which nature makes (gold), a great poet also creates "that which [nature] never did." Lull is not quite as impressive as Homer. But still, the point remains: while perhaps not at the same level of artistry, a good poet and a good alchemist both initiate their work by artificial means, but then proceed to a form of creativity that occurs in nature and models God: "an Imitator is but an Artificer, when as the Original Author is a Creator, and ought to be accounted of, and respected, and worship'd as Divine."[66]

Often, to be sure, Cavendish relies upon the truism that alchemy is a sham. (This despite the fact that her beloved husband, William Cavendish, seems to have dabbled in alchemy [*Observations* xiii].) The Empress's alchemists in *The Blazing World*, for example, are ape-men, a reference to the cunningly mimetic ape of medieval beast fable that extends, in the form of court satire, at least as late as Spenser's *Mother Hubberds Tale* (1591). The problem with the ape-men alchemists' form of mimesis, however, is that it is purely imaginary. Elsewhere, in *The Worlds Olio* (1655), Cavendish pooh-poohs the plausibility of the alchemical homunculus, "Paracelsus little Man," on the grounds that Paracelsus, seeing "some Dregs gathered together in a Form . . . perswaded himself it was like the Shape of a Man, as Fancies will form, and liken the Vapours that are gathered into Clouds, to the Figures of several things."[67] Similarly, the ape-men's alchemical theories in *The Blazing World* hold no water for the Empress because their opinions on which are the fundamental elements are so various, so malleable, and so ephemeral that they are a set of inapplicable fancies and unsatisfying stories.

In contrast, however, the Empress is extremely interested in the ape-men's account of a desert rock that produces a gum that, when given to "an old decayed man," will make him young again (155). This rock has all the properties of the philosopher's stone: it is found "in the parts of that world, which contained the golden sands"; it comes to perfection after the impossibly long ritualized duration of "a hundred years"; and the last stage of its application to the patient is the similarly ritualized span of nine months, "which is the time of a child's formation in the womb" (155–56). Moreover, the rock partakes of the properties of the Paracelsian mummy, the alchemical balm that conveys life (discussed in Chapter 2). Here the process is one of literal mummification. The old man is first purged of all bodily fluids, then his entire body scabs over, then he sheds the scab, and finally he "is wrapped into a cere-cloth, prepared of certain gums and juices," from which he emerges a young man of twenty (156). The Empress at first finds this account implausible. But ultimately she accepts it, for two interdependent reasons. First, because "the gum did grow naturally" and was not "a medicine prepared by art" (156–57). Second, because the story of the gum reminds her of other alchemical stories she knows from her native world, "great reports" of the efficacy of the philosopher's stone and of "a certain liquor called alkahest, which by the virtue of its own fire, consumed all diseases" (156). This confluence of nature with narrative, truth with artifice, allows the Empress's conference with the ape-men to end far differently than it began: with her granting credence to alchemy, "for she knew that nature's works are so various and wonderful, that no particular creature is able to trace her ways" (157).

Cavendish's point is more than simply that fictional creation is like alchemy. It is that fictional creation *is* alchemy. Whereas Sidney's alchemical metaphor for the literary enterprise was only that, metaphorical, Cavendish has something much more extreme in mind: a fictional enterprise that begins where alchemy begins, with the very substrate of physical matter. Thinking of alchemy as a fiction both fully natural and fully artificial aligns with Cavendish's project of framing her entire theory of material reproduction as a theory also of mimesis.

Here is how that theory goes. Revising her natural philosophy to oppose an Epicurean-Hobbesian-Cartesian matter theory that would subdivide the universe into inanimate, undifferentiated particles, Cavendish subscribes, as Eileen O'Neill puts it in her introduction to Cavendish's *Observations upon Experimental Philosophy*, to a view of nature as "a single, continuous self-subsistent organism" whose parts, like the parts of the human body, have specialized functions and individuated means of operation (xxvii).[68] To the extent that nature employs seeds as reproductive tools, then, those seeds are merely one of many modes by which those individual parts of nature engage in motion and replication: "nature hath many more ways of productions, than by seeds or seminal principles. . . . [F]or nature being infinite, also has infinite ways of acting in her particulars" (68). In this way Cavendish subscribes to the largest possible version of the one-sex model of reproduction: all of nature is a single body. Furthermore, that body includes a kind of intelligence. Nature is self-moving, sensitive, and rational, and her intelligence in turn manifests itself in the intelligences of her individual parts: "every part or particle of nature, as it is self-moving, so it is also self-knowing and perceptive" (113).[69] And part of those particles' self-knowledge includes the capacity for making new substances, objects, and creatures through imitation. Generally speaking, the natural philosopher attempting to understand nature through experiment is thus merely imitating nature's own mimetic operations: "all or most artificial experiments, are the best arguments to evince, there is perception in all corporeal parts of nature: for, as parts are joined, or commix with parts, so they move or work accordingly into such or such figures, either by the way of imitation, or otherwise" (113).

If intelligently crafted artificial experiment merely reproduces nature's own intelligently crafted artifice, it follows that Cavendish can view natural reproduction itself as a kind of fictional enterprise. This view emerges in Cavendish's repeated assertion that nature reproduces by means of "figures." When the Blazing World's Empress inquires after how vegetables reproduce themselves from seed, since "a particular part cannot increase of itself," the worm-men, her consultants on botany and zoology, reply that seeds "increase not barely of themselves, but by joining and commixing with other parts, which do assist them in their productions, and by way of imitation form or figure their own parts into such or such particulars" (152). Like Sidney defending poetry, Cavendish must then defend these natural parts' figured artistry from charges of lying. The Empress wants to know "what disguise these seeds put on, and how they do conceal themselves in their transmutations." The worm-men explain by way of rejoinder that "seeds did no ways disguise or conceal, but rather divulge themselves in the multiplication of their off-spring; only they did hide and conceal themselves from their sensitive perceptions so, that their figurative and productive motions were not perceptible by animal creatures" (152). Nothing affirming, therefore nothing lying, as Sidney would put it, nature reproduces "figuratively." Cavendish reaches back here to her description in *Philosophicall Fancies* (1653) of the "sensitive" parts of nature as quicksilver, that mercurial element. Those parts arrange themselves poetically, "severall ways placing themselves in several Figures, sometimes moving in measure, and in order."[70]

When the Empress and her scribe the Duchess of Newcastle resolve, upon the advice of spirits, "to create two worlds within themselves" (186), they thus achieve in microcosm what nature does by way of reproduction: they create through means of fiction. An author, like nature itself, "may make a world full of veins, muscles, and nerves, and all these to move by one jolt or stroke" (186). We would expect that the question of sex would begin to enter in here, since in the context of *The Blazing World*, a narrative that is in part a defense of the female authorial imagination, this natural production of the world is also an invention of the female mind. Furthermore, because nature is typically described as female in Cavendish's work, and because *The Blazing World*'s two creators of worlds—the Empress and the Duchess, the latter Cavendish herself—are female, we might be led to describe this model of reproduction specifically as that unusual thing, a feminine one-sex model. Certainly Cavendish is interested in staking out authorial capability and privileges for women. But because her vision of reproduction is imaginative as well as embodied, such that even the material of the world is reproduced according to the imaginative capacities of that world's parts, reproduction in *The Blazing World* is, paradoxically, a one-sex model that is strikingly unconnected to theories of reproductive anatomy. Cavendish imagines both for her Empress and for the Blazing World over which she reigns an "interior bodilessness," as Mary Baine Campbell puts it, at whose center is not the womb but rather—as if in a series of Chinese boxes—the author of *The Blazing World* itself.[71] As a result, Cavendish's world can be built on mind motions rather than birthing. While Cavendish may indeed achieve self-authorization through the rhetoric of conjugality, as Kate Lilley suggests, Cavendish does not draw upon the images of *coniunctio* that mark theories of natural reproduction derived from Aristotelian hylomorphism.[72] Her reproductive imagery, as we have seen, is of craftsmanship or artistry—of the will and motion of parts toward their own recombination and assemblage—rather than of sexual union.

The product of that reproduction, therefore, is truly an independent creation, not a child.[73] As the worm-men in *The Blazing World* explain to the Empress, the life of worms and other underground creatures "is their own, and not their parents; for no part or creature of nature can either give or take away life, but parts do only assist and join with parts, either in the dissolution or production of other parts and creatures" (153). Cavendish's commitment is to a potentially feminine but always nonsexualized creativity. Whether she is describing alchemical, fictional, or simply natural creation, gendered reproductive function simply does not come up. None of what nature, the alchemist, or the poet makes is conceived or birthed in sexualized fashion. As in the discussion of Homer and Raymond Lull in *A Comical Hash*, quoted above, what is made is simply "wrought." Thus Cavendish's alchemical reproduction is ultimately allied to the radical, emancipatory poetic space ascribed to this text by Nicole Pohl in her account of *The Blazing World*'s genre.[74] That alliance comes about because Cavendish, perhaps recollecting Paracelsus's panactive alchemical elements, refuses to assign especially feminine or especially masculine qualities either to nature or to its literary analogue, the authorial mind. Rather, nature, the authorial mind, and their productions are all so thoroughly hermaphroditic, such a successful recombination of all possible qualities, that their gender affiliation is impossible to discern.[75] In an era in which the normative authorial mind is a masculine one, desexualized authorship leaves space for female-authored fictions.

If, as I argued in Chapter 4, the conjunction of alchemy and gynecology in certain texts signals an optative epistemological moment—the choice of one way of knowing rather than another—then Cavendish's substitution of infinite, alternative alchemical fictions for finite physiognomic conceptions is a claim for radical optionality both in fiction and in physics. That is to say, Cavendish has created her Blazing World through the same kind of nonsexual intellectual production that she attributes to nature: she has organized "the parts of [her] mind" (224) in the same way that parts of nature—plants, animals, minerals, elements—combine and recombine in order to form novel productions, equally natural and aesthetic. Since all of those natural parts possess volition in the same way that the parts of Cavendish's mind possess volition, every alternative assemblage of parts into whole represents an alternative choice. De-gendering this reproductive process only increases volitional options in mathematical terms, since no recombinatory part is limited in its choices by its sexual role. Cavendish's preference for a nonsexualized reproduction thus contributes to what Stephen Clucas, quoting Robert Boyle, calls her preference for a "heap of bare Probabilities" over certainty and uniformity: science as Erasmian rhetorical *copia*.[76] There is no limit to what can be chosen, because there is no limit to the parameters within which choices may be made. Cavendish's epilogue in fact imagines an infinite future of choices. Some may be made by her: "though I have made my Blazing World, a peaceable world, allowing it but one religion, one language, and one government; yet could I make another world, as full of factions, divisions, and wars, as this is of peace and tranquility" (224). Some may be made by others: "if any should like the world I have made, and be willing to be my subjects, they may imagine themselves such . . . but if they cannot endure to be subjects, they may create worlds of their own, and govern themselves as they please" (224–25).

In considering Cavendish's alternative worlds, it is important to emphasize how she does not think of those worlds as purely intellective and immaterial. Rather, they draw upon and alter options for reshaping the physical universe. For Cavendish, fiction is everywhere, everyone's, everything's. Occupying all physical space and involving all physical matter, Cavendish's fiction making quite obviously contrasts with Jonson's restriction of the literary arts to the bounds of the house of alchemy. And yet Cavendish's radical democratization of fiction—so radical that it has all things in the universe making art both individually and together—is, in its own way, as innovatively posthumanist as Jonson's is. Perhaps even more innovative in that it goes head-to-head with that other version of posthumanism, Cartesian skepticism. Cavendish's posthumanism shares its contours with Bruno Latour's: it is a knowledge system that is no longer "constructed through contrast with the object," the thing that, conceived as separate from human judgment, "has been abandoned to epistemology."[77] Cavendish's knowledge system, however, is more complex (and more cognizant of the creativity of nature) than what results from Latour's sense of the nonhuman as "quasi-objects," things that act in and of themselves while they are at the same time constructed socially by humans' needs and desires for them.[78] Her material universe exists and changes not simply by means of action within a human/nonhuman network but by means of an ongoing process of fiction making.

This democratization of literary creation represents Cavendish's challenge to classical Cartesian epistemology, but she poses her challenge by expanding Cartesian wonder.[79] On the one hand, Cavendish's one-body vitalism, in which all things, creatures, minds, and elemental particles are rational actors within the single (and equally rational) body of nature, obviates the Cartesian mind-body split that tends to instantiate perception and ratiocination as masculine/active and the object of perception and ratiocination as feminine/passive.[80] On the other hand, Cavendish's attribution of both motion and volition to all those parts of nature expands the capacity for Cartesian wonder from the perceiver to the perceived. In the passage in *Passions of the Soul* that I discussed in Chapter 4, René Descartes proposes that the brain in a state of wonder is the brain in a state of heightened motion: "objects of the senses that are novel affect the brain in certain parts where it is not normally affected; and . . . since those parts are more tender or less firm than those hardened through frequent agitation, the effects of the movements produced in them are thereby increased."[81] When Cavendish argues for an entire world as one mind-body that both thinks and moves, she thus also implicitly postulates, perhaps based on her own reading of *Passions of the Soul*, that individual parts of that mind-body must be constantly in a mutually reciprocal state of inducing and experiencing wonder.[82] Creating through motion rather than insemination, the parts of Cavendish's universe assemble themselves in wondrous and unlimited artistry.

Because she places fiction at the very heart of being, it would be possible to construe Cavendish as some kind of superhumanist, one who promotes literary creation from the primarily social, moral, and ethical function it had in a humanistic education to the status of governing principle, the equivalent of Paracelsus's alchemical life spark that inhabits all matter, earthly and heavenly. It would be more accurate, however, to describe Cavendish's literary particle physics as liberating literature from humanism. First of all, for Cavendish, fiction is not necessarily associated with text. Without text, the primary philological operations upon which humanism depends collapse. Second, because her fictions proliferate infinitely, there can be no governing truth. Cavendish's fictions are universal in the sense of being ubiquitous, but they are not universal in the sense of being universally applicable.

Jonathan Goldberg's comments on the meaning of Cavendish's illegible handwriting—an issue that the character of the Duchess of Newcastle mentions in *The Blazing World* when the Empress asks for her services as a scribe—are apropos here. While other critics, notably Sandra Sherman, have considered how Cavendish creates individual subjectivity in dialectic with a textuality that threatens to dissolve the self, Goldberg connects the peculiarity of Cavendish's handwriting—indeed, the peculiarity of her entire writing and publishing practice—to her positing both a social community and a physical world in which "everyone is connected to and yet at the same time utterly different from everyone else. . . . Matter and mind, the animate and the inanimate, are all one, even as they are each different."[83] Textuality matters to Cavendish, as does community. But neither textuality nor community works in the service of some real or desired totality. Cavendish's Blazing World, unlike the King of Navarre's academy at the opening of *Love's Labour's Lost*, does not feature a circle of the learned seeking Truth with a capital *T*. Rather, each person, each creature, each particle has its own tale to tell.

In many ways, the ambitious Cavendish attempted to install herself in precisely the laureate lineage that English authors developed from humanist precedent.[84] She deeply desired literary fame: she was, as Clucas reminds us, "arguably the first Englishwoman to fashion herself as an author," achieving "publication on an unprecedented scale" and submitting copies of her books to the Oxford and Cambridge university libraries.[85] And yet, in the way that her works grant fiction's power to each subunit of the physical universe, Cavendish invented a knowledge system that no one had yet imagined, and that remained unimaginable by anyone else in her day—and challenging even in ours. The utter unorthodoxy of Cavendish's theories on matter and its generation also upends all prior theory of what and whom literature is for. Literature neither changes the world, as early humanism would have it, nor does it exist apart from the world, as *The Alchemist* would have it. Literature *is* the world.

Cavendish's marriage of matter to fiction is thus at the heart of why her works could find no place in seventeenth-century thought: despite her royalist affiliations, her work nonetheless levels all hierarchy from (literally) the ground up. Humanism's male-authored, academically endorsed, Christian syncretism is out; highly individualized conceptions are in. Conceptions that extend even to previously disesteemed entities like things, and women.[86] In Cavendish's fiction-making universe, Hamlet's theory of everything would have to coexist with Horatio's, and Gertrude's, and the Ghost's, and maybe even Yorick's skull's. We can imagine Hamlet protesting. "This?" he would ask Cavendish, just as he asks the gravedigger about the skull, in the single instance in the play in which he seems truly to seek another's opinion. And with the gravedigger, Cavendish would reply, "E'en that" (*Hamlet*, 5.1.176–77). Through the making of fiction, Cavendish engages in disknowledge on the grandest possible scale: she trades all that is known about how and what to learn for a fanciful and untried alternative. Through the making of fiction, she propels learning into a vastly uncertain but vastly optimistic future, past the systematic practices, customary texts, and restricted student population that humanism had addressed in its making of knowledge. Through the making of fiction, she makes learning the provenance of whoever will take it up.

Afterword

My argument in this book has been founded on the close relation between humanism and alchemy as knowledge-making systems. That close relation helps crack one of the enduring puzzles of late seventeenth-century intellectual culture: Why did groundbreaking geniuses of mathematics, science, and political theory such as Isaac Newton, John Locke, Gottfried Leibniz, and Robert Boyle remain enamored of alchemy, long after its foundational texts had been exposed as far less ancient than claimed, and despite centuries of doubt over its methods and results? Recent work by intellectual historians and historians of science has suggested a number of persuasive and fascinating rationales having to do with alchemy's lingering explanatory power. For example, Newton saw gravity as similar to occult rather than mechanistic forces; Locke found alchemy's treatment of arcana applicable to his desire for secret knowledge; Leibniz used the metaphysics of alchemy to elaborate his ideas of composite substances; and Boyle, like John Dee before him, hoped that alchemical practice would facilitate communication with angels, bridging the human and the divine.[1] One unifying factor may underlie these individual rationales, however. The education that all these men received habituated them to the humanistic practices, both scrupulous and sloppy, that were ingrained in alchemical thinking. Thus, alchemy seemed plausible to the likes of Boyle, Newton, and Locke whether it did or did not support their chemistry, physics, mathematics, or political theory.

Like humanistic practices, then, alchemy does not entirely disappear at the end of the seventeenth century. The question of where alchemy goes, however, will get you different answers depending on whom you ask. Historians of science, interested as they are in how problem-solving strategies change over time, have for the most part answered the question of where alchemy went by

looking at its relation to seventeenth- and eighteenth-century scientific practice. Either alchemy's outmoded practice and inferior problem-solving strategies gave way in the eighteenth century to chemistry (the old answer), or
alchemy lent its protoscientific practice and its useful problem-solving strategies to late seventeenth-century empirical science (the more recent answer).
Historians and literary scholars who focus on Hermeticism and other esoteric
discourses, in contrast, have argued that alchemy survived in the symbolic register, diffused into the language of practices as various as Rosicrucianism,
Masonry, theosophy, and Jungian psychology.

Unlike these approaches, my method in this book has been to treat alchemy less as its own set of practices or its own semiotic system and more as
an interventional maneuver deployed by other practices and other discourses.
Alchemy's potential to be taken up by other intellectual endeavors would make
it possible, I suspect, to find alchemical discourse positioned in relation to
almost every avenue of early modern thinking, even though I have chosen
just a few to discuss in this book. A full account of the early modern use of
alchemy for the purposes of disknowledge, if one were possible, would look
beyond scientific practice or esoteric thought to trace how all of early modern
learning goes about its business: its requirements, ideologies, agendas, and ambitions but also its blind spots, shortcuts, evasions, and hubrises. And a full
account of alchemy's afterlife would trace how all of these maneuvers and habits are taken up by later generations, ones that do not necessarily recognize
their learning environment's debt to alchemically inflected intellective and
rhetorical patterns.

Based on their common history, a related question to where alchemy goes
after the seventeenth century is where humanism goes. If what the early seventeenth century forecasts for the future of humanism is the choice between
the disknowledge of William Shakespeare's *Hamlet* and the disknowledge of
Ben Jonson's *The Alchemist*—the choice, that is, between disastrous large-scale
theory and inconsequential small-scale fictions—then those of us who live in
that future may well despair. That despair is well founded, it seems to me,
when we notice the survival of Hamlet's humanistic habits in intellectual work
that has the potential for doing tremendous harm. To skip ahead from the
end of the seventeenth century to the present day, the kind of disknowledge
that implements theory designed rhetorically rather than empirically influences everything from medical research—much of which still assumes, for
example, that the male body is the normative body, even though everyone now
knows that is not so—to U.S. economic policy, which bows to patently un-

true truisms like the idea that taxing capital gains as ordinary income discourages business investment. In other words, it is not just the most blatant varieties of conspiracy theory, from intelligent design to the denial of the Holocaust or of climate change, that deploy disknowledge knowingly in intellectual realms. Disknowledge governs theory of all kinds, including, as Bruno Latour argues, the academic theory that is eager to critique all forms of cherished belief except for its own.[2] Far from having been either left behind in the scientific revolution or absorbed into rigorous experimental practice, the careless, cheerful, knowing acceptance of the countertruth that the age of late humanism attributed to alchemy is perhaps the habit of mind that most marks modernity. And the intellectual class is no freer than anyone else from modernity's worst intellectual habits.[3]

I am much more sanguine, however, about *The Alchemist*'s and Margaret Cavendish's posthumanistic approaches to disknowledge. Both craft a benign and even salutary form of disknowledge that has been a thread throughout this book and that has consequences not only for literature's production but also for its study. Take Jonson first. *The Alchemist*'s approach of deploying alchemy to show how literature, itself a form of disknowledge, may be cordoned off into a discipline of its own has its appeal. It is true enough that the current crisis of the humanities finds its historical origins in the late seventeenth-century establishment of the sciences as separate disciplines from letters and the arts. Pointing out those long-ago historical origins, though, only suggests how foolish it is to bewail the fact that literary studies has been labeled inconsequential. That ship sailed long ago. Yet in Jonson's powerful but contained symbiosis between the literary and the alchemical we may find the foundation of an epistemological status that will prove to be boon more than bane, not only for literature but also for literary studies. Possessing its own corner of the academy, its own redoubt of disknowledge, grants literary studies—as long as that redoubt lasts—the same pleasures that Lovewit and Face both claim for the house of alchemy. They are the pleasures of unbridling the imagination, the satisfactions of concocting intricate schemes out of one's brains and one's desires. Furthermore, literature's pleasures may safely be indulged in because they have veracity only within bounds. If it cannot often be credited for real effect, literary studies also cannot usually be blamed for real harm.

This combination of free imaginative rein and limited material consequence is what assures literary studies its continued place in the academy. There is a power in straitened disciplinarity. As Stanley Fish has argued, it is when literary studies diffuses itself into the "interdisciplinary" that it is most likely to lose its privileged status: "the hope that we can put all the jobs of work—all the so-called disciplines—together and form one large and unified field of knowledge (call it cultural studies) . . . is dashed when one realizes that different forms of disciplinary work, rather than being co-partners in a single teleological and utopian task, are engaged in performing the particular tasks that would pass away from the earth were they to lose themselves in the name of some grand synthesis."[4] Similarly skeptical about whether "interdisciplinarity" is the next newfound land of literary criticism, Linda Hutcheon suggests that we call such work merely "interdiscursive," one discipline attempting for its own peculiar purposes to talk the talk of another.[5] Both Fish and Hutcheon recognize how disciplinary boundaries help further the work that literary criticism does best on its own.

It is important to emphasize, however—as Fish often fails to do—that the work of literary criticism constitutes a separate discipline not merely because it has a separate object of study than does history or linguistics or physics. It also has a separate modus operandi. Here, both Jonson's *The Alchemist* and Cavendish's *The Blazing World* provide a cogent analysis. In designating the house of alchemy as the house of fiction, *The Alchemist* conspicuously declines to aspire to make the discipline of literature a science in the mold of I. A. Richards's practical criticism. Rather, as I have suggested, *The Alchemist* forecasts, through alchemy, the fate of literature to be the one discipline that lacks discipline—something more like F. R. Leavis's paradoxical "discipline of sensibility, judgment and thought . . . concerned with training a nonspecialist intelligence."[6] Similarly, if more radically, *The Blazing World* refuses to make literature the domain of any privileged class of people, or even the domain of humans in general as a privileged class of creatures or of material substance. Literature is different from science for Cavendish because it is bigger than science, because its operations are at work wherever we look. We do not cross disciplines when we think literarily about any topic at all; rather, we practice our discipline where it already resides. In short, Cavendish has already started the project that Henry Turner, drawing from Bruno Latour, Paul Feyerabend, and others, recommends: we must rejoin science to poetry by viewing contemporary sciences like genetic sequencing as poetically inventive sign-creating systems.[7] Thus, while Jonson and Cavendish offer widely different visions of the scope of literary study—one boutique, one universal—those visions are not necessarily mutually exclusive. While Jonson's house of alchemy models the delimited sphere of scholars of literature, both Jonson's nondisciplinary discipline and Cavendish's ubiquitous literariness pertain to the way we teach our students, very few of whom will embark upon a lifetime of literary scholarship, but all of whom, we hope, will apply literary thinking in a lifetime of analyzing whatever they come across.

As a scholar of literature I frankly acknowledge that *The Alchemist*'s boutique mode of disknowledge is my own. Outside the front door of literature's house its schemes vanish, as evanescent as the philosopher's stone. How sad. But yet, says Jonson, how fun. Asked by Dol, "say lord General, how fares our camp?"—the opening line (after the prologue) of *The Spanish Tragedy*— *The Alchemist*'s Face converts the looming tragedy of Dol's source text into the comedy of insular disciplinarity. He replies that their camp fares

> As, with the few, that had entrenched themselves
> Safe, by their discipline, against a world, Dol:
> And laughed, within those trenches, and grew fat
> With thinking on the booties, Dol, brought in
> Daily, by their small parties.
>
> (3.3.33–38)

We scholar-soldiers of literary study may be stuck in trenches that are narrow in comparison to the world beyond. The sorties we conduct from those trenches may be small. And yet, there we are safe; there we laugh. And there we grow fat with thinking, feeding upon falsehoods taken quite consciously for true.

Where did alchemy go after the seventeenth century? Sad to say, it went everywhere. Happy to say, it went into the work of literary critics, from F. R. Leavis to the author of this book. As it turns out, disknowledge has its uses.

NOTES

INTRODUCTION

1. William Shakespeare, *Hamlet*, ed. Harold Jenkins (London: Methuen, 1982), 1.5.174–75. All subsequent references to this play are to this edition and will be cited parenthetically in the text by act, scene, and line numbers.

2. William N. West, *Theatres and Encyclopedias in Early Modern Europe* (Cambridge: Cambridge University Press, 2002), 1.

3. Ann M. Blair, *Too Much to Know: Managing Scholarly Information Before the Modern Age* (New Haven, CT: Yale University Press, 2010).

4. Lucien Febvre and Henri-Jean Martin, *The Coming of the Book: The Impact of Printing 1450–1800*, trans. David Gerard (London: NLB, 1976), 280–81.

5. Maurice Blanchot, "Inner Experience," in *Faux Pas*, trans. Charlotte Mandell (Stanford, CA: Stanford University Press, 1991), 37–41.

6. Peter Sloterdijk, *Critique of Cynical Reason*, trans. Michael Eldred (Minneapolis: University of Minnesota Press, 1987), 5.

7. Harry Berger, Jr., *The Allegorical Temper: Vision and Reality in Book II of Spenser's Faerie Queene* (New Haven, CT: Yale University Press, 1957), 122.

8. See Tara Nummedal, *Alchemy and Authority in the Holy Roman Empire* (Chicago: University of Chicago Press, 2007); Marcos Martinón-Torres and Thilo Rehren, "Alchemy, Chemistry and Metallurgy in Renaissance Europe: A Wider Context for Fire-Assay Remains," *Historical Metallurgy* 39 (2005): 14–28; Warren Alexander Dym, "Alchemy and Mining: Metallogenesis and Prospecting in Early Mining Books," *Ambix* 55 (2008): 232–54; and Pamela H. Smith, *The Body of the Artisan: Art and Experience in the Scientific Revolution* (Chicago: University of Chicago Press, 2004), 129–51.

9. William R. Newman and Lawrence M. Principe, *Alchemy Tried in the Fire: Starkey, Boyle, and the Fate of Helmontian Chymistry* (Chicago: University of Chicago Press, 2002). Brian Vickers has taken Newman and Principe to task for overemphasizing alchemy's technological and protoscientific aspects and de-emphasizing its other dimensions, including its lack of success and its reputation for falsehood; see "The 'New Historiography' and the Limits of Alchemy," *Annals of Science* 65 (2008): 127–56; and William R. Newman, "Brian Vickers on Alchemy and the Occult: A Response," *Perspectives on Science* 17 (2009): 482–506.

10. Frances A. Yates, *Giordano Bruno and the Hermetic Tradition* (Chicago: University of Chicago Press, 1964); Frances A. Yates, *The Rosicrucian Enlightenment* (London: Routledge and Kegan Paul, 1972). See also Keith Thomas, *Religion and the Decline of Magic: Studies in Popular Beliefs in Sixteenth- and Seventeenth-Century England* (1971; repr., London: Penguin, 1991).

11. Although we may speak of practical and theoretical alchemy as distinct enterprises, the same people often practiced both. Stanton J. Linden points to engravings that show the alchemist's laboratory divided into two halves—one filled with equipment, the other with alchemical books; see Linden, *Darke Hierogliphicks: Alchemy in English Literature from Chaucer to the Restoration* (Lexington: University Press of Kentucky, 1996), 8–10. For one alchemist who was both theorist and practitioner, see Walter W. Woodward, *Prospero's America: John Winthrop, Jr., Alchemy, and the Creation of New England Culture, 1606–1676* (Chapel Hill: University of North Carolina Press, 2010).

12. For often sympathetic rebuttals to the "Yates thesis" of Hermetic tradition see, e.g., Brian Vickers, "Introduction," in *Occult and Scientific Mentalities in the Renaissance*, ed. Brian Vickers (Cambridge: Cambridge University Press, 1984), 1–56; Brian P. Copenhaver, "Natural Magic, Hermeticism, and Occultism in Early Modern Science," in *Reappraisals of the Scientific Revolution*, ed. David C. Lindberg and Robert S. Westman (Cambridge: Cambridge University Press, 1990), 261–302; H. Floris Cohen, *The Scientific Revolution: A Historiographical Inquiry* (Chicago: University of Chicago Press, 1994), 169–83; and Stephen Clucas, "'Wondrous Force and Operation': Magic, Science and Religion in the Renaissance," in *Textures of Renaissance Knowledge*, ed. Philippa Berry and Margaret Tudeau-Clayton (Manchester, UK: Manchester University Press, 2003), 35–57. For a smart discussion of how it is and is not useful to speak of "Western esoteric thought," see Kocku von Stuckrad, *Locations of Knowledge in Medieval and Early Modern Europe: Esoteric Discourse and Western Identities* (Leiden: Brill, 2010), 43–64. For the popularity of alchemical symbology in the works of artists and artisans, see, e.g., Smith's discussion of Bernard Palissy in *Body of the Artisan*, 100–106; and Jacob Wamberg, "A Stone and Yet Not a Stone: Alchemical Themes in North Italian Quattrocentro Landscape Imagery," in *Art and Alchemy*, ed. Jacob Wamberg (Copenhagen: Museum Tusculanum Press, 2006), 41–82.

13. Karen Pinkus, *Alchemical Mercury: A Theory of Ambivalence* (Stanford, CA: Stanford University Press, 2010), 65.

14. Nummedal asserts that the frequent charges of fraud leveled against alchemists do not indicate that all alchemists were viewed as frauds. I see her point, but I also agree with her contention in *Alchemy and Authority*, 6, that the charge of fraud that so often accompanied alchemy became "a focal point for a much broader discussion about alchemy's cultural meaning."

15. John Lyly, *Gallathea*, in *Drama of the English Renaissance*, vol. 1: *The Tudor Period*, ed. Russell A. Fraser and Norman Rabkin (New York: Macmillan, 1976), 2.3.32–34.

16. Linden, *Darke Hierogliphicks*.

17. Peggy Ann Knapp, "The Work of Alchemy," *Journal of Medieval and Early Modern Studies* 30 (2000): 575–99; William H. Sherman, "'Gold is the strength, the sinnewes of the world': Thomas Dekker's *Old Fortunatus* and England's Golden Age," *Medieval and Renaissance Drama in England* 6 (1993): 85–102; David Hawkes, *Idols of the Marketplace: Idolatry and Commodity Fetishism in English Literature, 1580–1680* (New York: Palgrave, 2001), 143–67.

18. Robert N. Proctor, "Agnotology: A Missing Term to Describe the Cultural Production of Ignorance (and Its Study)," in *Agnotology: The Making and Unmaking of Ignorance*, ed. Robert N. Proctor and Londa Schiebinger (Stanford, CA: Stanford University Press, 2008), 1–36; Londa Schiebinger, *Plants and Empire: Colonial Bioprospecting in the Atlantic World* (Cambridge, MA: Harvard University Press, 2004), 8.

19. Lorraine Daston, "Historical Epistemology," in *Questions of Evidence: Proof, Practice, and Persuasion Across the Disciplines*, ed. James Chandler, Arnold I. Davidson, and Harry Harootunian (Chicago: University of Chicago Press, 1994), 282–88, quotations on 282–83; Arnold I. Davidson, *The Emergence of Sexuality: Historical Epistemology and the Formation of Concepts* (Cambridge, MA: Harvard University Press, 2001).

20. Michel Foucault, *The Order of Things: An Archaeology of the Human Sciences* (New York: Vintage, 1994), 380.

21. Thomas S. Kuhn, *The Structure of Scientific Revolutions*, 4th ed. (Chicago: University of Chicago Press, 2012), 66–91.

22. David Glimp, "*Utopia* and Global Risk Management," *ELH* 75 (2008): 263–90, quotation on 263.

23. Schiebinger, *Plants and Empire*, 226–41.

24. For a subtle account of early modern authors as agents of their own censorship, see Richard Burt, *Licensed by Authority: Ben Jonson and the Discourses of Censorship* (Ithaca, NY: Cornell University Press, 1993).

25. Paul W. Mapp, *The Elusive West and the Contest for Empire, 1713–1763* (Chapel Hill: University of North Carolina Press, 2011).

26. Mary Poovey, *A History of the Modern Fact: Problems of Knowledge in the Sciences of Wealth and Society* (Chicago: University of Chicago Press, 1998).

27. Anthony Grafton, *Defenders of the Text: The Traditions of Scholarship in an Age of Science, 1450–1800* (Cambridge, MA: Harvard University Press, 1991).

28. See, e.g., Andrew Martin, *The Knowledge of Ignorance: From Genesis to Jules Verne* (Cambridge: Cambridge University Press, 1985); Stanley Cavell, *Disowning Knowledge in Six Plays of Shakespeare* (Cambridge: Cambridge University Press, 1987); Michael Smithson, *Ignorance and Uncertainty: Emerging Paradigms* (New York: Springer-Verlag, 1989); Christopher Herbert, *Victorian Relativity: Radical Thought and Scientific Discovery* (Chicago: University of Chicago Press, 2001); Philip Weinstein, *Unknowing: The Work of Modernist Fiction* (Ithaca, NY: Cornell University Press, 2005); and Andrew Bennett, *Ignorance: Literature and Agnoiology* (Manchester, UK: Manchester University Press, 2009).

29. Bruno Latour, "Why Has Critique Run Out of Steam? From Matters of Fact to Matters of Concern," *Critical Inquiry* 30 (2004): 225–48.

30. Roger Ariew, "G. W. Leibniz, Life and Works," in *The Cambridge Companion to Leibniz*, ed. Nicholas Jolley (Cambridge: Cambridge University Press, 1995), 18–42, quotation on 21.

31. For Leibniz's use and eventual repudiation of alchemy, see Stuart Brown, "Some Occult Influences on Leibniz's Monadology," in *Leibniz, Mysticism, and Religion*, ed. Allison P. Coudert, Richard H. Popkin, and Gordon M. Weiner (Dordrecht: Kluwer, 1998), 1–21.

1. HOW TO SUSTAIN HUMANISM

1. Arthur Kinney, *Humanist Poetics: Thought, Rhetoric, and Fiction in Sixteenth-Century England* (Amherst: University of Massachusetts Press, 1986), 446.

2. Virginia Woolf, *Mr. Bennett and Mrs. Brown* (London: Hogarth, 1924), 4.

3. For the persistence of the humanist curriculum in grammar schools, see Ian Green, *Humanism and Protestantism in Early Modern English Education* (Farnham, UK: Ashgate, 2009), 83–84, 131–45. For the same phenomenon at Oxford, see Mordechai Feingold, "The Humanities," in *The History of the University of Oxford*, vol. 4: *Seventeenth-Century Oxford*, ed. Nicholas Tyacke (Oxford: Clarendon, 1997), 211–358. For humanism's continuing influence on science, see Nancy G. Siraisi, *History, Medicine, and the Traditions of Renaissance Learning* (Ann Arbor: University of Michigan Press, 2007); and Grafton, *Defenders*. On Hobbes, see Quentin Skinner, *Reason and Rhetoric in the Philosophy of Hobbes* (Cambridge: Cambridge University Press, 1996). On Locke, see Feingold, "The Humanities," 238–39; and Gary Remer, *Humanism and the Rhetoric of Toleration* (University Park: Pennsylvania State University Press, 1996), 231–36. Kent Cartwright, while arguing that English humanism in its university-drama form enabled the growth of the public theater, also notes that part of what made humanism interesting for the public stage was its shortcomings—that is, the gap between book learning and experience; see Cartwright, *Theatre and Humanism: English Drama in the Sixteenth Century* (Cambridge: Cambridge University Press, 1999), 15–16. To challenge Kinney on the early robustness of English humanism, we might look to Alan Stewart, who describes how humanism was derided as early as William Tyndale; see Stewart, "The Trouble with English Humanism: Tyndale, More and Darling Erasmus," in *Reassessing Tudor Humanism*, ed. Jonathan Woolfson (New York: Palgrave, 2002), 78–98.

4. Brian Cummings, *The Literary Culture of the Reformation: Grammar and Grace* (Oxford: Oxford University Press, 2002).

5. For the humanistic disciplines—especially rhetoric—as the foundation of the Tudor education of the *vir civilis*, see Skinner, *Reason and Rhetoric*, 19–110.

6. Feingold, "Humanities," 235–42; Mordechai Feingold, "Reversal of Fortunes: The Displacement of Cultural Hegemony from the Netherlands to England in the Seventeenth and Early Eighteenth Centuries," in *The World of William and Mary: Anglo-Dutch Perspectives on the Revolution of 1688–89*, ed. Dale Hook and Mordechai Feingold (Stanford, CA: Stanford University Press, 1996), 234–61.

7. Kinney, *Humanist Poetics*, 441. See Luciano Floridi, *Sextus Empiricus: The Transmission and Recovery of Pyrrhonism* (Oxford: Oxford University Press, 2002). For the history of pre-Cartesian skepticism in nominalism and other late medieval strands of thought, see Susan E. Schreiner, *Are You Alone Wise? The Search for Certainty in the Early Modern Era* (Oxford: Oxford University Press, 2011), 3–35; for its history in demonology and theories of vision and art, see Stuart Clark, *Vanities of the Eye: Vision in Early Modern European Culture* (Oxford: Oxford University Press, 2007).

8. Philip Melanchthon, *Erotemata dialectices*, in *Corpus reformatorum*, vol. 13: *Philippi Melanthonis opera quae supersunt omnia*, ed. Carl Bretschneider (Heidelberg: Schwetschke, 1846), column 646, quoted and trans. in Joel B. Altman, *The Improbability of Othello: Rhetorical Anthropology and Shakespearean Selfhood* (Chicago: University of Chicago Press, 2010), 116. Anthony Grafton and Lisa Jardine lay humanism's abandonment of moral truths at the feet of Peter Ramus, who "separat[ed] oratorical practice from any moral underpinning"; see Grafton and Jardine, *From Humanism to the Humanities: Education and the Liberal Arts in Fifteenth- and Sixteenth-Century Europe* (Cambridge, MA: Harvard University Press, 1986), 189. For the efforts of rhetoricians to reconcile humanism with skepticism, see Altman, *Improbability*, 93–117.

9. William Bouwsma, *The Waning of the Renaissance 1550–1640* (New Haven, CT: Yale University Press, 2000), 36.

10. Frances E. Dolan, *True Relations: Reading, Literature, and Evidence in Seventeenth-Century England* (Philadelphia: University of Pennsylvania Press, 2013).

11. Kinney, *Humanist Poetics*, 447.

12. Schreiner, *Are You Alone Wise?*, 79–129.

13. John Milton, *Paradise Regained*, in *John Milton: Complete Poems and Major Prose*, ed. Merritt Y. Hughes (New York: Odyssey, 1957), 4.318–20. For Protestant disapprobation of humanist reading, see Erika Rummel, *The Confessionalization of Humanism in Reformation Germany* (Oxford: Oxford University Press, 2000), 30–49; Grafton, *Defenders*, 17; and Wouter J. Hanegraaff, *Esotericism and the Academy: Rejected Knowledge in Western Culture* (Cambridge: Cambridge University Press, 2012), 78–93.

14. Margo Todd, *Christian Humanism and the Puritan Social Order* (Cambridge: Cambridge University Press, 1987), 206–38; Markku Peltonen, *Rhetoric, Politics, and Popularity in Pre-Revolutionary England* (Cambridge: Cambridge University Press, 2013).

15. See Sean Keilen, *Vulgar Eloquence: On the Renaissance Invention of English Literature* (New Haven, CT: Yale University Press, 2006), 2–3.

16. Hiram Haydn, *The Counter-Renaissance* (New York: Grove, 1950), xiii.

17. William Gilbert, *On the Magnet*, trans. Sylvanus Thompson (London: Chiswick, 1900), ii.

18. James I of England, *Basilikon doron* (Edinburgh, 1599), 113 (Q1r).

19. Jeff Dolven, *Scenes of Instruction in Renaissance Romance* (Chicago: University of Chicago Press, 2007), 11.

20. For the temporal demarcations of late humanism as opposed to early empiricism see, e.g., Stephen Toulmin, *Cosmopolis: The Hidden Agenda of Modernity* (Chicago:

University of Chicago Press, 1992), 5–87; and Bouwsma, *Waning*, 35–51, 179–97. Scholars have recently emphasized how much empiricism in its early stages depended on late-humanistic method; see Grafton, *Defenders*; and Gianna Pomata and Nancy G. Siraisi, eds., *Historia: Empiricism and Erudition in Early Modern Europe* (Cambridge, MA: MIT Press, 2005).

21. The timing of England's increasing interest in alchemy in the 1590s had to do in part with issues of textual transmission like the relatively late access in England to the works of Paracelsus; see my discussion of Paracelsianism in the work of John Donne in Chapter 2. It also, however, had to do with the unstable state of learning. Mary Thomas Crane argues that interest in alchemy and other esoteric discourses surged in the sixteenth century in response to Aristotelian natural philosophy's demotion; see Crane, *Losing Touch with Nature: Literature and the New Science in Sixteenth-Century England* (Baltimore: Johns Hopkins University Press, 2014), 15–16. Crane's study was published as this book went into press, and I regret that I could not incorporate her insights more fully into my argument.

22. The foundational work on humanism's interest in Hermeticism is Yates, *Giordano Bruno*. While Yates's case is overstated and has been challenged on that basis, much of her analysis of Hermeticism's structures and rhetoric remains useful. Hanegraaff, *Esotericism*, 12–17, argues that early humanists like Ficino were interested in a constellation of ancient sages, not just the wisdom of Hermes Trismegistus; he calls this constellation "Platonic Orientalism." See also Florian Ebeling, *The Secret History of Hermes Trismegistus: Hermeticism from Ancient to Modern Times*, trans. David Lorton (Ithaca, NY: Cornell University Press, 2007), 59–70; and Margaret Healy, *Shakespeare, Alchemy and the Creative Imagination: The Sonnets and* A Lover's Complaint (Cambridge: Cambridge University Press, 2011), 24–32.

23. Bruce Janacek, *Alchemical Belief: Occultism in the Religious Culture of Early Modern England* (University Park: Pennsylvania State University Press, 2011).

24. Comenius visited England twice in the 1640s on the invitation of Samuel Hartlib, who sought his advice on reforming schools along Baconian lines. However, "Baconian" did not mean "posthumanist" or "scientific" in modern terms. Comenius and Hartlib both rejected Baconian induction in favor of presuming that all knowledge and all creation proceed from an inclusive, divinely created universal frame. See William R. Newman, *Gehennical Fire: The Lives of George Starkey, An American Alchemist in the Scientific Revolution* (Cambridge, MA: Harvard University Press, 1994), 55–58; J. T. Young, *Faith, Medical Alchemy and Natural Philosophy: Johann Moriaen, Reformed Intelligencer, and the Hartlib Circle* (Aldershot, UK: Ashgate, 1998), 101–12; and Paolo Rossi, *Logic and the Art of Memory: The Quest for a Universal Language*, trans. Stephen Clucas (Chicago: University of Chicago Press, 2000), 133–38. Comenius's inclusion of alchemy in the scheme of universal knowledge followed his mentor, Johann Heinrich Alsted, who addresses alchemy quite seriously despite including it among the "Farragines disciplinarum" in his *Encyclopedia* (1630); see Howard Hotson, *Johann Heinrich Alsted, 1588–1638: Between Renaissance, Reformation, and Universal Reform* (Oxford: Clarendon, 2000), 153–63.

25. Hanegraaff, *Esotericism*, 204–5. I generally use the terms *theoretical alchemy* and either *practical alchemy* or *experimental alchemy* to distinguish between text-based and hands-on alchemy. William Newman and Lawrence Principe advocate for the term *chymistry* to describe practical or experimental alchemy, but so far this term has not caught on beyond a small coterie of historians of science.

26. Lawrence M. Principe, *The Secrets of Alchemy* (Chicago: University of Chicago Press, 2013), 181; see also Hanegraaff, *Esotericism*, 191–94.

27. Charles Webster, *From Paracelsus to Newton: Magic and the Making of Modern Science* (Cambridge: Cambridge University Press, 1982), 10.

28. Lawrence M. Principe, "The Alchemies of Robert Boyle and Isaac Newton: Alternate Approaches and Divergent Employments," in *Rethinking the Scientific Revolution*, ed. Margaret J. Osler (Cambridge: Cambridge University Press, 2000), 201–20.

29. Stephanie H. Jed, *Chaste Thinking: The Rape of Lucretia and the Birth of Humanism* (Bloomington: Indiana University Press, 1989).

30. Then as now, of course, sloppy scholarly habits and brilliant scholarly accomplishment are not mutually exclusive, as Anthony Grafton points out in a review of recent books on the Italian polymath Athanasius Kircher; see Grafton, "He Had Fun," *London Review of Books* 35, no. 21 (2013): 25–27.

31. Charles G. Nauert, Jr., *Humanism and the Culture of Renaissance Europe* (Cambridge: Cambridge University Press, 1995), 194–95, 214–15.

32. For an analysis of *copia* as encouraging a literary culture of detachable components that may be disassembled and reassembled, see Richard Halpern, *The Poetics of Primitive Accumulation: English Renaissance Culture and the Genealogy of Capital* (Ithaca, NY: Cornell University Press, 1991), 45–49.

33. Howard Hotson, *Commonplace Learning: Ramism and Its German Ramifications, 1543–1630* (Oxford: Oxford University Press, 2007), 51–68.

34. Blair, *Too Much to Know*. Work on the early modern perception of excess information—not only the proliferation of books but also the proliferation of newly observed natural phenomena—has itself proliferated in the last decade. For some of the foundational questions involved, see Daniel Rosenberg, "Early Modern Information Overload," *Journal of the History of Ideas* 64 (2003): 1–9. Haydn, in *Counter-Renaissance*, 76–130, was perhaps the first modern scholar to discuss a Renaissance backlash against the proliferation of books.

35. Martin, *Knowledge of Ignorance*, 26–27.

36. Blair, *Too Much to Know*, 59.

37. Nummedal, *Alchemy and Authority*, 27.

38. Anthony Grafton, *Commerce with the Classics: Ancient Books and Renaissance Readers* (Ann Arbor: University of Michigan Press, 1997), 97.

39. For the reformation of curiosity from a vice to a virtue, see Peter Harrison, "Curiosity, Forbidden Knowledge, and the Reformation of Natural Philosophy in Early Modern England," *Isis* 92 (2001): 265–90; and Neil Kenny, *The Uses of Curiosity in Early Modern France and Germany* (Oxford: Oxford University Press, 2004).

40. Ian Hacking, *Historical Ontology* (Cambridge, MA: Harvard University Press, 2002), 197.

41. John Locke, *John Locke's "Of the Conduct of the Understanding,"* ed. Francis W. Garforth (New York: Teacher's College Press of Columbia University, 1966), 72.

42. Robert Fludd, *Mosaicall Philosophy* (London, 1659), 42 (G1v).

43. Poovey, *Modern Fact*, 8–11.

44. Michael Sendivogius [Michal Sedziwój], *A New Light of Alchymie* (London, 1650), 1–2 (B1r–v).

45. Hanegraaff, *Esotericism*, 9. For early modern quarrels over how to interpret one fundamental alchemical text, the *Emerald Tablet* of Hermes Trismegistus, see Peter Forshaw, "Alchemical Exegesis: Fractious Distillations of the Essence of Hermes," in *Chymists and Chymistry: Studies in the History of Alchemy and Early Modern Chemistry*, ed. Lawrence M. Principe (Sagamore Beach, MA: Chemical Heritage Foundation, 2007), 25–38.

46. William Eamon, *Science and the Secrets of Nature: Books of Secrets in Medieval and Early Modern Culture* (Princeton, NJ: Princeton University Press, 1994); Allison Kavey, *Books of Secrets: Natural Philosophy in England, 1550–1600* (Urbana: University of Illinois Press, 2007); and Neil Kamil, *Fortress of the Soul: Violence, Metaphysics, and Material Life in the Huguenots' New World, 1517–1751* (Baltimore: Johns Hopkins University Press, 2005). See also Pamela O. Long, *Openness, Secrecy, Authorship: Technical Arts and the Culture of Knowledge from Antiquity to the Renaissance* (Baltimore: Johns Hopkins University Press, 2001).

47. Isaac Casaubon, *De rebis sacris et ecclesiasticis XVI exercitationes ad Cardinalis Baronii* (London, 1614). See Grafton, *Defenders*, 145–61; and Anthony Grafton and Joanna Weinberg, *"I Have Always Loved the Holy Tongue": Isaac Casaubon, the Jews, and a Forgotten Chapter in Renaissance Scholarship* (Cambridge, MA: Harvard University Press, 2011), 30–42. Casaubon's work built upon the work of other scholars that began in the 1560s; see Hanegraaff, *Esotericism*, 75. For the continued credence granted to the *Corpus Hermeticum* in the seventeenth century, see Yates, *Giordano Bruno*, 398–431; and Ebeling, *Secret History*, 91–114.

48. Neil Rhodes, *The Power of Eloquence and English Renaissance Literature* (New York: St. Martin's, 1992), 25.

49. Rhodes, *Power of Eloquence*, 61–62.

50. Kinney, *Humanist Poetics*, 427.

51. Thomas Sprat, *The History of the Royal-Society of London for the Improving of Natural Knowledge* (London, 1667), 112–13.

52. Brian Vickers, *In Defence of Rhetoric* (Oxford: Clarendon, 1988), 201.

53. Brian Vickers, "The Myth of Francis Bacon's 'Anti-Humanism,'" in *Humanism and Early Modern Philosophy*, ed. Jill Kraye and M. W. F. Stone (London: Routledge, 2000), 135–58.

54. See Warren Boutcher, "Humanism and Literature in Late Tudor England: Translation, the Continental Book and the Case of Montaigne's *Essais*," in *Reassessing Tudor Humanism*, ed. Woolfson, 242–68.

55. Rhodes, *Power of Eloquence*, 45, 59–60.

56. Mordechai Feingold, "English Ramism: A Reinterpretation," in *The Influence of Petrus Ramus: Studies in Sixteenth and Seventeenth Century Philosophy and Sciences*, ed. Mordechai Feingold, Joseph S. Freedman, and Wolfgang Rother (Basel: Schwabe, 2001), 127–76. For analyses of Ramus as against rhetoric and against humanism see, e.g., Walter Ong, *Ramus, Method, and the Delay of Dialogue: From the Art of Discourse to the Art of Reason* (Cambridge, MA: Harvard University Press, 1958); and Grafton and Jardine, *Humanism to the Humanities*, 161–200. Peter Mack argues that Ramus's separation of rhetoric from logic does not mean he disparaged or ignored rhetoric in his educational method; see Mack, "Ramus and Ramism: Rhetoric and Dialectic," in *Ramus, Pedagogy and the Liberal Arts: Ramism in Britain and the Wider World*, ed. Emma Wilson and Steven Reid (Farnham, UK: Ashgate, 2011), 7–24.

57. See Robert Goulding, "Method and Mathematics: Peter Ramus's Histories of the Sciences," *Journal of the History of Ideas* 67 (2006): 63–85.

58. Ryan Stark, *Rhetoric, Science, and Magic in Seventeenth-Century England* (Washington, DC: Catholic University of America Press, 2009), 19, 13. Stark points out that the mythical origin story of the orator as magical founder of civilization is found in Cicero's *De inventione*, Quintilian's *Institutio oratoria*, and Horace's *Ars poetica*, and that versions of the story made their way into, for example, Thomas Wilson's *Art of Rhetoric* (1560) and George Puttenham's *Art of English Poesy* (1589); see Stark, *Rhetoric, Science, and Magic*, 19.

59. John French, "To the Reader," in *The Divine Pymander of Hermes Mercurius Trismegistus*, trans. John Everard (London, 1649), A6r.

60. Principe, *Secrets*, 179–80.

61. Ibid.

62. Daniel Sennert, *De chymicorum cum Aristotelicis et Galenicis consensu ac dissensu* (1619), translated by Nicholas Culpeper and Abdiah Cole as *Chymistry Made Easie and Useful, Or, The Agreement and Disagreement of the Chymists and Galenists* (London, 1662), 134–35. Noting Sennert's efforts to distinguish practical alchemy from a belief in the power of language that is equally occultist and humanist, Stark, *Rhetoric, Science, and Magic*, 11–23, proposes that the seventeenth-century advocacy of a Baconian "plain style" in prose represents both a repudiation of humanism's beloved Ciceronian rhetoric and a repudiation of the idea that language itself may be charmed.

63. Bruce T. Moran, *Distilling Knowledge: Alchemy, Chemistry, and the Scientific Revolution* (Cambridge, MA: Harvard University Press, 2005), 40-42; Vannoccio Biringuccio, *The Pirotechnia of Vannoccio Biringuccio*, trans. Cyril Stanley Smith and Martha Teach Gnudi (1959; repr., New York: Dover, 1990), 337.

64. For example, alchemist George Starkey designed unique symbols to guard his proprietary information about how to make the philosopher's stone; see Starkey, *Alchemical Laboratory Notebooks and Correspondence*, ed. William R. Newman and Lawrence M. Principe (Chicago: University of Chicago Press, 2004), 305.

65. Basilius Valentinus, *The Last Will and Testament of Basil Valentine* (London, 1671), illustration facing 1 (B1r).

66. Nicholas H. Clulee, *John Dee's Natural Philosophy: Between Science and Religion* (London: Routledge, 1988), 96.

67. Reginald Scot, *The Discoverie of Witchcraft*, ed. Brinsley Nicholson (London: Elliot Stock, 1886), 294.

68. Ben Jonson, *Mercury Vindicated from the Alchemists at Court*, in *Ben Jonson: The Complete Masques*, ed. Stephen Orgel (New Haven, CT: Yale University Press, 1969), lines 45–48. All subsequent references to Ben Jonson's masques are to this edition and will be cited parenthetically in the text by line number.

69. Ben Jonson, *The Alchemist*, ed. Elizabeth Cook (London: A & C Black, 1991), 1.1.64–72.

70. Desiderius Erasmus, "Alchemy/*Alcumistica* 1524," in *Colloquies*, trans. and ed. Craig R. Thompson (Toronto: University of Toronto Press, 1997), 1:546–47.

71. As the editor of Erasmus's *Colloquies*, Craig R. Thompson, explains, *longatio* and *curtatio* are not available in contemporaneous alchemical vocabularies, "nor were they ever alchemical terms, so far as can be determined, until Erasmus made them so" (Erasmus, "Alchemy/*Alcumistica*," in *Colloquies*, 1:554n6).

72. George Ripley, *The Compound of Alchymie*, in *Theatrum chemicum Britannicum*, ed. Elias Ashmole (London, 1652), illustration facing 117. This diagram was specially engraved for Ripley's treatise in this volume, as evidenced by the fact that the number of the facing page in the volume appears in the engraving itself.

73. Benedek Láng, *Unlocked Books: Manuscripts of Learned Magic in the Medieval Libraries of Central Europe* (University Park: Pennsylvania State University Press, 2008), 142.

74. Thomas M. Greene, *The Light in Troy: Imitation and Discovery in Renaissance Poetry* (New Haven, CT: Yale University Press, 1982), 20. I have borrowed the connection between the alchemical emblem and Greene's *mundus significans* from Bernhard F. Scholz, "Alchemy, Metallurgy and Emblematics in the Works of the Seventeenth-Century Dutch 'Bergmeester' Goossen van Vreeswijck (1626–after 1689)," in *Emblems and Alchemy*, ed. Alison Adams and Stanton J. Linden (Glasgow: University of Glasgow, 1998), 3–24.

75. Hacking, *Historical Ontology*, 170–71; Kuhn, *Scientific Revolutions*; Paul Feyerabend, *Against Method: Outline of an Anarchistic Theory of Knowledge* (London: New Left, 1975). Hacking advises that we must avoid thinking of the contest between old and new—in this case, the contest between alchemy and what was to become chemistry—in terms from modern science anachronistically applied to the past. Reviewing the influence of Foucault's *The Order of Things*, Hacking, in *Historical Ontology*, 89, cautions that Foucault has been misread as assigning a scientific "system" to premodern science, a system whose founding principles are as provable, in that system's own terms, as those of modern science. Recent historians of alchemy like Newman and Principe, even while they have established alchemy's status as a sort of evolutionary contributor to modern chemistry, have also expressed this caution. It is not as if alchemy has a coherent set of tenets that is replaced by the equally coherent (if more sensible) set of tenets of the scientific method.

76. Marco Beretta, "The Role of Symbolism from Alchemy to Chemistry," in *Non-Verbal Communication in Science Prior to 1900*, ed. Renato G. Mazzolini (Florence: Leo S. Olschki/Istituto e Museo di Storia della Scienza, 1993), 285.

77. Beretta, "Symbolism," 303. Györgi E. Szőnyi has argued, in fact, that the alchemical illustration lends itself to allegory and thus to narrative: "Since a narrative always unfolds in time, the reader has to decipher the meaning step by step, thus, necessarily engaging in a consecutive translation as well as in a discursive cognitive process"; see Szőnyi, "Architectural Symbolism and Fantasy Landscapes in Alchemical and Occult Discourse: Revelatory Images," in *Emblems and Alchemy*, ed. Adams and Linden, 49–72, quotation on 57. For the emblem and especially the *impresa* as participating in *inventio*, and particularly in a kind of theatrical staging of moral dilemma, see Karen Pinkus, *Picturing Silence: Emblem, Language, Counter-Reformation Materiality* (Ann Arbor: University of Michigan Press, 1996), 129–82.

78. Umberto Eco, *The Search for the Perfect Language*, trans. James Fentress (Oxford: Blackwell, 1985).

79. Alastair Hamilton, *The Apocryphal Apocalypse: The Reception of the Second Book of Esdras (4 Ezra) from the Renaissance to the Enlightenment* (Oxford: Clarendon, 1999), 33.

80. Eco, *Perfect Language*, 185–90. As Clulee, *Dee's Natural Philosophy*, 86, details, "What distinguishes Dee's 'holy language' of the 'real' kabbalah from that of the Hebrews is that Dee's is a kabbalah of 'that which is' while Hebraic kabbalah is merely a grammar of 'that which is said' and 'rests on well-known letters that can be written by man.'" Clulee cites C. H. Josten, "A Translation of John Dee's *Monas Hieroglyphica* (Antwerp, 1564), with an Introduction and Annotations," *Ambix* 12 (1964): 134–35. For seventeenth-century English attempts to produce a universal and/or purely symbolic language, see Rossi, *Logic*, 145–75.

81. For the generative powers of the monad see Josten, "Dee's *Monas Hieroglyphica*," 99–111; Clulee, *Dee's Natural Philosophy*, 105–115; and Györgi E. Szőnyi, *John Dee's Occultism: Magical Exaltation Through Powerful Signs* (Albany: State University of New York Press, 2004), 161–73. Szőnyi, *Dee's Occultism*, 166–67, identifies one of the *Monas*'s main sources as Ficino's *Index eorum*, which is similarly interested in magically generative language.

82. Lee Patterson, "The Place of the Modern in the Late Middle Ages," in *The Challenge of Periodization: Old Paradigms and New Perspectives*, ed. Lawrence Besserman (New York: Garland, 1996), 58–59.

83. Robert Boyle, *The Sceptical Chymist* (London: Dent/Everyman, 1911), 113; Pierre Joseph Macquer, *Elements of the Theory and Practice of Chymistry*, trans. Andrew Reid (London, 1758), 1:viii–ix.

84. Hacking, *Historical Ontology*, 170.

85. *OED Online*, s.v. "metaphor, n. 1a," last modified 2001, accessed 18 August 2014, http://0-www.oed.com.libraries.colorado.edu/view/Entry/117328; Thomas Norton, *Thomas Norton's Ordinal of Alchemy*, ed. John Reidy (London: Oxford University Press for the Early

English Text Society, 1975), 6, lines 62–64. Reidy's edition is based on the two earliest known manuscripts, British Library Add. 10302 (late fifteenth century) and, where that is defective, British Library Sloane 1198 (mid-sixteenth century?), which uses a Middle English style of spelling. Despite its claim to clarity, the *Ordinal*'s explanation of alchemical processes is hardly straightforward.

86. My hunch that *metaphor* as a specific word enters English on the wings of alchemy is hardly definitive, of course; an earlier instance may be lurking out there. Previous to *metaphor*, the English language used the word *figure*, even though the word *metaphora* was available in Britain in medieval Latin. The *Dictionary of Medieval Latin from British Sources*, ed. R. E. Latham et al. (London: Oxford University Press for the British Academy, 1975–2013), fasc. 6, 1781, cites as the first use of *metaphora* the seventh-century *Biblical Commentaries from the Canterbury School of Theodore and Hadrian* and quotes from Bede's lengthy definition in his late seventh-century *De schematibus et tropis*. Early uses of *metaphor, trope*, and the rhetorical sense of *figure* in English seem, on the evidence of the *Oxford English Dictionary* and Early English Books Online, to cluster around questions of biblical interpretation such as how to read Christ's statement "this is my body." (William Tyndale calls this an instance of "trope" in *The Souper of the Lorde*, 1532). Other European vernaculars, in contrast, appear to have adopted *metaphor* considerably earlier than English, and not in contexts having to do with either alchemy or biblical interpretation. The *Dictionnaire de l'ancienne langue Française*, ed. Frédéric Godefroy (Paris: F. Vieweg, 1881–1902), 10:148, cites Jean de Meun's late thirteenth-century portion of the *Roman de la Rose* (line 7229); and the *Grande dizionario della lingua italiana*, ed. Salvatore Battaglia, Giorgio Bárberi Squarotti, and Edoardo Sanguineti (Turin: Unione Tipografico-Editrice Torinese, 1961–2009), 10:248, cites Giovanni Boccaccio's 1370s commentary on Dante's *Divine Comedy*.

87. Paul de Man, "The Epistemology of Metaphor," *Critical Inquiry* 5 (1978): 13–30; see especially de Man's treatment of the metaphors in Locke's discussion of the properties of substances in the *Essay Concerning Human Understanding* (17–22).

88. Nicolas Flamel, *His Exposition of the Hieroglyphicall Figures (1624)*, ed. Laurinda Dixon (New York: Garland, 1994), 29–30. This popular text was first published in France in 1612 and appeared in English in 1624. In 1761, the Abbé Villain established that "Flamel"— supposedly a fourteenth-century Parisian scrivener—was not the author of this text, which was likely written in the seventeenth century by P. Arnauld de la Chevalerie; see Laurinda Dixon, "Introduction," in Flamel, *Hieroglyphicall Figures*, xiii.

89. For the tendency of the occult sciences—including alchemy—to reify language into materiality, see Brian Vickers, "Analogy versus Identity: The Rejection of Occult Symbolism, 1580–1680," in *Occult and Scientific Mentalities*, ed. Vickers, 95–164.

90. Maureen Quilligan, *The Language of Allegory: Defining the Genre* (Ithaca, NY: Cornell University Press, 1979).

91. Gordon Teskey, *Allegory and Violence* (Ithaca, NY: Cornell University Press, 1996).

92. Judith H. Anderson, *Reading the Allegorical Intertext: Chaucer, Spenser, Shakespeare, Milton* (New York: Fordham University Press, 2008), 5.

93. George Puttenham, *The Art of English Poesy: A Critical Edition*, ed. Frank Whigham and Wayne A. Rebhorn (Ithaca, NY: Cornell University Press, 2007), 271.

94. Angus Fletcher, *Allegory: The Theory of a Symbolic Mode* (Ithaca, NY: Cornell University Press, 1964), 329.

95. Puttenham, *Art of English Poesy*, 271; emphasis added.

96. Harry G. Frankfurt's essay "On Bullshit," originally published in *The Importance of What We Care About: Philosophical Essays* (Cambridge: Cambridge University Press, 1988), 117–33, was reprinted as an enormously popular trade volume, *On Bullshit* (Princeton, NJ: Princeton University Press, 2005). Frankfurt's terms are often playful, but his argument has struck a nerve not only in the popular imagination but also in philosophy, the philosophy of science, psychology, and other fields. For scholarly responses see, e.g., G. A. Cohen, "Deeper into Bullshit," and Harry Frankfurt, "Reply to G. A. Cohen," in *The Contours of Agency: Essays on Themes from Harry Frankfurt*, ed. Sarah Buss and Lee Overton (Cambridge, MA: MIT Press, 2002), 321–39 and 340–44, respectively.

97. Frankfurt, *On Bullshit*, 56.

98. Anderson, *Allegorical Intertext*, 6–8.

99. Even where it was avidly received, alchemy was never accepted in the university curriculum; it was tainted by its associations with *techne* and manual labor. See William R. Newman, *Atoms and Alchemy: Chymistry and the Experimental Origins of the Scientific Revolution* (Chicago: University of Chicago Press, 2006), 26; and William R. Newman, "Technology and Alchemical Debate in the Late Middle Ages," *Isis* 80 (1989): 423–45. Patterson, "Place of the Modern," 60, notes that many authors of medieval alchemy texts "were lower clerics or friars who did their intellectual work outside the university."

100. William R. Newman, *Promethean Ambitions: Alchemy and the Quest to Perfect Nature* (Chicago: University of Chicago Press, 2004), 34–114.

101. Newman, "Technology and Alchemical Debate," 440.

102. Heinrich Cornelius Agrippa, *Of the Vanity and Vncertaintie of Artes and Sciences*, ed. Catherine M. Dunn (Northridge: California State University Press, 1974), 328. First printed in Latin in 1530, Agrippa's text went through twenty-four more Latin editions in the sixteenth and seventeenth centuries, as well as numerous translations into Italian, English, French, Dutch, and German; see Catherine M. Dunn, "Introduction," in Agrippa, *Vanity of Artes and Sciences*, xxiv. Dunn's edition is of the 1569 English translation by James Sanford. For Agrippa's involvement with alchemy, see Charles G. Nauert, Jr., *Agrippa and the Crisis of Renaissance Thought* (Urbana: University of Illinois Press, 1965), 17–25.

103. Agrippa, *Vanity of Artes and Sciences*, 380.

104. See Nauert, *Agrippa*; Yates, *Giordano Bruno*, 131; and Barbara C. Bowen, "Cornelius Agrippa's *De vanitate*: Polemic or Paradox?," *Bibliotheque d'humanisme et Renaissance* 34 (1972): 249–56.

105. Michael H. Keefer, "Agrippa's Dilemma: Hermetic 'Rebirth' and the Ambivalences of *De vanitate* and *De occulta philosophia*," *Renaissance Quarterly* 41 (1988): 614–53, quotation on 622.

106. The author who exposes other forms of alchemy as misguided and his own form as correct is a common stance of alchemical texts. George Starkey, for example, contrasts a careless, vainglorious, and foolish alchemist to a careful, modest, and effective one in *Pyrotechny Asserted and Illustrated to Be the Surest and Fastest Means for Art's Triumph over Nature's Infirmities* (London, 1658). Similarly, Gabriel Platte, a respectable mid-seventeenth-century writer on such useful topics as animal husbandry and mining, exposes the bulk of the history of alchemy as a cheat—in the service, however, of requesting space and funding from the English commonwealth for his own, true alchemy; see Platte, "Gabriel Plats Caveat for Alchymists," in Samuel Hartlib, *Chymical, Medicinal, and Chyrurgical Addresses Made to Samuel Hartlib* (London, 1655), 51–88 (E2r–G3v).

107. Geoffrey Chaucer, *The Canon Yeoman's Prologue*, in *The Riverside Chaucer*, ed. Larry D. Benson (Boston: Houghton Mifflin, 1987), lines 678–79.

108. The founding essay in ignorance studies is Wilbert E. Moore and Melvin M. Tumin, "Some Social Functions of Ignorance," *American Sociological Review* 14 (1949): 787–95. For "agnotology" see Proctor, "Agnotology: A Missing Term." The bibliography in ignorance studies is large and growing; for some interesting recent work, see, e.g., Casey High, Ann H. Kelly, and Jonathan Mair, eds., *The Anthropology of Ignorance: An Ethnographic Approach* (New York: Palgrave Macmillan, 2012); Joanna Kempner, Jon F. Merz, and Charles L. Bosk, "Forbidden Knowledge: Public Controversy and the Production of Non-knowledge," *Sociological Forum* 26 (2011): 475–500; and Eviatar Zerubavel, *The Elephant in the Room: Silence and Denial in Everyday Life* (Oxford: Oxford University Press, 2006).

109. Eve Kosofsky Sedgwick, *Tendencies* (Durham, NC: Duke University Press, 1993), 25. The essay in which Sedgwick describes this dynamic, "Privilege of Unknowing," was originally published in *Genders* 1 (1988): 102–24, and some of its material reappears in *Epistemology of the Closet* (Berkeley: University of California Press, 1990), 4–8. Sedgwick relies on the equation of "knowing" with sexual knowledge that Foucault explores in *The History of Sexuality*, vol. 1: *An Introduction*, trans. Robert Hurley (New York: Vintage, 1978). I explore this equation further in Chapter 4.

110. Avital Ronell, *Stupidity* (Urbana: University of Illinois Press, 2002), 43.

111. Bruno Latour, *Reassembling the Social: An Introduction to Actor-Network Theory* (Oxford: Oxford University Press, 2005).

112. Barry Barnes, David Bloor, and John Henry, *Scientific Knowledge: A Sociological Analysis* (Chicago: University of Chicago Press, 1996), 120.

113. See, e.g., Matthias Gross, *Ignorance and Surprise: Science, Society, and Ecological Design* (Cambridge, MA: MIT Press, 2010); and Stuart Firestein, *Ignorance: How It Drives Science* (Oxford: Oxford University Press, 2012).

114. See, e.g., Linsey McGoey, "The Logic of Strategic Ignorance," *British Journal of Sociology* 63 (2012): 553–76.

115. Michael Taussig, *Defacement: Public Secrecy and the Labor of the Negative* (Stanford, CA: Stanford University Press, 1999), 5; emphasis in the original.

116. Bruno Latour, *We Have Never Been Modern*, trans. Catherine Porter (Cambridge, MA: Harvard University Press, 1993), 13–48.

117. Poovey, *Modern Fact*, 55. The separation of language from science is detailed by Foucault in *The Order of Things*.

118. Sloterdijk, *Critique of Cynical Reason*, 5.

119. Slavoj Žižek, *The Sublime Object of Ideology* (London: Verso, 1989), 29, 32.

120. Sigmund Freud, "Negation (1925)," in *The Standard Edition of the Complete Psychological Works of Sigmund Freud*, trans. James Strachey (London: Hogarth, 1953–74), 19:235–39.

121. Sigmund Freud, *An Outline of Psycho-Analysis (1940 [1938])*, in *Standard Edition*, 23:204.

122. Friedrich Nietzsche, *Beyond Good and Evil: Prelude to a Philosophy of the Future*, ed. Rolf-Peter Horstmann and Judith Norman (Cambridge: Cambridge University Press, 2002), 6–7.

123. For Bourdieu's unacknowledged dependence upon Lacan's description of the symbolic order and Althusser's practice of symptomatic reading, see George Steinmetz, "Bourdieu's Disavowal of Lacan: Psychoanalytic Theory and the Concepts of 'Habitus' and 'Symbolic Capital,'" *Constellations* 13 (2006): 445–64. In describing Lacanian psychoanalysis as a model of "traumatic epistemology," Dany Nobus and Malcolm Quinn could be speaking for the main current of recent thought when they note that the end point for Lacan is "a practice of non-recognition in which knowledge appears as a foreign substance"; see Nobus and Quinn, *Knowing Nothing, Staying Stupid: Elements for a Psychoanalytic Epistemology* (London: Routledge, 2005), 111.

124. Jean-Paul Sartre, *Being and Nothingness: A Phenomenological Essay on Ontology*, trans. Hazel E. Barnes (New York: Washington Square, 1992), 89.

125. For Žižek's further elaboration on the way that the subject who recognizes her disavowal is only caught up in the Lacanian disavowal writ large of the symbolic order, see Slavoj Žižek, *The Plague of Fantasies* (London: Verso, 1997), 107–60.

126. Shaun Gallagher and Dan Zahavi, "Phenomenological Approaches to Self-Consciousness," *The Stanford Encyclopedia of Philosophy*, winter 2010 ed., ed. Edward N. Zalta, accessed 18 August 2014, http://plato.stanford.edu/archives/win2010/entries/self-consciousness-phenomenological.

127. Hubert L. Dreyfus, "Response to McDowell," *Inquiry* 50 (2007): 371–77. An idea of a consciousness that is not reflective has been advanced by recent work in behavioral economics, cognitive science, and neuroscience on why we act contrary to what we know to be true. Daniel Kahneman, for example, proposes that because the part of the mind that produces automatic, quick judgments will always overrule the part of the mind that engages in sustained, controlled analysis, there is no such thing as a rational economic choice; see Kahneman, *Thinking, Fast and Slow* (New York: Farrar, Straus and Giroux, 2011). V. S. Ramachandran has suggested that self-delusion is the result when the left brain's tendency to promote continuity of thought overpowers the right brain's tendency toward skepticism; see Ramachandran, "The Evolutionary Biology of Self-Deception, Laughter, Dreaming and Depression: Some Clues from Anosognosia," *Medical Hypotheses* 47 (1996): 347–62. I was led to Ramachandran's work by Dan McCormack's suggestion that I read

Errol Morris's remarkable *New York Times* blog essays on anosognosia—a condition in which a disabled or diseased person vehemently denies the existence of her disability or disease; see, e.g., Morris, "The Anosognosic's Dilemma: Something's Wrong But You'll Never Know What It Is (Part 4)," *New York Times*, 23 June 2010, accessed 18 August 2014, http://opinionator.blogs.nytimes.com/tag/anosognosics-dilemma.

128. For a succinct summary of Jung's archetypal approach to alchemy, see Betty Jo Teeter Dobbs, *The Foundations of Newton's Alchemy, or, "The Hunting of the Greene Lyon"* (Cambridge: Cambridge University Press, 1975), 26–35.

129. Pinkus, *Alchemical Mercury*.

130. Paul de Man, *Blindness and Insight: Essays in the Rhetoric of Contemporary Criticism*, 2nd ed. (Minneapolis: University of Minnesota Press, 1983), 117–19.

131. Richard Halpern usefully distinguishes between the kind of recognition that is "the moment of emergence from disavowal into enlightenment" and the "shocked recognition" that "places the seal on disavowal by insisting (falsely) that up until that moment one didn't know"; see Halpern, *Norman Rockwell: The Underside of Innocence* (Chicago: University of Chicago Press, 2006), 46. The text that ostentatiously overplays disavowal then recognition into disavowal then *shocked* recognition is more ethical in the sense that it registers, in its shock, the lie inherent in not taking responsibility. Similarly, Harry Berger, Jr., looking in Shakespeare's plays for characters' degree of conscious awareness of their own denial, notes those "shades of expression that display or betray sensitivity to the failure of acknowledgment—the failure, that is, to acknowledge one's complicity in what has been done to others or to oneself"; see Berger, *Making Trifles of Terrors: Redistributing Complicities in Shakespeare* (Stanford, CA: Stanford University Press, 1997), xiii.

132. Amélie Oksenberg Rorty, "Self-Deception, *Akrasia* and Irrationality," in *The Multiple Self*, ed. Jon Elster (Cambridge: Cambridge University Press, 1985), 115–32.

133. Sartre, *Being and Nothingness*, 97–98. The cheerfulness of the position of bad faith is frequently omitted in depictions of the modern condition, but we should not forget that Friedrich Nietzsche describes the "free spirit" of *Human, All Too Human*—the modern philosopher who has given up seeking the "truth"—as being in an exuberant state of good health; see Nietzsche, *Human, All Too Human: A Book for Free Spirits*, trans. Marion Faber (Lincoln: University of Nebraska Press, 1986), 7–9.

134. Martin Luther, *D[octo]ris Martini Lutheri colloquia mensalia: or, Dr Martin Luther's Divine Discourses at His Table*, trans. Henry Bell (London, 1651), 480. See Martin Luther, *D. Martin Luthers Werke: kritische Gesamtausgabe: Tischreden* (1912; repr., Weimar: Hermann Böhlaus Nachfolger, 1967), 1:566. In the context of an anti-Semitic remark about Jews as alchemists and con artists, Luther declared that "this practising of alchemy is a disgraceful deception, for all know money cannot be made by this sophistry"; Martin Luther to the elector Joachim II of Brandenburg, 9 March 1545, in *The Letters of Martin Luther*, ed. and trans. Margaret A. Currie (London: Macmillan, 1908), 451.

135. Francis Bacon, *The Advancement of Learning*, ed. Michael Kiernan (Oxford: Clarendon, 2000), 30. For the magical and alchemical foundations of Bacon's scientific

thought, see Paolo Rossi, *Francis Bacon: From Magic to Science*, trans. Sacha Ravinovitch (Chicago: University of Chicago Press, 1968), 1–35. Newman, *Promethean Ambitions*, 256–71, specifically argues that Bacon owes his defense of the "artifice" involved in experiment to alchemical discourse. Janacek, *Alchemical Belief*, 89–98, describes Bacon as expressing his admiration for alchemy indirectly, through messages deeply hidden within his open contempt. Linden, *Darke Hierogliphicks*, 104–17, astutely analyzes Bacon's mixed attitude toward alchemy across his oeuvre. For Bacon's attraction to the Hermetic tradition as *prisca theologia*, see Stephen A. McKnight, *The Modern Age and the Recovery of Ancient Wisdom: A Reconsideration of Historical Consciousness, 1450–1650* (Columbia: University of Missouri Press, 1991), 127–42.

136. Bacon, *Advancement of Learning*, 27.

137. Ibid. Bacon repeats this Aesopian analogy between the well-worked vineyard and alchemy in the *Novum organum*, book 1, aphorism 85; see Francis Bacon, Novum organum *with Other Parts of* The Great Instauration, trans. and ed. Peter Urbach and John Gibson (Chicago: Open Court, 1994), 95.

138. Graham Oddie, "Truthlikeness," in *The Stanford Encyclopedia of Philosophy*, summer 2014 ed., ed. Edward N. Zalta, accessed 18 August 2014, http://plato.stanford.edu /archives/sum2014/entries/truthlikeness/.

139. "*Truthiness* Voted 2005 Word of the Year by American Dialect Society," 6 January 2006, accessed 18 August 2014, http://www.americandialect.org/Words_of_the_Year _2005.pdf.

140. Knapp, "Work of Alchemy."

141. Lee Patterson, "Perpetual Motion: Alchemy and the Technology of the Self," *Studies in the Age of Chaucer* 15 (1993): 25–57.

142. Sherman, "Gold is the strength." Hawkes, *Idols of the Marketplace*, 143–67, develops a detailed and persuasive account of the similarities between alchemical fantasies and Marx's commodity fetishism. Tara Nummedal confirms the point of alchemy's ushering in capitalist conceptual frameworks from the standpoint of commercial legal history: early modern alchemists and their patrons, who were often involved in mining operations, increasingly signed contracts for future product, an arrangement that limited the financial risk for the employers; see Nummedal, "On the Utility of Alchemical Fraud," in *Chymists and Chymistry*, ed. Principe, 173–80.

143. Wiebe E. Bijker, *Of Bicycles, Bakelites, and Bulbs: Toward a Theory of Sociotechnical Change* (Cambridge, MA: MIT Press, 1995), 7. Crane's study of how sixteenth-century England retained Aristotelianism as a knowledge framework is an important treatment of the utility of outmoded science in the Renaissance; see Crane, *Losing Touch with Nature*.

144. Umberto Eco, "An *Ars Oblivionalis*? Forget It!," *PMLA* 103 (1988): 254–61.

145. Sybille Krämer, "Das Vergessen nicht vergessen! Oder, ist das Vergessen ein defizienter Modus von Erinnerung?," *Paragrana* 9 (2000): 251–75; David Lowenthal, "Preface," in *The Art of Forgetting*, ed. Adrian Forty and Suzanna Küchler (Oxford: Berg, 1999), xi–xiii.

146. Bacon, *Advancement of Learning*, 3; Thomas Browne, *Sir Thomas Browne's Pseudodoxia Epidemica*, ed. Robin Robbins (Oxford: Clarendon, 1981), 1:1.

147. For a fascinating analysis of *Pseudodoxia Epidemica* as an exercise in forgetting modeled on alimentary purgation, see Grant Williams, "Textual Crudities in Robert Burton's *Anatomy of Melancholy* and Thomas Browne's *Pseudodoxia Epidemica*," in *Forgetting in Early Modern English Literature and Culture: Lethe's Legacies*, ed. Christopher Ivic and Grant Williams (London: Routledge, 2004), 67–82.

148. Browne, *Pseudodoxia Epidemica*, 1:28.

149. Henry More, *The Apology of Henry More* (1664), quoted in Sarah Hutton, "The Cambridge Platonists," in *A Companion to Early Modern Philosophy*, ed. Steven Nadler (Malden, MA: Blackwell, 2002), 313.

150. See Didier Kahn, "Alchemical Poetry in Medieval and Early Modern Europe: A Preliminary Survey and Synthesis, Part I—Preliminary Survey," *Ambix* 57 (2010): 249–74.

151. Robert M. Schuler, ed., *Alchemical Poetry 1575–1700: From Previously Unpublished Manuscripts* (New York: Garland, 1995), xxvii, xxix–xxxi. See also Robert M. Schuler, *English Magical and Scientific Poems to 1700: An Annotated Bibliography* (New York: Garland, 1979).

152. Joshua Poole, *The English Parnassus, or, a Helpe to English Poesie* (London, 1657), A3v. Stanton Linden makes the point that a huge portion of alchemical writing was done in verse, a fact that establishes it as a self-consciously literary genre; see Linden, "Introduction," in George Ripley, *George Ripley's Compound of Alchymy (1591)*, ed. Stanton J. Linden (Aldershot, UK: Ashgate, 2001), xlii–xliii.

153. Eirenaeus Philalethes [George Starkey], *Secrets Reveal'd* (London, 1669), 4 (B2v), 6 (B3v).

2. HOW TO FORGET TRANSUBSTANTIATION

1. Robert Southwell, "The Burning Babe," in *The Poems of Robert Southwell, S. J.*, ed. James H. McDonald and Nancy Pollard Brown (Oxford: Clarendon, 1967), 15–16, lines 3, 7. All subsequent references to this poem are to this edition and will be cited parenthetically in the text by line number.

2. Lancelot Coelson, *Philosophia maturata: An Exact Piece of Philosophy Containing the Practick and Operative Part Thereof in Gaining the Philosophers Stone* (London, 1668), 19.

3. Miri Rubin, *Corpus Christi: The Eucharist in Late Medieval Culture* (Cambridge: Cambridge University Press, 1991), 13; for the institution of transubstantiation as doctrine, see chap. 1, esp. 14–34.

4. The disparity of Ambrose's and Augustine's opinions acquired more specificity in the ninth-century debate between two Frankish monks: Paschasius Radbert, who took the Ambrosian view that the bread and wine of the Eucharist are equivalent in essence to

the body and blood of Jesus Christ, and Ratrumnus, who argued in Augustinian terms that the sacraments are "visible words"; Rubin, *Corpus Christi*, 15–16.

5. Since a statement is invalidated if its subject is altered or removed by its predicate, argued Berengar, the verb *is* in Christ's assertion "This [bread] is my body" makes sense only if the subject ("this bread") remains intact at the end of the sentence. Thus, the Eucharistic bread cannot materially change; Heinrich Fichtenau, *Heretics and Scholars in the High Middle Ages, 1000–1200*, trans. Denise A. Kaiser (University Park: Pennsylvania State University Press, 1998), 290.

6. Rubin, *Corpus Christi*, 18–19. James F. McCue points out that it was not Berengar's queries about Christ's physical body but his crediting the notion that the Eucharist was entirely symbolic that necessitated his recantation; see McCue, "The Doctrine of Transubstantiation from Berengar Through Trent: The Point at Issue," *Harvard Theological Review* 61 (1968): 385–430. Brian Stock argues that Berengar's skepticism about transubstantiation was based not simply on grammar but rather on a very sophisticated theory of allegorical interpretation; see Stock, *The Implications of Literacy: Written Language and Models of Interpretation in the Eleventh and Twelfth Centuries* (Princeton, NJ: Princeton University Press, 1983), 272–81.

7. Ross Hamilton, *Accident: A Philosophical and Literary History* (Chicago: University of Chicago Press, 2007), 12–13.

8. Ibid., 52.

9. Thomas Aquinas, *Summa theologica*, trans. Fathers of the English Dominican Province, 2nd ed. (1920), IIIa, q.77, a.1, accessed 18 August 2014, http://www.newadvent.org/summa.

10. Aquinas, *Summa theologica*, IIIa, q.77, a.1–7. For an excellent account of the fine distinctions Aquinas makes regarding the Eucharistic accident of quantity, see Stephen E. Lahey, *John Wyclif* (Oxford: Oxford University Press, 2009), 102–34.

11. For the ongoing debates over transubstantiation, see McCue, "Transubstantiation from Berengar through Trent"; Robert Whalen, *The Poetry of Immanence: Sacrament in Donne and Herbert* (Toronto: University of Toronto Press, 2002), 3–21; and Lee Palmer Wandel, *The Eucharist in the Reformation: Incarnation and Liturgy* (Cambridge: Cambridge University Press, 2006). For medieval Scholasticism's difficulties in aligning Aristotelian metaphysics with the doctrine of transubstantiation, see Rubin, *Corpus Christi*, 12–82; Gary Macy, "The Dogma of Transubstantiation in the Middle Ages," *Journal of Ecclesiastical History* 45 (1994): 11–41; David Burr, *Eucharistic Presence and Conversion in Late Thirteenth-Century Franciscan Thought* (Philadelphia: American Philosophical Society, 1984); and Richard Cross, *The Metaphysics of the Incarnation: Thomas Aquinas to Duns Scotus* (Oxford: Oxford University Press, 2002).

12. Marcus Hellyer, *Catholic Physics: Jesuit Natural Philosophy in Early Modern Germany* (Notre Dame, IN: University of Notre Dame Press, 2005), 93–100.

13. Rubin, *Corpus Christi*, 32. Aquinas himself resorted to the circular reasoning of proving transubstantiation is true by asserting that it is true: "Some have held that the substance of the bread and wine remains in this sacrament after the consecration. But

this opinion cannot stand: first of all, because by such an opinion the truth of this sacrament is destroyed, to which it belongs that Christ's true body exists in this sacrament"; Aquinas, *Summa theologica*, IIIa, q.75, a.2.

14. Rubin, *Corpus Christi*, 325. Explicitly influenced by William of Ockham, Wyclif was condemned by the Council of Constance in 1414 for (among other things) his physics, including his assertion that "it is impossible for two corporeal substances to be co-extensive"—an assertion that denies Aquinas's proposition that the accidents of the bread and wine are spatiotemporally coterminous with the substantial form of Christ's body and blood; Lahey, *John Wyclif*, 103.

15. Lahey, *John Wyclif*, 128. The language of Wyclif's followers similarly displays a fairly sophisticated understanding of how transubstantiation did not comport with Aristotelian physics; see Fritz Kemmler, "Entrancing 'tra(u)ns/c': Some Metamorphoses of 'Transformation, Translation, and Transubstantiation,'" *Disputatio: An International Transdisciplinary Journal of the Late Middle Ages* 3 (1998): 176–222.

16. For the persistence of Aristotelian physics in Renaissance learning and beyond, see Charles H. Lohr, "Metaphysics and Natural Philosophy as Sciences: The Catholic and the Protestant Views in the Sixteenth and Seventeenth Centuries," in *Philosophy in the Sixteenth and Seventeenth Centuries: Conversations with Aristotle*, ed. Constance Blackwell and Sachiko Kusukawa (Aldershot, UK: Ashgate, 1999), 280–95; Henry S. Turner, "Nashe's Red Herring: Epistemologies of the Commodity in *Lenten Stuffe* (1599)," *ELH* 68 (2001): 529–61, esp. 538–40; and Crane, *Losing Touch with Nature*.

17. John Calvin, *Institutes of the Christian Religion*, trans. Henry Beveridge (1845; repr., Grand Rapids, MI: Eerdmans, 1989), 2:571. See Kilian McDonnell, *John Calvin, the Church, and the Eucharist* (Princeton, NJ: Princeton University Press, 1967), 32–39.

18. Pietro Redondi, *Galileo Heretic*, trans. Raymond Rosenthal (Princeton, NJ: Princeton University Press, 1987), 9–11.

19. Redondi's discovery of a report penned by the Holy Office of the Inquisition was the smoking gun in establishing that the church found Galileo's *The Assayer* (1623), which posits atomism on the basis of his and others' experiments with light, problematic primarily because Galileo's atomism disproves that the substance of bread and wine is annihilated in the transubstantiated Eucharist. The Inquisition official writes, "if one admits [Galileo's] philosophy of accidents is true, it seems to me, that makes greatly difficult the existence of the accidents of the bread and wine which in the Most Holy Sacrament are separated from their substance . . . one will also have to say . . . according to this doctrine that there are the very tiny particles with which the substance of the bread first moved our senses, which if they were substantial . . . , it follows that in the Sacrament there are substantial parts of bread or wine, which is the error condemned by the Sacred Tridentine Council"; Redondi, *Galileo Heretic*, 334. See also Rubin, *Corpus Christi*, 350.

20. Hellyer, *Catholic Physics*, 103–4. Descartes's philosophical works were placed on the Roman Catholic Index of Forbidden Books in part because his revision of matter theory debunked Aquinas's transubstantiative physics. Descartes, like William of Ockham, denied that a body's "quantity" or extension could be separated from that body, and

furthermore denied that accidents existed at all except in the mind of the perceiver; Hellyer, *Catholic Physics*, 100–107. For the origins of Descartes's matter theory in the Eucharistic puzzle, see Tomaso Cavello, "Real Accidents, Surfaces and Digestions: Descartes and the 'very easily explained' Transubstantiation," in *The Poetics of Transubstantiation: From Theology to Metaphor*, ed. Douglas Burnham and Enrico Giaccherini (Aldershot, UK: Ashgate, 2005), 11–25; and Steven M. Nadler, "Arnauld, Descartes, and Transubstantiation: Reconciling Cartesian Metaphysics and Real Presence," *Journal of the History of Ideas* 49 (1988): 229–46.

21. McDonnell, *John Calvin*, 63; McCue, "Transubstantiation from Berengar to Trent," 413. Luther's training at the University of Erfurt qualified him to discuss matter theory with authority, both in relation to the Eucharist and more generally. He cited William of Ockham as one of his great influences, and in 1517, at about the same time he was writing the Ninety-Five Theses, he was also planning a commentary on Aristotle's *Physics*; see Martin Luther to John Lang, 8 February 1517, in *Luther's Works*, ed. Jaroslav Pelikan and Helmut T. Lehmann (St. Louis, MO: Concordia, 1955–86), 48:38.

22. William N. West, "What's the Matter with Shakespeare? Physics, Identity, Playing," *South Central Review* 26, nos. 1–2 (2009): 103–26.

23. Church of England, *The Book of Common Prayer* (Oxford: W. Baxter, 1825), 907–908n. At one moment, the Order for Holy Communion declares that when communicants receive the Sacrament, they "eat the flesh of [God's] dear Son Jesus Christ, and . . . drink his blood." At another, it avers that communicants merely "*spiritually* eat the flesh of Christ, and drink his blood"; John E. Booty, ed., *The Book of Common Prayer 1559: The Elizabethan Prayer Book* (Charlottesville: University Press of Virginia for the Folger Shakespeare Library, 1976), 263, 258; emphasis added.

24. William Tyndale to John Frith, 1536, in John Foxe, *The Acts and Monuments of John Foxe*, ed. George Townsend (London: Seeley, Burnside, and Seeley, 1845), 5:133.

25. Richard Hooker, *Of the Laws of Ecclesiasticall Politie the Fift Book* (London, 1597), 177 (Q5r). J. R. Parris argues that Hooker takes a Calvinist position on the Eucharist, rejecting anything but Christ's symbolic presence; still, Parris acknowledges, Hooker is not eager to make the denial of transubstantiation a matter of faith; see Parris, "Hooker's Doctrine of the Eucharist," *Scottish Journal of Theology* 16 (1963): 151–65.

26. Michel de Montaigne, *Apology for Raymond Sebond*, trans. Roger Ariew and Marjorie Grene (Indianapolis: Hackett, 2003), 88.

27. Avicenna's text was translated in the early thirteenth century by Alfred of Sareshal as *Liber de congelatione et conglutinatione lapidum* (The book of the congealing and concretion of stones). It was initially attributed to Aristotle because it was appended to a manuscript of Aristotle's *Meteorology*. See Newman, *Promethean Ambitions*, 36–44.

28. Newman, *Promethean Ambitions*, 56. Newman points out that the *Margarita decreti*, a synopsis of Gratian's twelfth-century canon law encyclopedia, the *Decretum*, was incorporated into copies of that influential text.

29. As the *Aurora consurgens* attributed to Thomas Aquinas puts it, the end product of alchemy, the philosopher's stone, "separateth the purer parts from the impure, that the

impure parts being cast away, the work may be fulfilled with the pure"; Marie-Louise von Franz, ed., *Aurora consurgens: A Document Attributed to Thomas Aquinas on the Problem of Opposites in Alchemy* (New York: Bollingen Foundation/Pantheon, 1966), 95. Whereas von Franz dates the *Aurora consurgens* to the thirteenth century, contemporary to Aquinas, Lynn Thorndike dates it to the fifteenth in *A History of Magic and Experimental Science* (New York: Columbia University Press, 1923–58), 4:335.

30. The *Breve breviarum* (ca. 1270) falsely attributed to Roger Bacon, for example, argues that "the specific form can be dissociated from a given portion of [for example] silver, whose matter can then be informed by the specific form of gold. The form itself is indivisible and even impassible, but by its participation in matter it creates a new substance"; Newman, *Promethean Ambitions*, 68.

31. Alchemy's claim to reduce material to prime matter also ran afoul of the doctrine of transubstantiation. Margaret D. Garber relates a mid-seventeenth century quarrel at Prague's Charles-Ferdinand University between J. Marcus Marci, dean of the faculty of medicine, and the Jesuit Roderigo Arriaga, dean of the faculty of arts. Marci postulated, *contra* Aquinas, that two substantial forms can coexist, basing his theory on the way alchemists create the philosopher's stone: first they strip gold of its accidents by using a solvent, then they combine it with "philosophical mercury" to create an alchemical elixir in which the substantial forms of both the gold and the mercury remain. But if two substantial forms can coexist, so too might the substantial forms of bread and wine coexist in the Eucharist with the substantial forms of the body and blood of Christ. See Garber, "Transitioning from Transubstantiation to Transmutation: Catholic Anxieties over Chymical Matter Theory at the University of Prague," in *Chymists and Chymistry*, ed. Principe, 63–76. Garber also describes how Marci's theoretical physics tended toward atomism, another schema that, as described above, would void transubstantiation.

32. Walter Pagel, *Paracelsus: An Introduction to Philosophical Medicine in the Era of the Renaissance*, 2nd ed. (Basel: S. Karger, 1982), 82–125.

33. Charles Webster, *Paracelsus: Medicine, Magic and Mission at the End of Time* (New Haven, CT: Yale University Press, 2008), 131–68.

34. Allen Debus notes that while English writers referenced Paracelsus largely for his medicinal theories and practices, he was also recognized as theologically dangerous. According to Debus, Paracelsian theory did not gain currency in England until the 1570s, and did not really take off until the first decade of the seventeenth century, when Thomas Tymme's translations of sections of the Paracelsian alchemist Joseph Dechesne were published as *The Practise of Chymicall, and Hermeticall Physicke* (London, 1605). Tymme's introduction to this text argues that alchemy and theology concur because both the Creation and the Last Judgment were/will be alchemical processes. Allen G. Debus, *The English Paracelsians* (London: Oldbourne, 1965), 49, 88.

35. Andrew Weeks describes how Paracelsus deliberately inserted himself into the Lutheran-Zwinglian-Erasmian quarrel over the nature of Christ's Real Presence in the bread and wine of Holy Communion; see Weeks, *Paracelsus: Speculative Theory and the Crisis of the Early Reformation* (Albany: State University of New York Press, 1997),

110–11. See also Ute Frietsch, "Zwischen Transmutation und Transsubstantiation: zum theologischen subtext der *Archedoxis*-Schrift des Paracelsus," *Nova Acta Paracelsica* 19 (2005): 29–51.

36. Indeed, Paracelsus determined that the resurrected Christ does not possess human flesh, but rather has only the eternal, spiritual body any Christian receives in baptism and reinhabits at the time of her resurrection; Webster, *Paracelsus*, 200. For Paracelsus's views on the nature of Christ's body, see Dane T. Daniel, "Coping with Heresy: Suchten, Toxites, and the Early Reception of Paracelsus's Theology," in *Chymists and Chymistry*, ed. Principe, 53–62.

37. "[E]r sagt, do er das Brot in der Hand hat: Das ist mein Leib, do er den Wein hat: das ist mein Blut. . . . [W]ir vom Fleisch seind, und nit ohn Fleisch, des himmlischen Fleischs, das durch den heiligen Geist inkarniert ist worden. . . . Darumb ist er in uns und wir in ihm, darumb von deswegen, dass wir aus Gott geboren seind und seind des Fleischs und Bluts, das vom Himmel gestiegen ist, dass das Wort, das Fleisch ist worden in unsern Händen." Paracelsus, "Erklärung des 1 Kap. Joh.," in *Schriften Theophrasts von Hohenheim genannt Paracelsus*, ed. Hans Kayser (Leipzig: Insel-Verlag, 1921), 457–58; my translation. Andrew Weeks notes that in his *Eleven Treatises on the Origin, Causes, Signs, and Cure of Specific Diseases*, Paracelsus explicitly takes the Eucharist as evidence for the relation between the macrocosm (the universe) and the microcosm (the human body): just as Christ is invisibly in the Host, so too is the macrocosm invisibly in the human body; Weeks, *Paracelsus*, 122.

38. Paracelsus's work was proscribed by the faculty of the University of Paris in 1578 and gained mention on the Index of Forbidden Books in 1583 (where it remained until 1897); see Frietsch, "Transmutation und Transsubstantiation," 30. Paracelsus himself had died long before, in 1541. Hugh Trevor-Roper associates the censoring of Paracelsus's work with his becoming associated with a dissenting and antimonarchist position via his popularity among Calvinist alchemists; see Trevor-Roper, "Paracelsianism Made Political 1600–1650," in *Paracelsus: The Man and His Reputation, His Ideas and Their Transformation*, ed. Ole Peter Grell (Leiden: Brill, 1998), 119–33. For the gamut of Paracelsus's ideas on the Eucharist, see Hartmut Rudolph, "Hohenheim's Anthropology in the Light of His Writings on the Eucharist," in *Paracelsus*, ed. Grell, 187–206.

39. Norton, *Ordinal of Alchemy*, 78, lines 2519–20. For the identity of Thomas Norton, see John Reidy, "Introduction," in Norton, *Ordinal of Alchemy*, xxvii–lii. Kemmler, "Entrancing 'tra(u)ns/c,'" speculates that the length of time it took for the word *transubstantiation* to enter the English vernacular indicates the skepticism with which the doctrine of transubstantiation was viewed.

40. Von Franz, ed., *Aurora consurgens*, 129, 131.

41. This connection between the Eucharist and Christ's incarnation was what fueled some truly gruesome medieval visions of Christ as a child being sacrificed on the altar during Holy Communion; see David Aers, *Sanctifying Signs: Making Christian Tradition in Late Medieval England* (Notre Dame, IN: University of Notre Dame Press, 2004), 10–11.

42. Johann Valentin Andreae, *The Hermetick Romance: Or the Chymical Wedding*, trans. E. Foxcroft (London, 1690), 3, 200–201.

43. Nicholas Melchior Cibinensis, "Addam et processum sub forma missae," in *Theatrum chymicum*, ed. Lazarus Zetzner (Frankfurt, 1659), 3:758–63. Cibinensis's work first appeared in the 1602 edition of the *Theatrum chymicum*. Cibinensis has not been identified; the name is probably a pseudonym. For a summary of scholarly speculation on this author's identity, see Láng, *Unlocked Books*, 158–61.

44. The relevant illustration from Maier's *Symbola aureae mensae* (1617) is reproduced in Johannes Fabricius, *Alchemy: The Medieval Alchemists and Their Royal Art* (Copenhagen: Rosenkilde and Bagger, 1976), 138, fig. 258. Maier explains that he "saw the perfection of [the Philosopher's Stone]. . . . in the nativity, life, passion, death, and resurrection of Christ as commemorated in the Eucharist." See John Warwick Montgomery, *Cross and Crucible: Johann Valentin Andreae (1586–1654), Phoenix of the Theologians* (The Hague: Martinus Nijhoff, 1973), 18–19. For the philosopher's stone as the "philosopher's child" of the "chemical wedding" of sulfur and mercury, see Lyndy Abraham, *A Dictionary of Alchemical Imagery* (Cambridge: Cambridge University Press, 1998), 148–50.

45. Mary Baine Campbell, "Artificial Men: Alchemy, Transubstantiation, and the Homunculus," *Republics of Letters: A Journal for the Study of Knowledge, Politics, and the Arts* 1, no. 2 (2010): 8, accessed 18 August 2014, http://arcade.stanford.edu/sites/default/files/article_pdfs/roflv01i02_02campbell_comp3_083010_JM_0.pdf.

46. Gabriel Naudé, *The History of Magick*, trans. John Davies (London, 1657), 274 (T1v); originally published as *Apologie pour tous les grands personnages qui ont esté faussement soupçonnez de magie* (The Hague, 1625).

47. Lynn Staley argues that a reformist equation between transubstantiation and alchemy took place even long before Protestantism took hold, in Chaucer's portrayal of the alchemist-priest in the *Canon's Yeoman's Tale*; see Staley, "Chaucer and the Postures of Sanctity," in David Aers and Lynn Staley, *The Powers of the Holy: Religion, Politics, and Gender in Late Medieval English Culture* (University Park: Pennsylvania State University Press, 1996), 179–259, esp. 212.

48. William Prynne, *Aurum reginae* (London, 1668), 131. Henry VI's hiring priests to undertake alchemy because of their transubstantiative expertise has been taken as historical fact by generations of scholars working on alchemy, but as the passage quoted indicates, Prynne fabricates this story in order to reinforce his point that priests were no better than alchemists. The mistake of treating Prynne's anecdote as a true account of Henry VI's alchemy policy may be traced back to Charles Mackay's not picking up on Prynne's sarcasm; see Mackay, *Memoirs of Extraordinary Popular Delusions* (London: Richard Bentley, 1841), 3:50.

49. Benjamin Lany [or Laney], *A Sermon Preached Before His Majesty at Whitehall, April 5. 1663* (London, 1663), 4 (A3v).

50. John Donne, "A Sermon Preached at Pauls Cross to the Lords of the Council, and other Honorable Persons, 24. Mart. 1616. [1616/17]," in John Donne, *Sermons,*

ed. George R. Potter and Evelyn M. Simpson (Berkeley: University of California Press, 1953–62), 1:203.

51. George Goodwin, "Of That Loude Lye, and Fond Fiction of Transubstantiation," in *Babels Balm: or The honey-combe of Romes religion*, trans. John Vickers (London, 1624), 65 (L1r). This edition is a translation of Goodwin's *Melissa religionis pontificae* (1620).

52. Milton, *Paradise Lost*, in *Complete Poems and Major Prose*, 5.436–42; emphasis added.

53. William Vaughan, *The Soules Exercise* (London, 1641), 226.

54. Donne, "A Sermon Preached in Saint Pauls in the Evening, November 23. 1628," in Donne, *Sermons*, 8:288–89.

55. For example, Scot, *Discoverie of Witchcraft*, 294, baldly states that alchemy is "otherwise called Multiplication."

56. Norton's defense of true alchemy as not "multiplication" is based on the alchemical claim discussed above, that alchemy is not artificial but natural; Norton, *Ordinal of Alchemy*, 17, lines 439–42. For alchemists' description of the penultimate stage of purification as "multiplication," see Abraham, *Dictionary of Alchemical Imagery*, 132–33. The image alchemists associated with "multiplication" was the pelican, who feeds her young with her blood; this is Eucharistic imagery as well.

57. Alexander Ross, *Arcana microcosmi* (London, 1652), 253.

58. When I say that Donne was nostalgic for transubstantiation as nonsense, I do not mean to imply that the Protestant Donne regarded all other aspects of Roman Catholic doctrine as nonsensical. I would agree, for example, with Roberta Albrecht, who reads Donne's alchemical imagery as reconstructing the Roman Catholic adoration of the Virgin Mary in an acceptably Protestant form; see Albrecht, *The Virgin Mary as Alchemical and Lullian Reference in Donne* (Selinsgrove, PA: Susquehanna University Press, 2005).

59. Ramie Targoff, *John Donne: Body and Soul* (Chicago: University of Chicago Press, 2008). Robert N. Watson calls this fantasy of an exceptional, incorruptible earthly body Donne's wish for personal immortality; see Watson, *The Rest Is Silence: Death as Annihilation in the English Renaissance* (Berkeley: University of California Press, 1994), 156–252.

60. Arnold Hunt, "The Lord's Supper in Early Modern England," *Past and Present* 161 (1998): 39–83.

61. John Donne, *Ignatius His Conclave*, ed. T. S. Healy (Oxford: Clarendon, 1969), 9.

62. Donne, "A Sermon upon the XX. Verse of the V. chapter of the Booke of Judges. . . . Preached at the Crosse the 15th of September. 1622," in *Sermons*, 4:206.

63. Donne, "Preached at S. Pauls upon Christmas day. 1626," in *Sermons*, 7:295. Whalen, *Poetry of Immanence*, 90–93, argues that in this sermon Donne displays affinities to transubstantiative theology as a means of critiquing the more extreme varieties of Calvinist election. See also R. V. Young, *Doctrine and Devotion in Seventeenth-Century Poetry: Studies in Donne, Herbert, Crashaw, and Vaughan* (Cambridge: D. S. Brewer, 2000), 95–99.

64. Donne, "Preached at S. Pauls upon Christmas Day. 1626," in *Sermons*, 7:296.

65. Donne, "The First Sermon Preached to King Charles, at Saint James: 3rd April. 1625," in *Sermons*, 6:249–50.

66. Donne, "Preached at S. Pauls, June 21. 1626," in *Sermons*, 7:191.

67. A number of critics have usefully discussed alchemy and purification in Donne. See especially Linden, *Darke Hierogliphicks*, 154–92; Edgar Duncan Hill, "Donne's Alchemical Figures," *ELH* 9 (1942): 257–85; and Jocelyn Emerson, "Donne and the Noble Art," in *Textual Healing: Essays on Medieval and Early Modern Medicine*, ed. Elizabeth Lane Furdell (Leiden: Brill, 2005), 195–221.

68. John Donne, "The Canonization," in *The Complete Poetry of John Donne*, ed. John T. Shawcross (Garden City, NY: Anchor/Doubleday, 1967), lines 23–35. All subsequent references to Donne's poems, unless otherwise noted, are to this edition and will be cited parenthetically in the text by line number. While I give the spelling of Donne's poems as it appears in Shawcross's edition, I have modernized the spelling of the poems' titles for familiarity's sake. For the alchemical significance of the "phoenix riddle," see Linden, *Darke Hierogliphicks*, 174–80.

69. Previous critics have explored manifestations of the Eucharist in Donne's secular poems. Regina Schwartz argues that Donne's secular love poems unite mortal and immortal bodies in sacramental fashion; see Schwartz, *Sacramental Poetics at the Dawn of Secularism: When God Left the World* (Stanford, CA: Stanford University Press, 2008), 87–160. Whalen, *Poetry of Immanence*, 22–60, sees Eucharistic elements in the way Donne's secular poetry endows profane elements with sacred status.

70. Hamilton, *Accident*, 52.

71. My discussion of Paracelsian alchemy in the "Nocturnal" and "Love's Alchemy" comments (though with much different emphasis) on many of the images discussed in W. A. Murray, "Donne and Paracelsus: An Essay in Interpretation," *Review of English Studies* 25, no. 98 (1949): 115–23.

72. Kathleen H. Dolan interprets the metaphorical alchemical process of the "Nocturnal" as a fairly straightforward one: the speaker's self begins in prime matter, proceeds through a stage of "death" or putrefaction, and is rebegotten into new life; see Dolan, "*Materia in potentia*: The Paradox of the Quintessence in Donne's 'A Nocturnall upon S. Lucies Day,'" *Renascence* 32 (1979): 13–20. This reading depends, however, on equating the "nothing" from which the elixir is made with prime matter. Prime matter, although it is pure potentiality, is not nothing. The chaos from which God formed the world was prime matter, but Christian theologians, who necessarily endorsed God's creating the earth *ex nihilo*, took care to stress that chaos was preceded by nothingness.

73. Malcolm Mackenzie Ross initiated the argument that Donne's poems seek Eucharistic status in *Poetry and Dogma: The Transfiguration of Eucharistic Symbols in Seventeenth Century English Poetry* (New Brunswick, NJ: Rutgers University Press, 1954). For other major studies along these lines, see James S. Baumlin, *John Donne and the Rhetorics of Renaissance Discourse* (Columbia: University of Missouri Press, 1991), 159–90; Eleanor J. McNees, *Eucharistic Poetry: The Search for Presence in the Writings of John Donne, Gerard*

Manley Hopkins, Dylan Thomas, and Geoffrey Hill (Lewisburg, PA: Bucknell University Press, 1992), 33–68; Theresa M. DiPasquale, *Literature and Sacrament: The Sacred and the Secular in John Donne* (Pittsburgh: Duquesne University Press, 1999); and Catherine Gimelli Martin, "Unmeete Contraryes: The Reformed Subject and the Triangulation of Religious Desire in Donne's *Anniversaries* and *Holy Sonnets*," in *John Donne and the Protestant Reformation: New Perspectives*, ed. Mary Arshagouni Papazian (Detroit: Wayne State University Press, 2003), 193–220.

74. Frances Cruickshank, *Verse and Poetics in George Herbert and John Donne* (Farnham, UK: Ashgate, 2010); Targoff, *John Donne*.

75. See Debus, *English Paracelsians*; and Charles Webster, *The Great Instauration: Science, Medicine and Reform, 1626–1660* (New York: Holmes and Maier, 1976), 273–79. As T. S. Healy reminds us in his edition of *Ignatius His Conclave* (1610), a work in which the iconoclastic alchemist himself makes an appearance, Donne owned a copy of Paracelsus's *Chirurgia Magna* and seemed to know other Paracelsian works, as well; Healy, "Introduction," in Donne, *Ignatius His Conclave*, xxxi. See also Geoffrey Keynes, *A Bibliography of Dr. John Donne*, 4th ed. (Oxford: Oxford University Press, 1973), 270, 273.

76. Donne, *Ignatius His Conclave*, 21.

77. John Donne, *Devotions upon Emergent Occasions*, ed. Anthony Raspa (Oxford: Oxford University Press, 1987), 61.

78. Paracelsus was never entirely consistent on whether the life-giving balsam and mummy were exactly the same or whether mummy merely had balsamic qualities; see Pagel, *Paracelsus*, 101; and Webster, *Paracelsus*, 138, 151.

79. For the early modern confusion over what constituted mummy, see Richard Sugg, *Mummies, Cannibals, and Vampires: The History of Corpse Medicine from the Renaissance to the Victorians* (London: Routledge, 2011), 20–26. For a compelling analysis of mummy as a commodity circulating between England and the Mediterranean, see Philip Schwyzer, *Archaeologies of English Renaissance Literature* (Oxford: Oxford University Press, 2007), 151–74.

80. Katharine Park attributes Paracelsus's enthusiasm for using freshly dead bodies as mummy to northern European folk belief that the life force remained in the recently deceased. Indeed, Paracelsus preferred to employ the bodies of those who met violent deaths, since their life force was unabated by illness or old age. See Park, "The Life of the Corpse: Division and Dissection in Late Medieval Europe," *Journal of the History of Medicine and Allied Sciences* 50 (1995): 111–32. See also Karl H. Dannenfeldt, "Egyptian Mumia: The Sixteenth Century Experience and Debate," *Sixteenth Century Journal* 16 (1985): 163–80, esp. 173; and Sugg, *Mummies*, 77–90, 181–88. Robert Fludd explains the superiority of mummy from the hanged or strangled corpse by the fact that, whereas corpses that are consigned to the earth (by burial), to water (by drowning), or to fire (by burning) are immediately given over to corruption, bodies that are consigned to the air (by hanging or strangling) "will remain incorrupted. . . . [T]his airy kind of Microcosmicall Mummy, is most proper for the conservation of vitall spirits in the living man." See Fludd, *Mosaicall Philosophy*, 248 (I4v).

81. John French, *The Art of Distillation* (London, 1653), 90 (O1v). Since French's two active ingredients, mummy and turpentine, both had the reputation of being highly "balsamical" or preservative, his elixir is doubly engineered to heighten the body's alchemical efficiency. For medicinal cannibalism in the early modern period and beyond, see Sugg, *Mummies*; and Louise Noble, *Medicinal Cannibalism in Early Modern English Literature and Culture* (New York: Palgrave Macmillan, 2011), 17–34.

82. Richard Sugg, "'Good Physic But Bad Food': Early Modern Attitudes to Medicinal Cannibalism and Its Suppliers," *Social History of Medicine* 19 (2006): 225–40; Noble, *Medicinal Cannibalism*, 115–26. Schwyzer, *Archaeologies*, 158, also connects the ingestion of mummy with transubstantiation.

83. For an analysis of the use of mummy as both threatening and curative, see Noble, *Medicinal Cannibalism*. Richard Halpern's suggestion that Shakespeare and Donne associate women with the stinking "waste products" of alchemy might usefully be applied to one aspect of the horror of Eucharistic cannibalism, that the ingested body and blood of Christ are eventually mingled with the communicant's feces; see Halpern, *Shakespeare's Perfume: Sodomy and Sublimity in the Sonnets, Wilde, Freud, and Lacan* (Philadelphia: University of Pennsylvania Press, 2002), 14–17. For the problem of the fecal "material remainder" of the Host, see Stephen Greenblatt, "The Mousetrap," in Stephen Greenblatt and Catherine Gallagher, *Practicing New Historicism* (Chicago: University of Chicago Press, 2001), 136–62.

84. Daniel Featley, *The Grand Sacrilege of the Church of Rome* (London, 1630), 296 (Ss4v).

85. Paracelsus [attrib.], *Of the Nature of Things*, in Sendivogius, *New Light of Alchymie*, 53 (Gg3r). David A. Hedrich Hirsch cleverly attributes another of Donne's scientific interests, atomistic theory, to the fact that atomists who followed Lucretius described atoms as perfect and indestructible—properties that would extend, if atomism is true, to the human body itself; see Hirsch, "Donne's Atomies and Anatomies: Deconstructed Bodies and the Resurrection of Atomic Theory," *Studies in English Literature 1500–1900* 31 (1991): 69–94.

86. John Donne to Henry Goodyer, in John Donne, *Letters to Several Persons of Honour* (London, 1651), 98; Donne, *Devotions*, 61. For Donne's interest in "balsam," see Don Cameron Allen, "John Donne's Knowledge of Renaissance Medicine," *Journal of English and Germanic Philology* 42 (1943): 322–42; and Joseph A. Mazzeo, "Notes on John Donne's Alchemical Imagery," *Isis* 48 (1957): 103–23.

87. Donne, *Devotions*, 117.

88. Ambroise Paré, *The Workes of that Famous Chirurgion Ambrose Parey*, trans. Thomas Johnson (London, 1634), 448 (Qq2v).

89. See "To the Countess of Bedford [Reason is our soul's left hand, faith her right]," which describes the Countess as in possession of the eternal "Balsamum" (22–24); and "To the Countess of Huntingdon [Man to God's image]," which proposes that in this countess's (miraculous) case a woman may be virtuous because she has been alchemically, rather than eucharistically, transubstantiated (25–28). For a comprehensive analysis of Donne's use of alchemical imagery to compliment female patrons, see Linden, *Darke Hieroglyphicks*, 162–69.

90. John Donne, *The Elegies and the Songs and Sonnets*, ed. Helen Gardner (Oxford: Clarendon, 1965), 216.

91. As Hawkes, *Idols of the Marketplace*, 164–67, describes it, alchemy in this poem is attractive to Donne because, relying on a now outmoded physics in which the earthly and divine correspond, it invests the otherwise purely commodified material of this world with spiritual meaning. Noble, *Medicinal Cannibalism*, 142–59, reads Elizabeth Drury's body as medicine that is regenerative for Donne precisely because it is absent and hence not burdened by gross human (and especially feminine) corporeality.

92. John Donne, *Essays in Divinity*, ed. Evelyn M. Simpson (Oxford: Clarendon, 1952), 88.

93. Isabel Karremann, Cornel Zwierlein, and Inga Mai Groote, "Introduction," in *Forgetting Faith? Negotiating Confessional Conflict in Early Modern Europe*, ed. Isabel Karremann, Cornel Zwierlein, and Inga Mai Groote (Berlin: De Gruyter, 2012), 15–16.

94. Patterson, "Perpetual Motion"; Patterson, "Place of the Modern."

95. Thomas Docherty is perhaps the most eloquent spokesperson for the position that Donne's interest in the new science and in a Montaignean skeptical secularism, which are of a piece with his poetic experimentation, represent Donne's "fall into history" and hence into modernity; see Docherty, *John Donne, Undone* (London: Methuen, 1986). Drawing from Stanley Cavell's analysis of a Shakespearean proto-Cartesian skepticism that threatens to undo the whole world, Anita Gilman Sherman argues that Donne's wit is a hedge against such skeptical undoing; see Sherman, *Skepticism and Memory in Shakespeare and Donne* (New York: Palgrave Macmillan, 2007), 41–64.

96. Donne, "Preached at the Funerals of Sir William Cokayne Knight," in *Sermons*, 7:260. This sermon acknowledges that dead bodies are not useful as medicine: "Jezabels dust is not Ambar, nor Goliahs dust *Terra sigillata*, Medicinall" (7:272).

97. George Herbert, "The Altar," in *The Works of George Herbert*, ed. F. E. Hutchinson (Oxford: Clarendon, 1941), 26, line 15. All subsequent references to Herbert are to this edition, unless otherwise noted, and will be cited parenthetically in the text by line number in the case of poetry or page number in the case of prose. I obviously disagree with Richard Strier, who declares that "The Altar" "does not in any way refer to the Eucharist"; see Strier, *Love Known: Theology and Experience in George Herbert's Poetry* (Chicago: University of Chicago Press, 1983), 191. Strier argues more generally for Herbert's Calvinist leanings on the question of the Eucharist. Herbert's theological positioning on the spectrum from Laudian to Puritan continues to be a matter of debate, but surely Gene Edward Veith, Jr., is correct in identifying Herbert's poetry as voicing a range of stances on the question of Christ's presence in the Eucharist; see Veith, *Reformation Spirituality: The Religion of George Herbert* (Lewisburg, PA: Bucknell University Press, 1985), 205–20. For criticism that attends to how Herbert views the sacrament as a means toward union or at least conversation with God, see Heather A. R. Asals, *Equivocal Predication: George Herbert's Way to God* (Toronto: University of Toronto Press, 1981), 46–51; Schwartz, *Sacramental Poetics*, 117–37; Whalen, *Poetry and Immanence*, 110–26; and Young, *Doctrine and Devotion*, 106–40. Generally speaking, these critics view Herbert as promoting

an Augustinian view of language as sacramental, the Word made flesh. This kind of reading owes much to Stanley Fish, for whom Herbert's poems are self-consuming artifacts that require the reader to experience what each poem describes; see Fish, *Self-Consuming Artifacts: The Experience of Seventeenth-Century Literature* (Berkeley: University of California Press, 1972), 157–223.

98. Booty, ed., *Book of Common Prayer 1559*, 248.

99. Christ's blood is "balsam" in *The Temple*'s "The Sacrifice" and "An Offering" and *Passio discerpta*'s Poem XIII ("Christus in cruce"). Christ's gaze in "The Glance" causes the speaker to feel "a sugred strange delight, / Passing all cordials made by any art, / Bedew, embalme, and overrunne my heart" (5–7); and Christ's mother the Virgin Mary in "To all Angels and Saints" is "the holy mine, whence came the gold, / The great restorative for all decay / In young and old" (11–13).

100. On the grounds of the abstractness of the imagery, Strier, *Love Known*, 46, denies that either "The Agonie" or the similarly themed "Divinitie" has anything to do with the Eucharist. I disagree; my sense is that the Eucharist is evoked in the changeability denoted in the metaphors. Ryan Netzley notes that Herbert stands at arm's (or at least tongue's) length from Eucharistic controversy in "The Agonie," as he does elsewhere in *The Temple*, by making the experience of Holy Communion one of taste, not ingestion; see Netzley, *Reading, Desire, and the Eucharist in Early Modern Religious Poetry* (Toronto: University of Toronto Press, 2011), 23–65.

101. For the revisions of "The Elixir" from the Williams manuscript to the first print edition of *The Temple* (1633), see Herbert, *Works*, 185, note to lines 21–24. Yaakov Mascetti reads Herbert's revisions of this poem as an increasing commitment to alchemy as a figure for refining the dross both of the speaker's sinful state and of the poem itself; see Mascetti, "'This is the famous stone': George Herbert's Poetic Alchemy in 'The Elixir,'" in *Mystical Metal of Gold: Essays on Alchemy and Renaissance Culture*, ed. Stanton J. Linden (New York: AMS, 2007), 301–24.

102. Herbert, *Works*, 435, 436. Herbert translated Bacon's *The Advancement of Learning* into Latin for its incorporation into *De augmentis scientiae* (1623). Bacon acknowledges "The paines, that it pleased [Herbert] to take, about some of [Bacon's] Writings" in his dedication to Herbert of his *Translations of Certaine Psalmes into English Verse* (1625); F. E. Hutchinson, "Introduction," in Herbert, *Works*, xl. For Herbert's acquaintance with Bacon and specifically his admiration for Bacon's scientific works, see Cristina Malcolmson, *George Herbert: A Literary Life* (New York: Palgrave Macmillan, 2004), 81–86. For the way Herbert's poetry evidences both an attraction to and reservations about Baconian science, see Harold Tolliver, *George Herbert's Christian Narrative* (University Park: Pennsylvania State University Press, 1993), 22–33.

103. Bacon, *Novum organum*, 55–56, 46; emphasis in the original.

104. Ibid., 133, 142.

105. Michel Serres, *The Birth of Physics*, trans. Jack Hawkes, ed. David Webb (Manchester, UK: Clinamen, 2000); Jonathan Goldberg, *The Seeds of Things: Theorizing Sexuality and Materiality in Renaissance Representations* (New York: Fordham University

Press, 2009); Stephen Greenblatt, *The Swerve: How the World Became Modern* (New York: W. W. Norton, 2011). Some English thinkers attempted to reconcile atomism and Aristotelianism; see Stephen Clucas, " 'The Infinite Variety of Formes and Magnitudes': 16th- and 17th-century English Corpuscular Philosophy and Aristotelian Theories of Matter and Form," *Early Science and Medicine* 2 (1997): 251–71.

106. Serres, *Birth of Physics*, uncovers the affinities between Lucretian physics' basis in a theory of complex flow and contemporary physics' and mathematics' interests in post-Cartesian fluid mechanics and in nonlinear contingency. Goldberg, *Seeds of Things*, describes how Epicurean atomism shares with poststructuralist philosophy and literary theory an emphasis on a universe consisting of ongoing possibility. Greenblatt, *The Swerve*, emphasizes the freedom Lucretius gave early modern writers to view the world with secular skepticism.

107. Gerard Passannante, *The Lucretian Renaissance: Philology and the Afterlife of Tradition* (Chicago: University of Chicago Press, 2011).

108. Montaigne, *Apology for Raymond Sebond*, 73.

109. Robert Hugh Kargon, *Atomism in England from Hariot to Newton* (Oxford: Clarendon, 1966), 47–48.

110. In important work on the *Summa perfectionis*, an influential thirteenth-century text attributed to the Arab alchemist Jābir ibn Hayyān or "Geber," Newman, *Atoms and Alchemy*, 23–44, not only posits that the text was written by the monk Paul of Taranto but also argues that it propounds a kind of experimentally based atomism rather than an Aristotelian theory of alchemy; see also Geber, *The* Summa perfectionis *of Pseudo-Geber: A Critical Edition, Translation and Study*, trans. and ed. William R. Newman (Leiden: Brill, 1991). Alan Chalmers replies that Geber's descriptions of alchemical experimentation depended on a "rough and ready" sense of how mercury and sulfur behave in alchemical use rather than on a truly atomistic physical theory; see Chalmers, *The Scientist's Atom and the Philosopher's Stone: How Science Succeeded and Philosophy Failed to Gain Knowledge of Atoms* (Dordrecht: Springer-Verlag, 2009), 83–86. Similarly, Chalmers, 88–94, counters Newman's argument (in *Atoms and Alchemy*, 85–153) that Daniel Sennert developed an early seventeenth-century theory of atomism based on alchemical experiment by claiming that Sennert accommodated his experiments to his pre-existing atomistic theory, rather than the reverse. For French natural philosopher Pierre Gassendi's Christianized atomism, see Kargon, *Atomism in England*, 65–68. For an excellent account of seventeenth-century atomism and protoexperimentalism leading up to Boyle, see Christopher Meinel, "Early Seventeenth-Century Atomism: Theory, Epistemology, and the Insufficiency of Experiment," *Isis* 79 (1988): 68–103.

111. Epicurean atoms, as Goldberg, *Seeds of Things*, 34, points out, are "imperceptible, colorless, tasteless . . . lack[ing] almost every feature by which bodies can be known, virtually every characteristic that characterizes matter." For the eager reception of Descartes's and Gassendi's physical theories at Oxford and Cambridge in the 1640s and 1650s, see Mordechai Feingold, "Mathematical Sciences and New Philosophies," in *Seventeenth-Century Oxford*, ed. Tyacke, 405–12.

112. René Descartes, "Author's Replies to the Fourth Set of Objections," in *The Philosophical Writings of Descartes*, trans. John Cottingham, Robert Stoothoff, and Dugald Murdoch (Cambridge: Cambridge University Press, 1985–91), 2:173. For Montaigne's influence on Descartes, see Philip Ford, "Lucretius in Early Modern France," in *The Cambridge Companion to Lucretius*, ed. Stuart Gillespie and Philip Hardie (Cambridge: Cambridge University Press, 2007), 227–41.

113. Jonathan Gil Harris, *Untimely Matter in the Time of Shakespeare* (Philadelphia: University of Pennsylvania Press, 2009), 32–65. Cruickshank, *Verse and Poetics*, connects Herbert's love of ordinary matter to his Eucharistic imagery.

114. David Glimp, "Figuring Belief: George Herbert's Devotional Creatures," in *Go Figure: Energies, Forms, and Institutions in the Early Modern World*, ed. Judith H. Anderson and Joan Pong Linton (New York: Fordham University Press, 2011), 112–31.

115. Herbert, *Works*, 258.

116. Ibid., 257.

117. Hawkes, *Idols of the Marketplace*, 124–25.

118. The lack of a need for God in Descartes's system was an inference that he fully recognized but upon which he declined to make a definitive pronouncement. Geoffrey Gorham argues that Descartes's theories of space and motion tried to have it both ways: he posited God's continuous involvement in the ongoing creation of motion, but he also posited that intermediary intelligences (that is, humans) can initiate motion. Thus Pascal was and was not right when he claimed that Descartes needed God only to set the world in motion. Geoffrey Gorham, "Cartesian Causation: Continuous, Instantaneous, Overdetermined," *Journal of the History of Philosophy* 42 (2004): 389–423.

119. Bacon, *Novum organum*, 141; Kargon, *Atomism in England*, 61.

120. Alan Rudrum, "'These fragments I have shored against my ruins': Henry Vaughan, Alchemical Philosophy, and the Great Rebellion," in *Mystical Metal*, ed. Linden, 325–38.

121. Thomas Vaughan, *The Works of Thomas Vaughan*, ed. Alan Rudrum (Oxford: Clarendon, 1984), 14. Comparing Henry Vaughan's translations of Henry Nollius to Thomas Vaughan's publications, Ralph M. Wardle finds that Henry Vaughan relied entirely on Thomas Vaughan's work for all Paracelsianism beyond that which pertained to the Paracelsian medicine Henry Vaughan practiced; see Wardle, "Thomas Vaughan's Influence upon the Poetry of Henry Vaughan," *PMLA* 51 (1936): 936–52.

122. Thomas Vaughan, *Anthroposophia theomagica* (1650), in *Works*, 51. Thomas Vaughan habitually refers to Aristotelian physics as a religion in need not just of reformation but of demolition: "Thou wilt tell me perhaps, this is new Philosophy and that of Aristotle is old. It is indeed, but in the same sence as Religion is at Rome"; Vaughan, *Anthroposophia theomagica*, in *Works*, 53.

123. Thomas Vaughan, *Anima magica abscondita* (1650), in *Works*, 106.

124. Thomas Vaughan, *Anthroposophia theomagica*, in *Works*, 55. For Thomas Vaughan as protoexperimental scientist in partnership with his wife, Rebecca Vaughan, see Thomas Vaughan, *Thomas and Rebecca Vaughan's "Aqua vitae: non vitis" (British Library MS, Sloane*

1741), trans. and ed. Donald R. Dickson (Tempe: Arizona Center for Medieval and Renaissance Studies, 2001).

125. Thomas Vaughan, *Anthroposophia theomagica*, in *Works*, 47; Donald Dickson, "Thomas Vaughan and the Iatrochemical Revolution," *The Seventeenth Century* 15 (2000): 18–31, esp. 19. Dickson's essay ably describes Thomas Vaughan's dual commitments to esoteric alchemy and the seemingly incompatible experimental protochemistry.

126. Henry Vaughan, *Henry Vaughan: The Complete Poems*, ed. Alan Rudrum (New Haven, CT: Yale University Press, 1976), 142. All subsequent references to Vaughan's poems are to this edition and will be cited parenthetically in the text by line number.

127. Jonathan F. S. Post describes Vaughan's poetry written during the Civil War as an effort to instill patience in the face of worldly strife, and to look either backward to an Edenic past or forward to the Resurrection; see Post, *Henry Vaughan: The Unfolding Vision* (Princeton, NJ: Princeton University Press, 1982). Nigel Smith asserts that this seeming detachment is actually a royalist resistance to populist revolt; see Smith, *Literature and Revolution in England, 1640–1660* (New Haven, CT: Yale University Press, 1994), 267–73.

128. Rudrum, "These fragments," 335.

129. Alan Rudrum, "Vaughan, Henry (1621–1695)," *Oxford Dictionary of National Biography* (Oxford: Oxford University Press, 2004), accessed 18 August 2014, http://www .oxforddnb.com/view/article/28130.

130. For an excellent summary of the ongoing historical debate over whether religion (or theology) and science (or natural philosophy) came to be separate spheres during the seventeenth century, see Margaret J. Osler, "Mixing Metaphors: Science and Religion or Natural Philosophy and Theology in Early Modern Europe," *History of Science* 36 (1998): 91–113. Webster, *Great Instauration*, argues that Puritan millenarian eschatology encouraged a science that saw the current world as imminently perfectible. True enough, but millenarianism did not instruct seventeenth-century Puritans to work out theological principles' application to the structure of basic matter.

131. For Vaughan's alchemical imagery, see especially Wilson O. Clough, "Henry Vaughan and the Hermetic Philosophy," *PMLA* 48 (1933): 1108–30; Richard H. Walters, "Henry Vaughan and the Alchemists," *Review of English Studies* 23 (1947): 107–22; Alan Rudrum, "The Influence of Alchemy in the Poems of Henry Vaughan," *Philological Quarterly* 49 (1970): 469–80; Thomas O. Calhoun, *Henry Vaughan: The Achievement of Silex Scintillans* (Newark: University of Delaware Press, 1981), 100–130; and Linden, *Darke Hierogliphicks*, 224–46.

132. See, for example, "St Mary Magdalen," "The Feast," and "The Law, and the Gospel."

3. HOW TO SKIM KABBALAH

1. Khunrath (1560–1605) worked in the court of Rudolf II in Prague as well as for other patrons, including Count Wilhelm von Rosenburg, who was also a patron of the polymathic scholar-mathematician-Hermeticist-alchemist John Dee. For Khunrath's admiration

for Dee and his work, see Peter Forshaw, "'Alchemy in the Amphitheatre': Some Consideration of the Alchemical Content of the Engravings in Heinrich Khunrath's *Amphitheatre of Eternal Wisdom* (1609)," in *Art and Alchemy*, ed. Wamberg, 204; and Ursula Szulakowska, *The Alchemy of Light: Geometry and Optics in Late Renaissance Alchemical Illustration* (Leiden: Brill, 2000), 125–26. Dee's mysterious alchemical symbol, the Monas, appears in the engravings added to the second edition of Khunrath's *Amphitheatrum*.

2. Forshaw, "Alchemy in the Amphitheatre." Khunrath influenced, for example, the *Atalanta fugiens* (1617) of Michael Maier.

3. Forshaw, "Alchemy in the Amphitheatre," 197–98. The second edition of 1609 added five black-and-white double-page rectangular drawings.

4. The many surviving copies of the 1609 edition of Khunrath's *Amphitheatrum* have the illustrations bound in many different, seemingly random orders, but the 1595 edition, of which there are only four surviving printed copies, has the four circular illustrations all in the same order; Forshaw, "Alchemy in the Amphitheatre," 198. It is thus highly likely that Khunrath meant the reader to see these four circular illustrations as a progression.

5. For descriptions and analysis of the circular engravings in Khunrath, I am indebted to Peter Forshaw, "Curious Knowledge and Wonder-Working Wisdom in the Occult Works of Heinrich Khunrath," in *Curiosity and Wonder from the Renaissance to the Enlightenment*, ed. R. J. W. Evans and Alexander Marr (Aldershot, UK: Ashgate, 2006), 107–29.

6. Raphael Patai, *The Jewish Alchemists: A History and Source Book* (Princeton, NJ: Princeton University Press, 1994), 156–57. Among these divine names is a Pentagrammatic version of the name of God, YHSWH, whose significance I explain below.

7. Patai, *Jewish Alchemists*, 156. Gershom Scholem notes that Khunrath derives kabbalism from "a compendium published by Johann Nidanus Pistorius, *Artis Cabalisticae* (Basel, 1587), in which two authentic texts of Kabbalah are grouped with Christian-kabbalistic writings," all of which are "accepted by Pistorius as kabbalist without, as far as I can see, naming any sources"; Scholem, *Alchemy and Kabbalah*, trans. Klaus Ottmann (Putnam, CT: Spring, 2006), 88–89. Khunrath was singled out for mockery by Jewish kabbalist Jacob ben Ḥayyim Ẓemaḥ as an example of the errors of Christian Kabbalah (Scholem, *Alchemy and Kabbalah*, 89).

8. Tessa Watt, *Cheap Print and Popular Piety, 1550–1640* (Cambridge: Cambridge University Press, 1991), 161.

9. This Hebrew phrase is no doubt intended to be *hokhmah El*, "wisdom God," even though the illustrator in this case has misspelled *hokhmah* ("wisdom"), a word that appears correctly in the "EMES VERITAS" engraving. The left-most letter of *El* ("God"), however, is ambiguously engraved: it is the letter *lamed*, but the fact that its upper serif disappears into the crosshatching of the valence makes it look like the letter *resh* instead. What we see thus looks like הכ מה אר, resh-alef/heh-mem/kaf-heh: a set of letters that, mixing conventions for reading the Hebrew and the Latin alphabets (reading right to left but in three left-to-right dyads), transliterates as "kh hm[n] ra."

10. For analysis of the alchemist's physical relation to the ritual objects in this engraving's "Lab-Oratorium" and of the engraving's unification of mystical and alchemical tradition, see Peter Forshaw, "'Behold, the dreamer cometh': Hyperphysical Magic and Deific Visions in an Early-Modern Theosophical Lab-Oratory," in *Conversations with Angels: Essays Towards a History of Spiritual Communication, 1100–1700*, ed. Joad Raymond (New York: Palgrave Macmillan, 2011), 175–200. This image was drawn by Netherlandish architect, painter, and landscape designer Hans (Jan) Vredeman de Vries (1527–1606), renowned for his two-part illustrated *Studies in Perspective* (1604–5). For the perspectival scheme of this engraving, see Szulakowska, *Alchemy of Light*, 134–35. The perspectival view is common in early modern depictions of spaces of knowledge such as the library, the museum, and the wonder chamber: it indicates, Paula Findlen argues, not only the depth of knowledge itself but also the "openness, sociability, and publicity" of the trend toward civic rather than private collections; Findlen, *Possessing Nature: Museums, Collecting, and Scientific Culture in Early Modern Italy* (Berkeley: University of California Press, 1994), 117.

11. Forshaw, "Alchemy in the Amphitheatre," 210.

12. Szulakowska, *Alchemy of Light*, 123.

13. The two divine names written in Hebrew in the third circular engraving are the Tetragrammaton and *Ruach Elohim*, "Spirit of God."

14. Martin Luther, *Lectures on Genesis, Chapters 1–5*, in *Works*, 1:264.

15. Stephen G. Burnett, *Christian Hebraism in the Reformation Era (1500–1660): Authors, Books, and the Transmission of Jewish Learning* (Leiden: Brill, 2012), 93.

16. Gershom Scholem, *Kabbalah* (New York: Quadrangle/New York Times Book Company, 1974), 8–22.

17. Scholem, *Kabbalah*, 23. The Sefer Yetzirah was written between the third and sixth centuries.

18. Scholem, *Kabbalah*, 45.

19. Ibid., 53–61.

20. For the *sefirot* as "emanations" of the divine and for how they mediate between God and the created world, see Scholem, *Kabbalah*, 96–105. While there is no canonical list of the *sefirot*, their number is fixed at ten, and they reflect distinct aspects or planes of divine activity. They are also often subdivided into different groups based on shared domains of the divine nature. One frequent grouping divides the three higher *sefirot*, which pertain to God's will and God's wisdom, from the seven lower ones, the divine attributes that most closely approach the human and natural condition and that are most brought to bear upon physical change—attributes such as love, judgment, and compassion; see Scholem, *Kabbalah*, 96–107.

21. Harold Bloom, *Kabbalah and Criticism* (New York: Continuum, 1975), 25. Also see Scholem, *Kabbalah*, 105–16.

22. Jewish Kabbalists seem to have been well aware that there were commonalities between their work and Christian concepts. As well, post-Expulsion Jews working in Italy absorbed large doses of Neoplatonism and other current philosophical trends into their

kabbalistic writing; see Moshe Idel, *Kabbalah: New Perspectives* (New Haven, CT: Yale University Press, 1988), 256. Post-Expulsion Kabbalah also began to take on decidedly messianic tones among Jewish thinkers; see Gershom Scholem, *Origins of the Kabbalah*, ed. R. J. Zwi Werblowsky, trans. Allan Arkush (Princeton, NJ: Princeton University Press, 1987), 353–54; see also Scholem, *Kabbalah*, 67–86.

23. Scholem, *Alchemy and Kabbalah*, 13–19, 40–54. Scholem finds evidence of alchemical influence upon the thirteenth-century Zohar, but notes that, for the most part, early kabbalistic writings took care to distinguish the mystical perfection for which their work aims from the physical purification of alchemy (25–36). See also Patai, *Jewish Alchemists*, 154.

24. There were, of course, Jewish alchemists. The work of one, the author of the lost treatise *Esh Mezaref* (Purifying fire), has been identified by Scholem as having been translated from the Hebrew by Christian Knorr von Rosenroth for use in his influential 1677 text *Kabbala denudata* (Kabbalah unveiled). This author assigns the lower seven *sefirot* to the seven metals (silver, gold, iron, tin, lead, copper, and mercury) and the three upper ones to "the wellspring of all things metallic," perhaps reflecting the influence of Paracelsus. See Scholem, *Alchemy and Kabbalah*, 62–71, 76–77; for the text with commentary, see Patai, *Jewish Alchemists*, 322–35.

25. See Joseph Dan, "The Kabbalah of Johannes Reuchlin and Its Historical Significance," in *The Christian Kabbalah: Jewish Mystical Books and Their Christian Interpreters: A Symposium*, ed. Joseph Dan (Cambridge, MA: Harvard College Library, 1997), 55–96, esp. 62–67.

26. For Christian Kabbalah, see especially Joseph Blau, *The Christian Interpretation of the Cabala in the Renaissance* (1944; repr., Port Washington, NY: Kennikat, 1965); François Secret, *Les kabbalistes Chrétiens de la Renaissance* (Paris: Dunod, 1964); Moshe Idel, *Kabbalah in Italy, 1280–1510: A Survey* (New Haven, CT: Yale University Press, 2011), 227–35; Philip Beitchman, *Alchemy of the Word: Cabala of the Renaissance* (Albany: State University of New York Press, 1998); Wilhelm Schmidt-Biggemann, *Geschichte der christlichen Kabbala*, 4 vols. (Stuttgart: Frommann-Holzboog, 2012–14); and Bernard McGinn, "Cabalists and Christians: Reflections on Cabala in Medieval and Renaissance Thought," in *Jewish Christians and Christian Jews: From the Renaissance to the Enlightenment*, ed. Richard H. Popkin and Gordon M. Weiner (Dordrecht: Kluwer, 1994), 11–34.

27. For an invaluable summary of alchemy's absorption of (primarily Christian) Kabbalah, see Peter Forshaw, "*Cabala Chymica* or *Chemia Cabalistica*—Early Modern Alchemists and Cabala," *Ambix* 60 (2013): 361–89.

28. Giovanni Pico della Mirandola, *Syncretism in the West: Pico's 900 Theses (1486)*, trans. and ed. S. A. Farmer (Tempe, AZ: Medieval and Renaissance Texts and Studies, 1998), conclusion 9>15, 499.

29. See Scholem, *Alchemy and Kabbalah*, 85–87; Chaim Wirszubski, *Pico della Mirandola's Encounter with Jewish Mysticism* (Cambridge, MA: Harvard University Press, 1989); Yates, *Giordano Bruno*, 84–116; and Pico, *900 Theses*, 11. Pico explains in his *Commento* that he wishes to learn Hebrew so that he can learn Kabbalah; see Wirszubski,

Jewish Mysticism, 3. It is unclear how much Kabbalah Pico was actually familiar with at the time of his composition of the *Conclusiones*. Pico's editor, S. A. Farmer, disputes Wirszubski's argument that Pico's nine hundred theses were influenced by Mithridates' translations of Kabbalah, which may have been completed after the theses were written. Farmer acknowledges that Pico was certainly, however, influenced by Menahem Recanati's *Hebrew Commentary on the Pentateuch*, on which he may have been coached by Mithridates; Pico, *900 Theses*, 344–45.

30. Although Pico opens the "Oration on the Dignity of Man" with a quotation from one of the urtexts of alchemy, the *Asclepius* attributed to Hermes Trismegistus ("A great miracle, Asclepius, is man"), his understanding of matter and of the natural magic that brings about material change is not alchemical; Giovanni Pico della Mirandola, "Oration on the Dignity of Man," in *The Renaissance Philosophy of Man*, ed. Ernst Cassirer, Paul Oskar Kristeller, and John Herman Randall, Jr. (Chicago: University of Chicago Press, 1948), 223.

31. Heiko A. Oberman, "Reuchlin and the Jews: Obstacles on the Path to Emancipation," in *The Challenge of Periodization*, ed. Besserman, 67–93. See also David H. Price, *Johannes Reuchlin and the Campaign to Destroy Jewish Books* (Oxford: Oxford University Press, 2011), 59–94.

32. Price, *Reuchlin and Jewish Books*, 81–83.

33. Erika Rummel, "Humanists, Jews, and Judaism," in *Jews, Judaism, and the Reformation in Sixteenth-Century Germany*, ed. Dean Phillip Bell and Stephen G. Burnett (Leiden: Brill, 2006), 3–32, esp. 14.

34. Blau, *Christian Interpretation of the Cabala*, 48; Christopher I. Lehrich, *The Language of Demons and Angels: Cornelius Agrippa's Occult Philosophy* (Leiden: Brill, 2003), 158n25; Price, *Reuchlin and Jewish Books*, 63.

35. "[H]ic lapis philosophorum, longe quidem eum exuperans, de quo archimici errantes contendunt"; Johannes Reuchlin, *De verbo mirifico*, in *Sämtliche Werke*, ed. Widu-Wolfgang Ehlers, Hans-Gert Roloff, and Peter Schäfer (Stuttgart: Frommann-Holzboog, 1996), 1.1:401, lines 15–17; my translation.

36. "Gentlemen, you now have access to words with which you can do more than mutter secretly to yourselves in the depths of your hearts. . . . You can summon whatever angel you like by his own symbolic name"; Johannes Reuchlin, *On the Art of the Kabbalah*, trans. Martin and Sarah Goodman (Lincoln: University of Nebraska Press, 1993), 273. For Reuchlin's acquisition of expertise in Kabbalah see Dan, "Kabbalah of Reuchlin," 76–77. Charles Zika argues that Reuchlin already had Kabbalah's alliance with this sort of magic in mind when he wrote *De verbo mirifico*; Zika, *Exorcising Our Demons: Magic, Witchcraft, and Visual Culture in Early Modern Europe* (Leiden: Brill, 2003), 21–68.

37. We know that *De arte cabalistica* was read, for example, by Erasmus (who didn't think much of it, but who corresponded about it with John Colet and gave a copy to John Fisher, the bishop of Rochester) as well as by Henry Howard, Earl of Northampton; see Blau, *Christian Interpretation of the Cabala*, 34–35.

38. Patai, *Jewish Alchemists*, 158.

39. Forshaw, "*Cabala Chymica*," 373–74.

40. For Agrippa's lectures on Reuchlin, see Lehrich, *Demons and Angels*, 26. For Agrippa's debt to and personal relationship with Johannes Trithemius, see Szőnyi, *Dee's Occultism*, 107. Frances Yates calls Agrippa's aim in *Occult Philosophy* "precisely that of providing the technical procedures for acquiring the more powerful and 'wonder-working' philosophy which Reuchlin had called for"; Yates, *The Occult Philosophy in the Elizabethan Age* (London: Routledge and Kegan Paul, 1979), 55.

41. Heinrich Cornelius Agrippa, *Three Books of Occult Philosophy*, trans. James Freake, ed. Donald Tyson (Woodbury, MN: Llewellyn, 1993), 45. For Agrippa's attitude toward alchemy, see Lehrich, *Demons and Angels*, 76–91.

42. Szőnyi, *Dee's Occultism*, 117–18.

43. Scholem, *Alchemy and Kabbalah*, 28–31, 86.

44. Ibid., 90.

45. Flamel, *Hieroglyphicall Figures*, 8–9. The *Exposition of the Hieroglyphical Figures* appeared in French in 1612, in English in 1624, and in German in 1673, with multiple editions in each language throughout the seventeenth and early eighteenth centuries; see Laurinda Dixon, "Introduction," in Flamel, *Hieroglyphicall Figures*, xlii–xliii.

46. John Taylor, *All the Workes of John Taylor the Water-poet* (London, 1630), Aaa6v.

47. "Summa von 100. Juden hast du ein ganz Jahr 1248 lot[h] ☉"; Benedictus Figulus, *Rosarium novum Olympicum et benedictum* (Basel, 1608), part 1, tractatus 4, 31; my translation.

48. Jeffrey S. Shoulson, *Fictions of Conversion: Jews, Christians, and Cultures of Change in Early Modern England* (Philadelphia: University of Pennsylvania Press, 2013), 117–18.

49. The word *Kabbalah* means something like "reception" as well as "traditional wisdom." Agrippa even implies that Kabbalah was the revelation Moses received when God allowed him to see what the Vulgate calls God's "posteriora" and the Geneva Bible his "back parts"; Beitchman, *Alchemy of the Word*, 18, 85–86.

50. Patai, *Jewish Alchemists*, 158.

51. Giordano Bruno, *The Cabala of Pegasus*, trans. Sidney L. Sondergard and Madison U. Sowell (New Haven, CT: Yale University Press, 2002), 39.

52. For the supposed Mosaic origins of Kabbalah, see Gershom Scholem, "The Beginnings of the Christian Kabbalah," in *Christian Kabbalah*, ed. Dan, 17–51. Christian kabbalists also assumed that Christ and the apostles were familiar with Kabbalah. Jewish kabbalists, in turn, assumed that Christ was familiar with Kabbalah, but misinterpreted it; see Wirszubski, *Jewish Mysticism*, 109. The nonantique origins of Kabbalah were not taken seriously by Jewish scholars until the early seventeenth century. See Idel, *Kabbalah*, 3; and Yaacob Dweck, *The Scandal of Kabbalah: Leon Modena, Jewish Mysticism, Early Modern Venice* (Princeton, NJ: Princeton University Press, 2011), 59–100.

53. See Yates, *Giordano Bruno*, 87–106. For the way that Kabbalah may be used to practice magic, see Moshe Idel, "The Magical and Neoplatonic Interpretations of the Kabbalah in the Renaissance," in *Jewish Thought in the Sixteenth Century*, ed. Bernard Dov Cooperman (Cambridge, MA: Harvard University Press, 1983), 186–242.

54. Eco, *Perfect Language*, 8.

55. Ibid., 31.

56. "[S]uper vires humanas mirabilium operum ipsimet effectores sumus, simulque in natura constituti, supra naturam dominamur, et monstra, portenta, miracula divinitatis insignia, nos mortales uno verbo: quod iam pridem vobis explicare ausus sum prodigimus"; Reuchlin, *De verbo mirifico*, in *Sämtliche Werke*, 1.1:98, lines 5–9; trans. Jerome Friedman, "The Myth of Jewish Antiquity: New Christians and Christian-Hebraica in Early Modern Europe," in *Jewish Christians*, ed. Popkin and Weiner, 37.

57. Idel, *Kabbalah in Italy*, 231–32.

58. Blau, *Christian Interpretation of the Cabala*, 8. *Gematria* caught on with Christian kabbalists in part because it reminded them of the predecessor *ars combinatoria* of Raymond Lull; see Yates, *Giordano Bruno*, 96. For the popularity of kabbalistic anagrammatizing and *gematria*, see Idel, *Kabbalah*, 263.

59. As Pico's editor S. A. Farmer points out, with the use of what Pico called the "science of the revolution of the alphabet," "any required reading could be gotten from any text"; Pico, *900 Theses*, 521, 65.

60. Karen Silvia de León-Jones, *Giordano Bruno and the Kabbalah: Prophets, Magicians, and Rabbis* (New Haven, CT: Yale University Press, 1997).

61. Naudé, *History of Magick*, 12 (B6v).

62. Desiderius Erasmus to Wolfgang Capito, 26 February 1517, in *The Correspondence of Erasmus*, trans. R. A. B. Mynors, et al. (Toronto: University of Toronto Press, 1974–), 4:267. See also Zika, *Exorcising Our Demons*, 69–98.

63. Idel, "Magical and Neoplatonic Interpretations," 186–87.

64. Erasmus to Wolfgang Capito, 13 March 1518, in *Correspondence*, 5:347.

65. Rummel, "Humanists, Jews, and Judaism," 19–21.

66. See Hanegraaff, *Esotericism*, 55–58. The impulse to read the Hebrew Bible as always having been Christian follows the lead of Luther, who revered the Hebrew Bible but believed it had been corrupted and perverted by the rabbis who had had charge of it. Luther supported the confiscation of rabbinic books so that they might be accessed only by Christians; see Oberman, "Reuchlin and the Jews," 81. Other Christian thinkers supposed that in the hands of Christians, Hebrew books might assist in the conversion of the Jews; see Rummel, "Humanists, Jews, and Judaism," 11. Missionary activity had been a stated reason for learning Hebrew since at least the foundation of the Franciscan and Dominican orders; see David Daiches, *The King James Version of the English Bible: An Account of the Development and Sources of the English Bible of 1611 with Special Reference to the Hebrew Tradition* (Chicago: University of Chicago Press, 1941), 100–109.

67. Martinus Rulandus (Martin Ruland), *A Lexicon of Alchemy* (Frankfurt, 1612), trans. Arthur E. Waite (1893; repr., London: Kessinger, 1964), 76.

68. Pico, "Oration," 249; Pico, *900 Theses*, conclusion 11>5, 523. Kathleen Biddick argues that Pico's work, like early modern cartographies, attempts to create the "classic" Jew—the Jew that is the model of pre-Christian truth—and to marginalize contemporary Jews. The effect, she says, is to construct the classic Jew as a "paper Jew," in relation to whom

contemporary Jews serve only as relics. Biddick, *The Typological Imaginary: Circumcision, Technology, History* (Philadelphia: University of Pennsylvania Press, 2003), 29, 41–44.

69. Johannes Reuchlin, *De verbo mirifico*, in *Sämtliche Werke*, 1.1:106, lines 25–33; trans. Price, *Reuchlin and Jewish Books*, 84.

70. Agrippa, *Occult Philosophy*, 485.

71. Pagel, *Paracelsus*, 213. In practice, Paracelsus seems to have used "Kabbalah" as a synonym for "magic," with Kabbalah's divine origins as some kind of guarantee of his own magic's nondemonic status (Webster, *Paracelsus*, 156–68).

72. Giordano Bruno, *Spaccio della bestia trionfante*, in *Dialoghi Italiani*, ed. Giovanni Gentile and Giovanni Aquilecchia, 3rd ed. (Florence: Sansoni, 1958), 799–800; trans. Yates, *Giordano Bruno*, 223. For Bruno and Kabbalah, see also Yates, *Giordano Bruno*, 257–74. For Bruno's efforts to de-Judaize Kabbalah, see de León-Jones, *Giordano Bruno and the Kabbalah*, 118–27.

73. Scholem, *Kabbalah*, 199.

74. Neoplatonist and Christian kabbalist Francesco Giorgi's *De harmonia mundi* (1525) and *In sacram scripturam problemata* (1536) were quite influential in Europe and in England; see Yates, *Occult Philosophy*, 33–42; and Healy, *Shakespeare, Alchemy and the Creative Imagination*, 83–84. Copies of kabbalistic texts in Hebrew would have been confined in England to academic libraries such as Oxford's Bodleian Library. Daiches, *King James Version*, 166, notes that the Bodleian catalog of 1605, among its works in Hebrew, includes "quite a disproportionate number of minor cabalistic works."

75. Thomas Vaughan, *Magia Adamica*, in *Works*, 178; see also Beitchman, *Alchemy of the Word*, 209–92.

76. E. J. Holmyard, *Alchemy* (1957; repr., New York: Dover, 1990), 106. Robert of Chester is often confused with Robert of Ketton, another English Arabist who worked in Spain in the mid-twelfth century. See Charles Burnett, "Ketton, Robert of (fl. 1141–1157)," in *Oxford Dictionary of National Biography*, accessed 18 August 2014, http://www.oxforddnb.com/view/article/23723.

77. Lisa Jardine and Anthony Grafton, " 'Studied for Action': How Gabriel Harvey Read His Livy," *Past and Present* 129 (1990): 30–78.

78. The scholarly skimmer thus occupies a middle ground between Leah Price's opposing terms of those who see books as content to be read and those who use books as physical objects to be circulated, hurled, bought, sold, ignored, abandoned, and so on; Price, "From *The History of a Book* to a 'History of the Book,' " *Representations* 108 (2009): 120–38. Daniel Wakelin suggests that the late-medieval authorial display of superficial reading—throwing in, say, bits of Aristotle and Boethius just to demonstrate one has read them—might actually have encouraged and bolstered unpredictable and freeing ideas, such as a concern for the commonweal rather than an attachment to class; Wakelin, *Humanism, Reading, and English Literature 1430–1530* (Oxford: Oxford University Press, 2007), 21–22. Pierre Bayard argues that scholarly skimming produces the most essential kind of knowledge of a book: its relation to other books; Bayard, *How to Talk About Books You Haven't Read*, trans. Jeffrey Mehlman (New York: Bloomsbury, 2007), 14–31.

79. Roger Bacon [attrib.], *The Mirror of Alchimy* (London, 1597), 63 (I2r).

80. Frank Klaasen, *The Transformations of Magic: Illicit Learned Magic in the Later Middle Ages and Renaissance* (University Park: Pennsylvania State University Press, 2013), 9.

81. Grafton, *Defenders*, 23–46, points out that the very same humanists who were models of philological and historical rigor in their use of ancient texts were also prone to reading allegorically, so that those texts were made to say something quite other than what they actually said. In the same vein, Ann Blair notes that one of the effects of extracting quotes for commonplace books was to "[make] a 'matter of fact' out of someone else's evidence, neutralizing its original argumentative value, so that it can be used to a different, even exactly opposite, purpose"; Blair, *The Theater of Nature: Jean Bodin and Renaissance Science* (Princeton, NJ: Princeton University Press, 1997), 75. Grafton and Jardine, *Humanism to the Humanities*, xiii–xiv, describe selective reading as suiting a newly absolutist governmentality that requires texts and libraries carefully edited to fit its purposes. Halpern, *Poetics of Primitive Accumulation*, 47, identifies the humanistic rhetorical practice of reading for *copia* as a system for atomizing textual meaning into "dissociated bits of elocutionary material" that neutralize undesirable ideology.

82. Historians continue to explore and debate the many sources of Dee's blend of magic, natural philosophy, and alchemy. See, e.g., Stephen Clucas, "John Dee's Angelic Conversations and the *Ars Notoria*: Renaissance Magic and Mediaeval Theurgy," in *John Dee: Interdisciplinary Studies in English Renaissance Thought*, ed. Stephen Clucas (Dordrecht: Springer-Verlag, 2006), 231–73.

83. William H. Sherman, *John Dee: The Politics of Reading and Writing in the English Renaissance* (Amherst: University of Massachusetts Press, 1995); Stephen Clucas, "False Illuding Spirits and Cownterfeiting Deuills: John Dee's Angelic Conversations and Religious Anxiety," in *Conversations with Angels*, ed. Raymond, 150–74; Deborah Harkness, *John Dee's Conversations with Angels* (Cambridge: Cambridge University Press, 1999); and Glyn Parry, *The Arch-Conjuror of England: John Dee* (New Haven, CT: Yale University Press, 2011).

84. Dee's 1583 collection of Hebrew and Aramaic books is enumerated in G. Lloyd Jones, *The Discovery of Hebrew in Tudor England: A Third Language* (Manchester, UK: Manchester University Press, 1983), 275–77.

85. Jones, *Discovery of Hebrew*, 170. Harkness, *Dee's Conversations*, 85–86, points out the intensity of Dee's book-buying binges in volumes of Christian Kabbalah. Szulakowska, *Alchemy of Light*, 60, on the other hand, describes Dee as relying on just a few authors—Reuchlin, Paracelsus, Pico, and Guillaume Postel—for his knowledge of Kabbalah, and perhaps also on the pseudo-Lullian *De auditu cabbalistico*.

86. John Dee, *John Dee's Actions with Spirits, 22 December 1581 to 23 May 1583*, ed. Christopher Whitby (New York: Garland, 1988), 2:334.

87. Harkness, *Dee's Conversations*, 162.

88. Dee, *Actions with Spirits*, 2:65.

89. Dee refers to Galatino in the margins of his angel conversations; his copy is recorded in his library catalog. See Harkness, *Dee's Conversations*, 162; and Julian Roberts

and Andrew G. Watson, eds., *John Dee's Library Catalogue* (London: Bibliographical Society, 1990), #216. Though the edition of *De arcanis catholicae veritatis* I have been able to examine (Frankfurt am Main, 1672) is later than the one Dee used, it nevertheless reveals that Dee copied the angel's first Hebrew passage and its Latin translation directly from book 2, chapter 12, column 89 of Galatino; Dee has made one interpolation into the Latin, which he indicates in brackets. The second Hebrew passage is copied from Galatino's book 2, chapter 12, column 88; Dee has made a few errors transcribing the Hebrew but has quoted the Latin exactly. The third passage is copied from Galatino's book 3, chapter 11, column 136; Dee has rearranged the Hebrew words by copying the first five words last and the last six words first, an error that may have reflected his copying the second line of Galatino's Hebrew before the first.

90. Dee, *Actions with Spirits*, 2:65. Harkness, *Dee's Conversations*, 164–65, cites Dee's annotations in several books he owned as further evidence that he knew Hebrew, but the volumes she cites that I have been able to examine do not bear out her speculation that Dee was able to do more than basic letter-forming and sounding out of words:

1. Harkness notes some underscoring and annotations in Dee's copy of Elias Levita's *Composita verborum & nominum Hebraeicorum* (Basel, 1525; Cambridge University Library K*.6.36[F]; Roberts and Watson, #1594), but she does not explain why she, unlike Roberts and Watson, believes the annotations in this volume to be by Dee rather than someone else.

2. Harkness incorrectly describes Dee's making marginal annotations on or in Hebrew in Wigando Happellio's *Linguae sanctae canones grammatici* (Basel, 1561; Cambridge University Library K*.6.37[F]; Roberts and Watson, #1600). This volume's single marginal note is the Latin comment "Radix" (99), and the underscoring in the volume includes only one Hebrew word, in the context of a discussion of Hebrew "radicals" or roots (98).

3. Harkness describes Dee as correcting "an exegesis of the tetragrammaton" in his heavily annotated copy of Henricus de Herph, *Theologiae mysticae* (Cologne, 1556; Cambridge University Library, H*.1.10(B); Roberts and Watson, #223). The page she cites (B3r) includes one short Hebrew annotation, and the surrounding pages (B2r, B3v) are annotated with the Tetragrammaton in a different hand. Given that this book was subsequently owned by Richard Holdsworth, professor of theology at Cambridge University and bequeather to the Cambridge University Library of a sizable Hebraica collection, it is likely that Dee did none of these annotations, or only the Tetragrammaton.

I have not been able to examine two other books that Harkness cites to establish Dee's Hebrew proficiency: a Hebrew primer by Sanctes Pagninus, *Hebraicarum institutionum libri IIII* (Paris, 1549; Bodleian Library 4° P 47(1) Art.Seld; Roberts and Watson, #1570); and a bilingual edition of Saint Matthew the Evangelist's letter to the Hebrews with a

Latin commentary by Sebastian Münster, *Evangelium secundum Matthaeum in lingua Hebraica* (Basel, 1557; Bodleian Library 8° Z 202 Th; Roberts and Watson, #1588).

91. Jones, *Discovery of Hebrew*, 169.

92. Sherman, *John Dee*, 79–100. The markings in Dee's surviving Hebrew primers and Hebrew-language related books are as follows. Levita's *Composita verborum & nominum Hebraeicorum* (cited above) has very little in the way of notes and markings—and those, as Roberts and Watson, *Dee's Library Catalogue*, 103, point out, may be by someone other than Dee. Happellio's *Linguae sanctae canones grammatici* (cited above) has sparse notes and underscoring, almost entirely on pp. 33–99 of a volume spanning more than six hundred pages. Two more such books have no marks at all: Nicolaus Clenardus, *Tabulae in grammaticam Hebraeam* (Cologne, 1561; Cambridge University Library K*.6.46² [F]; Roberts and Watson, #1596); and Johannes Cheradamus, *Rudimenta quaedam Hebraicae* (Paris, 1523; Cambridge University Library Dd*.3.49¹[E]; Roberts and Watson, #1574).

93. Roberts and Watson, *Dee's Library Catalogue*, 29. For unmarked Hebrew books owned by Dee see, for example, *Proverbia Salomonis*, trans. Sebastian Münster (Basel, 1524; Cambridge University Library A*.10.43[F]; Roberts and Watson, #1604); and Angelo Canini, *Institutiones linguae Syriacae, Assyriacae atque Thalmudicae* (Paris, 1554; Cambridge University Library S822c.55.2; Roberts and Watson, #1624).

94. Desiderius Erasmus to John Colet, ca. December 1504, in *Correspondence*, 2:87.

95. Even the fact that Dee took most of his Hebrew books with him when beginning his European travels in 1583 may be put down to the fact that he needed them to augment the works of Christian Kabbalah that he also took with him, including those of Reuchlin and Giorgi. Or perhaps he intended to keep working on learning Hebrew, but didn't get around to it.

96. Matthew McLean, *The Cosmographia of Sebastian Münster: Describing the World in the Reformation* (Aldershot, UK: Ashgate, 2007), 22–23.

97. Sebastian Münster, *Messias Christianorum et Iudaeorum Hebraicem & Latinem* (Basel, 1539; Cambridge University Library K*.6.60[F]; Roberts and Watson, #1616), A8r, B1r, G6r.

98. Roberts and Watson, *Dee's Library Catalogue*, 29, note Dee's habit of connecting Kabbalah with angelology.

99. Hamilton, *Apocryphal Apocalypse*, 33.

100. Eco, *Perfect Language*, 123.

101. Webster, *Paracelsus*, 159; Blau, *Christian Interpretation of the Cabala*, 85–86.

102. William N. West, "'But this will be a mere confusion': Real and Represented Confusions on the Elizabethan Stage," *Theatre Journal* 60 (2008): 217–33; Carla Mazzio, *The Inarticulate Renaissance: Language Trouble in an Age of Eloquence* (Philadelphia: University of Pennsylvania Press, 2009).

103. Harkness, *Dee's Conversations*, 166–72, 175. Dee was convinced—and claimed that the angels he conversed with confirmed—that a particular book in his possession, the *Book of Soyga*, was written in the Adamic language. Having located two manuscript copies, one of them likely Dee's, Harkness, *Dee's Conversations*, 44–45, 161, describes the

Book of Soyga as nothing special: it is written in Latin and English and contains numerical and alphabetical tables that resemble those in the angel conversations.

104. Szulakowska, *Alchemy of Light*, 62; Karen de León-Jones, "John Dee and the
Kabbalah," in *John Dee*, ed. Clucas, 143–58.

105. John Bender and Michael Marrinan, *The Culture of Diagram* (Stanford, CA:
Stanford University Press, 2010), 19. Dee was intensely interested in the kabbalistic tables
in Agrippa's *Occult Philosophy*, which derived the names of "the seventy-two angels, which
bear the name of God" by means of "the commutations of letters and numbers" (Agrippa,
Occult Philosophy, 538), and he frequently imitated Agrippa's diagrammatic reasoning
elsewhere in his work. See Jim Reeds, "John Dee and the Magic Tables in the *Book of
Soyga*," in *John Dee*, ed. Clucas, 177–204.

106. The astrological symbols that are either explicitly figured in or may be derived
from the Monas include the sun, the moon, Saturn, Jupiter, Mars, Venus, Mercury, and
Aries; Clulee, *Dee's Natural Philosophy*, 107–9. The first seven of these eight astrological
symbols correspond to the seven metals (respectively, gold, silver, lead, tin, iron, copper,
and mercury) and hence are also alchemical signs; the eighth, for the constellation Aries,
is the first of the three fire signs and thus has special alchemical significance. The Monas's
shape is also derived from the origins of geometry: the point, line, and circle. For the
Habsburg symbols evoked in the Monas, see Parry, *Arch-Conjuror*, 20–21.

107. Josten, "Dee's *Monas Hieroglyphica*," 159.

108. See Michael T. Walton, "John Dee's Monas Hieroglyphica: Geometrical Cabala,"
Ambix 23 (1976): 116–23; Clulee, *Dee's Natural Philosophy*, 86–96; and Håkan Håkansson,
Seeing the Word: John Dee and Renaissance Occultism (Lund: Lunds Universitet, 2001),
180–99. For the alchemical valence of Dee's kabbalistic technique, see Federico Caval-
laro, "The Alchemical Significance of John Dee's *Monas Hieroglyphica*," in *John Dee*, ed.
Clucas, 159–76.

109. Josten, "Dee's *Monas Hieroglyphica*," 135.

110. De León-Jones, "John Dee and the Kabbalah."

111. For Dee's alchemy as cosmic and apocalyptic, see Harkness, *Dee's Conversations*,
195–214; Clulee, *Dee's Natural Philosophy*, 110–15; and Håkansson, *Seeing the Word*, 223–
30, 318–31. For Dee's alchemy as bringing about an Elizabethan alchemical empire, see
Parry, *Arch-Conjuror*, 71–93, 108–13. For the influence of Dee's *Monas hieroglyphica* upon
physical alchemy, see William R. Newman, "Alchemical Symbolism and Concealment:
The Chemical House of Lebavius," in *The Architecture of Science*, ed. Peter Gallison and
Emily Ann Thompson (Cambridge, MA: MIT Press, 1999), 59–78; and Peter Forshaw,
"The Early Alchemical Reception of John Dee's *Monas Hieroglyphica*," *Ambix* 52 (2005):
247–69. For the influence of Dee's plans for a Christian kabbalistic alchemical world
order, see Janacek, *Alchemical Belief*, 16–42. These plans fuse alchemy with conversion to
Christianity in a way that anticipates mid-seventeenth-century writers such as alchemist
Thomas Vaughan and his brother, poet Henry Vaughan; see Shoulson, *Fictions of Conversion*, 133–51.

112. Josten, "Dee's *Monas Hieroglyphica*," 197n112.

113. While Dee's conversations with angels are not solely or even mainly about alchemy, they seem to build toward the cosmic alchemy described in the *Monas hieroglyphica*. The angels impart to him, in the divine language, the names of the stages of the alchemical process; Harkness, *Dee's Conversations*, 180. One of the "Governing Angels" who appears to Dee, Bornogo, declares that "I prevayle in Metalls: in the knowledge of them"; Dee, *Actions with Spirits*, 2:147–48. Some of the angelic tables conveyed to Dee claim to address "the knowledg, finding and use of Metals"; see John Dee, *A True & Faithful Relation of What Passed for Many Yeers between Dr. John Dee . . . and Some Spirits*, ed. Meric Casaubon (London, 1659), 179. And Christopher Whitby, editor of the angel conversations, points out that the seven "Ensigns of Creation," tables that the angels instructed Dee to make, correspond to the stages of the alchemical process; Dee, *Actions with Spirits*, 1:135–37.

114. Dee, *Actions with Spirits*, 2:234–35.

115. Dee, *Actions with Spirits*, 2:398.

116. Harkness, *Dee's Conversations*, 60–61.

117. John Dee, *The Private Diary of Dr. John Dee*, ed. James Orchard Halliwell (London: Camden Society, 1842), 59.

118. Parry, *Arch-Conjuror*, 20.

119. Christopher Marlowe, *Doctor Faustus: A- and B-Texts (1604, 1616): Christopher Marlowe and His Collaborator and Revisers*, ed. David Bevington and Eric Rasmussen (Manchester, UK: Manchester University Press, 1993), 1.1.119; Yates, *Occult Philosophy*, 136–37. All subsequent references to *Doctor Faustus* are to the Bevington and Rasmussen edition and will be cited parenthetically in the text by act, scene, and line numbers. I use the A-Text version of *Doctor Faustus* unless otherwise specified; the A-Text's significantly different emphasis on theological issues is important to my reading of the use of Kabbalah in the play. For an important recent treatment of the Hermetic elements in *Doctor Faustus*, see Andrew Duxfield, "New Directions: *Doctor Faustus* and Renaissance Hermeticism," in *Doctor Faustus: A Critical Guide*, ed. Sara Munson Deats (London: Continuum, 2010), 96–110.

120. For example, "son but est de faire des miracles par la force des lettres & caracteres" [its purpose is to perform miracles by the power of letters and characters]; see Jean Bodin, *De la demonomanie des sorciers* (Paris, 1580), 38; my translation. The fact that Agrippa's *Occult Philosophy* uses the phrase "letters *or* characters" ("literae sive characteres," "literae seu characteres") rather than Bodin's "letters *and* characters" suggests that Marlowe is drawing from Bodin here rather than from Agrippa.

121. Line 53 in this passage presents a textual crux: the A-Text version of the play has the illegible word "sceanes," and the B-Text version is of no help since it omits the word entirely. W. W. Greg conjectures "signs," Roma Gill "schemes," and Michael Keefer "seals." Bevington and Rasmussen follow Greg by using "signs," as do I.

122. The English Faust book has Faustus both consulting books and performing rituals: he attends to "figures, characters, conjurations, incantations, with many other ceremonies belonging to these infernal arts"; see John Henry Jones, ed., *The English Faust Book: A Critical Edition Based on the Text of 1592* (Cambridge: Cambridge University Press, 1994), 92.

123. Unlike the English Faust book's protagonist, who "accompanied himself with divers that were seen in those devilish arts and that had the Chaldean, Persian, Hebrew, Arabian and Greek tongues" and who plays his leg-removal trick on a Jew from whom he has borrowed money, Marlowe's Faustus never meets a Jew or seeks explicit acquaintance with Hebrew except for the "Hebrew Psalter" (1.1.157), discussed below; Jones, ed., *English Faust Book*, 92, 152–53.

124. For Marlowe's likely acquaintance with and use of the popular Pseudo-d'Abano volume and for this volume's showcasing of Kabbalah, see Gareth Roberts, "Necromantic Books: Christopher Marlowe, *Doctor Faustus* and Agrippa of Nettesheim," in *Christopher Marlowe and English Renaissance Culture*, ed. Darryll Grantley and Peter Roberts (Aldershot, UK: Scolar, 1996), 148–71.

125. Reuchlin, *On the Art of the Kabbalah*, 277, asserts that "the Kabbalists have excerpted from the Book of Psalms pious prayers addressed to God that necessarily consist of seventy-two verses. Each of these verses contains the Tetragrammaton with the name of one of the seventy-two angels."

126. See the notes to 5.1.91–110 in Marlowe, *Doctor Faustus*, ed. Bevington and Rasmussen. While I prefer to think of it as Marlowe's last play, dating to 1592 or so, the alternative date of 1589–90 that would make *Doctor Faustus* predate *Tamburlaine* does not greatly lessen the intensity of the intertextuality of these lines. Richard Halpern suggests that Helen's lack of substance here recalls the tradition that the Helen of the Trojan War was merely an *eidolon*, a phantom put into place while the real Helen was relocated to Egypt; see Halpern, "Marlowe's Theater of Night: *Doctor Faustus* and Capital," *ELH* 71 (2004): 455–95, esp. 486–89.

127. For Faustus's inhabitation of the literary as the inescapable grounds of his tragedy, see Graham L. Hammill, *Sexuality and Form: Caravaggio, Marlowe, and Bacon* (Chicago: University of Chicago Press, 2000), 97–127. Faustus's oscillation between seeing letters on the page as magically efficacious and resorting to them solely as a source of textual pleasure supports Genevieve Juliette Guenther's sense that the magic in *Doctor Faustus* would have been seen by the play's early modern audience as both consequential and illusory; see Guenther, *Magical Imaginations: Instrumental Aesthetics in the English Renaissance* (Toronto: University of Toronto Press, 2012), 62–85. James Kearney argues that Faustus's tragedy inverts other famous conversions that occur by reading, e.g., Augustine's and Luther's; Faustus idolizes the letter, rather than the spirit, of the text. See Kearney, *The Incarnate Text: Imagining the Book in Reformation England* (Philadelphia: University of Pennsylvania Press, 2009), 140–77. Like me, Kearney reads Faustus's encounter with Helen as an ecstasy of textuality.

128. West, *Theatres and Encyclopedias*, 178.

129. Faustus reverts from the New Testament to the Old Testament several times in the play, including when he first signs the diabolical contract. The inscription that appears on his arm, "*Homo, fuge!*" (2.1.77), quotes the New Testament: "thou, ô man of God, flee these things" (1Tim. 6:11). Faustus's reply, "Whither should I fly?" (2.1.77), cites the Old Testament: "whether [*sic*] shal I flee from thy presence?" (Pss.139:7). Faustus

neglects the Christian interpretation of this psalm, that the verse just after the one he cites describes not only the inability to escape God—"If I ascend into heaven, thou art there: if I lie downe in hel, thou art there" (Pss. 139:8)—but also the ubiquity of Christ's salvation.

130. Watt, *Cheap Print*, 161. The Tetragrammaton became the preferred Protestant pictorial depiction of God in England as early as the Coverdale Bible (1535). See Margaret Aston, "Symbols of Conversion: Proprieties of the Page in Reformation England," in *Printed Images in Early Modern Britain: Essays in Interpretation*, ed. Michael Hunter (Farnham, UK: Ashgate, 2010), 23–42.

131. Reuchlin, *On the Art of the Kabbalah*, 73. Reuchlin's source is the Sefer Raziel HaMalakh (Book of the Angel Raziel), a thirteenth-century compilation of Kabbalah and kabbalistic magic that existed in early modern Europe in many versions, many of them with Christian interpolations. See Sophie Page, "Uplifting Souls: The *Liber de essentia spirituum* and the *Liber Razielis*," in *Invoking Angels: Theurgic Ideas and Practices, Thirteenth to Sixteenth Centuries*, ed. Claire Fanger (University Park: Pennsylvania State University Press, 2012), 79–112.

132. Edward A. Snow, "Marlowe's *Doctor Faustus* and the Ends of Desire," in *Two Renaissance Mythmakers: Christopher Marlowe and Ben Jonson*, ed. Alvin Kernan (Baltimore: Johns Hopkins University Press, 1977), 70–110.

133. For burning one's books as a traditional gesture of renouncing magic, see Marlowe, *Doctor Faustus*, ed. Bevington and Rasmussen, 197n123. Andrew Cambers's interesting account of Protestant exorcisms makes the point that Protestant ritual often saw the book (the religious book, or the magic book) as simultaneously powerful for its words and powerful as an object; see Cambers, "Demonic Possession, Literacy and 'Superstition' in Early Modern England," *Past and Present* 202 (2009): 3–35. In the 1616 B-Text of *Doctor Faustus*, Mephistopheles reveals that he has been the one who governed Faustus's reading of the scriptures and thus "dammed up" his passage to heaven: "When thou took'st the book / To view the Scriptures, then I turned the leaves / And led thine eye" (Marlowe, *Doctor Faustus*, ed. Bevington and Rasmussen, B-Text, 5.2.99–101). This ex post facto explanation provides the B-Text's protagonist with an excuse for his exegetical deficiencies; the A-Text Faustus has no such excuse. I should emphasize here that time-worn ritual magic and up-to-date hermeneutic practice are not necessarily opposed in the way that *Doctor Faustus* ultimately opposes them; Dee's angel conversations are clearly examples of both activities' being conducted simultaneously. See Klaasen, *Transformations of Magic*, 167–73.

134. Snow, "*Doctor Faustus* and the Ends of Desire." Similarly, Garrett Sullivan, drawing upon Stephen Greenblatt's account of the "will to absolute play" of the Marlovian protagonist, registers Faustus's "self-forgetting"—a horrific error for a Protestant culture that urged the believer always to *remember him or herself*—as the engine of Renaissance discovery and invention and as the source of the alluring raptures of Renaissance theater. See Garrett A. Sullivan, Jr., *Memory and Forgetting in English Renaissance Drama: Shakespeare, Marlowe, Webster* (Cambridge: Cambridge University Press, 2005), 65–87;

and Stephen Greenblatt, *Renaissance Self-Fashioning from More to Shakespeare* (Chicago: University of Chicago Press, 1980), 157–92.

135. Paul Budra, "*Doctor Faustus*: Death of a Bibliophile," *Connotations* 1 (1991): 1–11. Sarah Wall-Randell describes Faustus's tendency to summarize and condense learning as modeled after the commonplace book and the encyclopedia; see Wall-Randell, "Doctor Faustus and the Printer's Devil," *Studies in English Literature 1500–1900* 48 (2008): 259–81.

136. For Faustus's increasingly bad scholarship, see A. N. Okerlund, "The Intellectual Folly of Dr. Faustus," *Studies in Philology* 74 (1977): 258–78; and Joseph T. McCullen, "Dr Faustus and Renaissance Learning," *Modern Language Review* 51 (1956): 6–16.

137. William Shakespeare, *The Tempest*, ed. Virginia Mason Vaughan and Alden T. Vaughan (Walton-on-Thames, UK: Thomas Nelson and Sons, 1999), 1.2.76–77. Subsequent references to this play are to this edition and will be cited parenthetically in the text by act, scene, and line numbers.

138. Julia Reinhard Lupton, *Citizen-Saints: Shakespeare and Political Theology* (Chicago: University of Chicago Press, 2005), 159–80.

139. Gershom G. Scholem, *On the Kabbalah and Its Symbolism*, trans. Ralph Manheim (New York: Schocken, 1965), 161. Psalm 139:15–16 was used to read the golem alchemically as the forging of Adam as a precious metal "beneth in the earth." Jean D'Espagnet writes in his *Arcanum Hermeticae philosophiae* (1623), "The Generation of the Philosophers Stone is not unlike the Creation of Adam, for the Mud was made of a terrestriall and ponderous Body dissolved by Water, which deserved the excellent name of *Terra Adamica*, wherein all the virtues and qualities of the Elements are placed"; see D'Espagnet, *Hermetick Secrets*, in Arthur Dee, *Fasciculus chemicus or Chymical Collections*, trans. Elias Ashmole (London, 1650), 215. By some accounts a golem is also alchemically made when Moses creates and then animates the golden calf, deploying for that purpose the Kabbalah that he has just received in oral form from God on Mount Sinai; see Moshe Idel, *Golem: Jewish Magical and Mystical Traditions on the Artificial Anthropoid* (Albany: State University of New York Press, 1990), 170.

140. Moshe Idel, "Hermeticism and Judaism," in *Hermeticism and the Renaissance: Intellectual History and the Occult in Early Modern Europe*, ed. Ingrid Merkel and Allen G. Debus (Washington, DC: Folger, 1988), 59–78, esp. 61; Scholem, *On the Kabbalah and Its Symbolism*, 184–88. For the development of the golem legend in the Middle Ages and Renaissance, see Idel, *Golem*; Scholem, *On the Kabbalah and Its Symbolism*, 158–204; and Idel, *Kabbalah in Italy*, 236–86.

141. Scholem, *On the Kabbalah and Its Symbolism*, 200–202; Idel, *Golem*, 207–11.

142. Reuchlin, *On the Art of the Kabbalah*, 333.

143. William Newman's fascinating account of alchemy's obsession with artificial life details how, while Arabic and medieval Christian alchemists indulged themselves only to a limited extent in speculation about creating an artificial person, sixteenth- and seventeenth-century alchemists began seriously to consider whether alchemy might get into the business of parthenogenetic reproduction. Discussion around the alchemical pro-

duction of life then shifted to consider whether the alchemist's creation is infused with a rational soul; Newman, *Promethean Ambitions*, 164–237. I take up the question of gender and sexuality in alchemical reproduction in Chapter 4. For the interpenetration of the golem story and theories of the alchemical homunculus, see Campbell, "Artificial Men." For discussions of the golem's ensoulment in thinkers influenced by Hermeticism and Christian Kabbalah, see Idel, "Hermeticism and Judaism."

144. Naudé, *History of Magick*, 249 (R5r).

145. Idel, *Golem*, 182.

146. Joseph Solomon Delmedigo, *Matsref la-Hokhmah* (Odessa: Belinson, 1864), 10a; quoted and translated in Scholem, *On the Kabbalah and Its Symbolism*, 199.

147. Shakespeare's use of Agrippa's *Occult Philosophy* is pointed out by Frank Kermode in his Second Arden edition of *The Tempest* (London: Methuen, 1954), xlviii–li, 142–43. Frances Yates argues, "Of the two branches, Magia and Cabala, set out in [*Occult Philosophy*], Prospero would seem to use mainly the Cabalistic conjuring magic"; see Yates, *Majesty and Magic in Shakespeare's Last Plays: A New Approach to* Cymbeline, Henry VIII, *and* The Tempest (London: Routledge and Kegan Paul, 1975), 94. Yates, *Majesty and Magic*, 95–96, 117–26, makes the case for Prospero as based on Dee and for *The Tempest* as a bookend to *The Alchemist*. For the play's alchemical language and structure and for Prospero as an alchemist, see Peggy Muñoz Simonds, "'My charms crack not': The Alchemical Structure of *The Tempest*," *Comparative Drama* 31 (1997–98): 538–70; and John Mebane, *Renaissance Magic and the Return of the Golden Age: The Occult Tradition and Marlowe, Jonson, and Shakespeare* (Lincoln: University of Nebraska Press, 1989), 181. The foundational text of recent decades on Shakespeare and alchemy is Charles Nicholl, *The Chemical Theatre* (London: Routledge and Kegan Paul, 1980). For Prospero as a Hermetic magus and working magician, see Barbara Mowat, "Prospero, Agrippa, and Hocus Pocus," *English Literary Renaissance* 11 (1981): 281–303; and Barbara Mowat, "Prospero's Book," *Shakespeare Quarterly* 52 (2001): 1–33.

148. Robert Grudin and David Kastan have each argued that Prospero was based in part on the Holy Roman Emperor Rudolf II, whose devotion to alchemical-Hermetic-kabbalistic learning was well known in England, whose court at Prague attracted a glittering array of alchemists, artists, and natural philosophers (including John Dee), and whose slipshod government led to his being deposed by his brother Mathias in 1611, the time of *The Tempest*'s writing. See Robert Grudin, "Rudolf II of Prague and Cornelius Drebbel: Shakespearean Archetypes?" *Huntington Library Quarterly* 54 (1991): 181–205; and David Scott Kastan, *Shakespeare after Theory* (New York: Routledge: 1999), 183–97. Rudolf II's unfitness for rule and deposition were well known to English diplomats on the Continent, as evidenced by dispatches preserved in the British Library's Thomas Edmondes Papers. See, for example, Mss. Stowe 168, fol. 5r–v; Stowe 170, fols. 1r–v, 55r–v, and 93r–v; and Stowe 172, fols. 32r–33r and 90r–91r.

149. Shakespeare has altered the nature of Prospero's servants from his source text in order to emphasize Caliban's earthiness. In Agrippa, *Occult Philosophy*, 257, 533, 536, Ariel is the name given to the principal spirit of the earth, but Shakespeare makes Ariel a spirit

of the air. The other possible source for the name Ariel is not terribly apposite: Isaiah 29:1–8 uses it as a name for the besieged city of Jerusalem. The Geneva Bible, unlike the Coverdale or Bishop's Bible, translates "Ariel" in this verse into "altar."

150. Lupton, *Citizen-Saints*, 165–67.

151. For Adam Kadmon (or Qadmon) and his relationship to the golem, see Scholem, *On the Kabbalah and Its Symbolism*, 159–63; and Idel, *Golem*, 111, 145–46, 148–49.

152. Abraham Abulafia, quoted in Idel, *Kabbalah in Italy*, 240–41.

153. Edmund Spenser, *The Faerie Queene*, ed. A. C. Hamilton, 2nd ed. (Harlow, UK: Longman, 2001), 3.6.48.

154. De León-Jones, "John Dee and the Kabbalah," 150.

155. Eva Johanna Holmberg, *Jews in the Early Modern English Imagination: A Scattered Nation* (Farnham, UK: Ashgate, 2011), 21. For an overview of Jewish demography, migration, and population growth in early modern Europe, see Dean Philip Bell, *Jews in the Early Modern World* (Lanham, MD: Rowman and Littlefield, 2008), 35–92.

156. Lupton, *Citizen-Saints*, 177.

157. James Shapiro, *Shakespeare and the Jews* (New York: Columbia University Press, 1996), 36–37, 171–73, 197.

158. For a reading of *The Tempest* as a "contact zone" in which the racialized colonial subject may be African, Native American, Irish, or other, see Kim F. Hall, *Things of Darkness: Economies of Race and Gender in Early Modern England* (Ithaca, NY: Cornell University Press, 1995), 141–53.

159. Even the Jewish commitment to the sacred text was paradoxically viewed as carnal, since (following Augustine) Christian thinkers viewed Jews as too given to the literal sense of scripture, too bound by the letter of the law. See Achsah Guibbory, *Christian Identity, Jews, and Israel in Seventeenth-Century England* (Oxford: Oxford University Press, 2010), 16–17; and Jeremy Cohen, *Living Letters of the Law: Ideas of the Jew in Medieval Christianity* (Berkeley: University of California Press, 1999), 59–65. For the perception of the "Jew-devil" as existing in a presymbolic mode, see Matthew Biberman, *Masculinity, Anti-Semitism and Early Modern English Literature: From the Satanic to the Effeminate Jew* (Aldershot, UK: Ashgate, 2004), 7–46.

160. Stephen Greenblatt, *Learning to Curse: Essays in Early Modern Culture* (New York: Routledge, 1990), 16–39.

161. For a history of the critical "Americanization" of Caliban through the 1980s, see Alden T. Vaughan and Virginia Mason Vaughan, *Shakespeare's Caliban: A Cultural History* (Cambridge: Cambridge University Press, 1991), 118–43. Some critics in the 1990s returned to analyzing the play as a European or Mediterranean power struggle. See Richard Wilson, "Voyage to Tunis: New History and the Old World of *The Tempest*," *ELH* 64 (1997): 333–57; Jerry Brotton, " 'This Tunis, sir, was Carthage': Contesting Colonialism in *The Tempest*," in *Post-Colonial Shakespeares*, ed. Ania Loomba and Martin Orkin (London: Routledge, 1998), 23–42; and Kastan, *Shakespeare after Theory*, 183–89. More recent arguments that *The Tempest* demonstrates the moment at which Europeans attempt to think through the unfixed categories of race, sexuality, and humanity are far more useful

to my own argument. Along with Lupton's *Citizen-Saints*, see Roland Greene, "Island Logic," in *The Tempest and Its Travels*, ed. Peter Hulme and William H. Sherman (Philadelphia: University of Pennsylvania Press, 2000), 138–45; Jonathan Goldberg, *Tempest in the Caribbean* (Minneapolis: University of Minnesota Press, 2004); and especially Richard Halpern, " 'The picture of Nobody': White Cannibalism in *The Tempest*," in *The Production of English Renaissance Culture*, ed. David Lee Miller, Sharon O'Dair, and Harold Weber (Ithaca, NY: Cornell University Press, 1994), 262–92.

162. This slippage is crystallized in *Othello*'s famous typographical crux, in which, depending on whether one reads the Quarto or the First Folio, Othello declares himself either a "base Indian" or a "base Judean," each of whom has thrown away a pearl richer than all his "tribe." A similar slippage may be present in Caliban's name, which could be an instance of kabbalistic triple anagrammatization: not only "Caliban/canibal," but also "Caliban/cabalin."

163. David S. Katz, *Philo-Semitism and the Readmission of the Jews into England, 1603–1655* (Oxford: Clarendon, 1982), 130; Christopher Columbus, *The Diario of Christopher Columbus's First Voyage to America, 1492–1493*, trans. and ed. Oliver Dunn and James E. Kelley, Jr. (Norman: University of Oklahoma Press, 1989), 129.

164. For the suspicion that Jews were cannibals, see Shapiro, *Shakespeare and the Jews*, 89–111.

165. Gregorio Garcia, *Origen de los Indios*, 2nd ed. (Madrid, 1729; facsimile ed., Mexico City: Fondo de Cultura Económica, 1981), 86–91. The theory of the Jewish origin of the native peoples of the Americas was voiced as early as Peter Martyr's *Decades of the New World* (published between 1511 and 1530) and reached a peak in England in the commonwealth period, during which Oliver Cromwell oversaw the readmission of the Jews to England. See Katz, *Philo-Semitism*; Amy H. Sturgis, "Prophesies and Politics: Millenarians, Rabbis, and the Jewish Indian Theory," *The Seventeenth Century* 14 (1999): 15–23; and Tudor Parfitt, *The Lost Tribes of Israel: The History of a Myth* (London: Weidenfeld and Nicolson, 2002), 58–101.

166. Giordano Bruno, *Cabala of Pegasus*, 40, argues that the Israelites were enslaved in Egypt because the "Hebrews by nature" are "a people always cowardly, servile, mercenary, solitary, incommunicative, and unsociable with other peoples." This point of view goes beyond Roman Catholic canon law, which consigned Jews to perpetual servitude based on their guilt for Christ's death; see Anna Foa, *The Jews of Europe after the Black Death*, trans. Andrea Grover (Berkeley: University of California Press, 2000), 27–28.

167. Goldberg, *Tempest in the Caribbean*, 120–24.

168. Hugh Broughton, *A Require of Agreement to the Grounds of Divinitie Studies* (London, 1611), A1v.

169. Josten, "Dee's *Monas Hieroglyphica*," 137. Both Harkness, *Dee's Conversations*, 150–52, and Jones, *Discovery of Hebrew*, 173–74, argue that Dee uses Kabbalah to promote an ultratolerant, universalized Christianity that would convert the Jews in the process. See Dee, *Actions with Spirits*, 1:168.

170. These palindromic syllables are noticeable in part because of the infrequency with which Shakespeare uses the word *own* as a verb or as the root of a participle. According to the Northwestern University WordHoard software tool (http://www.wordhoard .northwestern.edu, accessed 18 August 2014), *own* appears as a verb or participial root, rather than as an adjective, only six times in Shakespeare. In all of Shakespeare's works, *know* and *own* are paralleled as verbs only here.

171. Jeffrey S. Shoulson, *Milton and the Rabbis: Hebraism, Hellenism, and Christianity* (New York: Columbia University Press, 2001), 76. Halpern's account of *The Tempest* as an attempt to absorb New World culture, then to "disappear" that culture as if it were never part of either the colonialist imaginary or the humanist vision of the New World as golden world, is pertinent to my reading here; Halpern, "The picture of Nobody."

172. Barbara Mowat, "'Knowing I loved my books': Reading *The Tempest* Intertextually," in The Tempest *and Its Travels*, ed. Hulme and Sherman, 27–36; see also Jonathan Bate, *Shakespeare and Ovid* (Oxford: Clarendon, 1993), 252.

173. Kearney, *Incarnate Text*, 178–79.

174. Pico, *900 Theses*, 134.

175. Halpern, "The picture of Nobody."

176. J. H. Lupton, *A Life of John Colet D.D.* (London: George Bell, 1887), 225–26.

177. See Steven Shapin, "The House of Experiment in Seventeenth-Century England," in *The Scientific Enterprise in Early Modern Europe: Readings from* Isis, ed. Peter Dear (Chicago: University of Chicago Press, 1997), 273–304; Lisa Jardine, *Ingenious Pursuits: Building the Scientific Revolution* (New York: Doubleday, 1999).

178. *OED Online*, s.v. "project, n.," 2a, last modified June 2007, accessed 18 August 2014, http://0-www.oed.com.libraries.colorado.edu/view/Entry/152265.

179. For example, *The Mirror of Alchemy* attributed to Roger Bacon defines alchemy as "a science teaching how to make and compound a certaine medicine, which is called Elixir, the which when it is cast upon mettals or imperfect bodies, doth fully perfect them in the verie projection"; Bacon [attrib.], *Mirror of Alchimy*, 1 (A3v).

180. Pamela H. Smith, *The Business of Alchemy: Science and Culture in the Holy Roman Empire* (Princeton, NJ: Princeton University Press, 1994), 269; see also Abraham, *Dictionary of Alchemical Imagery*, 157–58.

181. For the sixteenth- and seventeenth-century mania for "projects" as constructive, commercial, and/or shady enterprises, see Joan Thirsk, *Economic Policy and Projects: The Development of a Consumer Society in Early Modern England* (Oxford: Clarendon, 1978). One of Thirsk's earliest examples of an English "project" is the formation by Queen Elizabeth I's top courtiers (Burghley, Leicester, etc.) of the alchemical and metallurgical "Society of the New Art," whose project was "transmuting iron, lead, and other mineral ores into copper and quicksilver" (11–12).

182. Simonds describes the quite detailed alchemical terminology included in these and the following lines; see Simonds, "My charms crack not." Vaughan and Vaughan note in their edition of the play that Prospero's project's "gather[ing] to a head" refers to the alchemical boil (*Tempest*, 5.1.1n).

183. *Love's Labour's Lost* is often also identified as a play for which Shakespeare did not draw on the plot of a prior work, but its opening situation and its ensuing concerns, as I discuss in Chapter 4, are heavily indebted to Pierre de la Primaudaye's *L'academie Française*, published in English translation in 1586.

4. HOW TO AVOID GYNECOLOGY

1. Ben Jonson, *Mercury Vindicated from the Alchemists at Court*, in *Ben Jonson: The Complete Masques*, ed. Stephen Orgel (New Haven, CT: Yale University Press, 1969), lines 99, 161–62, 172–73. All subsequent references to Ben Jonson's masques are to this edition and will be cited parenthetically in the text by line number.

2. For the push and pull in early modern medicine between empirical evidence and the humanistic reading of classical texts, see, for example, Siraisi, *History, Medicine*; Peter Dear, *Revolutionizing the Sciences: European Knowledge and Its Ambitions, 1500–1700*, 2nd ed. (Princeton, NJ: Princeton University Press, 2009), 36–40; Harold J. Cook, "Medicine," in *The Cambridge History of Science*, vol. 3: *Early Modern Science*, ed. Katharine Park and Lorraine Daston (Cambridge: Cambridge University Press, 2006), 407–34; and Vivian Nutton, "The Fortunes of Galen," in *The Cambridge Companion to Galen*, ed. R. J. Hankinson (Cambridge: Cambridge University Press, 2008), 355–90. It must be noted that the drive toward empiricism was prompted not only by challenges to Galen but by Galen himself—who, in newly rediscovered and/or edited texts, prompted an increased emphasis on empiricism and anatomical dissection; see Nutton, "Fortunes of Galen," 374–75. Andrea Carlino makes the important point that humanist rhetoric, not merely humanist reading practice, was important to medical humanism; see Carlino, "Medical Humanism, Rhetoric, and Anatomy at Padua, circa 1540," in *Rhetoric and Medicine in Early Modern Europe*, ed. Stephen Pender and Nancy S. Struever (Farnham, UK: Ashgate, 2012), 111–28.

3. D. E. Eichholz, "Aristotle's Theory of the Formation of Metals and Minerals," *Classical Quarterly* 43 (1949): 141–46.

4. Newman, *Promethean Ambitions*, 169–71.

5. Sally G. Allen and Joanna Hubbs, "Outrunning Atalanta: Feminine Destiny in Alchemical Transmutation," *Signs* 6 (1980): 220–29; Kathleen P. Long, "Odd Bodies: Reviewing Corporeal Difference in Early Modern Alchemy," in *Gender and Scientific Discourse in Early Modern Culture*, ed. Kathleen P. Long (Farnham, UK: Ashgate, 2010), 63–85.

6. Allison B. Kavey, "Mercury Falling: Gender Malleability and Sexual Fluidity in Early Modern Popular Alchemy," in *Chymists and Chymistry*, ed. Principe, 125–35.

7. Hanegraaff, *Esotericism*, 42, questions the accuracy of this story, which began with Paul Oskar Kristeller and was widely disseminated by Frances Yates.

8. Brian P. Copenhaver, trans. and ed., "Introduction," in Copenhaver, *Hermetica: The Greek* Corpus Hermeticum *and the Latin* Asclepius *in a New English Translation, with*

Notes and Introduction (Cambridge: Cambridge University Press, 1992), xlvii–l. The *Asclepius* had been the subject of considerable commentary since the twelfth century. The "Pimander" tractate is also known as the "Poemander" or "Poemadres."

9. Copenhaver, *Hermetica*, 4.

10. Ibid., 75.

11. Ibid., 79.

12. Joan Cadden, *Meanings of Sex Difference in the Middle Ages: Medicine, Science, and Culture* (Cambridge: Cambridge University Press, 1993), 13–53, 105–63. For the classical background, see especially Thomas Laqueur, *Making Sex: Body and Gender from the Greeks to Freud* (Cambridge, MA: Harvard University Press, 1990), 25–43. Laqueur makes the point that even though Aristotle sees an absolute physical distinction between the two sexes, he is less interested in that physical distinction than he is in a continuum of activity and passivity that comprises both sexes. Aristotle thus uses the rhetoric of one sex, no matter his physiological model (28–32). Neither Aristotle nor Galen, nor the medieval and early modern Aristotle-Galen hybrid, of course, describes the totality of even academic approaches to gender difference and biological reproduction in the Middle Ages and Renaissance, much less vernacular approaches. I take up some important early modern objections to both Aristotle and Galen below.

13. Bacon, *Mirror of Alchimy*, 16 (C2v). For medieval Latin versions of the *Emerald Tablet* see Tenney L. Davis, "The Emerald Table of Hermes Trismegistus: Three Latin Versions Which Were Current Among Later Alchemists," *Journal of Chemical Education* 3 (1926): 863–75.

14. Bacon, *Mirror of Alchimy*, 20–21 (C4v–D1r).

15. Kathleen P. Long, *Hermaphrodites in Renaissance Europe* (Aldershot, UK: Ashgate, 2006), 111–16. Leah DeVun details how the alchemical hermaphrodite dovetails with an image of Christ as hermaphrodite that began to take hold in the High Middle Ages; see DeVun, "The Jesus Hermaphrodite: Science and Sex Difference in Premodern Europe," *Journal of the History of Ideas* 69 (2008): 193–218. The confusion over the relative powers of masculine, feminine, and/or hermaphroditic elements in the alchemical process contributes to the difficulty of discerning the sex of the various humans and creatures depicted in alchemical illustrations. See M. E. Warlick, "Fluctuating Identities: Gender Reversals in Alchemical Imagery," in *Art and Alchemy*, ed. Wamberg, 103–28.

16. Abraham, *Dictionary of Alchemical Imagery*, 153.

17. *Menstruum* was associated with female menstruation in classical Latin, and seems to have been transferred to alchemy as *solvent* only in the late Middle Ages; see *OED Online*, s.v. "menstruum, n.," etymology, last modified September 2001, accessed 18 August 2014, http://0-www.oed.com.libraries.colorado.edu/view/Entry/116522. Aristotle posits that "the natural substance of the menstrual fluid," the passive component contributed by the woman to conception, "is to be classed as 'prime matter'"; see Aristotle, *Generation of Animals*, trans. A. L. Peck (Cambridge, MA: Harvard University Press, 1942), 729a30.

18. See Linden, *Darke Hieroglyphicks*, 17.

19. The apparatus of alchemy lent itself to images of human reproduction. Called, among other things, a "body," a "womb," or an "egg," the vessel in which the substances to be purified were heated had a round womblike shape with a slender outlet called the "neck" (Abraham, *Dictionary of Alchemical Imagery*, 6, 50, 66–67, 219). Whereas the "neck" of the womb generally designates the cervix in early modern anatomical usage, Helkiah Crooke applies "neck" to the vagina; see Crooke, *Mikrokosmographia: A Description of the Body of Man* (London, 1615), 216 (T6v). For the prevalence of egg-as-flask imagery in early modern engravings and paintings, see Smith, *Body of the Artisan*, 129–40. For a compilation of sources for alchemical *coniunctio* and gender it is still difficult to beat C. J. Jung, *Mysterium coniunctionis: An Inquiry into the Separation and Synthesis of Psychic Opposites in Alchemy*, trans. R. F. C. Hull, 2nd ed. (Princeton, NJ: Princeton University Press, 1970). Pinkus, *Alchemical Mercury*, 66–89, argues that the chemical wedding is not about gender so much as it is about the nature of coupling (in the abstract) and of ambivalence.

20. Ripley, *Compound of Alchymy*, 56. For a concise summary of alchemical endorsements of an Aristotelian-Galenic reproductive scheme and gender hierarchy, see Nancy Tuana, *The Less Noble Sex: Scientific, Religious, and Philosophical Conceptions of Women's Nature* (Bloomington: Indiana University Press, 1993), 25–34.

21. Ripley, *Compound of Alchemy*, 62.

22. Bacon, *Mirror of Alchimy*, 6 (B1v).

23. Paracelsus, *The Aurora of the Philosophers*, in *The Hermetic and Alchemical Writings of Aureolus Philippus Theophrastus Bombast, of Hohenheim, Called Paracelsus the Great*, ed. Arthur E. Waite (London: James Elliott, 1894), 1:66. Paracelsian ideas on generation were spread chiefly by Peter Severinus, whose *Idea medicinae philosophicae* appeared in 1571. See Walter Pagel, *William Harvey's Biological Ideas: Selected Aspects and Historical Background* (New York: Hafner, 1967), 239–47.

24. Paracelsus, *Aurora of the Philosophers*, in *Hermetic and Alchemical Writings*, 1:65–66.

25. Pagel, *Paracelsus*, 78–80, 85–88. For the role of the hermaphrodite in Paracelsus's alchemy, see Long, *Hermaphrodites*, 116–28. Recent analysis of Paracelsus's skeletal remains suggests Paracelsus himself was intersexed; Newman, *Promethean Ambitions*, 196–97.

26. Amy Eisen Cislo, *Paracelsus's Theory of Embodiment: Conception and Gestation in Early Modern Europe* (London: Pickering and Chatto, 2010), 22–36. Bruce T. Moran argues that Paracelsus's "seed" theory contributed not only to Jean Baptiste van Helmont's vitalism but also to late seventeenth-century advances in understanding female reproductive anatomy; see Moran, *Distilling Knowledge*, 89–98.

27. For the controversy over the authenticity of *De natura rerum*, see Newman, *Promethean Ambitions*, 199n58. The work has been variously identified as genuinely Paracelsian, as pseudo-Paracelsian, and as a reworking of a genuinely Paracelsian text. In my own text, I identify the author as "Pseudo-Paracelsus" in order to make clear that *De natura rerum* is not known with certainty to be by Paracelsus.

28. Paracelsus, *Of the Nature of Things*, 8 (Aa4v).

29. Newman, *Promethean Ambitions*, 202, 204, 218.

30. Ibid., 204. For *De natura rerum*'s diminution of the feminine role in conception, see also Long, *Hermaphrodites*, 120–28.

31. Laqueur, *Making Sex*, 40; Clara Pinto-Correia, *The Ovary of Eve: Egg and Sperm and Preformation* (Chicago: University of Chicago Press, 1997), 256–61.

32. Andreas Vesalius, *On the Fabric of the Human Body, Book V: The Organs of Nutrition and Generation*, trans. William Frank Richardson (Novato, CA: Norman, 2007), 186–87.

33. R. H. F. Hunter, *Physiology of the Graafian Follicle and Ovulation* (Cambridge: Cambridge University Press, 2003), 5.

34. Katharine Park, *Secrets of Women: Gender, Generation, and the Origins of Human Dissection* (New York: Zone Books, 2006), 213–16, 219.

35. Vivian Nutton, "Historical Introduction," in Andreas Vesalius, *Of the Fabric of the Human Body*, trans. and ed. Daniel Garrison and Malcolm Hast, 2003, accessed 18 August 2014, http://vesalius.northwestern.edu.

36. In 1672, Dutch anatomist Regnier de Graaf described the fallopian tubes as the passages through which an egg made its way to the uterus; see Hunter, *Graafian Follicle*, 3–11.

37. Eve Keller, *Generating Bodies and Gendered Selves: The Rhetoric of Reproduction in Early Modern England* (Seattle: University of Washington Press, 2007), 72–73; Laura Gowing, *Common Bodies: Women, Touch and Power in Seventeenth-Century England* (New Haven, CT: Yale University Press, 2003), 19.

38. For Vesalius's many corrections to Galen based upon dissection see, e.g., Andrea Carlino, *Books of the Body: Anatomical Ritual and Renaissance Learning*, trans. John Tedeschi and Anne C. Tedeschi (Chicago: University of Chicago Press, 1999), 202–7.

39. Mary E. Fissell, *Vernacular Bodies: The Politics of Reproduction in Early Modern England* (Oxford: Oxford University Press, 2004).

40. Janet Adelman, "Making Defect Perfection: Shakespeare and the One-Sex Model," in *Enacting Gender on the English Renaissance Stage*, ed. Viviana Comensoli and Anne Russell (Urbana: University of Illinois Press, 1999), 23–52.

41. See Keller, *Generating Bodies*, 47–70. Winfried Schleiner argues that opposition to Galen was limited and eccentric before the 1595 publication of French physician André Dulaurens's *Historia anatomica humani corporis*, which influenced Crooke; see Schleiner, "Early Modern Controversies About the One-Sex Model," *Renaissance Quarterly* 53 (2000): 180–91.

42. Crooke, *Mikrokosmographia*, 271 (Aa4r).

43. Jane Sharp, *The Midwives Book, Or the Whole Art of Midwifry Discovered*, ed. Elaine Hobby (New York: Oxford University Press, 1999), 103. According to editor Elaine Hobby, Sharp is echoing Nicholas Culpeper's *A Physical Directory* from 1649 (103n2). For the ways that Sharp, the first woman to author a printed work on reproductive anatomy, reversed the usual Galenic system in order to make the woman the ideal against which

the man is measured, see Caroline Bicks, "Stones Like Women's Paps: Revising Gender in Jane Sharp's *Midwives Book*," *Journal for Early Modern Cultural Studies* 7, no. 2 (2007): 1–27. As Clara Pinto-Correia, *Ovary of Eve*, 16–64, discusses, de Graaf took part in a serious seventeenth-century debate over whether, in fact, it was the female ovary—not the male sperm—that contained the entire form of the child to be, so much so that the entire human race was contained within Eve's ovary. For the early modern suspicion that parthenogenesis was possible for human females—or, at least, that female seed might overwhelm male seed—see Maurizio Calbi, *Approximate Bodies: Gender and Power in Early Modern Drama and Anatomy* (London: Routledge, 2005), 56–70.

44. *Aristotle's Master-piece: Or, the Secrets of Generation* (London, 1690), 111–12.

45. Patricia Parker, "Gender Ideology, Gender Change: The Case of Marie Germain," *Critical Inquiry* 19 (1993): 337–74, quotation on 340. For a trenchant critique of Laqueur and of Stephen Greenblatt's influential analysis of *Twelfth Night* based on Laqueur (Greenblatt, "Fiction and Friction," in *Shakespearean Negotiations: The Circulation of Social Energy in Renaissance England* [Berkeley: University of California Press, 1988], 66–93), see Valerie Traub, *The Renaissance of Lesbianism in Early Modern England* (Cambridge: Cambridge University Press, 2002), 191–97.

46. Keller, *Generating Bodies*, 101–24.

47. John Rogers, *The Matter of Revolution: Science, Poetry, and Politics in the Age of Milton* (Ithaca, NY: Cornell University Press, 1996), 119–20. Rogers's argument is that Harvey's account of nonseminal reproduction might, by extension, go so far as to undermine even the monarchical authority to which the royalist Harvey was so committed.

48. William Harvey, *Anatomical Exercitations Concerning the Generation of Living Creatures* (London, 1653), 543 (Mm8r). All subsequent references to Harvey's *De generatione*, unless otherwise specified, are to this translation and will be cited parenthetically in the text. John Rumrich argues that the fact that Harvey does not think the semen enters the uterus grants unusual generative power to the woman; see Rumrich, *Milton Unbound: Controversy and Reinterpretation* (Cambridge: Cambridge University Press, 1996), 103–7. I believe Rumrich has uncharacteristically misread the same passage that I quote when he argues that Harvey "makes the womb the equal of the brain" (104). Harvey's analogy is this: the artist's brain is to his artistic work as the "genitor's" (father's) idea is to the fetus. The uterus contains the fetus, but the uterus does not think. See Keller, *Generating Bodies*, 119–20, 214n31.

49. For Harvey's debt to Aristotle's theories of generation, see Pagel, *Harvey's Biological Ideas*, 234–37, 251–78.

50. For example, Crooke, *Mikrokosmographia*, 262 (Z5v), contends that in pregnant women, "the mouth or orifice of the wombe is so exquisitely shut and locked up that it will not admit the poynt of a needle." Harvey notes of the cervix of the female hind that "this is that Orifice, which Physitians affirm to be so closely compressed, sealed up, and concluded in a Virgin, and Woman with child, that it will not admit the point of the finest Needle" (400 [Cc8v]). It is possible that Crooke and Harvey are citing some common source, but it is far more likely that Harvey used Crooke, whose *Microcosmographia* was

published in five editions between 1615 and 1651, the year of the first edition of Harvey's *De generatione*.

51. Rogers, *Matter of Revolution*, 16–38; see also Pagel, *Harvey's Biological Ideas*, 251–65.

52. For the ways Harvey's theories of blood drew from Paracelsianism, see Pagel, *Harvey's Biological Ideas*, 94–103; and Peter Mitchell, *The Purple Island and Anatomy in Early Seventeenth-Century Literature, Philosophy, and Theology* (Madison, NJ: Fairleigh Dickinson University Press/Associated University Presses, 2007), 331–34. For the general influence of alchemy on various seventeenth-century theories of the mechanics and function of the blood, see Allen G. Debus, *Chemistry, Alchemy and the New Philosophy, 1550–1700: Studies in the History of Science and Medicine* (London: Variorum Reprints/Ashgate, 1987), 245–63.

53. For Harvey's replacement of Paracelsian spirit with blood, see Pagel, *Harvey's Biological Ideas*, 255.

54. Mitchell, *The Purple Island and Anatomy*, 331–34.

55. Gail Kern Paster argues that part of the reason Harvey was able to meet objections to his theory of the circulation of the blood was that, although he rejected the humoral theory of the refinement of the blood, he retained "refinement" as metaphor rather than fact; see Paster, *The Body Embarrassed: Drama and the Disciplines of Shame in Early Modern England* (Ithaca, NY: Cornell University Press, 1993), 72–73. Harvey's simultaneous exclusion of material substance from the womb and conversion of blood in the womb to "spirit" recalls, to some extent, Paracelsus's musings upon uterine conception as derived not from maternal fecundity but from a link between the minds of the couple and the mind of God; see Cislo, *Paracelsus's Theory of Embodiment*, 23–24.

56. See Jean Fernel, *Jean Fernel's On the Hidden Causes of Things: Forms, Souls and Occult Diseases in Renaissance Medicine*, ed. John M. Forrester and John Henry (Leiden: Brill, 2005), 681.

57. Elizabeth Spiller, *Science, Reading, and Renaissance Literature: The Art of Making Knowledge, 1580–1670* (Cambridge: Cambridge University Press, 2004), 91.

58. William Harvey, *Exercitationes de generatione animalium* (London, 1651), frontispiece.

59. Harvey's essay "Of Conception," appended to *De generatione*, recapitulates his avoidance of any feminine influence upon conception by cementing his commitment to the fictional. Like *De generatione*, "Of Conception" discounts feminine agency in conception, transfers responsibility for all postcoital creativity to the male, and repeats Harvey's analogy between reproductive conception and mental conception. Harvey then notes that this analogy is a mere fiction: "Aristotle saith, That Philosophers are in some sort lovers of Fables, because a Fable doth consist of strange things. . . . I plainly see that nothing at all doth remain in the Uterus after coition, whereunto I might ascribe the principle of generation; no more then remains in the braine after sensation, and experience, whereunto the principle of Art may be reduced; but finding the constitution to be alike in both, I have invented this Fable" (546 [Nn1v]).

60. Laqueur, *Making Sex*, 142–48. For *De generatione*'s noninfluence see Spiller, *Science, Reading, and Renaissance Literature*, 86–87.

61. Cavell, *Disowning Knowledge*, 94.

62. For these connections between Harvey's blood-circulation theory and his embryology I am indebted to Keller's brilliant account in *Generating Bodies*, 101–24. Like Keller, I am in turn indebted to Rogers's account in *Matter of Revolution*, 16–27, of Harvey's blood-circulation theory as tending—quite against Harvey's royalist sympathies—to promote the protoliberal, individualized self, independent of hierarchical authority.

63. Cavell, *Disowning Knowledge*, 10, 13.

64. Will Fisher, *Materializing Gender in Early Modern English Literature and Culture* (Cambridge: Cambridge University Press, 2006), 68–74; Jean Howard and Phyllis Rackin, *Engendering a Nation: A Feminist Account of Shakespeare's English Histories* (London: Routledge, 1997), 187–88.

65. Jonathan Sawday, *The Body Emblazoned: Dissection and the Human Body in Renaissance Culture* (London: Routledge, 1995), 245. See also Martina Mittag, *Gendered Spaces: Wandel des "Weiblichen" im englischen Diskurs der frühen Neuzeit* (Tübingen: Narr, 2002), 89–95.

66. Sawday, *Body Emblazoned*, 225.

67. Crooke, *Mikrokosmographia*, 197 (S3r).

68. Traub, *Renaissance of Lesbianism*, 122.

69. Johann Remmelin, *Catoptrum microcosmicum* (Augsburg, 1619).

70. Johann Remmelin, *An Exact Survey of the Microcosmus or Little World* (London, 1670), Wellcome Library EPB F.2277.

71. See Valerie Traub, "Gendering Mortality in Early Modern Anatomies," in *Feminist Readings of Early Modern Culture: Emerging Subjects*, ed. Valerie Traub, M. Lindsay Kaplan, and Dympna Callaghan (Cambridge: Cambridge University Press, 1996), 44–92, esp. 80–81.

72. Crooke, *Mikrokosmographia*, 197 (S3r).

73. For Pythagoreanism in the Renaissance, including its use by Spenser, see S. K. Heninger, *Touches of Sweet Harmony: Pythagorean Cosmology and Renaissance Poetics* (San Marino, CA: Huntington Library, 1974); for Neoplatonism in Spenser, see especially Jon Quitslund, *Spenser's Supreme Fiction: Platonic Natural Philosophy and* The Faerie Queene (Toronto: University of Toronto Press, 2001); and for Hermeticism in *The Faerie Queene*, see Douglas Brooks-Davies, *The Mercurian Monarch: Magical Politics from Spenser to Pope* (Manchester, UK: Manchester University Press, 1983), 11–84. For the body of Alma's castle as female, see Dorothy Stephens, *The Limits of Eroticism in Post-Petrarchan Narrative: Conditional Pleasure from Spenser to Marvell* (Cambridge: Cambridge University Press, 1998), 46–61.

74. Edmund Spenser, *The Faerie Queene*, ed. A. C. Hamilton, 2nd ed. (Harlow, UK: Longman, 2001), 3.6.43, 47–48; all subsequent references to this poem are to this edition and will be cited parenthetically in the text by book, canto, and stanza numbers. The vagueness of reproductive function in the Garden of Adonis is a subset of what Harry

Berger, Jr., identifies as the vagueness of form in the garden; see "Spenser's Gardens of Adonis: Force and Form in the Renaissance Imagination," in *Revisionary Play: Studies in the Spenserian Dynamics* (Berkeley: University of California Press, 1988), 131–53. For a splendid analysis of the ambiguity of male and female sexual traits and roles in the Garden of Adonis, see Anderson, *Allegorical Intertext*, 214–23.

75. For a discussion of how Alma's house "avoids" the genitals, see David Lee Miller, *The Poem's Two Bodies: The Poetics of the 1590* Faerie Queen (Princeton, NJ: Princeton University Press, 1988), 164–91.

76. "Aqua aeris. . . . Ipsa enim aqua solvit corpus in spiritum, & de mortuo facit vivum, & facit matrimonium inter viram & mulierem"; Michael Maier, *Atalanta fugiens* (Oppenheim, 1618), Dd2r; my translation.

77. No doubt Archimago designs this alchemically fleshed-out vision in part to mollify Redcrosse's gynephobic nightmare of what Una looks like under her skirt. For Redcrosse's displacement of the guilt of sexuality onto Una and Duessa, see Harry Berger, Jr., "Displacing Autophobia in *Faerie Queene* I: Ethics, Gender, and Oppositional Reading in the Spenserian Text," *English Literary Renaissance* 28 (1998): 163–82.

78. Abraham, *Dictionary of Alchemical Imagery*, 174. Robert M. Schuler notes that Spenser's "'virgin wex' may be an ironic glance at the mysterious but wonder-working *lac virginis* (virgin's milk) of the alchemists, and refers to an Elizabethan manuscript alchemical poem that claims that "Lac virgynen / [is] cauled virgins wax in our englysh tonge" (British Library Ashmole 1480, fol. 72a); see Schuler, "Alchemy," in *The Spenser Encyclopedia*, ed. A. C. Hamilton (Toronto: University of Toronto Press, 1990), 12–14, quotation on 13. Positing that the "burning lamps" used in False Florimell's construction signify sulfur, Alexandra Block and Eric Rothstein point out that vermilion, mercuric sulfide, is created by the compounding of mercury and sulfur. Block and Rothstein also collect a number of other ways in which False Florimell's career has alchemical associations; see "Argument and 'Representation' in *The Faerie Queene*, Book III," *Spenser Studies* 19 (2004): 177–207, esp. 183–84, 203n15.

79. *OED Online*, s.v. "franion, n.," last modified 1897, accessed 18 August 2014, http://0-www.oed.com.libraries.colorado.edu/view/Entry/74205. As far as I can determine, Spenser was the only sixteenth- or seventeenth-century English author to have applied the term *franion* not to a roistering man but to a loose woman.

80. Because the very existence and the meaning of the hymen were under debate in the early modern period, Artegall's suggestion of stripping the two Florimells would lead only to more epistemological quandaries. Margaret W. Ferguson argues that early modern literature uses the hymen "as focus for an instructional discourse on what constitutes proper masculine and feminine behavior at the threshold of the marital relation"; see Ferguson, "Hymeneal Instruction," in *Masculinities, Childhood, Violence: Attending to Early Modern Women—and Men*, ed. Amy E. Leonard and Karen L. Nelson (Plymouth, UK: Rowman and Littlefield, 2011), 97–130, quotation on 98.

81. William Shakespeare, *Hamlet*, ed. Harold Jenkins (London: Methuen, 1982), 3.2.117–19.

82. The only possible other instance of this joke on feminine "nothingness" I have located in *The Faerie Queene* is similarly attached to the false feminine, when the Palmer (perhaps incorrectly) suspects a siren-like woman who calls to Guyon for succor of being "*inly nothing* ill apayd, / But onely womanish fine forgery" (2.12.28; emphasis added). As I have noted elsewhere, I do not agree with Jonathan Goldberg's argument that Amoret's being restored as "perfect Whole" in the 1590 ending of book 3 constitutes a pun on femininity as vacuity or nothingness. See Jonathan Goldberg, *Endlesse Worke: Spenser and the Structures of Discourse* (Baltimore: Johns Hopkins University Press, 1981), 11; and Katherine Eggert, "Spenser's Ravishment: Rape and Rapture in *The Faerie Queene*," *Representations* 70 (2000): 1–26.

83. For an insightful discussion of how the prospects of knowing feminine anatomy also denote the pleasures and terrors of subjectivity, see Katharine Eisaman Maus, *Inwardness and Theater in the English Renaissance* (Chicago: University of Chicago Press, 1995), 182–209.

84. Brooks-Davies, *Mercurian Monarch*, 56–63, briefly discusses the alchemical valence of the Isis Church episode in his reading of *The Faerie Queene* as promoting a Hermetic sovereignty for England.

85. The Nile is metaphorically associated, for example, with the spontaneous generations of both Errour's brood and Chrysogone's pregnancy (1.1.21, 3.6.6–8). A slight alchemical tinge is added in the latter case by Chrysogone's name ("golden-born") and the Danae-like circumstances of her insemination, which hint that "Nilus inundation" in her case might turn the warmth of the sun to gold.

86. I have argued elsewhere that the mission in progress for Britomart at this point, her rescue of Artegall, draws from Isis's restoration of her husband's phallic power in Plutarch's *Of Isis and Osiris*; see Katherine Eggert, *Showing Like a Queen: Female Authority and Literary Experiment in Spenser, Shakespeare, and Milton* (Philadelphia: University of Pennsylvania Press, 2000), 41.

87. The hermaphroditic Venus in book 4's temple bears some resemblance to Britomart's dream in book 5 in that the feet and legs of book 4's Venus are "twyned . . . with a snake" (4.10.40). While this Venus is not alchemical, (s)he partakes of some of the same pool of Hermetic imagery that we see in Isis Church. The hermaphrodite formed by the embrace of Amoret and Scudamour in the 1590 ending of book 3 is primarily Ovidian, with no alchemical elements. Nevertheless, it is worth noting that alchemists made much of the fact that Ovid's Hermaphroditus is the son of Mercury.

88. Michael Maier, *Arcana arcanissima* (London, 1613), 33 (F1r). For alchemical crocodiles and kindred serpentine creatures, see Lyndy Abraham, "Alchemical Reference in *Antony and Cleopatra*," *Sydney Studies in English* 8 (1982): 100–104; and Laurence A. Breiner, "The Career of the Cockatrice," *Isis* 70 (1979): 30–47.

89. See Stanton J. Linden, "Alchemical Art and the Renaissance Emblem," in *Secret Texts: The Literature of Secret Societies*, ed. Marie Mulvey Roberts and Hugh Ormsby-Lennon (New York: AMS, 1995), 7–23.

90. Simonds, "My charms crack not."

91. Spiller, *Science, Reading, and Renaissance Literature*, 59–100.

92. Lowell Gallagher, *Medusa's Gaze: Casuistry and Conscience in the Renaissance* (Stanford, CA: Stanford University Press, 1991), 170.

93. Stephens, *Limits of Eroticism*, 81–89; Eggert, *Showing Like a Queen*, 22–50.

94. Lorraine Daston and Katharine Park, *Wonders and the Order of Nature, 1150–1750* (New York: Zone Books, 1998), 220. See also Mary Baine Campbell, *Wonder and Science: Imagining Worlds in Early Modern Europe* (Ithaca, NY: Cornell University Press, 1999), 2–9.

95. René Descartes, *The Passions of the Soul*, article 53, in *Philosophical Writings*, 1:350.

96. Sawday, *Body Emblazoned*, 231, associates the rise of science in the late seventeenth century with the suppression of the feminine, and he rightly credits Descartes's "mechanic philosophy" with encouraging the "conscious deployment of a gendered language of discovery" that enforced the image of the examined world as a subservient, submissive, and lesser body. But R. W. Hepburn, following Ludwig Wittgenstein, proposes that wonder is not incompatible with the causal explanations that are the grounds of modern science. If, for example, the object of wonder is "the sheer existence of a world," then "there is no good reason after all why that existential wonder should seem threatened by the network of causal relationships among the world's constituents"; see Hepburn, *"Wonder" and Other Essays: Eight Studies in Aesthetics and Neighbouring Fields* (Edinburgh: Edinburgh University Press, 1984), 140.

97. Descartes, *Passions of the Soul*, article 72, in *Philosophical Writings*, 1:354.

98. Luce Irigaray, *An Ethics of Sexual Difference*, trans. Carolyn Burke and Gillian C. Gill (Ithaca, NY: Cornell University Press, 1984), 75.

99. Grant Williams, "Early Modern Blazons and the Rhetoric of Wonder: Turning Towards an Ethics of Sexual Difference," in *Luce Irigaray and Premodern Culture: Thresholds of History*, ed. Theresa Krier and Elizabeth D. Harvey (London: Routledge, 2004), 126–37.

100. Traub, *Renaissance of Lesbianism*, 188–228.

101. Ibid., 195–97; Katharine Park, "The Rediscovery of the Clitoris: French Medicine and the Tribade, 1570–1630," in *The Body in Parts: Fantasies of Corporeality in Early Modern Europe*, ed. David Hillman and Carla Mazzio (New York: Routledge, 1997), 171–93; Bettina Mathes, "As Long as a Swan's Neck? The Significance of the 'Enlarged' Clitoris for Early Modern Anatomy," in *Sensible Flesh: On Touch in Early Modern Culture*, ed. Elizabeth D. Harvey (Philadelphia: University of Pennsylvania Press, 2003), 103–24.

102. Eggert, "Spenser's Ravishment."

103. Mazzio, *Inarticulate Renaissance*, 147–62. *Love's Labour's Lost*'s mockery of humanist rhetoric is the basis for assertions that the play satirizes this or that academic circle. Perhaps the Ralegh group, say M. C. Bradbrook in *The School of Night: A Study in the Literary Relationships of Sir Walter Ralegh* (Cambridge: Cambridge University Press, 1936) and Frances Yates in *A Study of* Love's Labour's Lost (Cambridge: Cambridge University Press, 1936). Or perhaps the scholars gathered by Henri IV of France, says Richard David in William Shakespeare, *Love's Labour's Lost*, ed. Richard David (London: Methuen, 1956), xxix. For the play as a rejection of the last gasps of scholasticism, see Eric C. Brown, "Shake-

speare's Anxious Epistemology: *Love's Labor's Lost* and Marlowe's *Doctor Faustus*," *Texas Studies in Literature and Language* 45 (2003): 20–41.

104. Jardine, *Ingenious Pursuits.*

105. Shapin, "House of Experiment."

106. See Michelle O'Callaghan, *The English Wits: Literature and Sociability in Early Modern England* (Cambridge: Cambridge University Press, 2007); and Andrew Barnaby and Lisa J. Schnell, *Literate Experience: The Work of Knowing in Seventeenth-Century English Writing* (New York: Palgrave Macmillan, 2002).

107. Steven Shapin and Simon Schaffer, *Leviathan and the Air-Pump: Hobbes, Boyle, and the Experimental Life*, 2nd ed. (Princeton, NJ: Princeton University Press, 2011), 113–14. For the coercive group work of humanism, see, e.g., Rebecca Bushnell, *A Culture of Teaching: Early Modern Humanism in Theory and Practice* (Ithaca, NY: Cornell University Press, 1996); and Alan Stewart, *Close Readers: Humanism and Sodomy in Early Modern England* (Princeton, NJ: Princeton University Press, 1997).

108. Nancy Tuana, "Coming to Understand: Orgasm and the Epistemology of Ignorance," in *Agnotology*, ed. Proctor and Schiebinger, 108–45; Malin Ah-King, Andrew B. Barron, and Marie E. Herberstein, "Genital Evolution: Why Are Females Still Understudied?" *PLoS Biology* 12, no. 5 (2014): 1–7.

109. Lynn Enterline, *Shakespeare's Schoolroom: Rhetoric, Discipline, Emotion* (Philadelphia: University of Pennsylvania Press, 2012), 62–94.

110. While it is unclear whether these men all knew each other, a chain of associations among them, their writings, and their interests makes it not unreasonable to connect them. See Mark Thornton Burnett, "Chapman, George (1559/60–1634)," *Oxford Dictionary of National Biography*, online edition (Oxford: Oxford University Press, 2004), May 2006, accessed 18 August 2014, http://www.oxforddnb.com/view/article/5118.

111. William Shakespeare, *Love's Labour's Lost*, ed. H. R. Woudhuysen (Walton-on-Thames, UK: Thomas Nelson and Sons, 1998), 4.3.251. All further references to *Love's Labour's Lost* are to this edition, unless otherwise specified, and will be cited parenthetically in the text by act, scene, and line numbers. For *Love's Labour's Lost* as a satire of the Ralegh circle, see Bradbrook, *School of Night*; for the play as Shakespeare's championing the practitioners of the *via activa* associated with the Earl of Essex against the academicians associated with Ralegh, see Yates, *Study of* Love's Labour's Lost. For Shakespeare's acquaintance with Bruno's works, specifically the play *Candelaio*, via the works of (and perhaps a personal acquaintance with) John Florio, see Amelia Buono Hodgart, "*Love's Labour's Lost* di William Shakespeare e il *Candelaio* di Giordano Bruno," *Studi secenteschi* 19 (1978): 3–21.

112. Mary Ellen Lamb, "The Nature of Topicality in *Love's Labour's Lost*," *Shakespeare Survey* 38 (1985): 49–59; see also E. A. Strathman, "The Textual Evidence for 'The School of Night,'" *Modern Language Notes* 56 (1941): 176–86.

113. Ingrid Rowland, "Introduction," in Giordano Bruno, *On the Heroic Frenzies: A Translation of* De gli eroici furori, trans. Ingrid Rowland (Toronto: University of Toronto Press, 2013), xxii.

114. Giordano Bruno, *The Heroic Frenzies*, trans. Paul Eugene Memmo, Jr. (Chapel Hill: University of North Carolina Press, 1964), 5. For the Italian of this passage, quoted below, see Bruno, *Gli heroici furori*, trans. Rowland, 4–6. For *Love's Labour's Lost* as a parody of Chapman's "Shadow of Night," see Brown, "Shakespeare's Anxious Epistemology," 33.

115. Elliott M. Simonson, *The Myth of Sisyphus: Renaissance Theories of Human Perfectibility* (Madison, NJ: Fairleigh Dickinson University Press, 2007), 216–17. For how Bruno's rejection of venereal sexuality in *The Heroic Frenzies* plays into his vision of seeking philosophical verities, see Hilary Gatti, *Essays on Giordano Bruno* (Princeton, NJ: Princeton University Press, 2011), 115–26.

116. *The Riddles of Heraclitus and Democritus* (London, 1598), B1v–B2r, *2v.

117. For a discussion of poetic production in Shakespeare's Sonnet 5 as drawing upon the alchemical process of sublimation, which separates the impure, excremental feminine remainder from the pure, masculine spirit, see Halpern, *Shakespeare's Perfume*, 14–16.

118. See Judith Perryman, " 'The Words of Mercury': Alchemical Imagery in *Love's Labour's Lost*," in *The Spirit of the Court: Selected Proceedings of the Fourth Congress of the International Courtly Literature Society (Toronto 1983)*, ed. Glyn S. Burgess and Robert A. Taylor (Cambridge: D. S. Brewer, 1985), 246–53; and Peggy Muñoz Simonds, " 'Love is a spirit all compact of fire': Alchemical *Coniunctio* in *Venus and Adonis*," in *Emblems and Alchemy*, ed. Adams and Linden, 133–56. See especially Margaret Healy, " 'Making the quadrangle round': Alchemy's Protean Forms in Shakespeare's Sonnets and *A Lover's Complaint*," in *A Companion to Shakespeare's Sonnets*, ed. Michael Schoenfeldt (Malden, MA: Blackwell, 2007), 405–25; and Healy, *Shakespeare, Alchemy and the Creative Imagination*.

119. As George Starkey's late seventeenth-century line-by-line exposition of George Ripley's *Compound of Alchemy* explains, "our Green Lyon . . . is indeed the greenest or rawest of the three: for it hath no manner of Metalline Sulphur, no not a grain, and therefore is Totally Volatile, and it is more raw than the common Water"; Eirenaeus Philalethes [George Starkey], *Ripley Reviv'd* (London, 1678), 29 (B8r). On alchemical green, see Bruce R. Smith, *The Key of Green: Passion and Perception in Renaissance Culture* (Chicago: University of Chicago Press, 2009), 64–68.

120. British Library Ms. Sloane 3747, fol. 5r, quoted in Jennifer M. Rampling, "Establishing the Canon: George Ripley and His Alchemical Sources," *Ambix* 55 (2008): 204.

121. See Gail Paster, *Humoring the Body: Emotions and the Shakespearean Stage* (Chicago: University of Chicago Press, 2004), 77–134; Winfried Schleiner, "Early Modern Green Sickness and Pre-Freudian Hysteria," *Early Science and Medicine* 14 (2009): 661–76; and Helen King, *The Disease of Virgins: Green Sickness, Chlorosis, and the Problems of Puberty* (London: Routledge, 2004).

122. Philalethes, *Ripley Reviv'd*, 8 (Cc2v); "Artephius His Secret Booke," in Flamel, *Hieroglyphicall Figures*, 65.

123. Hall, *Things of Darkness*, 67–69. Race and alchemy can be related concerns, of course. The whitening of the daughters of the Niger River in Ben Jonson's *Masque of Blackness* (1605), for example, is notably alchemical, from the sun's possessing a "light

sciential" that "refines / All things on which his radiance shines," to the transformed ladies' carrying fans on which are written Egyptian hieroglyphs (226, 234–35, 238).

124. Norton, *Ordinal of Alchemy*, 49, lines 1529–30.

125. Bacon, *Mirror of Alchimy*, 12–13 (B4v–C1r).

126. Perryman, "Words of Mercury," points out that each of the gentlemen brings up a different Aristotelian element when discussing how to woo his lady in act 4, scene 3—Longaville, earth; Navarre, water; Dumaine, air; and Berowne, fire. For a smart reading of Berowne's language as part of the gentlemen's efforts to "Petrarchify" their beloveds into purity, see Mark Breitenberg, *Anxious Masculinity in Early Modern England* (Cambridge: Cambridge University Press, 1996), 128–49.

127. For example, Boyet tells Rosaline that her future husband is bound to be a cuckold: "if thou marry, / Hang me by the neck if horns that year miscarry" (4.1.110–11).

128. See Perryman, "Words of Mercury," 252.

129. William Shakespeare, *King Henry IV, Part 2*, ed. A. R. Humphreys (London: Methuen, 1966), 3.2.324; emphasis added; Lyly, *Gallathea*, 5.1.20–27.

130. The "Tubal" pun, though not explicit in *Love's Labour's Lost*, proves to be one Shakespeare cannot long resist, as Shylock complains to his friend Tubal about his daughter Jessica's having stolen the family jewels; William Shakespeare, *The Merchant of Venice*, ed. John Russell Brown (London: Methuen, 1955), 3.1.72–82.

131. Jeffrey Masten, *Textual Intercourse: Collaboration, Authorship, and Sexualities in Renaissance Drama* (Cambridge: Cambridge University Press, 1997). The connections among excrement, alchemy, and reproduction are made clear by John Milton, who in his *Doctrine and Discipline of Divorce* (1644) contrasts a marriage of true minds to purely "carnal" marriage by calling the latter "the quintessence of an excrement," one in which the man regards his wife merely as a "vessell of voluptuous enjoyment"; see John Milton, *The Doctrine and Discipline of Divorce*, in *Complete Prose Works of John Milton*, ed. Don M. Wolfe et al. (New Haven, CT: Yale University Press, 1959), 2:248. The husband deposits semen—his "excrement" in the sense that it is his superfluity—in his wife's "vessell," and this act's "quintessence" may refer both to the child who may result from the sexual act and to the marriage itself. Milton later, in *Paradise Lost*, in *Complete Poems and Major Prose*, ed. Hughes, 6.482–515, associates alchemy with pregnancy when he depicts the rebel angels pillaging minerals from the soil of heaven to invent gunpowder. "These in thir dark Nativity the Deep / Shall yield us, pregnant with infernal flame," says Satan, just before his crew locates "The originals of Nature in thir crude / Conception" and refines them alchemically: "with subtle Art / Concocted and adusted they reduc'd [them] / To blackest grain." Malabika Sarkar correctly notes *Paradise Lost*'s association of alchemy with revolution gone wrong, but incorrectly describes the fallen angels as incapable of alchemy; see Sarkar, *Cosmos and Character in* Paradise Lost (New York: Palgrave, 2012), 161–83.

132. For Marcadé as "Mar-Arcadia" and as Mercury, see Shakespeare, *Love's Labour's Lost*, ed. Woudhuysen, 34, 65–66.

133. Patricia Parker, *Shakespeare from the Margins: Language, Culture, Context* (Chicago: University of Chicago Press, 1996), 20–55.

134. Flamel, *Hieroglyphicall Figures*, 28.

135. Paracelsus, *Of the Nature of Things*, 2 (Aa1v).

136. Bacon, *Mirror of Alchimy*, 45–46 (G1r–v). For Paracelsus's similar, if inconsistent, theory that conjunction precedes putrefaction, see Long, *Hermaphrodites*, 118–20.

137. See William Shakespeare, *Love's Labour's Lost*, ed. William C. Carroll (Cambridge: Cambridge University Press, 2009), 191.

5. HOW TO MAKE FICTION

1. Naudé, *History of Magick*, 8 (B4v).

2. Ibid., 6 (B3v).

3. Healy, "Making the quadrangle round"; Puttenham, *Art of English Poesy*, 233. For poetry's relation to alchemy in Renaissance English poetic theory, see also Healy, *Shakespeare, Alchemy and the Creative Imagination*, 52–56.

4. Philip Sidney, *A Defence of Poetry*, in *Miscellaneous Prose of Sir Philip Sidney*, ed. Katherine Duncan-Jones and Jan van Dorsten (Oxford: Clarendon, 1973), 78.

5. Ibid. In his account of Sidney's taking alchemical instruction from John Dee in 1577, Thomas Moffet either wittingly or unwittingly characterizes alchemy in the same way that Sidney characterizes poetry, as going nature one better: "he learned chemistry, that starry science, rival to nature." See Alan Stewart, *Philip Sidney: A Double Life* (New York: St. Martin's, 2000), 169.

6. Sidney, *Defence*, 100.

7. Margaret W. Ferguson, *Trials of Desire: Renaissance Defenses of Poetry* (New Haven, CT: Yale University Press, 1983), 11.

8. The date of Sidney's composition of *The Defense of Poetry* is unknown, but scholars generally put it at the time of his writing the *Arcadia*, which he began in the late 1570s; see Stewart, *Philip Sidney*, 228.

9. Sidney, *Defence*, 91.

10. Alan Macfarlane, "Civility and the Decline of Magic," in *Civil Histories: Essays Presented to Sir Keith Thomas*, ed. Peter Burke, Brian Harrison, and Paul Slack (Oxford: Oxford University Press, 2000), 145–59, quotation on 153. Macfarlane cites John Ziman, *Reliable Knowledge: An Exploration of the Grounds for Belief in Science* (Cambridge: Cambridge University Press, 1978).

11. See Timothy J. Reiss, "The Idea of Meaning and Practice of Method in Peter Ramus, Henri Estienne, and Others," in *Humanism in Crisis: The Decline of the French Renaissance*, ed. Philippe Desan (Ann Arbor: University of Michigan Press, 1991), 125–52.

12. For the "scholastic revival" in early modern philosophy, see John A. Trentman, "Scholasticism in the Seventeenth Century," in *The Cambridge History of Later Medieval Philosophy from the Rediscovery of Aristotle to the Disintegration of Scholasticism, 1100–1600*, ed. Norman Kretzmann, Anthony Kenny, and Jan Pinborg (Cambridge: Cambridge University Press, 1982), 818–37. For the contributions of and the religious constraints placed

on Jesuit science, see Mordechai Feingold, ed., *Jesuit Science and the Republic of Letters* (Cambridge, MA: MIT Press, 2003).

13. Iain Chambers, *Culture After Humanism: History, Culture, Subjectivity* (London: Routledge, 2001), 78.

14. Ibid., 93; Walter Benjamin, *The Origin of German Tragic Drama* (London: Verso, 1998), 175.

15. Margaret W. Ferguson, "*Hamlet*: Letters and Spirits," in *Shakespeare and the Question of Theory*, ed. Patricia Parker and Geoffrey Hartman (New York: Methuen, 1985), 292–309. The evidence of Hamlet's humanist training in his proposals and plans extends from the handwriting he uses to forge Rosencrantz's and Guildenstern's death warrants—handwriting prized by the "statists" who were themselves products of a humanist education (5.2.33)—to his imagining that his standing in future history will be determined by the status of a word, his own potentially "wounded [but preferably unwounded] name" (5.2.349).

16. William Shakespeare, *Hamlet*, ed. Harold Jenkins (London: Methuen, 1982), 1.5.99–101. All subsequent references to this play are to this edition and will be cited parenthetically in the text by act, scene, and line numbers.

17. See Joel B. Altman, *The Tudor Play of Mind: Rhetorical Inquiry and the Development of Elizabethan Drama* (Berkeley: University of California Press, 1978).

18. Despite his schemes' illogic, Hamlet's is the language in the play that claims logic and system. For example, whereas others in *Hamlet* more or less exclusively use *ground* to mean dirt, land, or kingdom and *reason* to mean sanity, Hamlet also deploys these terms as descriptors of sound analysis. He'll have "grounds / More relative" than the Ghost's appearance to condemn Claudius, just as he identifies the difference between man and beast as man's "large discourse" and "godlike reason" (2.2.599–600; 4.4.36–38).

19. Passannante, *Lucretian Renaissance*.

20. Abraham, *Dictionary of Alchemical Imagery*, 55–56. Alchemical imagery in *Hamlet* has not drawn extensive comment; instead, critics have dwelled upon, for example, the physiological implications of Hamlet's and the Ghost's descriptions of the human body. However, Sidney Warhaft, perhaps the first to use early modern humoral theory to defend the First Folio's "solid flesh" over the First and Second Quartos' "sallied" and Dover Wilson's "sullied," speculates that "some text in alchemy [may lie] behind the thaw-melt-resolve series. This is after all a form of transmutation of a base substance into a less base. *Resolution* also seems to have been applied to alchemical change; certainly *solution* is one of the alchemical processes." See Warhaft, "Hamlet's Solid Flesh Resolved," *ELH* 28 (1961): 21–30, quotation in 27n. Harold Jenkins's Second Arden edition of *Hamlet*, which I have otherwise used for quotations from the play, prefers Wilson's indefensible "sullied"; I have substituted "solid," the choice that best fits the metaphor of melting flesh.

21. Margreta de Grazia, *Hamlet Without Hamlet* (Cambridge: Cambridge University Press, 2007), 22–44, 129–57.

22. Jenkins chooses the Fifth Quarto in having Hamlet call Ophelia attractive "mettle" rather than "metal" (3.2.108); my sense of the pun is that either word will do, since both are meant.

23. Greenblatt, "Mousetrap."

24. I owe the insight that Hamlet's "quintessence of dust" violates Aristotelian science to Kristen Poole, *Supernatural Environments in Shakespeare's England: Spaces of Demonism, Divinity, and Drama* (Cambridge: Cambridge University Press, 2007), 1–2.

25. For the ways that Horatio both enables and subverts the story that Hamlet wishes to have told of himself, see Christopher Warley, *Reading Class Through Shakespeare, Donne, and Milton* (Cambridge: Cambridge University Press, 2014), 47–72. One more reference to the fate of flesh in *Hamlet* has possible alchemical resonances. Jumping into Ophelia's grave after Laertes, Hamlet proposes they both "drink up eisel, eat a crocodile," suggesting the kind of esoteric alchemical medicinal potion that—like the medicinal mummy I discussed in Chapter 3—requires an exotic, Egyptian meat dissolved in solvent, "eisel" or vinegar. The extravagance of Hamlet's vision at this point for what should be done with earth—that both he and Laertes be "buried quick" with Ophelia in a mound so high it will "Make Ossa like a wart"—argues for this speech as another instance in which Hamlet imagines an alchemical conversion of the linked matter of earth and flesh into something grander (5.1.271–78).

26. Paul A. Kottman, *A Politics of the Scene* (Stanford, CA: Stanford University Press, 2008), 141, 143. Kottman's only examples of Hamlet's engaging in this cowitnessing are, in fact, conspicuously one-sided: his dialogue with Yorick's skull and his bequeathing his story to Horatio (144–47). Elsewhere Kottman gives a quite different reading of community in *Hamlet* as failed, lost in the transition from (maimed) burial rites to (claimed) property rights; see *Tragic Conditions in Shakespeare: Disinheriting the Globe* (Baltimore: Johns Hopkins University Press, 2009), 44–77.

27. See Greenblatt, "Mousetrap"; and Sarah Beckwith, "Stephen Greenblatt's *Hamlet* and the Forms of Oblivion," *Journal of Medieval and Early Modern Studies* 33 (2003): 261–80, esp. 274. For a refutation of Greenblatt's and Beckwith's association of modernity with the rejection of Eucharistic transubstantiation, see Katherine Eggert, "*Hamlet*'s Alchemy: Transubstantiation, Modernity, Belief," *Shakespeare Quarterly* 64 (2013): 45–57. David Aers objects to the claim that modernity originates in the Protestant Reformation of the Eucharist; see "New Historicism and the Eucharist," *Journal of Medieval and Early Modern Studies* 33 (2003): 241–59.

28. Cavell, *Disowning Knowledge*, 179–92.

29. For Horatio's reworking of *Hamlet*'s genre into revenge tragedy, see Eggert, *Showing Like a Queen*, 118–19.

30. Warley, *Reading Class*, 47–60, brilliantly reads Horatio's "scholar" status as allied to the "emerging rational public" promised by science and economics, even while the play also undercuts the possibility of disinterested interpretation.

31. Thomas Hobbes, *Leviathan*, ed. Edwin Curley (Indianapolis: Hackett, 1994), 19. Skinner, *Reason and Rhetoric*, argues that Hobbes's moral and political philosophy reflects his training in humanism, as well as his subsequent rejection and eventual reincorporation of the humanistic disciplines. Ted H. Miller takes issue with Skinner's picture of Hobbes as moving in and out of a sympathy with humanism, contending that Hobbes's humanism informed his understanding of mathematics as the basis of sovereign power;

see Miller, *Mortal Gods: Science, Politics, and the Humanist Ambitions of Thomas Hobbes* (University Park: Pennsylvania State University Press, 2011).

32. Grafton and Jardine, *Humanism to the Humanities*.

33. For the slow shift from humanism's idea of "general learning" to specific, disciplinary learning, see Mordechai Feingold, *The Mathematicians' Apprenticeship: Science, Universities and Society in England, 1560–1640* (Cambridge: Cambridge University Press, 1984); and Feingold, "The Humanities," 238–42.

34. Bacon, *Advancement of Learning*, 27–30.

35. Grafton and Jardine, *Humanism to the Humanities*, 196–200.

36. I take this sense of "veridiction" from Michel Foucault's early work on disciplinarity, in which he describes how the "regime of truth" shifts from the "universal intellectual" to the scientist; see Foucault, "Truth and Power," in *Power/Knowledge: Selected Interviews and Other Writings, 1972–1977*, ed. Colin Gordon (New York: Pantheon), 109–33. In his late work, Foucault develops the idea of a "modality of veridiction" that explains an individual speaker's expression of what she believes to be the truth; it involves "the act of speaking which has its own forms and which entails a particular experience of language, of discourse; the mode of subjectivity which is capable of using language in the necessary way in order to articulate truth; and the domain or region of truth which is articulated in the act of speaking"; see Edward F. McGushin, *Foucault's Askēsis: An Introduction to the Philosophical Life* (Evanston, IL: Northwestern University Press, 2007), 9.

37. See Paul G. Bator, "The Formation of the Regius Chair of Rhetoric and Belles Lettres at the University of Edinburgh," *Quarterly Journal of Speech* 75 (1989): 40–64. For the Romantic period's further development of the study of literature as separate from the study of aesthetics, see Clifford Siskin, *The Work of Writing: Literature and Social Change in Britain, 1700–1830* (Baltimore: Johns Hopkins University Press, 1998), 29–99. My argument that the turn of the seventeenth century begins to invent literature as a narrow discipline owes much to Kathleen Wine's discussion of Honoré d'Urfé's *L'Astrée* (1607–28) as an example of a work that strenuously forgets humanism in order to establish itself as a work of literature; see Wine, *Forgotten Virgo: Humanism and Absolutism in Honoré d'Urfé's* L'Astrée (Geneva: Librairie Droz, 2000), as well as Alain Viala, *Naissance de l'écrivain: sociologie de la littérature à l'âge classique* (Paris: Éditions de Minuit, 1985). Keilen, *Vulgar Eloquence*, persuasively argues that English authors around the turn of the seventeenth century categorized their vernacular writing as literary, even if they called that category "eloquence" rather than "literature."

38. Alvin Kernan, "Introduction," in Ben Jonson, *The Alchemist*, ed. Alvin Kernan (New Haven, CT: Yale University Press, 1974), 15.

39. See Jonathan Goldberg, *James I and the Politics of Literature: Jonson, Shakespeare, Donne, and Their Contemporaries* (Stanford, CA: Stanford University Press, 1989), 60.

40. *The Alchemist* relies distantly on only one significant classical source, Plautus's *Mostellaria*, with its theme of a servant abusing his absent master's trust.

41. For Jonson's comprehensive knowledge and complex use of both theoretical and practical alchemical texts, see Linden, *Darke Hierogliphicks*, 118–53.

42. Ben Jonson, *The Alchemist*, ed. Elizabeth Cook (London: A & C Black, 1991), 2.3.203; William W. E. Slights, *Ben Jonson and the Art of Secrecy* (Toronto: University of Toronto Press, 1994), 108. All subsequent references to *The Alchemist*, unless otherwise noted, are to Cook's edition and will be cited parenthetically in the text by act, scene, and line numbers.

43. See Anne Barton, *Ben Jonson, Dramatist* (Cambridge: Cambridge University Press, 1984), 170–93.

44. Ibid., 190.

45. Subtle's accumulation of such expensive equipment puts him in rather elite scientific company. The magician, astrologer, and physician Simon Forman, Jonson's contemporary, had to practice ten years or more before he could afford the apparatus and materials to amalgamate metals, and his diary records his unhappiness at instances of breakage; see Lauren Kassell, *Medicine and Magic in Elizabethan London: Simon Forman: Astrologer, Alchemist, and Physician* (Oxford: Clarendon, 2005), 173. Similarly, seventeenth-century alchemist George Starkey reported in his notes on his experiments that just when he was about to perfect a curative "Arcanum," he was "hindred by the unfortunate breaking of a glasse"; see Starkey, *Laboratory Notebooks*, 27, 29.

46. Bruno Latour, "On the Partial Existence of Existing *and* Nonexisting Objects," in *Biographies of Scientific Objects*, ed. Lorraine Daston (Chicago: University of Chicago Press, 2000), 247–69, quotation on 257.

47. For early modern London as the microcosm of the nation, see Lawrence Manley, *Literature and Culture in Early Modern London* (Cambridge: Cambridge University Press, 1995), 131–32. For Lovewit's house as a microcosm of London, see James D. Mardock, *Our Scene Is London: Ben Jonson's City and the Place of the Author* (New York: Routledge, 2008), 84–86.

48. For the use of "memory houses" and "memory rooms" as mnemonic systems in the Middle Ages and Renaissance, see Frances A. Yates, *The Art of Memory* (Chicago: University of Chicago Press, 1966).

49. Used to mean "leave-taking" from Middle English to the seventeenth century, the word *department* then started to take on the sense of "division" and thence of "province or business assigned to a particular person"; Samuel Johnson, *A Dictionary of the English Language* (London, 1755), 1:566. Both John Shanahan and I have described *The Alchemist*'s house as a nascent version of the early modern laboratory, but it is important to qualify this comparison: whereas Shanahan sees in the artifice of Jonson's "unities" a model for the empirical practice that is to come, I argue that *The Alchemist*'s aims are always intended as matters of fiction, not matters of fact. See John Shanahan, "Ben Jonson's *Alchemist* and Early Modern Laboratory Space," *Journal for Early Modern Cultural Studies* 8 (2008): 35–66; and Katherine Eggert, "The Alchemist and Science," in *Early Modern English Drama: A Critical Companion*, ed. Garrett A. Sullivan, Jr., Patrick Cheney, and Andrew Hadfield (Oxford: Oxford University Press, 2006), 200–12.

50. Published posthumously in 1627 in the volume containing *Sylva sylvarum*, *New Atlantis* was likely composed in the early 1620s; see Francis Bacon, *New Atlantis*, in *Francis Bacon*, ed. Brian Vickers (Oxford: Oxford University Press, 1996), 786–87.

51. Bacon, *New Atlantis*, 486.

52. Bronwen Price, "Introduction," in *Francis Bacon's* New Atlantis: *New Interdisciplinary Essays*, ed. Bronwen Price (Manchester, UK: Manchester University Press, 2002), 1–27, esp. 13–14.

53. In its first, posthumous printing, *New Atlantis*—whether by Bacon's design or not—achieved the same separation of science from fiction bibliographically that Salomon's House does architecturally. Appended to *Sylva sylvarum* (London, 1627), Bacon's compendium of experiments, the fictional, utopian *New Atlantis* is given its own title page and its own page numbering, distinguishing it from the previous text. One of Bacon's most popular works, *New Atlantis* was, however, not necessarily taken for fiction by its seventeenth-century readership. According to Bacon's editor Brian Vickers, some readers thought it an authentic travel narrative, and there were a number of serious attempts to establish new institutions of learning according to the model of Salomon's House; Bacon, *New Atlantis*, 788–89.

54. Anthony Grafton, "Foreword (1993)," in *The Hieroglyphics of Horapollo*, trans. George Boas, 2nd ed. (Princeton, NJ: Princeton University Press, 1993), xi–xxi, esp. xvii–xix.

55. I am happy to credit Jonson for this pun on the term *crackpot* even if credit depends on his originating or at least gesturing toward the use of the term to mean "foolish." The gesture, at least, seems plausibly Jonsonian. While the *Oxford English Dictionary* notes the first use of *crackpot* as occurring in 1883, it cites "crack-brain" from 1570 and "crack-brained" from 1634. Lovewit's two uses of "crack," one connected with pots and one connected with his brain (5.5.40, 156), seem to associate the crack-brain with the crack-pot. See *OED Online*, s.v. "crackpot, n.," last modified 1972, http://0-www.oed.com.libraries.colorado.edu/view/Entry/43669; s.v. "crack-brain, n.," last modified 1893, http://0-www.oed.com.libraries.colorado.edu/view/Entry/43637; and s.v. "crack-brained, adj.," last modified 1893, http://0-www.oed.com.libraries.colorado.edu/view/Entry/43638; all accessed 18 August 2014. The association of foolishness with the words "crack" and "pot" may also have been familiar from Ecclesiastes 7:5–6, which in the Bishops' Bible used by the Church of England asserts, "It is better to geve eare to the chastening of a wyse man, then to heare the songue of fooles: For the laughyng of fooles is like the cracking of thornes under a pot: and that is but a vayne thing"; *The Holie Bible Conteynyng the Olde Testament and the Newe* (London, 1568), part 3, I1r.

56. Joseph Loewenstein, *Ben Jonson and Possessive Authorship* (Cambridge: Cambridge University Press, 2002), 123.

57. Ben Jonson, *Volpone, or the Fox*, ed. Brian Parker, 2nd ed. (Manchester: Manchester University Press, 1999), 68–69.

58. Ian Donaldson, *Jonson's Magic Houses: Essays in Interpretation* (Oxford: Oxford University Press, 1997), 74–84.

59. For Cavendish's ambivalence about whether Aristotelian natural philosophy was still valid, see Eileen O'Neill, "Introduction," in Margaret Cavendish, Duchess of Newcastle, *Observations upon Experimental Philosophy*, ed. Eileen O'Neill (Cambridge: Cambridge University Press, 2001), x–xi. All subsequent references to Cavendish's *Observations*

are to this edition and will be cited parenthetically in the text. For Cavendish's simultaneous humanist attentiveness to rhetoric and empiricist suspicion of rhetorical sophistry, see Jane Donawerth, ed., *Rhetorical Theory by Women Before 1900: An Anthology* (Lanham, MD: Rowman and Littlefield, 2002), 45–46.

60. Sidney, *Defense*, 78.

61. Fissell, *Vernacular Bodies*, 196–243. This shift helps explain why William Harvey's mid-seventeenth century work on generation, which discounted the female contribution to mammalian generation entirely, had so little influence after its publication, as was discussed in Chapter 4.

62. Cavendish's reading of Harvey on both the circulation of the blood and on generation is perhaps slyly signaled in her juxtaposition in *The Blazing World* of two topics of discussion between the Empress and the worm-men and the fish-men: whether worms, snails, maggots, and so on have blood that circulates; and how maggots are generated out of cheese; Margaret Cavendish, Duchess of Newcastle, *The Description of a New World Called the Blazing World and Other Writings*, ed. Kate Lilley (New York: New York University Press, 1992), 146–48. All subsequent references to *The Blazing World* are to this edition and will be cited parenthetically in the text.

63. See, for example, Cavendish's forthright detailing in her closet drama *The Convent of Pleasure* of the troubles and bodily harms brought about by marriage and childbearing.

64. Cavendish's observation in the *Observations* that alchemy is somewhere between natural and artificial represents something of a change of heart from her *Philosophicall Letters* (London, 1664), in which she asserts that "the Art of Fire cannot create and produce so, as Nature doth, nor dissolve substances so as she doth, nor transform and transchange, as she doth, nor do any effect like Nature" (283 [Cccc2r]).

65. Margaret Cavendish, Duchess of Newcastle, *The Comical Hash*, in *Plays Written by . . . the Lady Marchioness of Newcastle* (London, 1662), 561 (Ccccccc1r).

66. Ibid.

67. Margaret Cavendish, Duchess of Newcastle, *The Worlds Olio* (London, 1655), 176.

68. For Cavendish's evolution from mechanistic atomism to vitalism, see Rogers, *Matter of Revolution*, 185–90; and Stephen Clucas, "The Atomism of the Cavendish Circle: A Reappraisal," *The Seventeenth Century* 9 (1994): 247–73.

69. Every material body in Cavendish's natural philosophy possesses three kinds of matter: rational, sensitive, and inanimate. Thus, while not every particle is rational for Cavendish, all material bodies are rational. See Susan James, "The Philosophical Innovations of Margaret Cavendish," *British Journal for the History of Philosophy* 7 (1999): 219–44. James notes that Cavendish's ideas of the autokinetic powers of rational matter may have been influenced by Jean Baptiste van Helmont, whom Cavendish often refutes but whose idea of the "Archeus" or universal active spirit, derived from Paracelsian alchemy, resembles Cavendish's version of vitalism (233–34).

70. Margaret Cavendish, Duchess of Newcastle, *Philosophicall Fancies* (London, 1653), 39. For Cavendish's analogies between natural motion and alchemy, and for her

placement of fancy and the imagination at the center of material formation and motion, see Lisa T. Sarasohn, *The Natural Philosophy of Margaret Cavendish: Reason and Fancy During the Scientific Revolution* (Baltimore: Johns Hopkins University Press, 2010), 60–61, 85–93.

71. Campbell, *Wonder and Science*, 208. For Cavendish's Blazing World as an infinite regress of authorial-interior-imagining-external-world, see Catherine Gallagher, "Embracing the Absolute: The Politics of the Female Subject in Seventeenth-Century England," *Genders* 1 (1988): 24–39.

72. Kate Lilley, "Contracting Readers: 'Margaret Newcastle' and the Rhetoric of Conjugality," in *A Princely Brave Woman: Essays on Margaret Cavendish, Duchess of Newcastle*, ed. Stephen Clucas (Aldershot, UK: Ashgate, 2003), 19–39.

73. For example, Cavendish uses the term "quickening" to describe the motion of matter, not a stage in fetal development; Sarasohn, *Natural Philosophy*, 55–56.

74. Nicole Pohl, " 'Of Mixt Natures': Questions of Genre in Margaret Cavendish's *The Blazing World*," in *A Princely Brave Woman*, ed. Clucas, 51–68.

75. As O'Neill explains in the introduction to Cavendish, *Observations*, xxiv–xxv, Cavendish's theory that every substance is a mixture of animate (rational or sensitive) and inanimate parts led her to embrace mixture as a positive rather than a negative value. Cavendish seems to have been working out, in her own way, the same kinds of theories that led Robert Boyle and other seventeenth-century atomists to valorize mixture as the grounds of matter; see Wolfram Schmidgen's fine account of this development in *Exquisite Mixture: The Virtues of Impurity in Early Modern England* (Philadelphia: University of Pennsylvania Press, 2013), 24–58. Rogers, *Matter of Revolution*, 203, argues that the "rational" parts of material objects are feminine and the "sensitive" parts masculine in Cavendish's natural philosophy, but their union, as he points out, is one of working together on an architectural construction, not one of sexual intercourse.

76. Robert Boyle, *A Free Enquiry into the Vulgarly Receiv'd Notion of Nature* (London, 1686), A3r, quoted in Stephen Clucas, "Variation, Irregularity and Probabilism: Margaret Cavendish and Natural Philosophy as Rhetoric," in *A Princely Brave Woman*, ed. Clucas, 198–209, quotation on 201.

77. Latour, *We Have Never Been Modern*, 136.

78. Ibid., 51–55.

79. See Angus Fletcher's argument that Cavendish's emphasis on unregulated variety and restless motion in *The Blazing World* is manifested in her fictional aesthetic and her political philosophy as well as in her natural philosophy; Fletcher, "The Irregular Aesthetic of *The Blazing-World*," *Studies in English Literature 1500–1900* 47 (2007): 123–41.

80. See Londa Schiebinger, *The Mind Has No Sex? Women in the Origins of Modern Science* (Cambridge, MA: Harvard University Press, 1989), 51–52.

81. Descartes, *Passions of the Soul*, article 72, in *Philosophical Writings*, 1:354.

82. For Cavendish's reading of *Passions of the Soul*, see Cavendish, *Observations*, xvi; and Cavendish, *Philosophicall Letters*. For her response to Descartes in her *Philosophicall Letters* see Sarasohn, *Natural Philosophy*, 129–35. Misty Anderson's reading of Cavendish

as "anti-Cartesian" in her emphasis on tactility does not take Descartes's later writing on the passions into account; see Anderson, "Living in a Material World: Margaret Cavendish's *Convent of Pleasure*," in *Sensible Flesh*, ed. Harvey, 187–204. For Cavendish's blurring of the boundaries of selfhood, see Eve Keller, "Producing Petty Gods: Margaret Cavendish's Critique of Experimental Science," *ELH* 64 (1997): 447–71. Along with Descartes, Cavendish's philosophical interlocutors include Henry More and Thomas Hobbes, among others. Elizabeth Spiller, commenting on Cavendish as responding to both Hobbes's and Robert Hooke's theories of perception, argues that Cavendish postulates the reader as an active creator, one who "patterns" the world in the same way that Cavendish's "rational" substances organize themselves into new forms; see Spiller, *Science, Reading, and Renaissance Literature*, 137–77.

83. Goldberg, *Seeds of Things*, 144–45; Sandra Sherman, "Trembling Texts: Margaret Cavendish and the Dialectic of Authorship," *English Literary Renaissance* 24 (1994): 184–210.

84. See Richard Helgerson, *Self-Crowned Laureates: Spenser, Jonson, Milton, and the Literary System* (Berkeley: University of California Press, 1983).

85. Stephen Clucas, "Introduction," in *A Princely Brave Woman*, ed. Clucas, 1–15, quotation on 1.

86. For the way Cavendish's theories of matter eliminate the hierarchy of men and women, see Lisa T. Sarasohn, "A Science Turned Upside Down: Feminism and the Natural Philosophy of Margaret Cavendish," *Huntington Library Quarterly* 47 (1984): 289–307. Cavendish recognized that her matter theory was much more radical than her royalism would strictly allow; see Sarasohn, *Natural Philosophy*, 100–125.

AFTERWORD

1. Florian Ebeling, *Secret History*, 91–114, outlines the difficulties that Hermeticism faced in the seventeenth century in light of the debunking of the antiquity of its foundational texts. For the occult nature of Newton's gravitational force, see Richard S. Westfall, "Newton and Alchemy," in *Occult and Scientific Mentalities*, ed. Vickers, 315–36. For Locke's attraction to alchemical secrecy, see Peter Walmsley, *Locke's* Essay *and the Rhetoric of Science* (Lewisburg, PA: Bucknell University Press, 2003), 87–93. For Leibniz's alchemy, see Brown, "Occult Influences." For Boyle's motives for continued alchemical explorations, see Lawrence Principe, *The Aspiring Adept: Robert Boyle and His Alchemical Quest* (Princeton, NJ: Princeton University Press, 1998), 181–213. See also Betty Jo Teeter Dobbs, *The Janus Faces of Genius: The Role of Alchemy in Newton's Thought* (Cambridge: Cambridge University Press, 1991); Dobbs, *Newton's Alchemy*; and Peter R. Anstey, *John Locke and Natural Philosophy* (Oxford: Oxford University Press, 2011).

2. Latour, "Why Has Critique Run out of Steam?"

3. Describing modernity as the invention of the division between nature and culture, science and politics, Latour, *We Have Never Been Modern*, argues that this separation has always been theoretically unstable, even insupportable. In an important recent

study, Mark Morrison analyzes an astonishing example of such instability: the dependence of early twentieth-century nuclear physics—and, beyond it, early twentieth-century monetary theory, another arena shaken by the prospect of transmutable values—upon tropes and ideas generated by the late nineteenth-century alchemical revival; see Morrison, *Modern Alchemy: Occultism and the Emergence of Atomic Theory* (Oxford: Oxford University Press, 2007).

4. Stanley Fish, *Professional Correctness: Literary Studies and Political Change* (Oxford: Clarendon, 1995), 73.

5. Linda Hutcheon, "Disciplinary Formation, Faculty Pleasures, and Student Risks," *ADE Bulletin* 117 (1997): 19–22.

6. F. R. Leavis, *Education and the University: A Sketch for an "English School,"* 2nd ed. (London: Chatto & Windus, 1948), 43. For Richards versus Leavis on the subject of disciplinarity, see Joe Moran, *Interdisciplinarity*, 2nd ed. (London: Routledge, 2010), 24–32.

7. Henry S. Turner, *Shakespeare's Double Helix* (London: Continuum, 2007).

SELECT BIBLIOGRAPHY

I include here sources that I have cited multiple times. Full bibliographical information for every source cited is given at first mention in the notes.

Abraham, Lyndy. *A Dictionary of Alchemical Imagery*. Cambridge: Cambridge University Press, 1998.

Adams, Alison, and Stanton J. Linden, eds. *Emblems and Alchemy*. Glasgow: Glasgow Emblem Studies, 1998.

Agrippa von Nettesheim, Heinrich Cornelius. *Of the Vanity and Vncertaintie of Artes and Sciences*. Edited by Catherine M. Dunn. Northridge: California State University Press, 1974.

———. *Three Books of Occult Philosophy*. Translated by James Freake. Edited by Donald Tyson. Woodbury, MN: Llewellyn, 1993.

Altman, Joel B. *The Improbability of Othello: Rhetorical Anthropology and Shakespearean Selfhood*. Chicago: University of Chicago Press, 2010.

Anderson, Judith H. *Reading the Allegorical Intertext: Chaucer, Spenser, Shakespeare, Milton*. New York: Fordham University Press, 2008.

Aquinas, Thomas. *Summa theologica*. 2nd ed. Translated by Fathers of the English Dominican Province. 1920. http://www.newadvent.org/summa.

Bacon, Francis. *The Advancement of Learning*. Edited by Michael Kiernan. Oxford: Clarendon, 2000.

———. *New Atlantis*. In *Francis Bacon*, 457–89, 785–802. Edited by Brian Vickers. Oxford: Oxford University Press, 1996.

———. Novum organum *with Other Parts of* The Great Instauration. Translated and edited by Peter Urbach and John Gibson. Chicago: Open Court, 1994.

Bacon, Roger [attrib.]. *The Mirror of Alchimy*. London, 1597.

Barton, Anne. *Ben Jonson, Dramatist*. Cambridge: Cambridge University Press, 1984.

Beitchman, Philip. *Alchemy of the Word: Cabala of the Renaissance*. Albany: State University of New York Press, 1998.

Beretta, Marco. "The Role of Symbolism from Alchemy to Chemistry." In *Non-Verbal Communication in Science Prior to 1900*, 279–320. Edited by Renato G. Mazzolini. Florence: Leo S. Olschki, 1993.

Besserman, Lawrence, ed. *The Challenge of Periodization: Old Paradigms and New Perspectives*. New York: Garland, 1996.

Blair, Ann M. *Too Much to Know: Managing Scholarly Information Before the Modern Age*. New Haven, CT: Yale University Press, 2010.

Blau, Joseph. *The Christian Interpretation of the Cabala in the Renaissance*. 1944; reprint, Port Washington, NY: Kennikat, 1965.

Booty, John E., ed. *The Book of Common Prayer 1559: The Elizabethan Prayer Book*. Charlottesville: University Press of Virginia for the Folger Shakespeare Library, 1976.

Bouwsma, William. *The Waning of the Renaissance 1550–1640*. New Haven, CT: Yale University Press, 2000.

Bradbrook, M. C. *The School of Night: A Study in the Literary Relationships of Sir Walter Ralegh*. Cambridge: Cambridge University Press, 1936.

Brooks-Davies, Douglas. *The Mercurian Monarch: Magical Politics from Spenser to Pope*. Manchester, UK: Manchester University Press, 1983.

Brown, Eric C. "Shakespeare's Anxious Epistemology: *Love's Labor's Lost* and Marlowe's *Doctor Faustus*." *Texas Studies in Literature and Language* 45 (2003): 20–41.

Brown, Stuart. "Some Occult Influences on Leibniz's Monadology." In *Leibniz, Mysticism, and Religion*, 1–21. Edited by Allison P. Coudert, Richard H. Popkin, and Gordon M. Weiner. Dordrecht: Kluwer, 1998.

Browne, Thomas. *Sir Thomas Browne's Pseudodoxia Epidemica*. Edited by Robin Robbins. 2 volumes. Oxford: Clarendon, 1981.

Bruno, Giordano. *The Cabala of Pegasus*. Translated by Sidney L. Sondergard and Madison U. Sowell. New Haven, CT: Yale University Press, 2002.

———. *On the Heroic Frenzies: A Translation of* De gli eroici furori. Translated by Ingrid Rowland. Toronto: University of Toronto Press, 2013.

Campbell, Mary Baine. "Artificial Men: Alchemy, Transubstantiation, and the Homunculus." *Republics of Letters: A Journal for the Study of Knowledge, Politics, and the Arts* 1, no. 2 (2010): 4–15. http://rofl.stanford.edu/node/61.

———. *Wonder and Science: Imagining Worlds in Early Modern Europe*. Ithaca, NY: Cornell University Press, 1999.

Cavell, Stanley. *Disowning Knowledge in Six Plays of Shakespeare*. Cambridge: Cambridge University Press, 1987.

Cavendish, Margaret, Duchess of Newcastle. *The Comical Hash*. In *Plays Written by . . . the Lady Marchioness of Newcastle*, 558–78 (Bbbbbbb1r–Ggggggg1r). London, 1662.

———. *The Description of a New World Called the Blazing World and Other Writings*. Edited by Kate Lilley. New York: New York University Press, 1992.

———. *Observations upon Experimental Philosophy*. Edited by Eileen O'Neill. Cambridge: Cambridge University Press, 2001.

———. *Philosophicall Letters*. London, 1664.

Chalmers, Alan. *The Scientist's Atom and the Philosopher's Stone: How Science Succeeded and Philosophy Failed to Gain Knowledge of Atoms*. Dordrecht: Springer-Verlag, 2009.

Chambers, Iain. *Culture After Humanism: History, Culture, Subjectivity.* London: Routledge, 2001.

Cislo, Amy Eisen. *Paracelsus's Theory of Embodiment: Conception and Gestation in Early Modern Europe.* London: Pickering and Chatto, 2010.

Clucas, Stephen, ed. *John Dee: Interdisciplinary Studies in English Renaissance Thought.* Dordrecht: Springer-Verlag, 2006.

———, ed. *A Princely Brave Woman: Essays on Margaret Cavendish, Duchess of Newcastle.* Aldershot, UK: Ashgate, 2003.

Clulee, Nicholas H. *John Dee's Natural Philosophy: Between Science and Religion.* London: Routledge, 1988.

Copenhaver, Brian P., trans. and ed. *Hermetica: The Greek* Corpus Hermeticum *and the Latin* Asclepius *in a New English Translation, with Notes and Introduction.* Cambridge: Cambridge University Press, 1992.

Crane, Mary Thomas. *Losing Touch with Nature: Literature and Science in Sixteenth-Century England.* Baltimore: Johns Hopkins University Press, 2014.

Crooke, Helkiah. *Mikrokosmographia: A Description of the Body of Man.* London, 1615.

Cruickshank, Frances. *Verse and Poetics in George Herbert and John Donne.* Farnham, UK: Ashgate, 2010.

Daiches, David. *The King James Version of the English Bible: An Account of the Development and Sources of the English Bible of 1611 with Special Reference to the Hebrew Tradition.* Chicago: University of Chicago Press, 1941.

Dan, Joseph, ed. *The Christian Kabbalah: Jewish Mystical Books and Their Christian Interpreters: A Symposium.* Cambridge, MA: Harvard College Library, 1997.

———. "The Kabbalah of Johannes Reuchlin and Its Historical Significance." In *The Christian Kabbalah: Jewish Mystical Books and Their Christian Interpreters: A Symposium,* 55–96. Edited by Joseph Dan. Cambridge, MA: Harvard College Library, 1997.

De León-Jones, Karen Silvia. *Giordano Bruno and the Kabbalah: Prophets, Magicians, and Rabbis.* New Haven, CT: Yale University Press, 1997.

———. "John Dee and the Kabbalah." In *John Dee: Interdisciplinary Studies in Renaissance Thought,* 143–58. Edited by Stephen Clucas. Dordrecht: Springer-Verlag, 2006.

Debus, Allen G. *The English Paracelsians.* London: Oldbourne, 1965.

Dee, John. *John Dee's Actions with Spirits, 22 December 1581 to 23 May 1583.* Edited by Christopher Whitby. 2 volumes. New York: Garland, 1988.

Descartes, René. *The Philosophical Writings of Descartes.* Translated by J. Cottingham, Robert Stoothoff, Dugald Murdoch, and Anthony Kenny. 3 volumes. Cambridge: Cambridge University Press, 1985–91.

Dobbs, Betty Jo Teeter. *The Foundations of Newton's Alchemy, or, "The Hunting of the Greene Lyon."* Cambridge: Cambridge University Press, 1975.

Donne, John. *The Complete Poetry of John Donne.* Edited by John T. Shawcross. Garden City, NY: Anchor/Doubleday, 1967.

———. *Devotions upon Emergent Occasions.* Edited by Anthony Raspa. Oxford: Oxford University Press, 1987.

———. *Ignatius His Conclave*. Edited by T. S. Healy. Oxford: Clarendon, 1969.

———. *Sermons*. Edited by George R. Potter and Evelyn M. Simpson. 10 volumes. Berkeley: University of California Press, 1953–62.

Ebeling, Florian. *The Secret History of Hermes Trismegistus: Hermeticism from Ancient to Modern Times*. Translated by David Lorton. Ithaca, NY: Cornell University Press, 2007.

Eco, Umberto. *The Search for the Perfect Language*. Translated by James Fentress. Oxford: Blackwell, 1985.

Eggert, Katherine. *Showing Like a Queen: Female Authority and Literary Experiment in Spenser, Shakespeare, and Milton*. Philadelphia: University of Pennsylvania Press, 2000.

———. "Spenser's Ravishment: Rape and Rapture in *The Faerie Queene*." *Representations* 70 (2000): 1–26.

Erasmus, Desiderius. *Colloquies*. Translated and edited by Craig R. Thompson. 2 volumes. Toronto: University of Toronto Press, 1997.

———. *The Correspondence of Erasmus*. Translated by R. A. B. Mynors, et al. 15 volumes. Toronto: University of Toronto Press, 1974–.

Feingold, Mordechai. "The Humanities." In *The History of the University of Oxford*, vol. 4: *Seventeenth-Century Oxford*, 211–358. Edited by Nicholas Tyacke. Oxford: Clarendon, 1997.

Fissell, Mary E. *Vernacular Bodies: The Politics of Reproduction in Early Modern England*. Oxford: Oxford University Press, 2004.

Flamel, Nicolas. *His Exposition of the Hieroglyphicall Figures (1624)*. Edited by Laurinda Dixon. New York: Garland, 1994.

Fludd, Robert. *Mosaicall Philosophy*. London, 1659.

Forshaw, Peter. "'Alchemy in the Amphitheatre': Some Consideration of the Alchemical Content of the Engravings in Heinrich Khunrath's *Amphitheatre of Eternal Wisdom* (1609)." In *Art and Alchemy*, 195–220. Edited by Joseph Wamberg. Copenhagen: Museum Tusculanum Press, 2006.

———. "*Cabala Chymica* or *Chemia Cabalistica*—Early Modern Alchemists and Cabala." *Ambix* 60 (2013): 361–89.

Foucault, Michel. *The Order of Things: An Archaeology of the Human Sciences*. New York: Vintage, 1994.

Frankfurt, Harry. *On Bullshit*. Princeton, NJ: Princeton University Press, 2005.

Freud, Sigmund. *The Standard Edition of the Complete Psychological Works of Sigmund Freud*. Translated by James Strachey. 24 volumes. London: Hogarth, 1953–1974.

Frietsch, Ute. "Zwischen Transmutation und Transsubstantiation: zum theologischen Subtext der *Archedoxis*-Schrift des Paracelsus." *Nova acta Paracelsica* 19 (2005): 29–51.

The Geneva Bible: A Facsimile of the 1560 Edition. Madison: University of Wisconsin Press, 1969.

Goldberg, Jonathan. *The Seeds of Things: Theorizing Sexuality and Materiality in Renaissance Representations*. New York: Fordham University Press, 2009.

————. *Tempest in the Caribbean*. Minneapolis: University of Minnesota Press, 2004.

Grafton, Anthony. *Defenders of the Text: The Traditions of Scholarship in an Age of Science, 1450–1800*. Cambridge, MA: Harvard University Press, 1991.

Grafton, Anthony, and Lisa Jardine. *From Humanism to the Humanities: Education and the Liberal Arts in Fifteenth- and Sixteenth-Century Europe*. Cambridge, MA: Harvard University Press, 1986.

Greenblatt, Stephen. "The Mousetrap." In Stephen Greenblatt and Catherine Gallagher, *Practicing New Historicism*, 136–62. Chicago: University of Chicago Press, 2001.

————. *The Swerve: How the World Became Modern*. New York: W. W. Norton, 2011.

Grell, Ole Peter, ed. *Paracelsus: The Man and His Reputation, His Ideas and Their Transformation*. Leiden: Brill, 1998.

Hacking, Ian. *Historical Ontology*. Cambridge, MA: Harvard University Press, 2002.

Håkansson, Håkan. *Seeing the Word: John Dee and Renaissance Occultism*. Lund: Lunds Universitet, 2001.

Hall, Kim F. *Things of Darkness: Economies of Race and Gender in Early Modern England*. Ithaca, NY: Cornell University Press, 1995.

Halpern, Richard. "'The picture of Nobody': White Cannibalism in *The Tempest*." In *The Production of English Renaissance Culture*, 262–92. Edited by David Lee Miller, Sharon O'Dair, and Harold Weber. Ithaca, NY: Cornell University Press, 1994.

————. *The Poetics of Primitive Accumulation: English Renaissance Culture and the Genealogy of Capital*. Ithaca, NY: Cornell University Press, 1991.

————. *Shakespeare's Perfume: Sodomy and Sublimity in the Sonnets, Wilde, Freud, and Lacan*. Philadelphia: University of Pennsylvania Press, 2002.

Hamilton, Alastair. *The Apocryphal Apocalypse: The Reception of the Second Book of Esdras (4 Ezra) from the Renaissance to the Enlightenment*. Oxford: Clarendon, 1999.

Hamilton, Ross. *Accident: A Philosophical and Literary History*. Chicago: University of Chicago Press, 2007.

Hanegraaff, Wouter J. *Esotericism and the Academy: Rejected Knowledge in Western Culture*. Cambridge: Cambridge University Press, 2012.

Harkness, Deborah. *John Dee's Conversations with Angels*. Cambridge: Cambridge University Press, 1999.

Harvey, Elizabeth D., ed. *Sensible Flesh: On Touch in Early Modern Culture*. Philadelphia: University of Pennsylvania Press, 2003.

Harvey, William. *Anatomical Exercitations Concerning the Generation of Living Creatures*. London, 1653.

Hawkes, David. *Idols of the Marketplace: Idolatry and Commodity Fetishism in English Literature, 1580–1680*. New York: Palgrave, 2001.

Haydn, Hiram. *The Counter-Renaissance*. New York: Grove, 1950.

Healy, Margaret. "'Making the quadrangle round': Alchemy's Protean Forms in Shakespeare's Sonnets and *A Lover's Complaint*." In *A Companion to Shakespeare's Sonnets*, 405–25. Edited by Michael Schoenfeldt. Malden, MA: Blackwell, 2007.

————. *Shakespeare, Alchemy and the Creative Imagination: The Sonnets and* A Lover's Complaint. Cambridge: Cambridge University Press, 2011.

Hellyer, Marcus. *Catholic Physics: Jesuit Natural Philosophy in Early Modern Germany.* Notre Dame, IN: University of Notre Dame Press, 2005.

Herbert, George. *The Works of George Herbert.* Edited by F. E. Hutchinson. Oxford: Clarendon, 1941.

Hunter, R. H. F. *Physiology of the Graafian Follicle and Ovulation.* Cambridge: Cambridge University Press, 2003.

Idel, Moshe. *Golem: Jewish Magical and Mystical Traditions on the Artificial Anthropoid.* Albany: State University of New York Press, 1990.

————. "Hermeticism and Judaism." In *Hermeticism and the Renaissance: Intellectual History and the Occult in Early Modern Europe,* 59–78. Edited by Ingrid Merkel and Allen G. Debus. Washington, DC: Folger, 1988.

————. *Kabbalah in Italy, 1280–1510: A Survey.* New Haven, CT: Yale University Press, 2011.

————. *Kabbalah: New Perspectives.* New Haven, CT: Yale University Press, 1988.

————. "The Magical and Neoplatonic Interpretations of the Kabbalah in the Renaissance." In *Jewish Thought in the Sixteenth Century,* 186–242. Edited by Bernard Dov Cooperman. Cambridge, MA: Harvard University Press, 1983.

Janacek, Bruce. *Alchemical Belief: Occultism in the Religious Culture of Early Modern England.* University Park: Pennsylvania State University Press, 2011.

Jardine, Lisa. *Ingenious Pursuits: Building the Scientific Revolution.* New York: Doubleday, 1999.

Jones, G. Lloyd. *The Discovery of Hebrew in Tudor England: A Third Language.* Manchester, UK: Manchester University Press, 1983.

Jones, John Henry, ed. *The English Faust Book: A Critical Edition Based on the Text of 1592.* Cambridge: Cambridge University Press, 1994.

Jonson, Ben. *The Alchemist.* Edited by Elizabeth Cook. London: A & C Black, 1991.

————. *Ben Jonson: The Complete Masques.* Edited by Stephen Orgel. New Haven, CT: Yale University Press, 1969.

Josten, C. H. "A Translation of John Dee's *Monas Hieroglyphica* (Antwerp, 1564), with an Introduction and Annotations." *Ambix* 12 (1964): 84–221.

Kargon, Robert Hugh. *Atomism in England from Hariot to Newton.* Oxford: Clarendon, 1966.

Kastan, David Scott. *Shakespeare after Theory.* New York: Routledge: 1999.

Katz, David S. *Philo-Semitism and the Readmission of the Jews into England, 1603–1655.* Oxford: Clarendon, 1982.

Kearney, James. *The Incarnate Text: Imagining the Book in Reformation England.* Philadelphia: University of Pennsylvania Press, 2009.

Keilen, Sean. *Vulgar Eloquence: On the Renaissance Invention of English Literature.* New Haven, CT: Yale University Press, 2006.

Keller, Eve. *Generating Bodies and Gendered Selves: The Rhetoric of Reproduction in Early Modern England.* Seattle: University of Washington Press, 2007.

Kemmler, Fritz. "Entrancing 'tra(u)ns/c': Some Metamorphoses of 'Transformation, Translation, and Transubstantiation.'" *Disputatio: An International Transdisciplinary Journal of the Late Middle Ages* 3 (1998): 176–222.

Khunrath, Heinrich. *Amphitheatrum sapientiae aeternae.* Hamburg, 1595.

Kinney, Arthur. *Humanist Poetics: Thought, Rhetoric, and Fiction in Sixteenth-Century England.* Amherst: University of Massachusetts Press, 1986.

Klaasen, Frank. *The Transformations of Magic: Illicit Learned Magic in the Later Middle Ages and Renaissance.* University Park: Pennsylvania State University Press, 2013.

Knapp, Peggy Ann. "The Work of Alchemy." *Journal of Medieval and Early Modern Studies* 30 (2000): 575–99.

Kuhn, Thomas. *The Structure of Scientific Revolutions.* 4th ed. Chicago: University of Chicago Press, 2012.

Lahey, Stephen E. *John Wyclif.* Oxford: Oxford University Press, 2009.

Láng, Benedek. *Unlocked Books: Manuscripts of Learned Magic in the Medieval Libraries of Central Europe.* University Park: Pennsylvania State University Press, 2008.

Laqueur, Thomas. *Making Sex: Body and Gender from the Greeks to Freud.* Cambridge, MA: Harvard University Press, 1990.

Latour, Bruno. *We Have Never Been Modern.* Translated by Catherine Porter. Cambridge, MA: Harvard University Press, 1993.

———. "Why Has Critique Run Out of Steam? From Matters of Fact to Matters of Concern." *Critical Inquiry* 30 (2004): 225–48.

Lehrich, Christopher I. *The Language of Demons and Angels: Cornelius Agrippa's Occult Philosophy.* Leiden: Brill, 2003.

Linden, Stanton J. *Darke Hierogliphicks: Alchemy in English Literature from Chaucer to the Restoration.* Lexington: University Press of Kentucky, 1996.

———, ed. *Mystical Metal of Gold: Essays on Alchemy and Renaissance Culture.* New York: AMS, 2007.

Long, Kathleen P. *Hermaphrodites in Renaissance Europe.* Aldershot, UK: Ashgate, 2006.

Lupton, Julia Reinhard. *Citizen-Saints: Shakespeare and Political Theology.* Chicago: University of Chicago Press, 2005.

Luther, Martin. *Luther's Works.* Edited by Jaroslav Pelikan and Helmut T. Lehmann. 55 volumes. St. Louis, MO: Concordia, 1955–86.

Lyly, John. *Gallathea.* In *Drama of the English Renaissance*, vol. 1: *The Tudor Period*, 125–43. Edited by Russell A. Fraser and Norman Rabkin. New York: Macmillan, 1976.

Marlowe, Christopher. *Doctor Faustus A- and B-Texts (1604, 1616): Christopher Marlowe and His Collaborator and Revisers.* Edited by David Bevington and Eric Rasmussen. Manchester, UK: Manchester University Press, 1993.

Martin, Andrew. *The Knowledge of Ignorance: From Genesis to Jules Verne.* Cambridge: Cambridge University Press, 1985.

Mazzio, Carla. *The Inarticulate Renaissance: Language Trouble in an Age of Eloquence.* Philadelphia: University of Pennsylvania Press, 2009.

McCue, James F. "The Doctrine of Transubstantiation from Berengar Through Trent: The Point at Issue." *Harvard Theological Review* 61 (1968): 385–430.

McDonnell, Kilian. *John Calvin, the Church, and the Eucharist.* Princeton, NJ: Princeton University Press, 1967.

Milton, John. *John Milton: Complete Poems and Major Prose.* Edited by Merritt Y. Hughes. New York: Odyssey, 1957.

Mitchell, Peter. *The Purple Island and Anatomy in Early Seventeenth-Century Literature, Philosophy, and Theology.* Madison, NJ: Fairleigh Dickinson University Press/Associated University Presses, 2007.

Montaigne, Michel de. *Apology for Raymond Sebond.* Translated by Roger Ariew and Marjorie Grene. Indianapolis: Hackett, 2003.

Moran, Bruce T. *Distilling Knowledge: Alchemy, Chemistry, and the Scientific Revolution.* Cambridge, MA: Harvard University Press, 2005.

Naudé, Gabriel. *The History of Magick.* Translated by John Davies. London, 1657.

Nauert, Charles G., Jr. *Agrippa and the Crisis of Renaissance Thought.* Urbana: University of Illinois Press, 1965.

Newman, William R. *Atoms and Alchemy: Chymistry and the Experimental Origins of the Scientific Revolution.* Chicago: University of Chicago Press, 2006.

———. *Promethean Ambitions: Alchemy and the Quest to Perfect Nature.* Chicago: University of Chicago Press, 2004.

———. "Technology and Alchemical Debate in the Late Middle Ages." *Isis* 80 (1989): 423–45.

Noble, Louise. *Medicinal Cannibalism in Early Modern English Literature and Culture.* New York: Palgrave Macmillan, 2011.

Norton, Thomas. *Thomas Norton's Ordinal of Alchymy.* Edited by John Reidy. London: Oxford University Press for the Early English Text Society, 1975.

Nummedal, Tara. *Alchemy and Authority in the Holy Roman Empire.* Chicago: University of Chicago Press, 2007.

Nutton, Vivian. "The Fortunes of Galen." *The Cambridge Companion to Galen,* 355–90. Edited by R. J. Hankinson. Cambridge: Cambridge University Press, 2008.

Oberman, Heiko A. "Reuchlin and the Jews: Obstacles on the Path to Emancipation." In *The Challenge of Periodization: Old Paradigms and New Perspectives,* 67–93. Edited by Lawrence Besserman. New York: Garland, 1996.

Oxford Dictionary of National Biography. Edited by H. C. G. Matthew and Brian Harrison. Oxford: Oxford University Press, 2004.

Pagel, Walter. *Paracelsus: An Introduction to Philosophical Medicine in the Era of the Renaissance.* 2nd ed. Basel: S. Karger, 1982.

———. *William Harvey's Biological Ideas: Selected Aspects and Historical Background.* New York: Hafner, 1967.

Paracelsus. *The Hermetic and Alchemical Writings of Aureolus Philippus Theophrastus Bombast, of Hohenheim, Called Paracelsus the Great.* Edited by Arthur E. Waite. 2 volumes. London: James Elliott, 1894.

————[attrib.]. *Of the Nature of Things*. In *A New Light of Alchymie*, 1–143 (Aa2r–Ss4r). By Michael Sendivogius. London, 1650.

Parry, Glyn. *The Arch-Conjuror of England: John Dee*. New Haven, CT: Yale University Press, 2011.

Passannante, Gerard. *The Lucretian Renaissance: Philology and the Afterlife of Tradition*. Chicago: University of Chicago Press, 2011.

Patai, Raphael. *The Jewish Alchemists: A History and Source Book*. Princeton, NJ: Princeton University Press, 1994.

Patterson, Lee. "Perpetual Motion: Alchemy and the Technology of the Self." *Studies in the Age of Chaucer* 15 (1993): 25–57.

————. "The Place of the Modern in the Late Middle Ages." In *The Challenge of Periodization: Old Paradigms and New Perspectives*, 51–66. Edited by Lawrence Besserman. New York: Garland, 1996.

Perryman, Judith. "'The Words of Mercury': Alchemical Imagery in *Love's Labour's Lost*." In *The Spirit of the Court: Selected Proceedings of the Fourth Congress of the International Courtly Literature Society (Toronto 1983)*, 246–53. Edited by Glyn S. Burgess and Robert A. Taylor. Cambridge: D. S. Brewer, 1985.

Philalethes, Eirenaeus [George Starkey]. *Ripley Reviv'd*. London, 1678.

Pico della Mirandola, Giovanni. "Oration on the Dignity of Man." In *The Renaissance Philosophy of Man*, 215–54. Edited by Ernst Cassirer, Paul Oskar Kristeller, and John Herman Randall, Jr. Chicago: University of Chicago Press, 1948.

————. *Syncretism in the West: Pico's 900 Theses (1486)*. Translated and edited by S. A. Farmer. Tempe, AZ: Medieval and Renaissance Texts and Studies, 1998.

Pinkus, Karen. *Alchemical Mercury: A Theory of Ambivalence*. Stanford, CA: Stanford University Press, 2010.

Pinto-Correia, Clara. *The Ovary of Eve: Egg and Sperm and Preformation*. Chicago: University of Chicago Press, 1997.

Poovey, Mary. *A History of the Modern Fact: Problems of Knowledge in the Sciences of Wealth and Society*. Chicago: University of Chicago Press, 1998.

Popkin, Richard H., and Gordon M. Weiner, eds. *Jewish Christians and Christian Jews: From the Renaissance to the Enlightenment*. Dordrecht: Kluwer, 1994.

Price, David H. *Johannes Reuchlin and the Campaign to Destroy Jewish Books*. Oxford: Oxford University Press, 2011.

Principe, Lawrence M., ed. *Chymists and Chymistry: Studies in the History of Alchemy and Early Modern Chemistry*. Sagamore Beach, MA: Chemical Heritage Foundation, 2007.

————. *The Secrets of Alchemy*. Chicago: University of Chicago Press, 2013.

Proctor, Robert N. "Agnotology: A Missing Term to Describe the Cultural Production of Ignorance (and Its Study)." In *Agnotology: The Making and Unmaking of Ignorance*, 1–36. Edited by Robert N. Proctor and Londa Schiebinger. Stanford, CA: Stanford University Press, 2008.

Proctor, Robert N., and Londa Schiebinger, eds. *Agnotology: The Making and Unmaking of Ignorance*. Stanford, CA: Stanford University Press, 2008.

Puttenham, George. *The Art of English Poesy: A Critical Edition*. Edited by Frank Whigham and Wayne A. Rebhorn. Ithaca, NY: Cornell University Press, 2007.

Raymond, Joad, ed. *Conversations with Angels: Essays Towards a History of Spiritual Communication, 1100–1700*. New York: Palgrave Macmillan, 2011.

Redondi, Pietro. *Galileo Heretic*. Translated by Raymond Rosenthal. Princeton, NJ: Princeton University Press, 1987.

Remmelin, Johann. *Catoptrum microcosmicum*. Augsburg, 1619.

Reuchlin, Johannes. *On the Art of the Kabbalah/De Arte Cabalistica*. Translated by Martin and Sarah Goodman. Lincoln: University of Nebraska Press, 1993.

———. *Sämtliche Werke*. Edited by Widu-Wolfgang Ehlers, Hans-Gert Roloff, and Peter Schäfer. 17 volumes. Stuttgart: Frommann-Holzboog, 1996.

Rhodes, Neil. *The Power of Eloquence and English Renaissance Literature*. New York: St. Martin's, 1992.

Ripley, George. *George Ripley's Compound of Alchymy (1591)*. Edited by Stanton J. Linden. Aldershot, UK: Ashgate, 2001.

Roberts, Julian, and Andrew G. Watson, eds. *John Dee's Library Catalogue*. London: Bibliographical Society, 1990.

Rogers, John. *The Matter of Revolution: Science, Poetry, and Politics in the Age of Milton*. Ithaca, NY: Cornell University Press, 1996.

Rossi, Paolo. *Logic and the Art of Memory: The Quest for a Universal Language*. Translated by Stephen Clucas. Chicago: University of Chicago Press, 2000.

Rubin, Miri. *Corpus Christi: The Eucharist in Late Medieval Culture*. Cambridge: Cambridge University Press, 1991.

Rudrum, Alan. "'These fragments I have shored against my ruins': Henry Vaughan, Alchemical Philosophy, and the Great Rebellion." In *Mystical Metal of Gold: Essays on Alchemy and Renaissance Culture*, 325–38. Edited by Stanton J. Linden. New York: AMS, 2007.

Rummel, Erika. "Humanists, Jews, and Judaism." In *Jews, Judaism, and the Reformation in Sixteenth-Century Germany*, 3–32. Edited by Dean Phillip Bell and Stephen G. Burnett. Leiden: Brill, 2006.

Sarasohn, Lisa T. *The Natural Philosophy of Margaret Cavendish: Reason and Fancy During the Scientific Revolution*. Baltimore: Johns Hopkins University Press, 2010.

Sartre, Jean-Paul. *Being and Nothingness: A Phenomenological Essay on Ontology*. Translated by Hazel E. Barnes. New York: Washington Square, 1992.

Sawday, Jonathan. *The Body Emblazoned: Dissection and the Human Body in Renaissance Culture*. London: Routledge, 1995.

Schiebinger, Londa. *Plants and Empire: Colonial Bioprospecting in the Atlantic World*. Cambridge, MA: Harvard University Press, 2004.

Scholem, Gershom. *Alchemy and Kabbalah*. Translated by Klaus Ottmann. Putnam, CT: Spring, 2006.

———. *Kabbalah*. New York: Quadrangle/New York Times Book Company, 1974.

————. *On the Kabbalah and Its Symbolism*. Translated by Ralph Manheim. New York: Schocken, 1965.

Schreiner, Susan E. *Are You Alone Wise? The Search for Certainty in the Early Modern Era*. Oxford: Oxford University Press, 2011.

Schwartz, Regina. *Sacramental Poetics at the Dawn of Secularism: When God Left the World*. Stanford, CA: Stanford University Press, 2008.

Schwyzer, Philip. *Archaeologies of English Renaissance Literature*. Oxford: Oxford University Press, 2007.

Scot, Reginald. *The Discoverie of Witchcraft*. Edited by Brinsley Nicholson. London: Elliot Stock, 1886.

Sendivogius, Michael [Michal Sedziwój]. *A New Light of Alchymie*. London, 1650.

Serres, Michel. *The Birth of Physics*. Translated by Jack Hawkes. Edited by David Webb. Manchester, UK: Clinamen, 2000.

Shakespeare, William. *Hamlet*. Edited by Harold Jenkins. London: Methuen, 1982.

————. *Love's Labour's Lost*. Edited by H. R. Woudhuysen. Walton-on-Thames, UK: Thomas Nelson and Sons, 1998.

————. *The Tempest*. Edited by Virginia Mason Vaughan and Alden T. Vaughan. Walton-on-Thames, UK: Thomas Nelson and Sons, 1999.

Shapin, Steven. "The House of Experiment in Seventeenth-Century England." In *The Scientific Enterprise in Early Modern Europe: Readings from Isis*, 273–304. Edited by Peter Dear. Chicago: University of Chicago Press, 1997.

Shapiro, James. *Shakespeare and the Jews*. New York: Columbia University Press, 1996.

Sherman, William H. "'Gold is the strength, the sinnewes of the world': Thomas Dekker's *Old Fortunatus* and England's Golden Age." *Medieval and Renaissance Drama in England* 6 (1993): 85–102.

————. *John Dee: The Politics of Reading and Writing in the English Renaissance*. Amherst: University of Massachusetts Press, 1995.

Shoulson, Jeffrey S. *Fictions of Conversion: Jews, Christians, and Cultures of Change in Early Modern England*. Philadelphia: University of Pennsylvania Press, 2013.

Sidney, Philip. *A Defence of Poetry*. In *Miscellaneous Prose of Sir Philip Sidney*, 59–121. Edited by Katherine Duncan-Jones and Jan van Dorsten. Oxford: Clarendon, 1973.

Simonds, Peggy Muñoz. "'My charms crack not': The Alchemical Structure of *The Tempest*." *Comparative Drama* 31 (1997–98): 538–70.

Siraisi, Nancy G. *History, Medicine, and the Traditions of Renaissance Learning*. Ann Arbor: University of Michigan Press, 2007.

Skinner, Quentin. *Reason and Rhetoric in the Philosophy of Hobbes*. Cambridge: Cambridge University Press, 1996.

Sloterdijk, Peter. *Critique of Cynical Reason*. Translated by Michael Eldred. Minneapolis: University of Minnesota Press, 1987.

Smith, Pamela H. *The Body of the Artisan: Art and Experience in the Scientific Revolution*. Chicago: University of Chicago Press, 2004.

Snow, Edward A. "Marlowe's *Doctor Faustus* and the Ends of Desire." In *Two Renaissance Mythmakers: Christopher Marlowe and Ben Jonson*, 70–110. Edited by Alvin Kernan. Baltimore: Johns Hopkins University Press, 1977.

Southwell, Robert. *The Poems of Robert Southwell, S. J.* Edited by James H. McDonald and Nancy Pollard Brown. Oxford: Clarendon, 1967.

Spenser, Edmund. *The Faerie Queene.* Edited by A. C. Hamilton. 2nd ed. Harlow, UK: Longman, 2001.

Spiller, Elizabeth. *Science, Reading, and Renaissance Literature: The Art of Making Knowledge, 1580–1670.* Cambridge: Cambridge University Press, 2004.

Stark, Ryan. *Rhetoric, Science, and Magic in Seventeenth-Century England.* Washington, DC: Catholic University of America Press, 2009.

Starkey, George. *Alchemical Laboratory Notebooks and Correspondence.* Edited by William R. Newman and Lawrence M. Principe. Chicago: University of Chicago Press, 2004.

Stephens, Dorothy. *The Limits of Eroticism in Post-Petrarchan Narrative: Conditional Pleasure from Spenser to Marvell.* Cambridge: Cambridge University Press, 1998.

Stewart, Alan. *Philip Sidney: A Double Life.* New York: St. Martin's, 2000.

Strier, Richard. *Love Known: Theology and Experience in George Herbert's Poetry.* Chicago: University of Chicago Press, 1983.

Sugg, Richard. *Mummies, Cannibals, and Vampires: The History of Corpse Medicine from the Renaissance to the Victorians.* London: Routledge, 2011.

Szőnyi, Györgi E. *John Dee's Occultism: Magical Exaltation Through Powerful Signs.* Albany: State University of New York Press, 2004.

Szulakowska, Ursula. *The Alchemy of Light: Geometry and Optics in Late Renaissance Alchemical Illustration.* Leiden: Brill, 2000.

Targoff, Ramie. *John Donne: Body and Soul.* Chicago: University of Chicago Press, 2008.

Traub, Valerie. *The Renaissance of Lesbianism in Early Modern England.* Cambridge: Cambridge University Press, 2002.

Tyacke, Nicholas, ed. *The History of the University of Oxford*, vol. 4: *Seventeenth-Century Oxford.* Oxford: Clarendon, 1997.

Vaughan, Henry. *Henry Vaughan: The Complete Poems.* Edited by Alan Rudrum. New Haven, CT: Yale University Press, 1976.

Vaughan, Thomas. *The Works of Thomas Vaughan.* Edited by Alan Rudrum. Oxford: Clarendon, 1984.

Vickers, Brian, ed. *Occult and Scientific Mentalities in the Renaissance.* Cambridge: Cambridge University Press, 1984.

Von Franz, Marie-Louise, ed. *Aurora consurgens: A Document Attributed to Thomas Aquinas on the Problem of Opposites in Alchemy.* New York: Bollingen Foundation/Pantheon, 1966.

Wamberg, Jacob, ed. *Art and Alchemy.* Copenhagen: Museum Tusculanum Press, 2006.

Warley, Christopher. *Reading Class Through Shakespeare, Donne, and Milton.* Cambridge: Cambridge University Press, 2014.

Watt, Tessa. *Cheap Print and Popular Piety, 1550–1640*. Cambridge: Cambridge University Press, 1991.

Webster, Charles. *The Great Instauration: Science, Medicine and Reform, 1626–1660*. New York: Holmes and Maier, 1976.

———. *Paracelsus: Medicine, Magic and Mission at the End of Time*. New Haven, CT: Yale University Press, 2008.

Weeks, Andrew. *Paracelsus: Speculative Theory and the Crisis of the Early Reformation*. Albany: State University of New York Press, 1997.

West, William N. *Theatres and Encyclopedias in Early Modern Europe*. Cambridge: Cambridge University Press, 2002.

Whalen, Robert. *The Poetry of Immanence: Sacrament in Donne and Herbert*. Toronto: University of Toronto Press, 2002.

Wirszubski, Chaim. *Pico della Mirandola's Encounter with Jewish Mysticism*. Cambridge, MA: Harvard University Press, 1989.

Woolfson, Jonathan, ed. *Reassessing Tudor Humanism*. New York: Palgrave, 2002.

Yates, Frances A. *Giordano Bruno and the Hermetic Tradition*. Chicago: University of Chicago Press, 1964.

———. *Majesty and Magic in Shakespeare's Last Plays: A New Approach to* Cymbeline, Henry VIII, *and* The Tempest. London: Routledge and Kegan Paul, 1975.

———. *The Occult Philosophy in the Elizabethan Age*. London: Routledge and Kegan Paul, 1979.

———. *A Study of* Love's Labour's Lost. Cambridge: Cambridge University Press, 1936.

Young, R. V. *Doctrine and Devotion in Seventeenth-Century Poetry: Studies in Donne, Herbert, Crashaw, and Vaughan*. Cambridge: D. S. Brewer, 2000.

Zalta, Edward N., ed. *The Stanford Encyclopedia of Philosophy*. Stanford, CA: Metaphysics Research Lab, Center for the Study of Language and Information, Stanford University. http://plato.stanford.edu/.

Zika, Charles. *Exorcising Our Demons: Magic, Witchcraft, and Visual Culture in Early Modern Europe*. Leiden: Brill, 2003.

INDEX

Abraham, Lyndy, 272n44, 273n56, 300n180, 302n16, 303n19, 308n78, 309n88, 315n20
Abulafia, Abraham, 147
Adelman, Janet, 170
Aers, David, 271n41, 316n27
Agrippa, Heinrich Cornelius, 121, 123–25, 129, 135, 136, 153, 155, 286n49; *Occult Philosophy*, 39–40, 121, 137, 138, 146, 292n105, 293n120, 297n149; *The Vanity of Arts and Sciences*, 39–40, 208
Ah-King, Marlin, 195
Albrecht, Roberta, 273n58
alchemy: and allegory, 28, 35–38, 53, 259n77; and capitalism, 4, 6, 49, 224; and con games, 5, 6, 39, 40; and humanism, 19–25, 48, 50, 212; and Kabbalah, 119–24, 136–39; physics of, 13, 64–65, 70; practical, 4–5, 19, 28, 194; reading practices of, 21–22, 51–52, 128; relation of fiction to, 52–54, 220–21, 226–30, 233–39; and rhetoric, 27–28, 211; as sexual reproduction, 160–68, 187–88, 200–205, 232–33; and syncretism, 19–20, 21–22; theoretical, 5, 9, 19, 51, 53; and transubstantiation, 56, 65–75
allegory, 18, 28, 35–38, 227
Allen, Don Cameron, 276n86
Allen, Sally, 160
Alsted, Johann Heinrich, 254n24
Althusser, Louis, 44, 263n123
Altman, Joel B., 253n8, 315n17
Ambrose, 59, 266n4
Anderson, Judith, 36, 37, 308n74
Anderson, Misty, 321n82
Andreae, Johann Valentin, 67
Anstey, Peter, 322n1
Aquinas, Thomas, 146; on alchemy, 39, 269n29; on transubstantiation, 60–62, 67,

70, 72, 75–76, 100, 267n13, 268n14, 268n20, 270n31. See also *Aurora consurgens*
Aristotle, 23, 43, 140, 159, 211, 231, 254n21; dramatic unities of, 221; matter theory of, 10, 39, 56–62, 64–65, 69–70, 73, 75, 77–78, 83, 90–91, 98–102, 104, 164; *Meteorologica*, 160. See also alchemy: physics of; reproduction, human: Aristotelian "one seed" model of; reproduction, human: Aristotelian-Galenic "hybrid" model of
Asals, Heather, 277n97
Aston, Margaret, 295n130
atomism, 57, 62, 70, 99–100, 102, 107, 270n31, 276n85, 320n68
Augustine, 59, 266n4, 298n159
Aurora consurgens (attrib. to Thomas Aquinas), 66, 269n29
Avicenna, 39, 64, 269n27

Bacon, Francis, 6; *The Advancement of Learning*, 14, 46–48, 50, 226; and alchemy, 46–48, 50–51, 87, 219, 264n135, 265n137; empiricism of, 18–19, 24, 98–99, 102; and humanism, 2, 9, 14–16, 211–12, 254n24; *New Atlantis*, 226, 230; *Novum organum*, 98–99, 105; and rhetoric, 9, 26, 31, 211, 257n62; *Sylva sylvarum*, 318n50, 319n53
Bacon, Roger, 33, 39, 138, 270n30. See also *Mirror of Alchemy, The*
Barnaby, Andrew, 311n106
Barnes, Barry, 42
Barron, Andrew B., 195
Barton, Anne, 222, 318n43
Bate, Jonathan, 300n172
Bator, Paul G., 317n37
Baumlin, James S., 274n73

ACKNOWLEDGMENTS

Having written a book that is about both learning and ignorance, I am even more than usually conscious of my debts to the colleagues, friends, and family members who enlightened me during the long process of research and writing, often saving me from my own stupidity and always giving me smarter ways to think about my topic. I began writing this book in 2007–8 with the support of an Andrew W. Mellon Fellowship at the Folger Shakespeare Library, and I could not have asked for a more congenial and brilliant group of colleagues than that year's Folger Fellows. I thank Hannibal Hamlin, Linda Levy Peck, Julia Rudolph, and Wolfram Schmidgen for hours of delightful and illuminating conversation, as I do other companions at the Folger, especially Paula Blank, Bill Carroll, Kent Cartwright, the late Marshall Grossman, Gerry Passannante, Gail Paster, Rebecca Totaro, and Georgianna Ziegler. Colleagues and friends around the country listened patiently and responded helpfully to my ideas in conference rooms, over restaurant tables, and even on street corners. I look back with special warmth at conversations with Judith Anderson, David Baker, Harry Berger, Jr., Jeff Dolven, Andrew Escobedo, Margaret Ferguson, Paula Findlen, Valerie Forman, Richard Halpern, Bruce Holsinger, Lindsay Kaplan, Annette Mahoney, Katharine Maus, D. A. Miller, Tom Pavlik, Shankar Raman, Bill Sherman, and Peter Stallybrass. Seminars at conferences of the Shakespeare Association of America provided a crucial sounding board for early versions of parts of this book, and I thank Hannibal Hamlin, Thomas Herron, Carla Mazzio, Rebecca Lemon, Joe Loewenstein, and David Riggs for organizing and leading those seminars.

Closer to home, I have been blessed for many years at the University of Colorado with the company of exceptional colleagues both in the Department of English and elsewhere on campus. For intellectual aid both general and specific and support both material and moral, I am grateful to Fred Anderson, Marty Bickman, Chris Braider, Jeff Cox, Claire Farago, John Fisher, Jane Garrity, Sidney Goldfarb, Nan Goodman, Skip Hamilton, Paul Hammer,

Jill Heydt-Stevenson, Janice Ho, Stephen Graham Jones, Penny Kelsey, Mary Klages, William Kuskin, Catherine Labio, Thea Lindquist, Marjorie McIntosh, Richelle Munkhoff, Graham Oddie, Cathy Preston, Mike Preston, John-Michael Rivera, Ann Schmiesing, Elisabeth Sheffield, John Slater, Jeremy Smith, John Stevenson, Jim Symons, Teresa Toulouse, Eric White, and Laura Winkiel. Special thanks to then dean Todd Gleeson and then associate dean Graham Oddie of the College of Arts and Sciences for making it possible for me to take ten months' research leave in between terms as chair of my department. My Colorado graduate students past and present, many of them now colleagues at colleges and universities around the country, helped me formulate my thoughts for this book at all its stages; Jacob Clayton, Nodin de Saillan-Olsen, Ben Deneault, Maren Donley, Ruben Espinosa, B. G. Harding, Kat Lecky, Patricia Marchesi, Sara Morrison, Teresa Nugent, Melinda Pearson, Peter Remien, Rhonda Lemke Sanford, Michael Slater, Melanie Stein, and Ann Stockho, in particular, have all given me new points of view and much to ponder.

My deepest thanks—and their own paragraph—are reserved for the selfless friends who read chapters in progress and gave me the benefit of their extraordinary minds and their editorial advice: Jeffrey DeShell, David Glimp, Karen Jacobs, Dan McCormack, Chris Warley, and Will West. And for Mark Winokur, who listened to countless ideas for this book as they took shape, and made all of them better.

It is a great privilege to be able to work again with the University of Pennylvania Press and its superb staff. I am tremendously grateful to senior humanities editor Jerry Singerman for his guidance, patience, and good humor. Frances Dolan and Henry Turner provided invaluable, detailed suggestions for improving the manuscript, and I thank them for their time and thought.

An earlier version of part of Chapter 5 appeared in *Shakespeare Quarterly* 64, no. 1 (2013): 45–57, and has been reproduced by permission of the Johns Hopkins University Press. A few paragraphs scattered throughout the book were originally published in *Early Modern English Drama: A Critical Companion*, edited by Garrett A. Sullivan, Jr., Patrick Cheney, and Andrew Hadfield, and this material has been reproduced by permission of Oxford University Press (http://global.oup.com/academic/product/early-modern-english-drama-9780195153866).

The women of the Up & Running international running club kept my feet moving and my spirits light while I was finishing this book. My family kept me happy. Thanks especially, and always, to my brothers—Paul, Keith, Jim, and Kurt Eggert—for their kindness, wit, and good counsel. I have been the lifelong beneficiary of the support and wisdom of my beloved father, Richard Eggert, man of science and lover of a good story. This book is dedicated to him.